The Social Politics
of Medieval Diplomacy

STUDIES IN MEDIEVAL AND EARLY MODERN CIVILIZATION
Marvin B. Becker, General Editor

Charity and Children in Renaissance Florence:
The Ospedale degli Innocenti, 1410–1536
Philip Gavitt

Humanism in Crisis: The Decline of the French Renaissance
Philippe Desan, editor

Upon My Husband's Death: Widows in the Literatures
and Histories of Medieval Europe
Louise Mirrer, editor

The Crannied Wall: Women, Religion, and the Arts
in Early Modern Europe .
Craig A. Monson, editor

Wife and Widow in Medieval England
Sue Sheridan Walker, editor

The Rhetorics of Life-Writing in Early Modern Europe: Forms of
Biography from Cassandra Fedele to Louis XIV
Thomas F. Mayer and D. R. Woolf, editors

Defining Dominion: The Discourses of Magic and Witchcraft in
Early Modern France and Germany
Gerhild Scholz Williams

Women, Jews, and Muslims in the Texts
of Reconquest Castile
Louise Mirrer

The Culture of Merit: Nobility, Royal Service, and the Making of
Absolute Monarchy in France, 1600–1789
Jay M. Smith

Clean Hands and Rough Justice: An Investigating Magistrate
in Renaissance Italy
David S. Chambers and Trevor Dean

"Songes of Rechelesnesse": Langland and the
Franciscans
Lawrence M. Clopper

Godliness and Governance in Tudor Colchester
Laquita M. Higgs

The Social Politics of Medieval Diplomacy: Anglo-German Relations
(1066–1307)
Joseph P. Huffman

The Strozzi of Florence: Widowhood and
Family Solidarity in the Renaissance
Ann Crabb

The Social Politics
of Medieval Diplomacy

Anglo-German Relations (1066–1307)

Joseph P. Huffman

Ann Arbor

THE UNIVERSITY OF MICHIGAN PRESS

2003   2002   2001   2000   4   3   2   1

A CIP catalog record for this book is available from the British Library.

Library of Congress Cataloging-in-Publication Data

Huffman, Joseph P., 1959–
    The social politics of medieval diplomacy : Anglo-German relations
(1066–1307) / Joseph P. Huffman.
        p.   cm.
    Includes bibliographical references and index.
    ISBN 0-472-11061-6 (cloth : acid-free paper)
    1. Great Britain—Foreign relations—Germany.   2. Germany—Foreign
relations—Great Britain.   3. Great Britain—Foreign relations—
1066–1485.   I. Title.

DA47.2.H84   1999
327.41043—dc21
                                                              99-051933

Preface

This book was written with certain assumptions that should be made plain at the outset. I have not attempted here to write a comprehensive history of the English and German realms, which has been done for both separately and elsewhere more extensively than I would have the audacity to attempt or claim here. Rather, this is a history of the diplomatic relations *between* the two realms. Hence, this study assumes that the reader has a general familiarity with the political histories of medieval Germany and England. Major regional events and individuals will be referred to but not developed in detail for their own sake. They shall only appear when they have a bearing on Anglo-German diplomacy. Where appropriate, and in the bibliography, the reader is referred to studies of these events and individuals to enable further consideration.

In addition, although the English primary sources have been extensively examined, this study emphasizes the German side of the diplomatic equation. I have chosen this approach for two reasons—firstly, because the vast majority of Anglo-German diplomatic activity passed in one form or another through the city of Cologne. Since our reference point will most often be this flourishing Rhenish metropolis, one can expect that the story will be told with a distinctively German accent. There is, furthermore, a grave paucity of materials on any aspect of medieval German history in English, and so I have attempted to remedy the situation in some modest fashion. The notes and bibliography integrate both the sizable English- and German-speaking scholarly traditions, which is something often lacking in both German- and English-language texts. In an attempt to make German-language scholarship accessible to Anglophone readers, I have translated into English all passages quoted in the notes from German scholarly literature.

This book is not merely a narrative account of Anglo-German diplomatic discourse but one that uses the historical record as a springboard to considerations about the nature of medieval political life and about anachronisms in the existing modern historiography on this period. I hope to accomplish in some degree three goals: to make medieval Germany accessible and relevant to English-speaking, Anglo-French–oriented medievalists, to show the merits of a comparative use of regional sources, and to show the need to reevaluate traditional political history in the light of the insights afforded by social history. If I stimulate any further discussion in these areas, though parts or even all of my thesis might show frayed edges, I shall be satisfied.

Without the support of many the research and writing phases of this book would never have been completed. In particular I wish to thank the Deutscher Akademischer Austauschdienst for the generous research fellowship that made archival research possible. Appreciation for various writing and research grants goes to Messiah College. I extend special thanks to my two sons, Austin and Brendan, whose patience with my work and special wisdom about life have enabled me to love the past and live in the present. It is to them, my future, that I dedicate this book.

Contents

Abbreviations

Annalen	*Annalen des Historischen Vereins für den Niederrhein, insbesondere die alte Erzdiözese Köln*
Böhmer	*Regesta Imperii*, ed. J. F. Böhmer, rev. eds., vols. 3–6 (Innsbruck, 1881–1901; Vienna, Cologne, and Graz, 1951–84).
CCLR	*Calendar of Close Rolls Preserved in the PRO*
CLR	*Calendar of Liberate Rolls Preserved in the PRO*
CPR	*Calendar of Patent Rolls Preserved in the PRO*
CRC	*Chronica regia Coloniensis (Annales maximi Colonienses)*, ed. Georg Waitz, MGH SS rer. Germ., no. 18 (Hanover, 1880; reprint, 1978).
DA	*Deutsches Archiv für Erforschung des Mittelalters*
EHR	*English Historical Review*
Ennen/Eckertz	*Quellen zur Geschichte der Stadt Köln*, ed. Leonard Ennen and Gottfried Eckertz, 6 vols. (Cologne, 1860–79).
HGB	*Hansische Geschichtsblätter*
HUB	*Hansisches Urkundenbuch*
JKGV	*Jahrbuch des Kölnischen Geschichtsvereins*
MGH	Monumenta Germaniae Historica
MGH Const.	Monumenta Germaniae Historica: Constitutiones et acta publica imperatorum et regum
MGH DD	Monumenta Germaniae Historica: Diplomata
MGH Leges	Monumenta Germaniae Historica: Leges (folio)
MGH SS	Monumenta Germaniae Historica: Scriptores (folio)
MGH SS rer. Germ.	Monumenta Germaniae Historica: Scriptores rerum Germanicarum in usum scholarum separatim editi
MIÖG	*Mitteilungen des Instituts für Österreichische Geschichtsforschung*
MPCM	Matthew Paris, *Chronica majora*, ed. Henry Richards Luard, 7 vols., RS, no. 57, (London, 1872–73; reprint, 1964).

MPHA	Matthew Paris, *Historia Anglorum sive historia minor*, ed. Frederic Madden, 3 vols., RS, no. 44 (London, 1866–69; reprint, 1970).
MSAK	*Mitteilungen aus dem Stadtarchiv von Köln*
NF	Neue Folge
NS	New Series
PGRG	Publikationen der Gesellschaft für Rheinische Geschichtskunde
PL	*Patrologiae cursus completus, series latina*, ed. J. P. Migne, 234 vols. (Paris, 1844–1955).
PR	Pipe Rolls
PRO	Public Record Office
REK	*Die Regesten der Erzbischöfe von Köln im Mittelalter*
RNI	*Regestum Innocentii III papae super negotio Romani imperii*, ed. Friedrich Kempf, Miscellanea Historiae Pontificiae, no. 12 (Rome, 1947).
RS	Rerum Britannicarum Medii Aevi Scriptores (Rolls Series)
Rymer	*Foedera, conventiones, litterae etc.*, ed. Thomas Rymer, 2d rev. ed. by George Holmes, 20 vols. (London, 1727–35).
Shirley	*Royal and Other Historical Letters Illustrative of the Reign of Henry III*, ed. Walter W. Shirley, 2 vols., RS, no. 27 (London, 1862–68).
TRHS	*Transactions of the Royal Historical Society*
UGN	*Urkundenbuch für die Geschichte des Niederrheins*, ed. Theodor Josef Lacomblet, 4 vols. (Düsseldorf, 1840–58).
ZRG kan. Abt.	*Zeitschrift der Savigny-Stiftung für Rechtsgeschichte, kanonistische Abteilung*

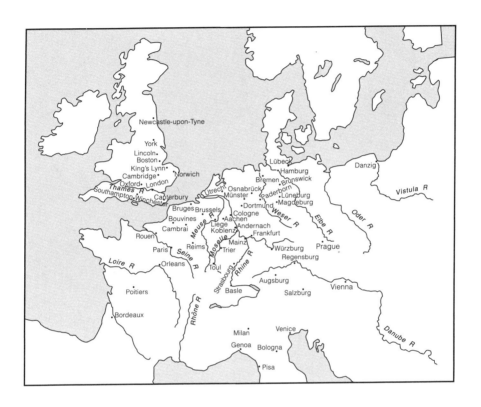

Newcastle-upon-Tyne

York

Lincoln
Boston
King's Lynn
Cambridge
Oxford London
Norwich
Thames R
Southampton Winchester
Canterbury
Utrecht
Bruges Brussels
Bouvines
Cambrai
Rouen
Paris
Reims
Orleans
Seine R
Loire R
Toul
Poitiers
Bordeaux
Rhône R
Strasbourg
Basle
Meuse R
Moselle R
Rhine R
Liege
Koblenz
Mainz
Trier
Andernach
Frankfurt
Würzburg
Regensburg
Augsburg
Salzburg
Milan
Genoa Bologna
Pisa
Venice
Vienna
Danube R
Lübeck
Hamburg
Bremen Brunswick
Osnabrück
Münster
Paderborn
Lüneburg
Magdeburg
Dortmund
Cologne
Aachen
Weser R
Elbe R
Oder R
Prague
Danzig
Vistula R

Introduction

Methodological Considerations

This book explores medieval European political life as a record of the social dynamics *between* political communities. Therefore, the social context of political activity will be of central importance. Our focus will be on the role of interpersonal and familial connections in the formation of political policies and in the subsequent implementation, success, or failure of these policies. In particular, we shall see the personal dimensions of political life as they were lived out in the sphere of diplomatic relations.

Such a social approach to political history has been the vanguard of a recent revival of interest in medieval politics. In a 1989 *American Historical Review* article, Charles T. Wood reviewed no fewer than seven major publications from the years 1979 through 1986 that employed such an approach.[1] Taken as a whole, the results of this (dare we say) "new political history" have restructured our understanding of the basis of medieval political life. Traditional modes of discourse about the origins of the modern nation state, political rhetoric, and the ideological underpinnings of power have given way to interest in the familial, economic, and religious realities of political activity. Each of the works Wood reviewed, however, studies political life in the social context of either France or England.[2] Yet in this "new political history," which no longer privileges

---

1. Charles T. Wood, "The Return of Medieval Politics," *American Historical Review* 94 (1989): 391–404.

2. John W. Baldwin, *The Government of Philip Augustus: Foundations of French Royal Power in the Middle Ages* (Berkeley and Los Angeles, 1986); William C. Jordan, *Louis IX and the Challenge of the Crusade* (Princeton, 1979); Andrew W. Lewis, *Royal Succession in Capetian France: Studies on Familial Order and the State* (Cambridge, MA, 1981); Joseph R. Strayer, *The Reign of Philip the Fair* (Princeton, 1980); Chris Given-Wilson, *The Royal Household and the King's Affinity: Service, Politics, and Finance in England, 1360–1413* (New Haven, 1986); Judith A. Green, *The Government of England*

institutional and state formation as the paradigm of political advancement, medieval Germany looks less "underdeveloped" than previous Anglophone scholarship has asserted and more akin to the Anglo-French political communities studied in the works reviewed by Wood. Therefore this book, while following in the footsteps of these earlier studies, applies this methodology in two new ways.

First, there is a geographical shift away from traditional Anglo-French historiography. As Alfred Haverkamp has argued, of all the regions of Europe, Germany was the most affected and transformed by the rapid changes occurring in European society during the Central Middle Ages. Indeed, Germany not only constantly received the cultural and economic impulses from western European and Mediterranean regions but also came to serve a mediating role between these regions and the north and east of Europe.[3] Medieval Germany should therefore be seen as moving inward from the periphery and beginning to merge with the currents of western European and Mediterranean civilization during the Central Middle Ages. This being the case, Germany is an especially suitable vantage point from which to consider the growing ties of the larger Western world with central Europe during this period of expansion.[4] The setting aside of former historical and historiographical boundaries established by earlier political writers seems eminently appropriate at the close of the twentieth century, and therefore it is time that Germany is grafted more soundly onto the historiography of the medieval West. This study is intended to contribute to such a needed integration, which bridges both modern political and intellectual boundaries through a distinctly interregional approach.[5]

Second, the insights of social history are applied here to a neglected

---

under Henry I (Cambridge, 1986); W. L. Warren, *The Governance of Norman and Angevin England, 1086–1272* (Stanford, 1987).

3. Alfred Haverkamp, *Medieval Germany (1056–1273)*, trans. Helga Braun and Richard Mortimer, 2d ed. (Oxford, 1992), 352.

4. Hagen Keller, *Zwischen regionaler Begrenzung und universalem Horizont: Deutschland im Imperium der Salier und Staufer, 1024–1250*, Propylaen Geschichte Deutschlands, no. 2 (Berlin, 1986), 49: "Common western developmental trends and unique regional structures, unification and differentiation intermingle so much with each other that a history of Germany can serve as a mirror for western history."

5. For a study of why medieval German history had faded from the Angloliterate academic world in the twentieth century see Edward Peters, "More Trouble with Henry: The Historiography of Medieval Germany in the Angloliterate World, 1888–1995," *Central European History* 28, no. 1 (1995): 47–72.

subcategory of political history—diplomacy. Virtually nothing has been written on the nature of medieval diplomacy since the fundamental works of Pierre Chaplais and G. P. Cuttino.[6] Yet since medievalists have reconsidered political history in general recently, it is equally appropriate to revisit the world of medieval diplomacy with an eye toward its social aspects. And this we shall do. Hence, to achieve the dual goals of considering the social world of medieval diplomacy and grafting medieval Germany more solidly onto western European historiography, the social history of diplomatic relations between Germany and England in the Central Middle Ages forms the substance of this book.

What specifically is the nature of the social approach to political history? In a word, it places less emphasis on the institutions and levers of power and more on the social groups that pull the levers and run the institutions. German scholars employ a most appropriate term for this process of combining medieval social and political history: family politics *(Familienpolitik)*.[7] From early research that reconstructed the social and kinship networks of Carolingian Europe[8] down to recent work on

6. Pierre Chaplais, *English Medieval Diplomatic Practice,* 2 vols. (London, 1975–82); idem, *Essays in Medieval Diplomacy and Administration* (London, 1981); G. P. Cuttino, *English Diplomatic Administration, 1259–1339,* 2d ed. (Oxford, 1971); idem, *English Medieval Diplomacy* (Bloomington, 1985). See also François Ganshof, *Le Moyen âge: Histoire des relations internationales I* (Paris, 1953).
7. The doyen of German historians of this approach is Gerd Tellenbach (see *Zur Bedeutung der Personenforschung fur die Erkenntnis des fruheren Mittelalters,* Freiburger Universitätsreden, NF, no. 25 [Freiburg im Breisgau, 1957]), who has been joined by such important medievalists as Karl Schmid, J. Wollasch, E. Hlawitschka, J. Fleckenstein, R. Sprandel, and K. F. Werner, to name a few; they are collectively known as the "Freiburg School." The work of Georges Duby and Leopold Genicot has led the way among French historians. The late Karl Leyser has also done his share of such research in England: see "The German Aristocracy from the Ninth to the early Twelfth Century: A Historical and Cultural Sketch," *Past and Present* 41 (1968): 25–53 (reprinted in *Medieval Germany and Its Neighbours, 900–1250* [London, 1982], 161–90); "Maternal Kin in Early Medieval Germany: A Reply," *Past and Present* 49 (1970): 126–34. German medievalists use the terms *Personenforschung, Personengeschichte,* and *Namenforschung* as well to emphasize the social and personalized nature of this historiography.
8. Gerd Tellenbach, "From the Carolingian Imperial Nobility to the German Estate of Imperial Princes," in *The Medieval Nobility: Studies in the Ruling Classes of France and Germany from the Sixth to the Twelfth Centuries,* ed. Timothy Reuter, Europe in the Middle Ages: Selected Studies, no. 14 (Amsterdam, New York, and Oxford, 1978), 203–42; idem, "Der Grossfränkische Adel und die Regierung Italiens in der Blütezeit des Karolingerreiches," *Studien und Vorarbeiten zur Geschichte des grossfränkischen und frühdeutschen Adels,* Forschungen zur Oberrheinischen Landesgeschichte, no. 4 (Freiburg im Breisgau, 1957); K. F. Werner, "Untersuchungen zur Frühgeschichte des Französischen Fürstentums," *Die*

Ottonian/Salian Germany,[9] crucial insights have been reached into the sociopolitical life of the Early Middle Ages. Here we shall move into a later period (the eleventh through the thirteenth centuries) and build on the firm foundation already laid.

What, then, is the result of understanding medieval politics from a social history perspective? Ironically, it is the dismantling of traditional categories of political history as established by the nineteenth- and early twentieth-century medievalists. When set next to the insights of the "sociopolitical" approach, the old themes of traditional political historiography appear anachronistic and more appropriate for nineteenth- and early twentieth-century political life than for anything medieval. When the pioneer professional historians of the nineteenth century wrote the first modern histories of the Middle Ages, their goal was to "tell of their nation's successes and of the unique national character that had made them possible."[10] In an age of profound nationalism and the rise of the modern nation-state, historians endeavored to find the seeds of these fruits in the origins of their national histories, deeply embedded in the Middle Ages. Such a preoccupation assumed the centrality of political institutions and nationalism in medieval life and also presupposed that one's contemporary national character (understood in political, not social, terms) existed in some incipient medieval form. Perhaps the most significant element in this view of the past was the formulation of all political history using the dichotomy of "national history" and "external history" (these are William Stubbs's words).[11] Such intellectual categories built on modern national

---

Welt als Geschichte 18 (1958): 255–89; 19 (1959): 146–93; 20 (1960): 87–119; Franz Irsigler, *Untersuchungen zur Geschichte des frühfränkischen Adels*, Rheinisches Archiv, no. 70 (Bonn, 1969).

9. Gerd Althoff, *Spielregeln der Politik im Mittelalter: Kommunikation in Frieden und Fehden* (Darmstadt, 1997); Winfrid Glocker, *Die Verwandten der Ottonen und ihre Bedeutung in der Politik: Studien zur Familienpolitik und zur Genaeologie des sächsischen Kaiserhauses*, Dissertationen zur mittelalterlichen Geschichte, no. 5 (Cologne and Vienna, 1989).

10. Wood, "Medieval Politics," 392.

11. William Stubbs, *The Constitutional History of England*, 3 vols. (Oxford, 1880), 1:v: "The growth of the English Constitution, which is the subject of this book, is the resultant of three forces, whose reciprocal influences are constant, subtle, and intricate. These are the national character, the external history, and the institutions of the people . . . the national character has been formed by the course of the national history quite as certainly as the national history has been developed by the working of the national character; and the institutions in which the newly conscious nation is clothed may be either the work of the constructive genius of the growing race, or simply the result of the discipline of its external history."

boundaries did much to hinder a true, comprehensive medieval European history; indeed, they ran counter to the concepts of Europe held by medieval people themselves.[12] This original foundation of medieval historiography remained thereafter the bedrock of historical scholarship well into the twentieth century.

The Anglo-American historiographical tradition was built around Whig notions of state building and modernization. The key theme for this tradition was the rise of constitutionalism, whereby the unique English national character expressed itself in balancing centralized, bureaucratic government with limited executive (i.e., royal) power. Conversely, the French traced the convergence of centralized political power and the personal power of the king. The common purpose of both Anglo-American and French historiography was to show how the rise of *impersonal* institutions shaped the state. Historians understood this process as something apart from the individuals who happened to staff and administer such institutions. Hence, political history was essentially institutional history, the story of political institutions that ultimately either buttressed or restricted royal power. Of course, such a historical paradigm naturally produced the conclusion in Anglo-French historiography that medieval Germany was simply backward in comparison to western Europe, since it proved unable to fashion a unified constitutional state like England and France—hence scholars have often cited a German "special path" *(Sonderweg)* into modernity. Germany maintained a *Personenverbandsstaat* (a social polity based on the relationships between ruler and magnates), while England and France were said to have developed a "state" complete with "government" (bureaucratic institutions) and "policy."

This interest in the state as a depersonalized institution remained the driving force in political historiography, both in Europe as well as in North America, until the close of the 1960s,[13] when the entire enterprise was undermined by the rise of a new generation of medievalists who produced the "new social history" and discarded political history as too narrow and socially elitist in focus. These scholars doubted the maxim

---

12. Karl Leyser, "Concepts of Europe in the Early and High Middle Ages," *Past and Present* 137 (November 1992): 25–47 (reprinted in *Communications and Power in Medieval Europe: The Carolingian and Ottonian Centuries*, ed. Timothy Reuter [London and Rio Grande, OH, 1994], 1–18).

13. See, for example, the classics by Heinrich Mitteis and Joseph Strayer: Mitteis, *Der Staat des hohen Mittelalters*, 8th ed. (Weimer, 1968); Strayer, *On the Medieval Origins of the Modern State* (Princeton, 1970).

that the modern nation-state was the focal point of human history; they relocated the center in society. And so it has been until the past decade, as social historians have begun to reconsider political history anew and integrate the two historiographies.

The German historiographical tradition also had its origins in the same nineteenth-century preoccupations of the nation-state and national character, but with decidedly different results. Nineteenth-century German historians lamented the lack of political unification and sought the origins of this modern *Sonderweg* predicament in the Middle Ages. It is crucial to remember that modern German historiography on the Middle Ages originated during an era dominated by the forces of unification, nationalism, and unprecedented European imperialism.[14] So just like their British contemporaries,[15] German scholars thought of medieval politics in terms of their own age.[16] Therefore, while Whiggish Anglophone historiography

---

14. Dietrich Schäfer (*Deutsches Nationalbewußtsein im Licht der Geschichte* [Jena, 1884]) described the nature of late nineteenth-century German historical scholarship in no uncertain terms: "It flows along predominantly within the national stream, is accompanied chiefly by the national idea which dominates the present, which can be summarized in the words: Germany for the Germans and the Germans for Germany only. It thereby becomes an important factor in our common intellectual life" (5).

15. Herbert Butterfield (*The Whig Interpretation of History* [London, 1931; reprint, 1959], 11–12) identified the limitations of a methodology that seeks merely to find the present in the past and thus perceives history as the march of progress toward advanced modern civilization: "It is part and parcel of the whig interpretation of history that it studies the past with reference to the present; and though there may be a sense in which this is unobjectionable if its implications are carefully considered, and there may be a sense in which it is inescapable, it has often been an obstruction to historical understanding because it has been taken to mean the study of the past with direct and perpetual reference to the present. . . . On this system the historian is bound to construe his function as demanding him to be vigilant for likenesses between the past and present, instead of being vigilant for unlikenesses; so that he will find it easy to say that he has seen the present in the past, he will imagine that he had discovered a 'root' or an 'anticipation' of the 20th century, when in reality he is in a world of different connotations altogether, and he has merely tumbled upon what could be shown to be a misleading analogy."

16. Joachim Ehlers, "Die Deutsche Nation des Mittelalters als Gegenstand der Forschung," in *Ansätze und Diskontinuität Deutscher Nationsbildung im Mittelalter*, ed. Joachim Ehlers, Nationes: Historische und philologische Untersuchungen zur Entstehung der europäischen Nationen des Mittelalter, no. 8 (Sigmaringen, 1989), 13–14: "If the late medieval imperial constitution can be described as 'anarchic,' as 'a caricature,' 'a nuisance,' 'a lie,' or 'chaos,' then this view was 'decisively influenced by the events of the nineteenth century, above all by the predominant position of Prussia, whose history was considered a decisive preparation for the establishment of a German state.' " Ehlers is quoting H. Sproemberg, "Betrachtung zur Geschichte der Reichsidee im Mittelalter," in *Mittelalter und demokratische Geschichtsschreibung*, Forschungen zur mittelalterlichen Geschichte, no. 18 (Berlin, 1971), 27–44, here 29.

marginalized medieval Germany as a failed experiment in constitutional development, nineteenth-century German historiography was constructed around a paradigm of imperialist competition for national legitimacy and power. Here we find a political history with constant references to the "empire-building" schemes and "strategic alliances" of medieval monarchs; in particular the historiography on medieval Anglo-German relations reads much more like an account of modern than medieval Anglo-German political relations.[17]

After the horrors of two world wars and the Nazi era, topics dealing with nationalism and an essential national character naturally faded in postwar German historiography. *Reichsgeschichte* (comprehensive imperial history) was supplanted by research on local and regional political traditions that shaped the regional diversity of the German people. The rise of territorial lordship became the new focus in medieval history, with scholarship on regional history *(Landesgeschichte* and *Territorialpolitik)* remaining prominent to this day.[18] Local and regional research has done much to illuminate the nature of medieval society and political order within its original local contexts. In particular, it has presented the medieval German aristocracy as positive contributors to the German political tradition rather than as destroyers of some imagined centralized state under royal control.[19] Yet these regional researches have left behind earlier

---

17. Hagen Keller, *Zwischen regionaler Begrenzung und universalem Horizont,* 13–14: "The nineteenth century became the era of Historicism not merely in the scientific and scientific-theoretical manner in which one customarily describes it. Perhaps no other epoch has attempted in this manner to legitimate from history its own present and particularly its own desires and objectives."

18. The early classic of this tradition is Otto Brunner's *Land und Herrschaft: Grundfragen der territorialen Verfassungsgeschichte Österreichs im Mittelalter* (Vienna, 1939; rev. ed., Darmstadt, 1973); for the English edition see *Land and Lordship: Structures of Governance in Medieval Austria,* Middle Ages Series (Philadelphia, 1992). Benjamin Arnold has produced regional studies in the *Landesgeschichte* tradition: *Count and Bishop in Medieval Germany: A Study of Regional Power, 1100–1350* (Philadelphia, 1991); *Princes and Territories in Medieval Germany* (Cambridge, 1991). For valuable surveys of German local and regional histories see Irmline Beit-Brause, "The Place of Local and Regional History in German and French Historiography: Some General Reflections," *Australian Journal of French Studies* 16 (1979): 447–78; John Freed, "Medieval German Social History: Generalizations and Particularism," *Central European History* 25, no. 1 (1992): 1–26; P. Fried, ed., *Probleme und Methoden der Landesgeschichte* (Darmstadt, 1978); K. Jordan, "Aspekte der Mittelalterforschung in Deutschland in den letzten fünfzig Jahren," in *Ausgewählte Aufsätze zur Geschichte des Mittelalters,* Kieler historische Studien, no. 29 (Stuttgart, 1980), 329–44.

19. Arnold, *Princes and Territories,* 5: "... the territorial structure of Germany followed not from the fragmentation or usurpation of imperial authority but rather from the

efforts at understanding medieval Germany in the larger context of Europe. Only recently has this subject reemerged, no doubt because of the momentous historical changes in Europe in the past few years.[20] Hence there is still a great deal of nineteenth-century prose on medieval German "power politics" *(Machtpolitik)* to be addressed and corrected.

Up to this point I have attempted to show the convergence of several trends in the historiography of medieval politics to indicate why a study of the social aspects of Anglo-German diplomatic relations is a worthwhile endeavor. In many ways it is the natural result of the convergence of the previously mentioned trends and will not only bridge the broad chasm between national history boundaries but also provide new insights into the social nature of medieval politics between communities. We shall find a political history that looks less like an account of imperial alliances and the building of modern nation-states and more like an account of medieval social groups building and maintaining local and regional bases of power. Political ideologies will not always be the central driving force in policy decisions but rather are reflections of the interests and goals of a given social group. Familial, social, personal, and religious motives will prove to be as important as institutional and geopolitical motives. What emerges is a paradigm that looks more medieval than modern and that reveals medieval Germany as more normative and intimately connected to the political communities of western Europe than the predominant Anglo-French historiography of Anglophone scholarship has hitherto suggested. Just because Germany cannot trace the origins of its modern nation-state and modern political institutions to the Middle Ages does not mean that it was therefore cut off or somehow disconnected from England and France, though these ties were not the stuff of imperialist competition either.[21]

---

creative political and juridical outlook of the richer prelates and dynasts located in the various German regions." This was certainly the case for the archbishops of Cologne.

20. See, for example, Keller, *Zwischen regionaler Begrenzung und universalem Horizont*; Alfred Haverkamp, ed., *Friedrich Barbarossa: Handlungsspielräume und Wirkungsweisen des staufischen Kaisers,* Vorträge und Forschungen, no. 40 (Sigmaringen, 1992); and the series Nationes: Historische und philologische Untersuchungen zur Entstehung der europäischen Nationen im Mittelalter, particularly the eighth volume appearing under the editorship of Joachim Ehlers: *Ansätze und Diskontinuität Deutscher Nationsbildung im Mittelalter* (Sigmaringen, 1989).

21. Timothy Reuter, "Pre-Gregorian Mentalities," *Journal of Ecclesiastical History* 45, no. 3 (July 1994): 474: "The alterity of European culture in the twelfth and thirteenth centuries, both sacred and secular, is badly in need of rediscovery and re-emphasis."

One final word concerning methodology is needed still, in regard to the merit of studying medieval diplomatic history. It is the one area of political life to which the social history approach has not been applied extensively (at least in medieval historiography). The traffic of embassies and negotiators from one court to another has still not been fully analyzed as a social history of interactions between political communities. There are three reasons for this. First, medieval diplomatic activity appears to many as the core of the "old elitist political history" that focused on an aristocratic minority of the population. This approach has emphasized administration (that is, institutions over people) and sought the origins of modern mechanisms of diplomatic discourse. Hence one reads more about the *office* of the ambassador than about the movement of an ambassador within an actual sociopolitical network that linked regions and kingdoms.[22] Second, the intellectual boundaries of scholarship on the Middle Ages tend to line up with the current political boundaries of Europe. Hence, given the political history of the twentieth century, there has been little interest among its British and German historians for such joint ventures. Third, with the growth of social history the emphasis on regionalism and local history has predominated over questions of interregional social and political intercourse. As we have seen, German scholars have emphasized regional studies at the expense of a comprehensive integration or interregional studies until quite recently, while British historiography has shown a profound lack of interest in Anglo-German relations and has favored the traditional Anglo-French paradigm.

Fortunately these are only perceived limitations. By the time of the Central Middle Ages, bourgeois participation in diplomatic activities was expanding along with its members' economic influence. Thus historians studying this period must begin to broaden the definition of diplomatic history beyond the merely aristocratic. We shall soon meet many merchant families who were deeply involved in Anglo-German diplomacy and who served as intermediaries between archbishops, dukes, and kings over great distances. In addition, a social study of diplomatic discourse is eminently suited to the pursuit of an interregional medieval historiography. There are few better means of crossing existing intellectual and political boundaries than by a comparative use of primary sources on activities that built unifying ties between regions in the Middle Ages.

---

22. Donald E. Queller, *The Office of the Ambassador in the Middle Ages* (Princeton, 1967).

These sources ultimately indicate that medieval Europe was much more interconnected than national, regional, and local histories imply. They also make clear that medieval Anglo-German diplomacy was characterized neither by a sharp disparity in political development nor by imperialist competition.

A Case Study: Cologne and Anglo-German Relations

The call for a comparative history of medieval European societies goes back to the voice of Marc Bloch crying in the wilderness.[23] Bloch would be pleased to find that in recent years there has developed an increasing interest in comparative history and in the study of interregional activity.[24] Yet relations between the English and German realms, as already mentioned, have received very limited attention thus far. This neglect contrasts markedly with the traditional historiography of Anglo-French and papal-imperial relations. These traditional political constellations obviously exist with good reason. The Norman Conquest and the subsequent English involvement in French continental holdings, on the one hand, or the preoccupation of the German emperors in Italy and their resultant conflicts with the papacy, on the other, explain why the history of the Central and Later Middle Ages has been written along these two main geopolitical axes. Nevertheless, activity between England and Germany represented a vital and at times no less influential interregional relationship, which has not received its due attention under such a framework.

Previous research on Anglo-German relations has emphasized either

---

23. Marc Bloch, "A Contribution towards a Comparative History of European Societies," in *Land and Work in Medieval Europe: Selected Papers by Marc Bloch*, trans. J. E. Anderson (Berkeley, 1967), 44–81. Bloch begins this essay as follows: "The comparative method has great possibilities; I consider that an improved and more general use of this method in historical study is one of the most urgent tasks for the present day. . . . Nevertheless it is obvious that the majority of historians are not yet fundamentally converted to it. They make polite gestures of assent, then go back to their work without effecting the slightest change in their habits" (44).

24. See, for example, R. H. Hilton, *English and French Towns in Feudal Society: A Comparative Study* (Cambridge, 1992); James Given, *State and Society: Gwynedd and Languedoc under Outside Rule* (Ithaca, 1990). I am specifically using Bloch's definition of the comparative method as stated in *Land and Work*: "This is to make a parallel study of societies that are at once neighbouring and contemporary, exercising a constant mutual influence, exposed throughout their development to the action of the same broad causes just because they are close and contemporaneous, and owing their existence in part at least to a common origin" (47).

political alliances or trade. These two topics of research have been almost wholly the domain of German scholars, who viewed England rather narrowly in the context of either its political involvement in papal-imperial conflicts and its cultivation of anti-French allies among the German princes or its role in the history of the German Hansa. Since political history has been eclipsed by social history in the past thirty years, little new scholarship has appeared to update this historiography. Furthermore, most of the research in economic history concentrated on the Hanseatic era *(Hansezeit)* in the Later Middle Ages, so that little work has been devoted to Anglo-German relations during the pre-Hansa era *(Vorhansezeit)*—that is, around A.D. 1000–1300. Of course, the dearth of quantifiable sources on trade in the earlier period accounts for the emphasis on the Later Middle Ages. The historiography on the pre-Hansa period, however, stands in the shadow of the Hanseatic era and has not been considered in the broader context of exchange between the regions and without reference to later developments. It, like the political histories of the nineteenth and early twentieth centuries, is characterized by categories not belonging to its own era.

Aside from a few notable endeavors, virtually nothing new on the Anglo-German connection has appeared for many years.[25] A conference held in 1987 at the German Historical Institute in London, entitled "Germany and England in the High Middle Ages: A Comparative Approach," was intended to create momentum among medievalists for the cultivation of this open field. Yet, beyond Karl Leyser's impressive research, the exhortation has received little response to date for the crucial period of the Central Middle Ages. It seems incredible that 1987 was the first time

---

25. Valuable new contributions are Julia Barrow, "Cathedrals, Provosts, and Prebends: A Comparison of Twelfth-Century German and English Practice," *Journal of Ecclesiastical History* 37, no. 4 (October 1986): 536–64; idem, "Education and the Recruitment of Cathedral Canons in England and Germany," *Viator* 20 (1989): 118–37; C. Stephan Jaeger, *The Envy of Angels: Cathedral Schools and Social Ideas in Medieval Europe, 950–1200* (Philadelphia, 1994); and selected portions of Veronica Ortenberg's *The English Church and the Continent in the Tenth and Eleventh Centuries: Cultural, Spiritual, and Artistic Exchanges* (Oxford, 1992). Worthy of note as well is a recent comparative effort in the area of urban historical geography: Dietrich Denecke and Gareth Shaw, eds., *Urban Historical Geography: Recent Progress in Britain and Germany*, Cambridge Studies in Historical Geography, no. 10 (Cambridge, 1988). But in that book Brian Graham concludes: "Finally, there is an awareness of the insular parochialism of much previous [British] work and ideas and rather belatedly more attention is being paid to continental studies both as comparisons and contrasts. Oddly, however, the revisions and reevaluations persist in their isolation of each other" (38).

English and German medievalists met to consider the merits of such cooperative research.[26] Not until nine years later did a volume of articles resulting from the conference finally appear.[27] The collection is an outstanding summary of the state of research on literacy, kingship and warfare, Jewish and crusading history, and the history of urban communities, manors, and social mobility. Yet unfortunately these articles still review English and German historiographical issues in isolation from one another and leave the reader to do the comparative work. Indeed, the volume does not contain even one study of any actual relations *between* the two realms.

The English and German historiographical traditions have developed so independently of one another that they often employ two separate, parallel systems of citation for primary sources, which further complicates any attempt to synthesize the body of secondary literature.[28] This unfortunate situation, together with the European political history of this century, may help to account for the lack of interest in such research, but it does not reflect the actual status of the primary sources themselves, which are rich in material concerning the multifaceted relations between these regions.

Little needs to be said about the sizable body of documents surviving from the English realm from the eleventh to the early fourteenth century, as its value and usefulness has been demonstrated over and over again. Yet despite the lack of a highly developed royal administration in Germany, a large amount of primary source material survives virtually untapped; one need only know where to look for it. A major source of available data can be found in the records of German cities, most signifi-

---

26. Alfred Haverkamp (Trier), Hanna Vollrath (Bochum), and Karl Leyser (Oxford) were the organizers of the symposium (1–4 July 1987). Their report noted that: "This conference seems to have been the first opportunity for British and German medieval historians to meet in order to discuss German and English history in this way" (*Bulletin of the German Historical Institute of London* 10, no. 2 [May 1988]: 23–26).

27. Alfred Haverkamp and Hanna Vollrath, eds., *England and Germany in the High Middle Ages* (Oxford, 1996).

28. This is best seen in the practice of German scholars citing English sources from the excerpts in MGH SS, volumes 27 and 28 (entitled "Ex rerum Anglicarum scriptoribus"), rather than from the standard complete editions as found in the English Rolls Series. In addition the use of separate charter books and *Urkundenbücher* (e.g., Rymer's *Foedera* and Böhmer's *Regesta Imperii*) has created many problems in the consistent dating of documents. Most recently, Ferdinand Opll's *Friedrich Barbarossa*, Gestalten des Mittelalters und der Renaissance (Darmstadt, 1990), made no use of Karl Leyser's extensive scholarship in English.

cantly in the municipal documents of the largest and most powerful of these cities—Cologne. Cologne has been chosen as our case study, based on its vast archival holdings as well as on its close diplomatic and economic relationship with the English kingdom. While Cologne enjoyed relations with England unequaled by other German cities during this period, a study of its contacts will confirm the value of comparative, interregional research and serve as an exhortation to consider similar research elsewhere in Germany and England.

The city of Cologne serves as an excellent case study for applying the methodology described earlier. Its highly developed ties to England rested on two firm foundations: the traditionally pro-English policies of its archbishops and the privileged legal and economic position held by Cologne merchants and citizens in the English realm. Cologne, situated along the Rhine-Thames trading route and on the eastern frontier of France, was a natural point of contact for the English. And the powerful position of the city's archbishops as regional princes made it all the more important. The Cologne archbishops accumulated a number of honors and powers, which led to their ultimate political dominance over the lower Rhine region. Many of these ecclesiastical lords were imperial chancellors, and they had exercised the right to crown the king-elect at Aachen since the pontificate of Archbishop Heribert (999–1021); thus they played a leading role in all royal elections. In addition to their superior ecclesiastical authority throughout northwest Germany, they also exercised imperial regalian rights. Close ties had existed between the archbishopric and the German monarchy since the pontificate of Bruno I of Saxony (953–65), who was the brother of Emperor Otto I. The emperor not only appointed his brother to the Cologne see but also made Bruno the duke of Lotharingia. From this time on, therefore, the Cologne archbishops were both secular and ecclesiastical princes. As imperial princes *(principes imperii)* they were heavily involved in the emperors' Italian politics (several died in Italy on imperial campaigns), and from 1031 each bore the title of archchancellor of Italy. A few even exercised royal authority in Germany as regents. Anno II (1056–75) served as regent during part of the minority of Henry IV, and Engelbert I (1215–25) exercised this authority during the almost permanent absence of Frederick II from Germany. Engelbert was also the guardian of Frederick's son Henry. The archbishops' regional political power as territorial lords *(Landesherr)* was ultimately solidified when, as a reward for military assistance to Emperor Frederick Barbarossa against Duke Henry the

Lion in Saxony, Archbishop Philip of Cologne was given the ducal dignity and lands of Westphalia in 1180. As we shall see, over time these powerful ecclesiastical princes developed close ties with the English royal house and therefore acted as diplomatic middlemen in virtually all political contacts between England and the German empire during this period.

The second foundation of the unique relationship between Cologne and England, the dominance of the Cologne merchants in German trade with English territories, is certainly in concert with the first. Cologne merchants were beneficiaries of a long tradition of royal privileges that exempted them from exactions and local legal authority in England. These grants were in turn reconfirmed by every English king during this period. The Cologne merchants also possessed their own guildhall in London, from which all other German merchants had to operate if they wished to participate in English trade. The Cologne merchants held a monopoly over German trade with England until the late thirteenth century, when, due to the newly developing Hanseatic League, Cologne was gradually replaced by Lübeck as the dominant economic power, with the London guildhall subsumed into the larger Hanseatic Steelyard complex.

Relations between medieval England and Germany were surely rich and varied and were at times as influential as the Anglo-French and papal-imperial axes—indeed all three axes were deeply intertwined. To keep this particular study at an appropriate length, we shall focus primarily on the role of the city of Cologne in Anglo-German diplomatic intercourse, although a lively history of interregional social, cultural, economic, and religious life forms the backdrop of this study and has been told elsewhere.[29] Yet even when restricting ourselves to the realm of interregional diplomacy, Cologne is eminently suited for our purposes. Both the city and its archbishops became regional powers that were tied intimately into the interregional network of political communities connecting England and Germany. Cologne's history cuts across the tradi-

---

29. Joseph P. Huffman, *Family, Commerce, and Religion in London and Cologne: Anglo-German Emigrants, c. 1000–c. 1300*, Cambridge Studies in Medieval Life and Thought, 4th ser., no. 39 (Cambridge, 1998), completes the spectrum of Anglo-Cologne relations by examining the extensive social, economic, religious, and cultural ties that existed. See also Huffman, "Prosopography and the Anglo-Imperial Connection: A Cologne *Ministerialis* Family and Its English Relations," *Medieval Prosopography* 11, no. 2 (autumn 1990): 53–134; "*Anglicus in Colonia:* Die juristische, soziale und ökonomische Stellung der Engländer in Köln während des 12. und 13. Jahrhunderts," *JKGV* 62 (1991): 1–62; "Documentary Evidence for Anglo-German Currency Movement in the Central Middle Ages: Cologne and English Sterling," *British Numismatic Journal* 65 (1995): 32–45.

tional Anglo-French and papal-imperial political narratives, yet it impinges directly on the political fortunes of both the English and German kingdoms. This fascinating intersection of interests will allow us to combine regional and interregional politics in a manner that provides a more comprehensive view of the actual dynamics of medieval political life and that at the same time integrates at least one region of Germany more fully into western European society. As a result, we have all the tools necessary to reevaluate earlier paradigms of medieval political life as essentially driven by state and empire building.

Historiographical Review: Scholarly Literature to Date

The first attempts at writing a history of relations between medieval Germany and England were an outgrowth of the era of German nationalism in the nineteenth century and reflected an initial attitude of kinship between the two regions as a result of a common Germanic heritage and the rule of the Hanoverians in England. Yet this initial Anglophilia faded by the last quarter of the century, as the emergence of a united Germany signaled a real threat to England's predominance in European affairs. Karl Heinrich Schaible wrote a popular history of the Germans in England in 1885, in the heyday of German unification, nationalism, and imperial competition with the other European powers.[30] Schaible's book was a sketch of German emigrants in England that did little to illuminate the English half of the equation. The first scholarly attempt at such a history appeared in the form of a dissertation by Felix Wissowa in 1889.[31] His seventy-six-page study was a survey of political relations between the two kingdoms, in which he asserted the thesis that England's consistent choice to support the papacy rather than the emperor in the papal-imperial conflicts of the Central Middle Ages made it possible not only for the empire to fragment but also for France to eventually drive the English out of their continental holdings. England, by choosing the pope over the emperor, had alienated the support of the empire against the French enemy.[32] Wissowa's thesis,

---

30. Karl Heinrich Schaible, *Geschichte der Deutschen in England von den ersten germanischen Ansiedlungen in Britannien bis zum Ende des 18. Jahrhunderts* (Strasbourg, 1885).

31. Felix Wissowa, *Politische Beziehungen zwischen England und Deutschland bis zum Untergang der Staufer* (Breslau, 1889).

32. Ibid., 76: "As we have seen, England chose the pope; this proved disastrous for the empire, but no less so for England itself. When through its stance against the emperor

formed as it was on the heels of the *Kulturkampf* and Franco-Prussian War, and influenced by the development of England's policy of "splendid isolation" under the Salisbury ministry (as seen in the Mediterranean Agreements of 1887), smacks more of the political machinations of the late nineteenth-century imperialist age than of the dynamics operating during the Central Middle Ages. Indeed, this would also be the problem with the next publication to appear, that of Friedrich Hardegen in 1905.[33] Hardegen's influential dissertation was an attempt to prove that Henry II of England had employed a complex master plan to extend the "Angevin Empire" in an effort not only to swallow up the French territories but also eventually to capture the Staufen empire. Once again the themes of imperialist competition appear, this time coupled with the thesis that there was a concerted "encirclement policy" *(Einkreisungspolitik)* against the German empire. We shall consider this in more detail later, since it has some bearing on the role of Cologne in such a policy. Although Hardegen's entire methodology and use of sources was repeatedly criticized as untrustworthy,[34] the notion of an anti-Staufen *Einkreisungspolitik* managed by the Angevin dynasty survived and continued to appear in many later, more respected German studies.[35]

Hardegen's thesis is a reminder of the increasingly harsh political atmosphere that had emerged in Anglo-German affairs by the turn of the century. This was only hardened further by the cataclysm of World War I. The nadir of this vein of German historical writing on medieval Anglo-German relations appeared in Heinz Zatschek's 1942 publication *England und das Reich*, which was a piece of Nazi polemic that presented

---

England robbed itself of the possibility of using him as an ally against France, it strengthened its most dangerous enemy [France] in an unimaginable way and made it possible for France to survive the vicissitudes of the fourteenth and fifteenth centuries and finally at the end of the Middle Ages to limit the English to that which they had possessed at the beginning, namely to their island."

33. Friedrich Hardegen, *Imperialpolitik König Heinrichs II. von England*, Heidelberger Abhandlungen zur mittleren und neueren Geschichte, no. 12 (Heidelberg, 1905).

34. See, for example, H. W. C. Davis's review in *EHR* 21 (1906): 363–67; Felix Leibermann's review in *Deutsche Literaturzeitung* 26 (December 9, 1905): cols. 3066–67; Ludwig Riess's review in *Historische Zeitschrift* 97 (1906): 670–71; Ferdinand Güterbock's review in *Österreichische Geschichtsforschung* 21 (1910): 628–29; Charles Bemont's review in *Revue historique* 94 (1907): 363.

35. Odilo Engels, *Die Staufer*, 3d ed. (Stuttgart, 1984): 99–100; Horst Fuhrmann, *Deutsche Geschichte im hohen Mittelalter*, Deutsche Geschichte, no. 2 (Göttingen, 1978; 2d ed., 1983), 187–88; Helmut Hiller, *Heinrich der Löwe: Herzog und Rebell* (Munich, 1978; reprint, Frankfurt am Main, 1985), 135, 139, 165, for example.

relations between England and Germany from the Middle Ages to the present as a pretext for showing England's continual anti-German political posture.[36] The English were said to be responsible for everything from the decline of the medieval German empire to the end of the Hanseatic League. The book reaches its lowest point when castigating Richard of Cornwall for involving Jewish moneylenders in the purchase of his election as King of the Romans.

Only one major scholarly study produced during the first half of the twentieth century holds long-standing value for this subject, Walter Kienast's enormous two-volume project on the role of German princes in the conflicts among the western rulers—meaning principally the rulers of England and France.[37] Vast in scope and research, this study had a decidedly French focus and concentrated more on the princes of the region we would now call the Benelux. Thus, unfortunately, it serves our purposes only now and again, without a thorough evaluation of the place of the archbishops of Cologne among the princes of the lower Rhineland. The planned third and final volume of this monumental effort never appeared, and the original material was subsequently re-published in a revised form, which better reflected Kienast's French interests.[38]

Not until 1961 did an authoritative work on medieval Anglo-German political relations appear, and this work, Fritz Trautz's inaugural dissertation *(Habilitationsschrift)*, has served as the standard work on the subject ever since.[39] It is extremely thorough and represents the first effort at synthesizing the English and German scholarly traditions. Trautz focused on the fourteenth century and therefore incorporated only a brief retrospective survey *(Rückblick)* on the Central Middle Ages. Therefore, while his work is invaluable with regard to methodology, Trautz produced only a brief history of the last thirty years of the thirteenth century.

36. Heinz Zatschek, *England und das Reich* (Vienna, 1942).

37. Walter Kienast, "Die Deutschen Fürsten im Dienste der Westmächte bis zum Tode Philipps des Schönen von Frankreich," *Bijdragen van het Instituut voor Middeleeuwsche Geschiedenis der Rijks-Universiteit te Utrecht,* nos. 10, 16 (Utrecht and Munich, 1924–31).

38. Walter Kienast, *Deutschland und Frankreich in der Kaiserzeit (900–1270): Weltkaiser und Einzelkönige,* Monographien zur Geschichte des Mittelalters, no. 9, 1–3 (Stuttgart, 1974–75). Kienast's modernist political interests are best represented in his article "Die Anfänge des europäischen Staatensystem im späteren Mittelalter," *Historische Zeitschrift* 153 (1936): 229–71.

39. Fritz Trautz, *Die Könige von England und das Reich 1271–1377: Mit einem Rückblick auf ihr Verhältnis zu den Staufern* (Heidelberg, 1961).

Since the appearance of Trautz's study little has followed on the subject. Jens Ahlers has superbly chronicled the history of relations between the English kings (from Henry II to Henry III) and the Welf dynasty as a result of the 1168 marriage between the English princess Matilda and Duke Henry the Lion of Saxony/Bavaria.[40] To his credit he has also reevaluated German historiographical conceptions of English involvement in German political affairs. Yet his study of Anglo-Welf relations naturally focused on Saxony rather than on the Rhineland, so he mentioned Cologne and its archbishops only in passing. Although he recognized the archbishop's dominant position among the princes of the lower Rhineland, here we shall see that the archbishop of Cologne was an integral member of the Anglo-Welf connection and was as influential as the other two parties of the triangle—indeed the Cologne archbishops' relations with the English royal house spanned a much longer period than did the Anglo-Welf kinship ties and were therefore more influential in the long run.

In the same year as Ahlers's book two publications by Dieter Berg appeared.[41] His book was a study of Anglo-Norman foreign policy with primary attention to western Europe. Relations with the empire, therefore, take up only a small portion of the discussion, and the study only touches on relations from the Norman Conquest to the end of Henry I's reign (1066–1135). Yet the book has the merit of presenting these relations from the perspective of the English kings. Further, Berg's article was a valuable addition to the debate among German scholars over the reality of an imperial ideology of world dominion *(Weltherrschaftsidee)*. Rather than relying exclusively on imperial polemical sources for this debate, as so many had before, Berg looked at the actual political developments themselves for evidence of a tangible implementation of such an alleged imperial sovereignty. In both of these works, however, the archbishops of Cologne find little place.

Despite their limitations for our purposes, the works of both Ahlers and Berg have made significant contributions to reevaluating modern German

---

40. Ahlers, *Die Welfen und die englischen Könige 1165–1235,* Quellen und Darstellungen zur Geschichte Niedersachsens, no. 102 (Hildesheim, 1987).

41. Dieter Berg, *England und der Kontinent: Studien zur auswärtigen Politik der anglonormannischen Könige im 11. und 12. Jahrhundert* (Bochum, 1987); "Imperium und Regna: Beiträge zur Entwicklung der deutsch-englischen Beziehungen im Rahmen der auswärtigen Politik der römischen Kaiser und deutschen Könige im 12. und 13. Jahrhundert," in *Zeitschrift für Historische Forschung Beihefte 5: "Bündnissystem" und "Außenpolitik" im späteren Mittelalter,* ed. Peter Moraw (Berlin, 1987), 13–37.

historiography's traditional view of the nature of medieval politics in general and in the political life of medieval Germany in particular. Even so, their work has not generated a widespread reconsideration of the traditional historiography on medieval Anglo-German politics and diplomacy. The traditional view remains, irrespective of the fact that it was shaped by the modern political interests of the early twentieth century.

It should be obvious by now that the bulk of the research has been done by German scholars; only a few articles by English historians have appeared on selected subjects. The only extended effort in English to date has been a popular history by Ian Colvin in 1915.[42] Ironic as was the appearance of this brief publication during World War I, it was not until the years surrounding World War II that A. L. Poole, Geoffrey Barraclough, and Charles C. Bayley introduced English-speaking scholars to topics on German political history.[43] This rather small corpus of Anglophone scholarship on medieval Germany was not substantially supplemented until some twenty years later. Geoffrey Barraclough, himself responsible for the renewal of interest in things German among Anglophone scholars, essentially abandoned the field after World War II.[44] The outstanding publications of Karl Leyser, which will find mention often in this study, sparked a muted revival in medieval German studies during the postwar years.[45] A

42. Ian Colvin, *The Germans in England, 1066–1598* (London, 1915). For an interesting study on this period see Stuart Wallace, *War and the Image of Germany: British Academics, 1914–1918* (Edinburgh, 1988).

43. In addition to Poole's contributions on Germany in the *Cambridge Medieval History,* see Austin Lane Poole, *Henry the Lion* (Oxford, 1912); "Die Welfen in der Verbannung," *Deutsches Archiv für Geschichte des Mittelalters* 2 (1938): 129–48; "Richard the First's Alliances with the German Princes in 1194," in *Studies in Medieval History Presented to F. M. Powicke,* ed. R. W. Hunt, W. A. Pantin, and R. W. Southern (Oxford, 1948), 90–99. See Geoffrey Barraclough, "Edward I and Adolf of Nassau, a Chapter of Medieval Diplomatic History," *Cambridge Historical Journal* 6 (1940): 225–62; *The Origins of Modern Germany,* 2d ed. (Oxford, 1947); ed., *Mediaeval Germany, 911–1250: Essays by German Historians,* 2 vols., Studies in Mediaeval Germany, nos. 1 and 2 (Oxford, 1948), the second volume of which contains a comparative essay by A. Brackmann, "The Birth of the National State in Medieval Germany and the Norman Monarchies" (281–300), which is primarily institutional and constitutional in focus; "Frederick Barbarossa and the Twelfth Century," in *History in a Changing World* (Oxford, 1955; reprint, 1957), 73–96. See Charles C. Bayley, "The Diplomatic Preliminaries of the Double Election of 1257 in Germany," *EHR* 62 (1947): 457–83; *The Formation of the German College of Electors in the Mid-Thirteenth Century* (Toronto, 1949).

44. For Barraclough's changing views on European history as a result of World War II see his essay "Europe in Perspective: New Views on European History," in *History in a Changing World* (Oxford, 1955; reprint, 1957), 168–84.

45. See the bibliography for Leyser's wide-ranging publications.

handful of other scholars publishing in English, such as Timothy Reuter, John Gillingham, Benjamin Arnold, John Freed, John Van Engen, and David Abulafia, have made important new contributions in the last decade or so on selected topics involving medieval Germany.[46] These works have enlightened non-German speakers about medieval Germany and at times have used a social approach to politics as well. For the most part they follow the German postwar historiographical tradition, focusing on regional and local studies rather than on interregional or diplomatic activity. Hence there exists to date a limited but growing body of Anglophone scholarship on medieval Germany during the Central Middle Ages. But with regard to Anglo-German diplomatic relations in particular nothing of length has been written to supersede the politically charged historiography of the early twentieth century. Only two brief surveys (of nine and eleven pages, respectively) have appeared, in which twentieth-century diplomatic terminology like *entente cordiale* and *détente* continues to modernize medieval politics.[47]

The literature on Anglo-German economic relations is worth considering briefly in this context, since commercial diplomacy will have a direct bearing on the political realities we shall discuss later. Once again we find the overwhelming preponderance of German scholarship. Research in economic relations between England and Germany has been deeply rooted in the soil of scholarship on the Hanseatic League. This work was stimulated by the fundamental study of the London Steelyard complex begun by Sartorius and completed by Lappenberg.[48] It was followed by a series of articles on the *Vorhansezeit*—that is, the period before the Hansa became a truly pan-German institution (ca. 1000–1300)—in the journal *Hansische Geschichtsblätter*.[49]

---

46. See the bibliography for works by these historians. For early medieval Germany see also John W. Bernhardt, *Itinerant Kingship and Royal Monasteries in Early Medieval Germany, c. 936–1075*, Cambridge Studies in Medieval Life and Thought, 4th ser., no. 21 (Cambridge, 1993).

47. B. Arnold, "England and Germany, 1050–1350," in *England and Her Neighbours, 1066–1453: Essays in Honour of Pierre Chaplais*, ed. Michael Jones and Malcolm Vale (London, 1989), 43–51; "Germany and England, 1066–1453," in *England in Europe, 1066–1453*, ed. Nigel Saul (New York, 1994), 76–87.

48. G. F. Sartorius, *Urkundliche Geschichte des Ursprungs der deutschen Hanse*, ed. John Martin Lappenberg, 2 vols. (Hamburg, 1830); J. M. Lappenberg, *Urkundliche Geschichte des Hansischen Stahlhofes zu London* (Hamburg, 1851; new ed., Osnabrück, 1967).

49. Konstantin Höhlbaum, "Kölns älteste Handelsprivilegien für England," *HGB* 3 (1882): 41–48; Karl Kunze, "Das erste Jahrhundert der deutschen Hanse in England,"

The focus in the *Vorhansezeit* research was a debate about the relationship between the original Cologne guildhall and the later Hanseatic Steelyard complex in London—specifically about when the former lost its dominance and was absorbed into the latter, signifying the true beginning of a united German Hansa in England under the leadership of Lübeck. The debate over how much one can consider Cologne a true Hansa city *(Hansestadt)* has continued up to the present.[50] Dollinger's standard history of the Hansa mentions the dominant role of Cologne in the *Vorhansezeit*, though its main focus was the period from the fourteenth to the sixteenth century.[51] The standard sourcebooks for the Hansa were edited by the same German scholars, and the bulk of their documents comes from the golden age *(Blütezeit)* of the Hansa, in the Later Middle Ages.[52]

Once again institutional history has predominated, with no thoroughgoing social analysis of the members of this institution. Although studies of German Hansa merchants in England have been promised, little has appeared to date.[53] Interest has recently been kindled among British

---

HGB 6 (1889): 129–54; Walther Stein, "Die Hansebruderschaft der Kölner Englandfahrer und ihr Stadt vom Jahre 1324," *HGB* (1908): 197–240; W. Kurzinna, "Der Name Stahlhof," *HGB* 18 (1912): 429–61; Martin Weinbaum, "Stahlhof und Deutsche Gildhalle zu London," *HGB* 33 (1928): 45–65.

50. Detlev Ellmers ("Die Entstehung der Hanse," *HGB* 103 [1985]: 3–40) has argued anew that the founding of Lübeck was the decisive event for the emergence of the German Hansa and not the Cologne guildhall in London, while Joachim Deeters (*Die Hanse und Köln: Ausstellung des Historischen Archivs der Stadt Köln zum 8. Hansetag der Neuzeit in Köln im September 1988* [Cologne, 1988]) has reaffirmed the contention that Cologne was the early leader among the *Hansestädte.*

51. Philippe Dollinger, *La Hanse* (Paris, 1964); *Die Hanse* (Stuttgart, 1966); *The German Hansa,* ed. and trans. D. S. Ault and S. H. Steinberg (London, 1970). Terence H. Lloyd's book *England and the German Hansa, 1157–1611: A Study of Their Trade and Commercial Diplomacy* (Cambridge, 1991) adds much to Dollinger's material on the Later Middle Ages, but little for the pre-Hansa period. Still useful is Etienne Sabbe, "Les relations économiques entre l'Angleterre et le Continent au Haut Moyen Age," *Le Moyen Age 56* (1950): 169–93. For the most recent work see Heinz Stoob, *Die Hanse* (Styria, 1995); Uwe Ziegler, *Die Hanse: Aufstieg, Blütezeit und Niedergang der ersten europaischen Wirtschaftsgemeinschaft: Eine Kulturgeschichte von Handel und Wandel zwischen 13. und 17. Jahrhundert,* 2d ed. (Bern, 1997).

52. See *HUB* vols. 1–3, ed. Konstantin Höhlbaum (Halle, 1876–86); vols. 4–6, ed. Karl Kunze (Halle, 1896; Leipzig, 1899–1905); vol. 7, ed. H. G. Runstedt (Weimar, 1939); vols. 8–11, ed. A. Stein (Leipzig and Munich, 1899–1916). See also Karl Koppmann, ed., *Hanserecesse: Die Recesse und andere Akten der Hansetage von 1256–1430,* vol. 1, *1256–1370* (Leipzig, 1870); Karl Kunze, ed., *Hanseakten aus England 1271 bis 1472,* Hansische Geschichtsquellen, no. 6 (Halle, 1891).

53. Natalie Fryde has promised such studies in "Deutsche Englandkaufleute in Frühhansischer Zeit," *HGB* 97 (1979): 1–14; "Arnold fitz Thedmar und die Entstehung der

historians by the discovery of the Cologne guildhall and the Steelyard complex during new building at the Cannon Street underground railway station in London.[54] Other noteworthy contributions to this work have been made by English scholars, but again it has been overwhelmingly the province of German historians.[55]

These trends in research on Anglo-German political and economic history in general apply even more so to the thin historiography on Anglo-Cologne diplomacy in particular. Karl Wand's 1957 article only begins to sketch the outline of political relations, but it clearly shows the potential for further detailed research.[56] Hugo Stehkämper's several valuable articles concerning the roles of the burghers of Cologne and their archbishops in the elections of Otto IV and Richard of Cornwall represent the extent of publications on the subject.[57] The bulk of the numerous studies on the archbishops of Cologne customarily focus on their regional

Grossen Deutschen Hanse," *HGB* 107 (1989): 27–42; "Hochfinanz und Landesgeschichte im Deutschen Hochmittelalter," *Blätter für Deutsche Landesgeschichte* 125 (1989): 1–12. She has produced one such study to date: *Ein mittelalterlicher deutscher Großunternehmer: Terricus Teotonicus de Colonia in England, 1217–1247*, Vierteljahrschrift für Sozial- und Wirtschaftsgeschichte, Beihefte no. 125 (Stuttgart, 1996).

54. Derek Keene, "New Discoveries at the Hanseatic Steelyard in London," *HGB* 107 (1989): 15–25; *Die Hanse: Lebenswirklichkeit und Mythos, Eine Ausstellung*, Museum für Hamburgische Geschichte (Hamburg, 1989), 2:47.

55. Travers Twiss, *On the Early Charters Granted by the Kings of England to the Merchants of Cologne* (London, 1881); A. Weiner, "Early Commercial Intercourse between England and Germany," *Economica* 11 (1922): 127–48; P. H. Sawyer, "The Wealth of England in the Eleventh Century," *TRHS*, 5th ser., 15 (1965): 145–64; Eleonora M. Carus-Wilson, "Die Hanse und England," in *Hanse in Europa: Brücke zwischen den Märkten 12.–17. Jahrhundert* (Cologne, 1973), 85–106; Pamela Nightingale, "The Evolution of Weight-Standards and the Creation of New Monetary and Commercial Links in Northern Europe from the Tenth Century to the Twelfth Century," *Economic History Review*, 2d ser., 38, no. 2 (May 1985): 192–209.

56. Karl Wand, "Die Englandpolitik der Stadt Köln und ihrer Erzbischöfe im 12. und 13. Jahrhundert," in *Aus Mittelalter und Neuzeit: Festschrift zum 70. Geburtstag von Gerhard Kallen*, ed. Josef Engel and Hans Martin Klinkenbert (Bonn, 1957), 77–95.

57. Hugo Stehkämper, "Konrad von Hochstaden, Erzbischof von Köln (1238–1261)," *JKGV* 36/37 (1961/62): 95–116; "England und die Stadt Köln als Wahlmacher König Ottos IV," *Köln, das Reich und Europa*, MSAK 60 (1971): 213–24; "Der Kölner Erzbischof Adolf von Altena und die deutsche Königswahl (1195–1205)," in *Historische Zeitschrift, Beihefte NF 2*, ed. Theodor Schneider, Beiträge zur Geschichte des mittelalterlichen deutschen Königtums (Munich, 1973), 5–83; "Geld bei deutschen Königswahlen des 13. Jahrhunderts," in *Beiträge zur Wirtschaftsgeschichte 4: Wirtschaftskräfte und Wirtschaftswege*, vol. 1, *Mittelmeer und Kontinent: Festschrift für Hermann Kellenbenz*, ed. Jürgen Schneider (Bamberg, 1978), 83–135; "Die Stadt Köln in der Salierzeit," in *Die Salier und das Reich*, ed. Stefan Weinfurter (Sigmaringen, 1991), 3:75–152.

politics *(Territorialpolitik)* in Westphalia and the lower Rhineland, with virtually nothing on their relations with England. In the area of economic ties between the regions little has been added to the material mentioned earlier concerning Hanseatic history. Horst Buszello and Franz Irsigler have done research on Anglo-Cologne commerce, but their attention has been once again on the fourteenth and fifteenth centuries.[58] A 1965 Cologne exhibition catalog contains an excellent sketch of sources surviving in the municipal archive, but it is not an exhaustive presentation of materials available, particularly in regard to English sources.[59] Since the historiography on economic history has been dominated by interest in the Hansa, the emphasis has naturally been the activities of the Germans in England.

The period covered in this study, ca. 1066–1307, has been chosen for a variety of reasons. At first glance these dates reflect an English chronology from the Norman Conquest to the end of Edward I's reign. Yet they are convenient markers in other respects. Although 1066 is a key point in English history, it also serves as an approximate marker for developments in Europe as a whole: Henry IV had begun his troubled minority in Germany ten years earlier, the French king Philip I had begun his long reign in 1060, and reform-minded popes (such as Nicholas II, Alexander II, and Gregory VII) were firmly entrenched in Rome by this time. When one adds the epoch-making cultural developments emerging from the second half of the eleventh century onward, it is not hard to understand why many historians consider the decade surrounding the 1050s as the beginning of the High, or Central, Middle Ages.[60] A practical consideration for this choice is, of course, that the surviving sources increase continually both in volume and detail from this time onward.

The end of Edward I's reign in England has been chosen as an ending

---

58. For example, Horst Buszello, "Köln und England (1468–1509)," *Köln, Das Reich und Europa, MSAK* 60 (1971): 431–67; Franz Irsigler, "Industrial Production, International Trade, and Public Finances in Cologne," *Journal of European Economic History* 6 (1977): 269–306; idem, *Die wirtschaftliche Stellung der Stadt Köln im 14. und 15. Jahrhundert,* Vierteljahrschrift für Sozial- und Wirtschaftsgeschichte, Beihefte no. 65 (Wiesbaden, 1979). For an emphasis on the Hansa see Walther Stein, *Die Hanse und England: Ein hansisch-englischer Seekrieg im 15. Jahrhundert,* 2d ed., Pfingstblätter des Hansischen Geschichtsvereins, no. 1 (Leipzig, 1905).

59. Hugo Stehkämper, ed., *England und Köln: Beziehungen durch die Jahrhunderte in archivalischen Zeugnissen.* (Cologne, 1965).

60. See, for example, Horst Fuhrmann, *Germany in the High Middle Ages (c. 1050–1200),* Cambridge Medieval Textbooks (Cambridge, 1986); Haverkamp, *Medieval Germany (1056–1273).* French historians also often use this dating scheme.

point for this study (though we shall stray beyond this boundary now and then) because by that point the German empire no longer held even the appearance of a unified force in European politics and by then the papacy's exile in Avignon had begun. Therefore Anglo-French conflicts would no longer have an imperial angle worth playing, and the papal-imperial conflicts which had defined an entire era were exhausted. In particular, however, the end of Edward I's reign has special significance for Cologne. With the issuance of the great Commercial Charter *(Carta Mercatoria)* in 1303 the long process that saw the erosion of Cologne's dominance over German trade with England had been completed. After this period Cologne lost its sole position of leadership to Lübeck, as the Hanseatic era was ushered in.

By this time the archbishops of Cologne had firmly established themselves as powerful regional princes operating completely independent of imperial restraint or fear of French interference. Therefore, their traditional attention to England faded increasingly in favor of territorial interests at home. By the end of Edward I's reign the elements that made up the special relationship between Cologne and England had ended. The early fourteenth century was the end of an era both for Anglo-German diplomacy in general and for relations between England and Cologne in particular.

The intention of this work is, then, to move beyond the traditional themes of geopolitical and Hanseatic alliances to see medieval political and commercial diplomacy within their social and interregional contexts. Such a perspective will free us from earlier paradigms of medieval diplomatic life as defined by state and empire building and instead allow us to comprehend and appreciate more fully both the social aspects of medieval political life and the vital nature of Anglo-German relations within the matrix of western European society. We shall therefore be considering Anglo-German relations from the perspective of its continental hub: the city of Cologne. And we shall be examining political life from a social, rather than from an institutional or ideological, context. To what extent, then, are the themes of state modernization and empire building legitimate in the medieval histories of England and Germany? To what extent is the absence of Anglo-German relations in the historiography of medieval European development legitimate? How "underdeveloped" was medieval Germany in comparison to medieval England (and the West in general)? Let us now move on to answer these questions.

1

Diplomatic Relations between the Anglo-Norman and Salian Kingdoms

A Review of Anglo-Saxon–Ottonian Relations

Although pre–Norman Conquest Anglo-Saxon ties to the Ottonian empire lie beyond the range of this study, it is important to define their nature as our starting point.[1] Suffice it to say that the foundations for lasting and continually expanding relations between the two kingdoms were laid before the arrival of the Normans in England.[2] Northern Germany had for a long time served as a place of exile for those aristocratic families that had lost power in the struggles between the Anglo-Saxon kingdoms. This may have developed out of a sense of kinship between the Anglo-Saxons in England and the Saxon ruling house in Germany. Early evidence of embassies[3] ultimately resulted in a dynastic marriage between

---

1. For a brief survey of these relations see Wissowa, *Politische Beziehungen*, 7–15. For introductory material on Ottonian Germany see Karl Leyser, "Henry I and the Beginning of the Saxon Empire," *EHR* 83 (1968): 1–32; "Ottonian Government," *Medieval Germany and Its Neighbours* (London, 1982), 69–101; "Die Ottonen und Wessex," *Frühmittel-alterliche Studien* 17 (1983): 73–97 (translated into English as "The Ottonians and Wessex," in *Communications and Power in Medieval Europe: The Carolingian and Ottonian Centuries*, ed. Timothy Reuter [London and Rio Grande, OH, 1994], 73–104); chapters in the *New Cambridge Medieval History*, vol. 3, ed. Timothy Reuter.

2. Veronica Ortenberg (*The English Church and the Continent*, 61–94) has identified the currents of exchange during this period. See also Janet L. Nelson, "England and the Continent in the Anglo-Saxon Period," in *England in Europe, 1066–1453*, ed. Nigel Saul (New York, 1994), 21–35; J. Campbell, "England, France, and Germany: Some Comparisons and Connexions," in *Ethelred the Unready: Papers from the Millenary Conference*, ed. David Hill, BAR British Series, no. 59 (Oxford, 1978); W. Levison, *England and the Continent in the Eighth Century* (Oxford, 1946).

3. Asser, "Asser's Life of King Alfred," in *Alfred the Great*, trans. S. D. Keynes and M. Lapidge (Harmondsworth, 1983), 63. Page 81 mentions the arrival of a Saxon monk named John at Alfred's court in the late ninth century, and a letter from a certain Immo to Bishop Azecho of Worms (*Die Ältere Wormser Briefsammlung*, ed. Walther Blust, MGH Epistolae: Die Briefe der Deutschen Kaiserzeit, no. 3 [Weimar, 1949], 20–22, no. 5) mentions the reception of an embassy from England by the empress in 1036.

Aethelstan's half sister Edith and the future emperor Otto I in 929.[4] This marriage venture led Bishop Ceonwald of Worcester to visit several monasteries in Germany, St. Gall being principal among them. These visits resulted in the establishment of prayer brotherhoods between the English and German monks to strengthen ties begun with the marriage alliance.[5]

At this early date the city of Cologne and its archbishop became central players in the growing Anglo-German nexus. The city had enjoyed a steady rise in both ecclesiastical and imperial importance since late Merovingian times. St. Boniface, who had originally intended Cologne as his see before removing to Mainz, dedicated the first cathedral there to St. Peter. In 689 the wife of Pepin II of Heristal, Plectrude, founded a house for female religious on the site of an old Roman temple, which was later known as St. Maria im Kapitol. The bishopric of Cologne was then raised to the archiepiscopal rank by Charlemagne in 812, and by the reign of Otto I the see was occupied by none other than the emperor's brother, Bruno I (953–65). Bruno received from his brother not only this powerful ecclesiastical position but also the duchy of Lotharingia. The combination of spiritual and secular power assured the future archbishops a major role in the life of the empire.[6]

By the early eleventh century the archbishop of Cologne had taken the lead in German diplomatic relations with England. In 1054 Bishop Ealdred of Worcester led a legation to Germany, which was warmly received in Cologne by Emperor Henry III and Archbishop Hermann II.[7]

---

4. Aethelstan's other half sister was married to Conrad, son of Rudolf, the king of Burgundy: see R. L. Poole, "Burgundian Notes: The Alpine Son-in-Law of Edward the Elder," *EHR* 26 (1911): 313–17. See especially Janet Nelson, "England and the Continent in the Anglo-Saxon Period," 28; Wolfgang Georgi, "Bischof Keonwald von Worcester und die Heirat Ottos I. mit Edgitha im Jahre 929," *Historisches Jahrbuch* 115(1995):1–40; and J. Sarnowsky, "England und der Kontinent im 10. Jahrhundert," *Historisches Jahrbuch* 114(1994):47–75.

5. Gerd Althoff, *Amicitiae et Pacta: Bündnis, Einung, Politik und Gebetsgedenken im beginnenden 10. Jahrhundert*, MGH Schriften, no. 37 (Hanover, 1992), 124–27. The archbishop of Cologne's name also appears in the *Verbrüderungsbuch* of St. Gall.

6. *Die Vita Brunonis des Ruotger*, ed. F. Lotter (Bonn, 1958).

7. *The Anglo-Saxon Chronicle*, ed. Benjamin Thorpe, RS, no. 23 (London, 1861; reprint, 1964), 2:155–56; *Chronica pontificum ecclesiae Eboracensis (The Historians of the Church of York and its Archbishops)*, ed. James Raine, RS, no. 71 (London, 1886; reprint, 1965), 2:345. Ealdred was bishop of Worcester and then was raised to archbishop of York by 1061: see Florence and John of Worcester, *Chronicon ex chronicis*, ed. Benjamin Thorpe, English Historical Society Publications (London, 1848–49), 1:218. Roger of Howden includes this account in his history: see *Chronica magistri Rogeri de Hovedene*, ed. William Stubbs, RS, no. 51 (London, 1868–71; reprint, 1964), 1:101.

No doubt the emperor and archbishop were well disposed toward the bishop of Worcester, since Ealdred's predecessor had come to Germany in 1036 accompanying King Cnut's daughter, Cunnigunde, on her way to marry the young Henry III.[8] And (as mentioned already) Bishop Ceonwald of Worcester had escorted two daughters of King Aethelstan into the Ottonian realm for an earlier double marriage to Otto I and the son of King Rudolf of Burgundy in 929. Ealdred's 1054 embassy, however, had come to obtain not a marriage but rather the return of the aetheling (king's son) Edward, son of Edmund Ironside, from Hungary, where he had been in exile under the protection of the emperor. Since King Edward the Confessor had no heir, the stability of the Anglo-Saxon kingdom necessitated the aetheling's return. Negotiations were apparently protracted, since the English legation remained in Cologne for about a year. In fact Edward returned to England only in 1057; the delay may have been due to Henry III's death and the outbreak of war in Hungary.[9]

Such growing dynastic ties between the royal households naturally stimulated cultural exchanges as well. Monastic and episcopal visits, the establishment of confraternities, and exchanges of manuscripts, Gospel books, relics, and liturgical practices became regular,[10] and English pilgrims passed through the Rhineland in increasing numbers on their way to Rome.[11] Economic exchange also expanded, and of all German cities Cologne benefited the most from this newly forged network. It became the central marketplace of the Rhine-Thames trading route, complete with an imperial palace and a guild system of merchants—with striking similarities to English guilds—whose political power was expanding along with the economy. It became possible, then, for an English abbess to pass many years in Cologne and for several Scottish monks to establish themselves in the most prestigious monasteries of the city.[12] There can be

---

8. *Hemingi Chartularium Ecclesiae Wigornensis,* ed. T. Hearne (Oxford, 1723), 1:267; H. Bresslau, ed., *Die Werke Wipos,* MGH SS rer. Germ., no. 61 (Hanover and Leipzig, 1915; reprint, Hanover, 1977), 54, 93.

9. Wissowa, *Politische Beziehungen,* 15.

10. Nelson, "England and the Continent in the Anglo-Saxon Period," 33.

11. Ortenberg, *The English Church and the Continent,* 61–94.

12. Aelfgifu became abbess of Nunnaminster after spending a number of years in Cologne: see S. J. Ridyard, *The Royal Saints of Anglo-Saxon England* (Cambridge, 1988), 34, 259–308 (appendix 1). The Scottish monks, who resided at the Benedictine houses of Groß St. Martin and St. Pantaleon under the dual abbacy of the reformer Elias (1019–42), experienced growing tension between themselves and the German contingent: "Propter religionem districtam disciplinamque nimiam et propter aliquos Scottus, quos secum habebat Helias Scottus abbas, qui monasterium Sancti Pantalionis et sancti Martini in

little doubt that by the early eleventh century England and Germany were much more similar and interrelated as European regions than is generally recognized.[13] This context is the starting point for this study.

Wars and Rumors of War:
Cologne and Norman-Salian Regionalism

The close diplomatic relations between England and Germany of the early eleventh century, which had undergirded and enabled the growing interregional economic and cultural ties, were given a new dynamic by the Norman Conquest of 1066. Initially the Norman rulers of England had little reason to seek ties with the Salian empire, for their attention was necessarily still drawn to the territories surrounding Normandy and to the consolidation of their new island kingdom. Traditional Saxon loyalties between the empire and the conquered Anglo-Saxons were further disturbed by papal support for the Conquest. Growing tensions between the papal and imperial parties would only have furthered this lack of common interests between the Norman and Salian rulers. The abrupt break in dynastic ties between the ruling houses of England and Germany was further punctuated by William the Conqueror's marriage to Matilda (1053), daughter of Count Baldwin V of Flanders, who had been the enemy of both Edward the Confessor and Emperor Henry III.

This being said, however, William of Poitiers reports that German mercenaries were allowed to participate in the conquest of England with the permission of Henry IV; indeed, Henry was supposed to have allowed this because "he was recently joined in friendship" *[noviter junctus fuit in amicitia]* with the Norman duke.[14] Some of the Flemish knights who took part were therefore from the imperial fiefs in Flanders. How, then, do we reconcile William's account with the apparent lack of common cause between the Norman and Salian houses?

Tacit Salian support for the Norman conquest of their Saxon cousins

Colonia pariter regebat . . ." (MGH SS, 5:556). See Hans Joachim Kracht, *Geschichte der Benedictinerabtei St. Pantaleon in Köln 965–1250,* Studien zur Kölner Kirchengeschichte, no. 11 (Siegburg, 1975), 56–59; Peter Opladen, *Groß St. Martin: Geschichte einer Stadt-kölnischen Abtei,* Studien zur Kölner Kirchengeschichte, no. 2 (Düsseldorf, 1954), 18–24.

13. Karl Leyser, "England and the Empire in the Early Twelfth Century," in *Medieval Germany and Its Neighbours (900–1250)* (London, 1982), 192; Janet Nelson, "England and the Continent in the Anglo-Saxon Period," 35.

14. William of Poitiers, *Histoire de Guillaume de la Conquérant,* ed. Raymonde Foreville (Paris, 1952), 154.

can be traced to the archbishop of Cologne, Anno II (1056–75). Here we discover the first of many such instances in which local and regional exigencies and the personal nature of medieval politics determined the political relationships between medieval kingdoms. The German king, Henry IV, had reached the age of fifteen by this time and therefore his majority, yet he was still under the firm control of Anno's faction of imperial princes. Anno became regent and thereafter was in a constant struggle with Archbishop Adalbert of Hamburg-Bremen for the control of the young prince. But in 1066 Anno had the upper hand and personal possession of Henry, after having abducted the young Salian along with the imperial regalia at Kaiserswerth in April 1062. As de facto regent, Anno directed an officially neutral imperial policy toward William's venture, even amid Anglo-Saxon pleas for help.[15] Such a pro-Norman policy led a later historian of Cologne to allege that Anno even supported William with money and troops.[16] The details of Anno's direct support are lacking, but his pro-Norman position was apparently enough of a matter of contention among the competing factions in Germany to be used against him a few years later. It was, in fact, Anno, rather than the young Salian king, who was *amicitia iunctus* with the Norman court, and this will not be the last time that an archbishop of Cologne's personal interests would set imperial diplomacy on a pro-English footing.[17]

Anno's shaping of imperial policy and control over the young Henry was bound to cause conflict, and such we find eight years later. In May 1074 Henry IV hastily cancelled his planned campaign against Hungarian rebels and moved his army to the Rhine when he received a surprising report in Regensburg.[18] Since the young king was in a very difficult political position in 1073–74, with a growing number of Saxon princes having turned against him and calling for his deposition, the news proved extremely disconcerting. According to members of Henry's court

---

15. Wissowa, *Politische Beziehungen*, 17.

16. Leonard Ennen, *Geschichte der Stadt Köln* (Cologne, 1860–79), 1:336–37. Although Ennen's claims of direct offensive and defensive support are exaggerated and without documentary foundation, Anno clearly held to a pro-Norman position.

17. Anno's Vita includes mention that he was "joined in friendship" with and received frequent embassies from England and Denmark: see *Vita Annonis archiepiscopi Coloniensis*, ed. R. Koepke, MGH SS, no. 11 (Hanover, 1854), 478–79. This activity was no doubt in connection with his role as regent.

18. Lampert of Hersfeld, *Lamperti monachi Hersfeldensis opera*, ed. Oswald Holder-Egger, MGH SS rer. Germ., no. 38 (Hanover and Leipzig, 1894; reprint, 1984), 195–97 (= MGH SS, 5:216). See also *REK*, 1:306–7, no. 1036.

(familiares), rumors were afoot that King William of England had been lured by the empty promises of Anno and was advancing an army through Lotharingia on his way to capture Aachen, the coronation city of the German kingdom. It appeared that Anno had joined the Saxon rebellion and even enlisted the aid of a foreign monarch. Henry first moved to Mainz—where he spent Pentecost (June 8)—and then, full of fury after discovering the rumor had no foundation, marched his army toward Cologne to confront Anno. The archbishop had meanwhile got wind of these events and made his own initiative, first sending an embassy to the king and then meeting him south of the city in Andernach. There he escaped the serious charge of treason by an oath of purgation before the king.

There was nowhere a more problematic region for Henry IV's rule than the northern duchy of Saxony, the heartland of Ottonian royal power. Upon achieving personal independence, the Salian monarch began a policy of castle-building and installing his Swabian ministerials *(ministeriales)* in Saxony in an attempt to regain his predecessors' basis of royal power, much of which had been lost to the nobility during the long years of his minority. Unlike his Norman contemporaries, King Henry lacked the power base needed for an active feudal policy, and so a castle-building strategy was the only alternative. In particular, he introduced a policy of reversion, whereby he reclaimed lands that the Saxon monarchs had granted out as private property *(in proprietatem)* and that had become the basis for noble independence and regional power. This aggressive reassertion of royal prerogatives induced a dangerous Saxon rebellion in 1073.[19] And there was a grave danger that Anno would join the Saxon rebels, thus leaving Henry in an even more precarious situation.[20] Anno's potential sympathy for the rebels was based on kinship ties: his nephew Burchard was the bishop of Halberstadt, and his brother Werner was

---

19. See Leyser, *Crisis in Medieval Germany;* "Gregory VII and the Saxons," in *La Riforma Gregoriana e l'Europa,* ed. Alphonso M. Stickler, Studi Gregoriani, no. 14, 2 (Rome, 1991), 231–38 (reprinted in *Communications and Power: The Gregorian Revolution and Beyond,* ed. Timothy Reuter [London and Rio Grande, OH, 1994], 69–76). Ministerials *(ministeriales)* were originally unfree professional retainers of kings and nobles; by the thirteenth century they had achieved freedom and the status of knighthood by virtue of their military and administrative services.

20. In *Erzbischof Anno II. von Köln (1056–1075) und sein politisches Wirken: Ein Beitrag zur Geschichte der Reichs' und Territorialpolitik im 11. Jahrhundert,* Monographien zur Geschichte des Mittelalters, no. 8, parts 1 and 2 (Stuttgart, 1974–75), 2:396–97, Georg Jenal has pointed out the strained relations between Henry IV and Anno and the danger for Henry of losing Anno to the rebels.

the archbishop of Magdeburg—indeed Anno had worked very hard to place these relatives in such high ecclesiastical positions in earlier years.[21] The centrality of familial ties and local interests in medieval political life threatened to overcome the archbishop's allegiance to the monarch.

Some have concluded that the rumor of a second Norman Conquest, which was effective enough to cause the German king to call off a fully organized campaign and move an army across the entire kingdom (indeed the historian Lampert of Hersfeld says the king was initially "territus"), shows what the Germans thought William capable of and how much unfriendly sentiment must have existed against the Norman king.[22] Yet there has been little discussion about why such a rumor was spread at this time and what connection it had to the archbishop of Cologne.[23] Once again, however, the answer lies with Anno himself. In his declaration of innocence, the archbishop asserted that he would never wish to surrender his land to barbarians *(patriam suam barbaris),* that is, to the Normans. He then declared that the rumor was spread by his rivals who had just recently expelled him from Cologne by force of arms and now were seeking again to overthrow him by lies.

Lampert of Hersfeld continues his account of the conflict, saying that the king was only checked in his fury but not completely freed from it by the Andernach meeting.[24] He therefore proceeded to Cologne to investigate this rebellion against Anno. Henry had hoped thereby to find further evidence against the archbishop or at least to stir up the population in order to drive him out of the city once again. Unable to achieve this, Henry then ordered Anno to pardon those who had rebelled against him and release them from excommunication. He also ordered the archbishop

21. Haverkamp, *Medieval Germany,* 108.

22. David Bates, *William the Conqueror* (London, 1989), 88–89; Berg, *England und der Kontinent,* 44 n. 184.

23. Wissowa (*Politische Beziehungen,* 18) states that the truth behind this report "can no longer be ascertained." Hugo Stehkämper ("Die Stadt Köln in der Salierzeit," 100) and Meyer von Knonau (*Jahrbücher des Deutschen Reiches unter Heinrich IV. und Heinrich V.* [Leipzig, 1894], 1:804–8) mention the rumor but do not pursue any extended consideration of it.

24. Lampert of Hersfeld, *Lamperti monachi,* 195–97 and MGH SS, 5:216: "Ita non extincto sed interim cohibito furore, Coloniam processit. Ibi postero die ad iudicandum populo assedit, sperans, per accusationem eorum, quos archiepiscopus propter iniurias suas poena affecerat, occasionem sibi futuram, ut eum, seditione concitata, rursus civitate exturbaret, vel propter oppressos per calumpniam innocentes saltem reum maiestatis faceret. Sed ille omnes accusationum strophas responsi veritate ac sententiarum gravitate tamquam aranearum telas dirupit."

to give him six hostages to assure compliance. This Anno refused to do in no uncertain terms, and an uneasy truce resulted.[25] Henry then proceeded to fortify Aachen and deal with those who had spread the rumor "about an attack of barbarians" *[de irruptione barbarorum]*.[26] What further steps he took are never specified, yet two conclusions can be drawn from this episode. Firstly, the young king had a falling out with Anno that would never be repaired—this necessitated his fortifying nearby Aachen in anticipation of Anno's joining the Saxon rebels. Secondly, Anno himself was experiencing an urban rebellion that seriously threatened to undermine his own local authority.

The rumors of an "Anglo-Anno" conspiracy were actually part of the first recorded rebellion of Cologne citizens against archiepiscopal authority. The rebellion, fueled by Anno's harsh lordship over the city and sparked by his overbearing treatment of wealthy merchants during a visit by the bishop of Münster at Easter in 1074, resulted in Anno barely escaping the city with his life.[27] He found refuge in the cathedral during a riot in the city, and he then escaped through the city wall at night, through a secret exit under the control of a cathedral canon. After fleeing with the bishop of Münster to Neuß, he returned to Cologne four days later with a large army and forced the burghers into submission. Anno humiliated the wealthy patrician merchants by demanding satisfaction and commanding them to come to him barefoot and ready for judgment. But inexplicably he delayed judgment against them until the following day, and in the night a number of these merchants (supposedly six hundred) escaped and fled to the king for help. The archbishop's men then wreaked justice on the rebellious city the next day by blinding the remaining leaders of the rebellion and burning and pillaging the city, while Anno excommunicated those who had fled to the king.

This was the background for Henry IV's stormy confrontation with Anno, yet to date no one has made the connection between the rumors of Anno's involvement in an Anglo-Norman plot and those merchants who

---

25. Jenal, *Erzbischof Anno II.,* 2:397. Despite this Anno did remain relatively loyal to Henry for the rest of his pontificate.

26. Lampert of Hersfeld, *Lamperti monachi,* 195–97 and MGH SS, 5:216–17.

27. See Lampert of Hersfeld, *Lamperti monachi,* 185–93 and MGH SS, 5:211–15, where Lampert discusses the rebellion in extensive detail. The burghers revolted after Anno seized a merchant ship when it was heavy laden and about to depart. The archbishop had intended the ship's services for his suffragan bishop, Frederick of Münster, yet Anno was entitled to such confiscation only when doing service to the king.

sought Henry's assistance sometime between Easter (April 20) and Pentecost (June 8) in 1074.[28] These merchants were surely involved in trade with England and, as citizens of the city, would have been aware of Anno's policy toward the new English king. Indeed, they themselves benefited from the pro-Norman diplomacy of the archbishop, since it likely encouraged trading advantages. In his personal politics Anno looked westward for two reasons. He sought to maintain the earlier beneficial economic ties established in preconquest England, and he also had to attend to a western border inhabited by the likes of the count of Flanders. Surely the cooperation of Norman monarchs became more crucial for the regional power of the archbishop of Cologne than for other German princes.

This rumor says much more about Anno and his probable efforts at maintaining the traditional relations between the Rhineland and England than about any intentions of William. Indeed it suggests that Anno was rather clear in his pro-Norman position within the empire, since the rumor of it had both believability and the power to elicit a strong negative response on the part of the German king. Henry IV's fears of Anno joining the widening Saxon rebellion had been triggered by the archbishop's kinship ties to some of the rebels and then heightened by the rumor of William the Conqueror's involvement. It looks as though the Cologne merchants had selected a perfect rumor to motivate the king against Anno, and this will not be the last time that the Cologne burghers would show initiative and independence from their archiepiscopal lord by playing the English card. It will also not be the last time we shall hear rumors of a supposed alliance between England, Cologne, and the princes of Saxony. In this case the urban uprising proved to be the undoing of the powerful and wily archbishop. Anno died shortly thereafter, in 1075.

For his part King William had no interest in engaging German affairs, since his attention was fully concentrated on consolidating his enormous gains in England and preserving his lordship in Normandy.[29] Indeed, it is reported that only a few months after the rumored "Anno conspiracy" Henry IV invited William, along with the kings of Denmark and France and the duke of Aquitaine, to join him in a campaign against the Saxon

---

28. The closest connection of this rumor to the political situation in Germany is Jenal's linking of it to the Saxon rebellion, yet no one has mentioned the rebellion facing Anno himself.

29. Bates, *William the Conqueror*, 89.

rebels. As an incentive the Salian king even offered "equivalent force" *[vicem aequam]* to assist William in his own troubles should there be the need. But, like the others, William declined, saying that his lands were too filled with warfare to leave them.[30] Henry had about as much chance in obtaining the Norman's military intervention as did Archbishop Anno. Local and regional political necessities predominated, even though talk of interregional cooperation was encouraged abroad.

In subsequent years Henry IV's growing conflicts with Pope Gregory VII and with his own son were mirrored by William Rufus's problems with Archbishop Anselm and his royal brother Robert Curthose. These internal conflicts perpetuated the unfavorable conditions that kept diplomatic relations between Germany and England distant. Familial and religious discord dominated political life in both kingdoms at this time and hindered, rather than helped, any kind of interregional political collaboration. Although a papal schism did arise and William Rufus considered using the German antipope to put pressure on Anselm, coordinated policies between the German and English monarchs never materialized. Concrete explorations of diplomatic cooperation came only under the more settled conditions of the reigns of Henry V in Germany and Henry I in England.

The nature of diplomatic and political activity thus far was one dominated by local and regional issues and shaped by the personal interactions of those within the circles of power. It was determined not by national or imperial ideologies or institutional forces but rather by the social and political realities of the respective regions. The rumor of an English invasion of Lotharingia was only plausible in the face of a regional conflict (the Saxon rebellion occasioned by an attempt to reassert royal prerogatives), a local conflict (the Cologne citizenry's rebellion precipitated by an attempt to assert archiepiscopal prerogatives), and a personal conflict (that between Anno and Henry IV) that had a long history dating back to the king's childhood. Though plausible, the rumor proved to be as elusive as the king of England, who was preoccupied with his own regional, local, and personal conflicts.

---

30. *Brunos Buch vom Sachsenkrieg,* ed. Hans-Eberhard Lohmann, MGH Deutsches Mittelalter, no. 2 (Leipzig, 1937), 38. William had earlier turned a deaf ear to Anselm of Lucca's appeal to come and free the Roman church from the hand of foreign oppressors: see *Briefsammlung der Zeit Heinrichs IV.,* ed. Carl Erdmann and Norbert Fickermann, MGH Epistolae: Die Briefe der deutschen Kaiserzeit, no. 5 (Weimar, 1950), 15–17, no. 1. This request was no doubt made in hopes of reciprocal support from William as a result of papal support for his conquest of England.

The Investiture Controversy and Norman France:
A Convergence of Regional Interests

Personal, local, and regional preoccupations continued to define the possibilities for Anglo-German diplomatic activity during the remainder of the eleventh century. For example, Cologne and its archbishops found their relations defined more by the Investiture Controversy than by shared economic ties to England.[31] At the death of Anno in 1075, the citizens of Cologne had hoped for a successor with a lighter hand, yet against their wishes Henry IV, mindful of the need for ecclesiastical support in his growing rift with Gregory VII, placed Hildolf (1076–78) in the see. In general, however, the burghers and the archbishops of Cologne supported Henry IV both before and after Canossa. Only the coup d'état of Henry's second son and namesake (1104–6) drove a wedge between people and archbishop, since Frederick I (1100–1131) supported the young Henry V while the burghers remained in their traditional allegiance to the king.

Henry IV fled in desperation to Cologne in the summer of 1106 and endured a siege there by his son. In the spring of that year Henry IV had obtained an oath from the Cologne burghers that they would extend the city walls for the defense of the king, and he had these new fortifications built apparently according to his own personal plans.[32] The city successfully withstood the siege by Henry V and remained a stout supporter of his father. Such royal grants to cities during the Investiture Controversy ultimately strengthened them. Though serving as royal fortifications, in time they enabled the citizens to resist both royal and episcopal authority and achieve a larger measure of independence. Cologne is a classic example of this development, and its burghers shall thereby play an increasingly important role in the political and diplomatic life of the city and surrounding region.

The death of Henry IV at Liège on August 7, 1106 altered political conditions radically, and the city, facing a punitive assault from Henry V, bought peace with the new king for the sizable amount of five thousand marks of silver.[33] Both this substantial tribute and the earlier fortification

---

31. Ursula Lewald, "Köln im Investiturstreit," in *Investiturstreit und Reichsverfassung,* ed. Josef Fleckenstein, Vorträge und Forschungen, no. 17 (Munich, 1973), 373–93.

32. *Annales Hildesheimenses,* ed. G. Pertz, MGH SS, no. 3 (Hanover, 1939; reprint, 1986), 110–11; Stehkämper, "Die Stadt Köln in der Salierzeit," 119–27.

33. *CRC,* 45: "Colonienses deditionem faciunt, insuper regi pro optinenda gratia sua 5,000 marcarum solvunt."

effort show the extent of the wealth and independent organization existing within the urban community of Cologne, which by this time had
developed into the primary trading center in Germany. The merchants'
prosperity depended as much on the new king as on English trade, and so
they awaited a happy confluence of these interests as the twelfth century
wore on.

Although diplomatic relations between England and the empire were
dormant during the closing years of the eleventh century, knowledge of
events in the respective territories seems well informed. The chronicles of
both Cologne and Magdeburg recorded the suspicious death of William
Rufus and included a curious legend about the appearance of Rufus's
ghost to his brother Henry I.[34] Among English chroniclers, Matthew
Paris inserted an account of the massacre of Jews in Cologne and Mainz
amid the religious fervor of the First Crusade,[35] and Robert of Torigni
condemned the rebellion of Henry V against his father and the siege of
Cologne.[36] With the reunification of Normandy and England in 1106 by
Henry I the potential role of the empire as an ally against the French king
became a real possibility for the first time, and the happy confluence of
interests hoped for by the Cologners was not far off. By this time Henry V
was well on his way to solidifying his position in Germany and was also
looking for an ally in his approaching showdown with Pope Paschal II.
Now the conditions were ripe for closer diplomatic ties between England
and the empire.

We get our first hint of such a development in a letter from Henry I in
Rouen to Archbishop Anselm dated March 1109, wherein he mentions
among other things that the matter under consideration between himself

---

34. Ibid., 41: "Rex Wilhelmus de Anglia sagitta interfectus est in venatione; frater vero
eius Heinricus dum vellet in eodem loco pro remedio animae eius monasterium construere,
apparuit ei, et duo dracones eum ferentes, dicens sibi nichil prodesse, eo quod suis temporibus
omnia destructa essent, quae sui antecessores in honorem Domini construxerant."

Annales Magdeburgenses, ed. G. Pertz, MGH SS, no. 16 (Hanover, 1859), 180:
"1100 . . . Rex Wilhelmus de Anglia sagitta interfectus est; Heinricus vero frater eius in
eodem loco pro remedio animae suae volens monasterium construere, apparuit ei, et duo
dracones ferentes eum, dicens, nichil sibi prodesse, eo quod suis temporibus omnia destructa essent, que antecessores sui in honorem Domini construxerent."

35. *MPHA,* 1:67; also in *MPCM,* 2:54.

36. Robert of Torigni, *Chronica,* ed. Richard Howlett, RS, no. 82 (London, 1882;
reprint, 1964), 4:87. Ralph de Diceto (*Abbreviationes Chronicorum,* ed. William Stubbs,
RS, no. 68 [London, 1876; reprint, 1964], 1:236) repeats Robert of Torigni's text.

and the emperor of the Romans was now completed, which would bring honor to God, the English ruling house, the Church, and all Christian people.[37] The matter was the engagement between Henry V and Matilda, the eight-year-old daughter of King Henry I. German envoys, described as exceedingly large and well dressed, came to the English court to confirm the agreement on Pentecost (June 13) of the same year.[38] In February 1110 the child Matilda began the trip to her new home, and in early March she passed through Liège, where Henry V received her.[39] On Easter Day at Utrecht (April 10) she was solemnly betrothed to Henry and assigned a dower. After sojourns in Cologne, Speyer, and Worms, the entourage reached Mainz, and on July 25 Matilda was anointed as queen by none other than Archbishop Frederick I of Cologne, as the archiepiscopal see of Mainz was then vacant.[40] Frederick was assisted by the archbishop of Trier, who subsequently took charge of Matilda's education and training in German customs.[41] And after four years of preparation for her royal duties, the marriage was consummated at Bamberg in January 1114.[42] At this time Henry V was at the height of his power at age thirty-eight or thirty-nine, and Matilda was not yet twelve years of age. Aside from the extreme youth of the new queen, we should note the

---

37. *Sancti Anselmi Cantuariensis Archiepiscopi Opera Omnia*, ed. F. S. Schmitt (Edinburgh, 1951), 5:410, no. 461: "Praeterea scias quoniam negotium, quod inter me et imperatorem Romanorum tractabatur, gratia Dei ad honorem Dei et nostrum et sanctae ecclesiae et Christiani populi ad finem perduximus." The king's scribes have conflated the titles of a German monarch. Henry V was still only the king of the Romans, since he had not yet been crowned emperor by the pope in Rome.

38. Henry of Huntingdon, *Historia Anglorum*, ed. Thomas Arnold, RS, no. 74 (London, 1879), 237; Robert of Torigni, *Chronica,* 89: "Missi sunt a Henrico imperatore Romano nuntii, mole corporis et cultus splendoribus excellentes, filiam regis Anglorum Henrici in domini sui conjugium postulantes. Tenens igitur curiam, apud Londoniam, qua nunquam splendidiorem tenuerat, sacramenta depostulans ad [sic] imperatoris recepit legatis ad Pentecosten."

39. *CRC,* 49.

40. Ibid., 49; Florence and John of Worcester (*Chronicon ex chronicis,* 67) incorrectly state that Matilda was crowned as empress and date the event incorrectly.

41. Marjorie Chibnall, *The Empress Matilda: Queen Consort, Queen Mother, and Lady of the English* (Oxford, 1991), 24–25; G. Meyer von Knonau, *Jahrbücher des deutschen Reichs unter Heinrich IV. und Henrich V.* (Leipzig, 1890–1909), 6:285ff. Trier was likely the best location for Matilda's education, since French and German language and culture were intermingled there.

42. *CRC,* 53; *Annales Hildesheimenses,* 113. See also F. J. Schmale and I. Schmale-Ortt, eds., *Anonymi Chronica Imperatorum Heinrico V dedicata,* Ausgewahlte Quellen zur Deutschen Geschichte des Mittelalters, no. 15 (Darmstadt, 1972), 262.

generous sum of money given as her dowry. A royal levy of three shillings on the hide was assessed in England to raise the ten thousand marks of silver sent along with Matilda to the German king.[43]

Although the English chronicle accounts attribute the initiative for this marriage union to Henry V, both monarchs must have welcomed the opportunity. For the Anglo-Norman monarch, whose royal house was only in its second generation, this link to the empire enhanced the prestige and legitimation of the Norman Conquest. The high value placed on this imperial connection by the English can be seen in the title used by Matilda upon return to her homeland after the death of Henry V. Although her status in Germany as empress is doubtful[44]—she bore no children of the emperor, her imperial coronations were at the hand of antipopes, she appears in the imperial diplomata as "queen" *[regina],* and her seal from Germany bore the title "queen of the Romans by the grace of God" *[Dei gratia Romanorum regina]*[45]—she nonetheless bore the title of "empress" *(imperatrix)* for the rest of her life in the Anglo-Norman realm.

In addition Henry I was in need of an ally to counterbalance the changed political situation in France as a result of the accession of Louis VI (1108–37). Louis was a king who sought to consolidate the power of the French kingdom and did not shy away from asserting his feudal lordship over such powerful vassals as the duke of Normandy. Louis had also gained the support of the duke of Burgundy and the counts of Flanders, Blois, and Nevers. Therefore an alliance with the German king would at least prevent the Salian from joining the Capetian camp and might eventually result in direct military support against the French. The marriage union was a great diplomatic success for the Anglo-Norman court and did not come about by chance, for it was concluded in the same year that Henry's first war with Louis VI began.[46]

The incentives for Henry V in this union were just as practical. While

43. Ordericus Vitalis, *The Ecclesiastical History,* ed. Marjorie Chibnall (Oxford, 1964–81), 5:200; *MPHA,* 1:210 and *MPCM,* 2:136, following Henry of Huntingdon, *Historia Anglorum,* 237.

44. Leyser, "England and the Empire," 196–99.

45. W. de Gray Birch, "A Fasciculus of the Charters of Mathildis, Empress of the Romans," *Journal of the British Archaeological Association* 31 (1875): 381; Percy Ernst Schramm, *Die Deutschen Kaiser und Könige in Bildern ihrer Zeit* (Leipzig, 1928), 1:216, 2: Abb. 118.

46. Berg, *England und der Kontinent,* 242–43; Trautz, *Die Könige,* 61.

he was in Liège to receive the English wedding party, another embassy of Germans arrived fresh from Rome. This embassy was probably part of the protracted negotiations with Paschal II, which had been going on since Henry seized his father's throne in 1106. The coordination of these embassies was no coincidence; Henry V's search for a wife converged with his attempts to achieve both a settlement between *regnum* and *sacerdotium* and an expedition to Rome for an imperial coronation to legitimate his monarchy. Henry needed an ally for the upcoming struggle in Rome. Certainly he hoped to strengthen his position vis-à-vis the papacy by this alliance, although there was never any English intercession before the popes on behalf of the German monarchs prior to the Concordat of Worms.[47] With the papacy finding increasing sympathy in France, England was the natural alternative among the western kingdoms. Henry V also needed an alliance that would bring legitimacy to his own kingship, which was after all usurped from his own father; furthermore Henry was facing financial difficulties due to his eastern campaigns and needed funding for the planned expedition to Rome.[48] A quick source of wealth could always be found in the dowry that went along with a royal bride, and Henry was an eligible bachelor.

This diplomatic initiative toward the West was a remarkable policy shift for the Salian kings, who had always focused their attention on an *Ostpolitik,* seeking both to exercise royal power in Saxony and to enforce a suzerainty in and collect tribute from Bohemia, Hungary, and Poland. This traditional policy had always been exercised by the force of military campaigns and not by diplomacy. The other traditional focus of Salian "foreign policy" was of course papal affairs, but an integration of traditional Salian politics into western affairs was something new.[49] This diplomatic policy shift is significant as it is a harbinger of Germany's growing integration into western European life during the twelfth and thirteenth centuries.

---

47. Kienast (*Deutschland und Frankreich,* 1:190) asserts, "The two kings stood shoulder to shoulder against the pope in the struggle over their investiture rights."

48. We have already seen expressed in English chronicles a negative view of Henry V's coup against his father, and this attitude was not unique. This must have weakened his negotiating position with the pope.

49. Berg, *England und der Kontinent,* 237–41. Berg declares that the marriage alliance with England was "a political novelty" for the Salian kings (237), and he points out that while the June 1109 embassy was concluding the agreement in London, Henry V was preparing for a campaign to Poland (240 n. 227).

The English king had more than a passing interest in the machinations surrounding the Investiture Controversy. He had grown impatient with the restrictions on royal investiture embodied in the 1107 Concordat of Westminster, while the German monarch continued to exercise the old practices with impunity. Indeed, in a letter by Archbishop Anselm to the pope dated October 12, 1108, Henry threatened to resume investing prelates with ring and staff again since the German ruler was allowed to do so.[50] He must also have known that the Roman expedition planned by Henry V for August 1110 had as its goals the recovery of the Italian kingdom, imperial coronation, and a settlement with the papacy over investiture, favorable to the German king. Thus it takes little imagination to determine the purposes for which the ten thousand English marks were reserved.[51] This vast sum was the largest single amount received by Henry V thus far in his reign, the Cologne burghers having paid him only half that much in 1106.[52] There is no account of Henry's difficulties in raising what was an enormous army for the Roman expedition, and this can be attributed to the liberal use of English money.[53]

The English court eagerly awaited news of the outcome of the Roman campaign, which came in a letter by a certain Burchard to Roger FitzRichard de Clare and to Gilbert, a chaplain to Henry I. Burchard was one of the imperial envoys who brought Matilda to Germany—he would eventually become bishop of Cambrai—and Roger FitzRichard de Clare had accompanied them. The letter arrived directly after the extorted treaty of Ponte Mammolo and subsequent imperial coronation had been completed in April 1111.[54] Burchard presents the text of the treaty as well as that of Paschal II's investiture privilege to Henry V. Such detailed and swiftly sent information about these affairs indicates how much interest Henry I had in the negotiations. Indeed, the personal nature of the letter between members of Matilda's entourage indicates the intimate character of English participation in Henry's Roman expedition.

Thus far it appears as if the new emperor had gained more concrete benefits from the alliance than did the English king. Although the ex-

---

50. *Sancti Anselmi Opera Omnia,* 5:399, no. 451.

51. Leyser, "England and the Empire," 204.

52. Ibid., 205.

53. Ibid., 206.

54. Walther Holtzmann, "Zur Geschichte des Investiturstreites: (Englische Analekten II, 3) England, Unteritalien und der Vertrag von Ponte Mammolo," *Neues Archiv* 50 (1935): 246–319, with the text of the letter on pages 300–301.

torted settlement was immediately repudiated by Paschal, English money had at least purchased an imperial coronation. Yet the alliance did bear fruit for Henry I on two different occasions several years later.[55] On February 2, 1123, Henry I gathered the ecclesiastical and secular lords of the realm at Gloucester to elect a new archbishop of Canterbury. The bishops, desiring a cleric rather than a monk, forced through the choice of William of Corbeil. The monks of Canterbury reluctantly acquiesced, and William was consecrated on February 16. Problems began, however, when William presented himself in Rome to receive the pallium. The reform-minded cardinals opposed his election on four grounds: William had been chosen at court and not in the cloister; he was elected by the bishops and not by the monks; the archbishop of York should have consecrated him (Archbishop Thurstan of York had been excluded in favor of suffragan bishops); and William was not a monk. Yet Calixtus II was willing to accept the election even though the cardinals disagreed with the election on canonical grounds. Such were the confounding conditions under which Henry I attempted to implement acceptable election procedures in his kingdom.

The emperor interceded on behalf of William with letters[56] and envoys.[57] The pope was anxious to honor the joint requests of king and emperor and set about to convince the cardinals to allow the election to stand, "for love of the emperor, who was recently reconciled to the Roman church" [pro amore imperatoris qui nuper ecclesiae Romanae reconciliatus erat].[58] The reconciliation mentioned here is of course the Concordat of Worms, which was promulgated on September 23, 1122. As Leyser has brilliantly pointed out, the formula for episcopal elections in

---

55. See Leyser, "England and the Empire," 210–13.

56. Hugh the Chanter, *Historians of the Church of York*, 2:201. These were letters of introduction carried on behalf of William of Corbeil. They appear also in Hugh the Chanter, *The History of the Church of York, 1066–1127*, ed. Charles Johnson, M. Brett, C. N. L. Brooke, and M. Winterbottom, Oxford Medieval Texts (Oxford, 1990), 188. Hugh the Chanter, being an intimate colleague of Archbishop Thurstan of York, was well informed about this crisis.

57. Simeon of Durham, *Historia regum (Symeonis monachi opera omnia)*, ed. Thomas Arnold, RS, no. 75 (London, 1882–85; reprint, 1965), 2:272.

58. Hugh the Chanter, *Historians of the Church of York*, 2:202; *History of the Church of York*, 190. The pope's formal pronouncement in favor of William is as follows (*History of the Church of York*, 192): "Quia ergo personam illius, que per Dei graciam honesta est et religiosa, ecclesiae profuturam confidimus, et pro amore filiorum nostrorum regis et imperatoris, amici quoque nostri Eboracensis archiepiscopi, eleccionem illius confirmamus, palleum ei concedimus."

the *Calixtinum* section of the Concordat of Worms served as justification for Calixtus II's argument that the cardinals accept William's election.[59] According to the *Calixtinum*, bishops and abbots could be elected in the presence of the monarch, and William of Corbeil had been chosen in a royal council. It also included the provision that if an election should be disputed the monarch should support the more reasonable party *(senior pars)* with the counsel of the metropolitan and bishops of the province.[60] One could argue that Henry I had already done this. The English king was one of the first to hear of the details of the treaty of Ponte Mammolo, and he certainly knew of the provisions of the Concordat of Worms. Therefore it would have been quite difficult for Paschal II to justify one set of concessions in Germany and another in England. One could say, therefore, that Henry I benefited directly from the Concordat of Worms. In fact the disputed Canterbury election of 1123 was one of the first cases in which Calixtus II's concessions to Henry V were actually applied. Although it took some time, Henry I's sizable investment of ten thousand marks did eventually pay some dividends.[61]

The second intervention of Henry V on behalf of the English king was less effective, yet it brought a new dynamic to relations between the empire and the western kingdoms. Barely having resolved the disputed archiepiscopal election, Henry I faced renewed rebellion in Normandy that was supported by Louis VI and his allies in eastern and northeastern France. Henry V, having been temporarily freed from the morass of papal affairs by the concordat, had also been active trying to pacify the turbulent regions of his empire, particularly in Saxony and northwestern Germany. Thus a geographical coordination of English and imperial attention on the Ile-de-France–Burgundy–Lotharingia–Flanders corridor may have contributed to an attempt at a concerted military action by both parties.[62] Imperial intercession in the previous year regarding the Canterbury election suggests that this was a period of particularly close relations

---

59. Leyser, "England and the Empire," 212–13.

60. MGH Const., 1:161, no. 108.

61. There were other benefits coming from the ties established through Matilda, such as the placement of the archdeacon Henry of Winchester (who went with the English bride to Germany) as the bishop of Verdun in 1117: see Laurentius de Leodio, *Gesta episcoporum Virdunensium et abbatum S. Vitoni,* ed. Georg Waitz, MGH SS, no. 10 (Hanover, 1852; reprint, 1987), 504–5. The Salian use of bishoprics as largesse was of course in direct conflict with papal proclamations and as such encountered resistance.

62. Berg, *England und der Kontinent,* 300 n. 65. The link of Lothar of Supplinburg's opposition to the emperor in Saxony and lower Lotharingia is important to note here.

between the monarchs. Henry V must have known of his father-in-law's new difficulties in Normandy and the Capetian role therein, and imperial relations with Capetian vassals appear to have been tense as well at the time. Matilda's planned visit with her father was cut short in 1122, when the count of Flanders would not allow her to pass through his territory on her way to England.[63]

Henry V therefore attempted to assist the English monarch militarily in the late summer of 1124 by bringing an army to the French frontier and threatening to attack Reims. It seems most likely, though, that the army was making this swing toward France as a diversionary tactic to draw some of the French army and thereby relieve Normandy indirectly—surely the original goal of Henry V's army, a campaign against Saxony, was never forgotten. In any case, this military maneuver signaled a new phase of involvement by Salian monarchs in western affairs. There was little to be gained by the emperor in this venture and so it was done solely for the support of his father-in-law.[64] Perhaps the active Matilda, who would later play a central role in the political fate of her homeland, was instrumental in obtaining her husband's involvement.

The venture was, however, flawed from the start. Henry V had called the princes to court at Bamberg (May 1124) to make preparations for an August military campaign against Duke Lothar of Saxony. But for some unexplained reason these plans were changed in the following months and redirected against the French king.[65] Ekkehard of Aura says that plans for an expedition against France had already been established at the Bamberg court, yet the subsequent paucity of German princes who took part in the venture suggests that the plans had been changed afterward. The majority of German princes did not take part, either because of the lack of time to adjust their plans or, more likely, because the princes were unwilling to leave the agreed-upon attack of Saxony and venture into

---

63. *Annales de Waverleia,* ed. Henry Richards Luard, RS, no. 36 (London, 1864–69; reprint, 1965), 2:218.

64. Suger (*Vita Ludovici Grossi Regis,* ed. A. Molinier, Collection de textes pour servir à l'étude et à l'enseignement de l'histoire, no. 4 [Paris, 1887], 144) claims that Henry V had intended as revenge to destroy Reims, a papal stronghold where the declaration of his excommunication had been promulgated in 1119. It seems unlikely, however, that Henry V was willing to risk war with France over a punitive raid on Reims, especially after the Concordat of Worms.

65. Ekkehard of Aura, *Chronica,* ed. F. J. Schmale and Irene Schmale-Ott, Ausgewählte Quellen zur Deutschen Geschichte des Mittelalters, Freiherr von Stein-Gedächtnisausgabe, no. 15 (Darmstadt, 1972), 368.

foreign lands. The army was made up only of contingents from the bishops of Eichstätt, Speyer, and Würzburg, the Count-Palatine Gottfried of Lotharingia, and a few Frankish and Lotharingian counts.[66]

The army reached Metz around August 13 under the leadership of the emperor. Yet the French king had somehow received news of the advancing troops, and the now legendary response of Louis VI ensued: he seized the *auriflamma* of St. Denis and called on the princes to support the French throne.[67] Louis quickly gathered the support of his local allies, the duke of Burgundy and the counts of Blois, Nevers, Champagne, Vermandois, and Flanders—a force primarily from northwestern France. Henry V learned of the sizable French army as well as of an uprising in the usually loyal city of Worms and quickly withdrew from the enterprise. Thus the attempt to intervene on behalf of the English monarch was as hastily abandoned as it had been organized. The failure of the campaign was caused by the lack of involvement by the German princes, who refused participation in foreign affairs, and by the decisive moves made by Louis VI. The princes were not willing, even at the request of their monarch, to engage in the affairs of others whose territories and personalities lay beyond the boundaries of their own daily concerns.

The question remains, how then did Louis get his information about the approaching invasion? Dieter Berg believes it came from the papal legate Cardinal William of Palestrina, who had traveled to the imperial court sometime after July 1 and who appears in an imperial charter for the monastery of Camoldoli issued at Worms on July 25. He certainly was in a position to learn of the plans and to have the news forwarded to papal allies in France.[68]

The aborted invasion had little political or military consequence for the English side. Indeed the effort had come a month too late, as Henry I had gained the upper hand in Normandy and was already showing a willingness to reach a settlement with Louis. It did perhaps preoccupy Louis VI enough to prevent him from sending troops to Normandy. Yet in France the effects were quite noticeable. Louis had rallied the local magnates behind him and gained a victory over the emperor without any

---

66. Berg, *England und der Kontinent*, 301.
67. Suger, *Vita Ludovici*, 142f.; see also Suger, *Vie de Louis VI le Gros*, ed. and trans. H. Waquet, Les Classiques de l'Histoire de France au Moyen Age, no. 11 (Paris, 1964), 220ff.
68. Berg, *England und der Kontinent*, 304–5.

shedding of blood. Much has been said about the French response as an early sign of national solidarity and self-confidence.[69] Although this is rather overplayed, still the negative effects on diplomatic relations between the Capetian and imperial courts were to be long lasting. Hitherto Henry V had been represented as a schismatic and enemy of the Church; now he appeared as an aggressor who threatened France for no reason.[70] From now on France would need to worry about being surrounded by enemies allied with one another should the English gain German support against them.

This initial phase of close Anglo-imperial diplomatic relations had important implications for the subsequent development of European political history. It signaled the end of German isolation from western politics and the emergence of a much more complex web of interregional diplomacy as a result of an Anglo-Norman kingdom with ties to England, France, and Germany (not to mention the Norman kingdom of Sicily). The conquest of England by the Normans and their later cultivation of ties with Germany drew both regions simultaneously out of their earlier eastern orientations and into close contact with affairs in the territories of France and Lotharingia. In addition, rising papal influence and the friction of papal-imperial politics were now fully injected into relations between the western kingdoms. Gone were the days when the empire was not a player in conflicts between English and French monarchs, and gone conversely were the days when an emperor's difficulties with the papacy had little direct impact on England or France. By 1125 all the important political players, whose diplomatic relations would shift with the changing conditions of the thirteenth through fifteenth centuries, had taken their place on the European stage.

It is important at this point to consider the forces that brought about the political realignment of the Central Middle Ages and that drew the German kingdom into the western European world. The increasing economic and cultural interdependency emerging throughout Europe during this era cannot be denied. Yet the defining forces that brought the regions of Europe together and encouraged such economic and cultural growth were political, though not of the modern variety. They were not those of nationalism, empire building, or the building of state institutions. Rather they were of a very personal nature and revolved around the regional

---

69. See particularly Kienast, *Deutschland und Frankreich,* 1:191ff.
70. Ibid., 1:194ff.

needs of the political leadership of western and central Europe. The interconnection of European politics was achieved through typical medieval means—marriage alliances between dynastic houses, military engagement (or threat of engagement) in an effort to enforce regional lordship, and the involvement of religious authorities in the temporal affairs of medieval Christian society. Where else have the marriage of an eleven-year-old child and the rules regarding the election of clergy greatly influenced the political possibilities of the entire emerging continent?

This kind of political life may appear "backward" or even "superstitious" to some when evaluated by modern expectations and values, but understood on its own social terms, rather than in the context of looking for a harbinger of something from a later age, it looks altogether human. In the absence of national ideologies, centralized bureaucratic states, and secularized religion, the means for establishing interregional ties were personal. Hence, we should expect that personal relations will be filled with those human, relational qualities lacking in the modern, impersonal state: local and regional ties based on private authority, marriage ties based on the personal commitments of individuals and communities, and the spiritual aspirations of individuals and communities. These qualities serve to create bonds of allegiance and cooperation. Medieval monarchs were constantly preoccupied in either maintaining existing or reasserting lost bonds of allegiance and cooperation. Hence any notions of imperialist conquest in Europe remained outside of the medieval political lexicon.

Given the private and personal nature of political life in this era, we should be impressed that cooperation reached such interregional proportions during the Norman-Salian era. We should not, however, be surprised when the weight of interregional ties becomes more than can be maintained when local and regional matters require concentrated attention, for the latter will always have preeminence.

The Collapse of Norman-Salian Diplomacy

In this era of increasingly complex interregional relations, we still find personal, local, and regional political exigencies defining the possibilities of political life. Nowhere better can we see the interplay between these political forces than in the history of Cologne's archbishops. They served as the key mediators in Anglo-German diplomatic relations and yet were deeply caught up in the local and personal conflicts of the Rhineland and of the regional matters of the German kingdom as a whole. From Archbishop Anno's pro-Norman policy to the involvement of Frederick I in the marriage of the English princess Matilda, Cologne and its archbishops were fast becoming the conduit for Anglo-German diplomacy. At the same time they were key political figures in Germany. Frederick I was among the most powerful supporters of Henry V during the 1111 Roman campaign in which Henry extracted the treaty of Ponte Mammolo and was crowned emperor.[71]

The archbishops of Cologne were likewise known for their own regional power and independence. Their regional and local exigencies would often complicate the diplomatic channel established between the royal courts of England and Germany, since it ran straight through Cologne. The first instance of this occurred barely after Henry V had achieved the double victory of a Roman triumph and a very lucrative marriage union with the English royal house. A rebellion of lower Lotharingian and Saxon princes, including Archbishop Frederick I, arose and interrupted Cologne's traditional allegiance to the emperor.

The first recension of the Cologne chronicle says that the rebellion had its origins even in the wedding festivities in Bamberg.[72] In later years Otto of Freising would look back on the feast as more of a conspiratorial meeting of the princes of the realm.[73] The cause of this uprising, which lasted throughout the year and left the districts of Cologne and Westphalia devastated, was Henry V's high-handed imprisonment of a certain nobleman named Ludwig. The imprisonment of the former chancellor and newly installed archbishop of Mainz, Adalbert I (1109–37), soon followed and was met with a rebellion in Saxony. Behind these arrests and the subsequent rebellion of princes from lower Lotharingia and Saxony lay the Salian's attempt to reintroduce his father's royal policy in Saxony and the upper Rhineland—it even appears that Henry may have desired to introduce a general tax modeled on English custom.[74] And as one would expect, the installation of ministerials, land reversion, and a general tax in these regions was as energetically rejected

---

71. *REK*, 2:12, nos. 76–77.

72. *CRC*, 53–54.

73. Otto of Freising, *The Two Cities*, trans. C. C. Mierow (New York, 1928), 421. Otto was Henry V's nephew and was thus perhaps informed concerning such matters.

74. On the tax see Karl Leyser, "The Anglo-Norman Succession, 1120–1125," *Anglo-Norman Studies* 13 (1991 for 1990): 233–39 (reprinted in *Communications and Power: The Gregorian Revolution and Beyond*, ed. Timothy Reuter [London, 1994], 97–114).

by the nobility as similar policies had been under Henry IV in 1073. Resistance to the extension of royal power into northern Germany was soon coupled with the papal reform movement, since the Investiture Controversy had not yet been resolved by this time. Archbishop Frederick I of Cologne, for example, saw a nice dovetailing of his own territorial ambitions with the goals of the religious reform movements.[75] Hitherto one of the most loyal of German prelates, he turned against Henry V and joined the rebellion in the hope of securing an independent basis for his regional power.[76]

Common cause between the Saxon and lower Lotharingian rebels in 1114 developed when Henry V led a large army into the territories of the lower Rhineland. This campaign must have ensued almost directly after the royal wedding at Bamberg. A beleaguered contingent of the archbishop of Cologne's army was rescued by the intervention of Duke Lothar of Saxony.[77] Soon Cologne itself was besieged a second time by Henry V, yet the Cologners broke the siege and defeated the royal army at Andernach. This victory was due in no small measure to the support of mercenary archers, whose tactics were not known outside England at this time.[78] In 1115 Archbishop Frederick I, the Cologne burghers, and many of the lower Lotharingian princes assisted Duke Lothar of Saxony in his struggle against the emperor, and collectively they handed Henry V a crushing defeat at Welfesholz on February 11, 1115. Henry was thus forced to flee northern Germany, thanks largely to the military contribution made by the citizens of Cologne and their archbishop.[79] News of

---

75. Frederick was an ardent supporter of monastic reform and as such a patron of St. Norbert of Xanten, who founded a Premonstratensian house in Cappenberg near Cologne (1122). At Steinfeld Frederick founded a house of Augustinian canons that later became Premonstratensian, and he founded the first Cistercian house in Germany (1122), located at Camp and filled with monks from Morimond. See Van Engen, *Rupert of Deutz*, 314, 324.

76. The clerical princes of Germany gained an important measure of independence from royal control as a result of the Investiture Controversy. They gained a constitutional position like the secular nobility and only owed feudal obligations to the king in return for their regalian rights. Hence, ecclesiastics like Frederick saw a confluence of goals by supporting the papal reform movement: both the reduction of royal influence over their elections and, at the same time, their integration among the regional princes of the realm, complete with an independent regional power base.

77. *CRC*, 52–53. See also Stehkämper, "Die Stadt Köln in der Salierzeit," 128–31.

78. Lewald ("Investiturstreit," 388) suggests that the mercenary archers, who proved so effective in driving off the army of Henry V, may have come from England. See also Haverkamp, *Medieval Germany*, 166.

79. *CRC*, 56 (Recensio II).

these events soon made their way into English chronicles, although with some confusion on the details.[80]

Tensions between the archbishop and the emperor continued throughout the remaining years of Henry V's reign.[81] Frederick himself pronounced the sentence of papal excommunication of Henry in Cologne in April 1115 and was thereafter an implacable foe.[82] Not surprisingly, therefore, Cologne was shut out of involvement in Henry's diplomacy with England during this time. We shall not see the Anglo-Cologne diplomatic connection revitalized until the archiepiscopate of Rainald of Dassel (1159–67), when its potential for political intrigue was fully developed. Once again, local and regional affairs, both colored a great deal by the personal and religious conflicts among the princes of Germany, eclipsed the promising diplomatic inroads with England. It is instructive to note that Henry V never used dynastic ties with the English king to his advantage during these difficult years of his reign and, likewise, that the decisive victories of the northern German armies were instrumental in forcing Henry V to reach a lasting reconciliation with the papacy in the form of the Concordat of Worms (1122).

Marjorie Chibnall has speculated on the possible English influence via Matilda during these last years of Henry V's reign.[83] It is remarkable to note, for example, that in 1117 Matilda was left behind in Italy when Henry V was forced to return to deal with rebels in Germany. She may have acted as regent there until she rejoined her husband in Lotharingia in 1119. While her personal power was limited by her age—she would have been no older than fifteen years of age—she did indeed preside over court sessions. It seems likely that her presence attached imperial authority to the proceedings and that her direct participation was minimal. Perhaps more important, however, were her personal ties to those involved in the negotiations resulting in the Concordat of Worms. Surely there were diplomatic contacts between the English and German courts, and perhaps the 1107 Concordat of Westminster even served as a model for the Worms settlement.[84] The fact that a kinsman of the emperor was

80. Florence and John of Worcester, *Chronicon,* 2:67–68. Roger of Howden borrows this passage for his *Chronica* (1: 169).

81. When in 1119 the citizens of Cologne allowed Henry V to enter the city during the absence of Archbishop Frederick I, the archbishop immediately placed the city under ecclesiastical interdict: see *CRC,* 59.

82. Van Engen, *Rupert of Deutz,* 228–29.

83. Chibnall, *Matilda,* 33–38.

84. Ibid., 35–37.

among those drowned at the sinking of the White Ship in 1120 makes this event all the more significant for Anglo-German diplomatic relations and assures us of continual contact between the courts.[85] We cannot determine the significance of this diplomatic channel, yet it should not therefore be lightly disregarded.

The diplomatic activity surrounding the Concordat of Worms was to be the last dynastic benefit of Matilda's marriage, as the constellation brought together by her marriage soon collapsed in the 1120s. We have already discussed the aborted military support offered to the English king against the French in 1124, which is symbolic of the limited nature of cooperation resulting from the Norman-Salian marriage union. The decisive shift occurred at the death of Henry V in 1125. The emperor had died childless,[86] and Matilda, having passed the imperial regalia to Archbishop Adalbert of Mainz, returned to the Anglo-Norman court—a court that she knew little of as a princess and that was itself growing increasingly unstable.[87] We shall meet up with her again. Lothar of Supplinburg, the duke of Saxony and bitter enemy of the late monarch, was declared king (1125–37) in a disputed election, and thus Henry I's kinship ties with Germany were quickly dissolved. With civil war surrounding Lothar's kingship, there was little likelihood of establishing useful ties with the new ruling house.

Archbishop Frederick I of Cologne had bitterly opposed Lothar's election. At first he suggested the candidacy of Count Charles the Good of Flanders (the same count who supported Louis VI in 1124). Wearied of the anticlerical Salian line, Frederick sought a successor who would be less heavy handed. He also sought to promote his own territorial ambitions. Since he had been extending his regional lordship *(Landesherrschaft)* into western Saxony he could not abide strengthening the duke of Saxony's hand by electing him king (we shall meet the same problem later with the kingship of Otto IV). From this point on the formerly coopera-

---

85. Ordericus Vitalis, *Ecclesiastical History*, 6:304–7.

86. In keeping with the negative representation of Henry V by Anglo-Norman chroniclers as a result of his role in the Investiture Controversy, Ordericus Vitalis asserts that Henry's sins kept him without a male heir (ibid., 5:200): "Imperator autem tam generosam coniugem admodum dilexit, sed peccatis exigentibus sobole imperio digna caruit unde imperiale stemma in aliam iubente Deo familiam transiit."

87. The Pipe Roll for 1130 indicates a disbursement made from royal revenues in Devonshire "quando Imperatrix venit in Anglia": see *The Pipe Roll of 31 Henry I, Michaelmas 1130,* ed. Joseph Hunter (London, 1929), 157.

tive relations between the dukes of Saxony and the archbishops of Cologne grew increasingly fractious as a result of conflicting territorial interests. Since most of the count of Flanders's lands lay in French territory he could be of little consequence in Germany and still preserve Cologne's positive economic and diplomatic relations with England. The latter would be assured by the influence Frederick would have over a candidate whose legitimacy depended on his endorsement. This was not the last time an archbishop of Cologne would proffer a foreign candidate to advance his *Territorialpolitik*.

The count refused the offer, primarily because he knew his candidacy was the invention of the archbishop of Cologne and had virtually no support elsewhere in Germany. Lothar, one of the most powerful princes in the realm, enjoyed support in lower Germany and was elected with the hope that he would reverse Salian policy in the North. The Salian party responded to the disputed election with a civil war in favor of their candidate, Conrad of Hohenstaufen (the nephew of Henry V who eventually succeeded Lothar as Conrad III). This dreary war dragged on for ten years, draining Lothar's political and military power. Lacking either the Salian territories or the ability to assert royal power outside Saxony, he was forced to curtail foreign diplomacy and concentrate on the difficult task of establishing his kingship within Germany. Thus he proved of little value to the English king, who sought, rather, to strengthen his own influence in lower Lotharingia and Flanders.

The king of England had problems of his own, the primary one being the establishment of a legitimate successor to his throne. Ironically, the two men who fashioned a marriage union between their houses were both without a legitimate male heir—in Henry's case this was so after the tragic loss of his son on the White Ship in 1120. Therefore Henry sought recognition of Matilda as the royal heir in 1127, and her role in the succession battle that ensued is well known.[88] The chaos in Germany only increased during the confused reign of the Staufer Conrad III (1138–52), which coincided with the chaos in England during the disputed kingship of Stephen (1135–54). Thus the quarter century from 1125 to

---

88. See Marjorie Chibnall, *Matilda*, 43–142; O. Rössler, *Kaiserin Mathilde, Mutter Heinrichs von Anjou, und das Zeitalter der Anarchie in England*, Historische Studien, no. 7 (Berlin, 1897); John T. Appleby, *The Troubled Reign of King Stephen* (London, 1969); Keith J. Stringer, *The Reign of Stephen: Kingship, Warfare, and Government in Twelfth-Century England*, Lancaster Pamphlets (London and New York, 1993).

1150 was a long winter of dormancy, after which the seeds of Anglo-imperial relations sown in the reigns of Henry V and Henry I would regenerate during the reigns of Frederick Barbarossa and Henry II. The succession struggles in England and Germany during this period once again remind us clearly how personal, local, and regional exigencies predominated over interregional diplomacy during the Middle Ages. And these exigencies resolved around the persons in power rather than around ideologies or notions of state or empire building.

There are only two dubious points of contact mentioned in the sources for the period 1125–52. The first is the assertion that Lothar's support of Innocent II in the papal schism was influential in Henry I's decision to support the pope in 1131.[89] The second is a letter of Conrad III to Emperor John of Constantinople dated February 12, 1142, in which Conrad boasts about the reception of daily embassies from numerous countries, England being among them.[90] Nothing concrete, however, ever emerged from whatever embassies he may have received—this is likely a boast from one hopeful successor of the Romans to another. And it remains difficult at best to prove a causal connection between German and English support for Innocent II other than shared views about the legitimacy of Innocent's pontificate. We must look elsewhere to find the kind of political cooperation symptomatic of an ever more integrated Europe of the Central Middle Ages.

The Second Crusade: A Sign of Growing Interregional Cooperation

Although little diplomatic activity occurred between the English and German monarchs at this time, the Second Crusade of 1147 resulted in another type of political cooperation between the two regions. The fall of Edessa in 1144 stirred up renewed interest in crusading, and both Conrad III and Louis VI of France took the cross in the first real European crusade. The Saxons preferred to stay near home and led a crusade against the Wends, while in the lower Rhineland and Flanders partici-

---

89. Wissowa, *Politische Beziehungen*, 23.

90. *Die Urkunden Konrads III. und Seines Sohnes Heinrich*, ed. Friedrich Hausmann, MGH DD: Die Urkunden der Deutschen Könige und Kaiser, no. 9 (Vienna, Cologne, and Graz, 1969), 121–23, no. 69, from Otto of Freising and Rahewin, *Gesta Frederici seu rectius Cronica*, ed. Franz-Josef Schmale, Ausgewählte Quellen zur deutschen Geschichte des Mittelalters, Freiherr von Stein-Gedächtnisausgabe, no. 17 (Berlin, 1965), 171–74.

pants chose to take the sea route around Europe. Among these crusaders were Cologne burghers, who had been spurred to action by the preaching of Bernard of Clairvaux in the city.[91] We have already seen the growing activism of the Cologne burghers in their revolts against archiepiscopal authority in 1074 and against imperial authority in both 1106 and 1114.[92] Now their civic confidence extended to participation in the crusading movement.

Accounts of this venture appear in many chronicles, with the eyewitness account *De expugnatione Lyxbonensi* as our main source.[93] The largest contingent of German ships, under the direction of Count Arnold of Aerschot and assembled at Cologne, left port in late April and arrived at the English harbor of Dartmouth on May 19. There they met Flemish participants under the leadership of Christian de Ghistelles and added to their number an English army from Norfolk and Suffolk under the leadership of Henry (or Hervey) Glanville, a prominent local landowner and

---

91. *REK*, 1:76, no. 446, dated January 13, 1147; Bernard is also there reputed to have healed a blind child in the presence of archbishop Arnold I. Prior to this visit, at the Frankfurt diet (November 1146), Bernard had convinced Conrad III to participate in the crusade: see Gaufridus, "Vita et res gestae sancti Bernardi, III," in *Recueil des historiens des Gaules et de la France,* ed. M. Bouquet et al. (Paris, 1877), 14:378; Odo of Deuil, *De profectione Ludovici VII in orientem,* ed. Virginia Berry (New York, 1948), 13.

92. Concerning the 1114 rebellion the royal chronicle of Cologne states that "Coniuratio Coloniae facta est pro libertate," which was directed against Henry V. See Joachim Deeters, "Die Kölner coniuratio von 1112," *Köln, das Reich und Europa, MSAK* 60 (1971): 125–48; Toni Diederich, "Coniuratio Coloniae facta est pro libertate: Eine quellenkritische Interpretation," *Annalen* 176 (1974): 7–19; Stehkämper, "Die Stadt Köln in der Salierzeit," 128.

93. Osbern, *De expugnatione Lyxbonensi,* ed. William Stubbs, RS, no. 38 (London, 1864; reprint, 1964), 1:cxliv–clxxxii—this text has also been edited and translated by C. W. David, as Columbia University Records of Civilization, no. 24 (New York, 1936); *CRC*, 84–86; *Annales de Waverleia,* 232; Robert of Torigni, *Chronica,* 155; *Annales Magdeburgenses,* 189; *Annales Sancti Disbodi,* ed. G. Waitz, MGH SS, no. 17 (Hanover, 1861; reprint, 1990), 27–28; *Gesta Alberonis Archiepiscopi auctore Balderico,* ed. G. Waitz, MGH SS, no. 8 (Hanover, 1848; reprint, 1992), 254–55; *Chronicon montis sereni,* ed. E. Ehrenfeuchter, MGH SS, no. 23 (Hanover, 1874; reprint, 1986), 147; Roger of Howden, *Chronica,* 210; Helmold of Bosau, *Slawenchonik,* ed. Heinz Stoob, Ausgewählte Quellen zur Deutschen Geschichte des Mittelalters, Freiherr von Stein-Gedächtnisausgabe, no. 19 (Darmstadt, 1973), 220; *REK,* 2:79, no. 460 (a letter sent by a Cologne priest named Winand to Archbishop Arnold I dated March 21, 1148, in which the priest tells Arnold about the conquest of Lisbon). See also Friedrich Kurth, "Der Anteil Niederdeutscher Kreuzfahrer an den Kämpfen der Portugiesen gegen die Mauren," *MIÖG Ergänzungsband* 8 (1911): 131–252; Giles Constable, "A Note on the Route of the Anglo-Flemish Crusaders," *Speculum* 28 (1953): 525–26; Christopher Tyerman, *England and the Crusades, 1095–1588* (Chicago, 1988), 32–35. For the development of crusading in Portugal see Carl Erdmann, "Der Kreuzzugsgedanke in Portugal," *Historische Zeitschrift* 141 (1930): 23–53.

constable in Suffolk. Henry apparently also held a general authority over additional participants from Kent, London, Southampton, Bristol, Hastings, Normandy, and even as far away as Scotland.[94] This massive flotilla is estimated to have comprised at least ten thousand crusaders.[95] At an average of seventy men per ship this required approximately one hundred and fifty ships, which is close to Osbern's report of one hundred and sixty-four ships. This amazing array of regional representatives certainly required some measure of organization and coordination. Oaths of unity and peace were taken, priests were placed on each ship for hearing confession and dispensing the Eucharist once a week, and weekly meetings among the lay and clerical leaders were held. For every one thousand men there were two men sworn as judges and jurors *(iudices et coniurati)* to maintain law and order.

The fleet left Dartmouth on May 23 and passed the western tip of Brittany two days later. En route they encountered a storm and the ships were separated, with the English landing at Gijon in the Austurias and fifty ships of the Germans and Flemish arriving at Gozon—some fifteen kilometers west of Gijon. This second party waited for the others to reassemble and, not finding them, set sail again on June 3, arriving at the mouth of the Tambre River, whence they made a pilgrimage to Santiago de Compostella to celebrate Pentecost on June 8. Upon their return they found the English contingent and set sail together on June 15. One day later they arrived at Oporto, the capital of the newly carved out "kingdom" of Portugal under the rule of Alfonso I (1129–85). Alfonso, the son of Count Henry of Burgundy, had founded the principality while himself on crusade and was negotiating with the papacy for recognition as a king by conquest.

Alfonso sought to use the good fortune of the crusaders' arrival as a means to conquer Lisbon from the Moors, and he enlisted the aid of the bishop of Oporto to warm the crusaders to the idea. The bishop preached to the crusaders that if they desired to make battle with the infidel they need not go clear to Palestine, since there were Muslims already in the vicinity. He also enticed them with promises not only of spiritual merit but also of rich estates. The English were reluctant at first and vowed to press

---

94. Bernard also stimulated crusading fervor in England, though by letter rather than by his personal presence: see *Letters of St. Bernard of Clairvaux*, ed. B. S. James (London, 1953), no. 391.

95. Kurth, "Kreuzfahrer," 135. The number could have been as high as thirteen thousand.

on to Jerusalem, arguing that such a detour could vitiate the emotional focus of pilgrimage to the Holy City that unified the fleet and gave the expedition a purpose. But clerical insistence that the act rather than the destination of crusading was the ultimate virtue led to the capitulation of constable Glanville and, thereafter, the entire English contingent. The ships sailed up the Tagus River while Alfonso brought his army by land, and the siege of Lisbon began on June 28, 1147.

The Moors valiantly defended the city, which capitulated after four months (on October 24), only after being given assurances that their lives and property would be spared. Yet once the city gates were opened a massacre ensued, in which the English, congratulating themselves on their virtuous choice, took a minor part.[96] After the conquest of Lisbon some of the crusaders continued on to Palestine, where they accomplished nothing. But many more stayed behind and settled under the favor of the new Portuguese monarchy. The coalition's conquest of Lisbon hastened the rise of Portugal as an independent Christian kingdom.

This venture shows the interregional cooperation and interaction created by crusading, as well as the dark side of the infusion of religious ideals into a military milieu. None seemed troubled by the treachery done at Lisbon; indeed the Cologne chronicle expresses conviction that the victory was of divine origin, occurring as it did on the day of the Feast of the Eleven Thousand Virgins, the special patron saints of Cologne.[97] Nonetheless, the joining of Cologne burghers, Anglo-Normans, Lotharingians, and Flemish in a far-flung common venture reflects the growing political and economic integration of these regions during the early twelfth century.

We must also note that this flotilla of crusaders was made up of the middle ranks of medieval society—small landholders, knights, burghers, and merchants. These minor political players were able to organize in a very sophisticated fashion and regulate their affairs with a high degree of

---

96. The *Annales Magdeburgenses* (189) are explicit about the actions of the Cologners and the English in the siege of the city. Steven Runciman (*A History of the Crusades* [Cambridge, 1954], 3:258) mentions only the participation of English, Flemish, and Frisian contingents; and Christopher Tyerman (*England and the Crusades, 1095–1588*, 32–35) refers to the German contingent only in general terms as from the Rhineland.

97. *CRC*, 86: "Consummata est autem haec divina, non humana victoria in ducentis milibus et quingentis viris Sarracenorum in festivitate 11,000 virginum. Quorundam christianorum corpora variis occisionibus exstincta, apud Ulixbonam sepulta, miraculis claruerunt." Thus those crusaders who died at the taking of Lisbon gave forth miracles in the same fashion as the eleven thousand legendary virgins who had been buried in Cologne after their martyrdom.

harmony and cooperation often uncharacteristic of their aristocratic betters. Since large numbers of German princes began crusading in the Second Crusade, and since English magnates did not begin to participate in crusading until the Third Crusade, it is actually those from the middling range of English and German society who have revealed the growing interregional cooperation and integration that was becoming increasingly typical of western Europe. Whereas regional and local political exigencies limited the magnates' interregional activities more, the small landholders and townsmen forged new channels of European cooperation and integration.

It should not escape our attention as well that the motive force bringing together a flotilla of European soldiers, remarkable for both their disparate origins as well as their numbers, was a religious one. Whatever we make of the religious fervor of the crusades, even when joined by economic and political motives, we cannot escape the fact that it was the sense of religious calling that moved these thousands of northern Europeans to join in a corporate venture so far away from home. Understood on its own, albeit violent, terms, the Second Crusade is symptomatic of a turning point in European history. In a world where localism and regionalism still predominated, there were forces underway that were interweaving the politics of regions and locales into a truly European context—a context that now included the territories of the German kingdom. No longer would the conflicts or events in one part of Europe have little or no impact on other Europeans. No longer would religious movements and controversies be restricted to the regions in which they originated. Now they would have consequences and repercussions elsewhere in Europe.

This was the new European context for renewed diplomatic ties between England, Cologne, and the empire during the reigns of Frederick Barbarossa and Henry II. Both monarchs understood the value of exploiting this growing integration of medieval Europe in the pursuance of their regional political goals. Yet so did the archbishops of Cologne—Rainald of Dassel and Philip of Heinsberg—in the pursuance of their own regional and local goals.

2

Renovatio Regnorum et Archiepiscoporum: Early Angevin-Staufen Relations and the Rise of Cologne

From the mid–twelfth century onward we find much more abundant source material, which informs us in detail about the specific individuals who participated in an ever more complex matrix of interregional diplomacy between Germany and England. The most important figures for our purposes are the new monarchs on the thrones of these respective kingdoms. In many ways Henry II of England and Frederick Barbarossa of Germany epitomize their era of medieval politics: they forcefully sought to recover lost royal rights in their kingdoms and also struggled with defining their proper roles within Christian society—particularly in determining the correct relationship between *regnum* and *sacerdotium*. One of the by-products of their political struggles was the rapid growth in royal diplomata issued in an effort to reassert royal authority. This documentation also allows us to understand with greater clarity the emerging relationship between the two kingdoms.

The Quest for the Holy Relic: Imperial Authority and the Personal Nature of Medieval Kingship

Contact between Henry the II and Frederick Barbarossa began very early in their respective reigns. In June 1156 Henry II sent an embassy to Würzburg bearing expensive gifts to Frederick in honor of his marriage to Beatrice of Burgundy.[1] Henry had just performed a feudal oath before Louis VII for his continental lands (Normandy, Anjou, Maine, Aquitaine,

---

1. *Böhmer*, 4, 2, part 1: 118, no. 398 from *Annales Herbipolenses*, ed. G. Pertz, MGH SS, no. 16 (Hanover, 1859), 9.

and Touraine) in February of this year, and no doubt a friendly monarch in Burgundy could help in disputes over asserting his lordship in French territories. Within a year Frederick sent a letter to Henry from Aachen.[2] Although addressing the English king as "brother" *[frater]* and "friend" *[amicus]*, Barbarossa took a rather superior tone and commended Abbot Gerald of Solignac and the abbey to Henry's protection. Ties of confraternity surrounding the cult of St. Remaclus had existed between Solignac and Stavelot (Stablo), the abbey of Wibald of Corvey. Thus it appears that Abbot Gerald had obtained the good offices of Wibald for this letter.

Wibald, abbot of Stavelot (Stablo) from 1130 and of Corvey from 1146, was the leading figure among Barbarossa's early advisors at court. Solignac had been harassed by the local nobility, and Gerald must have felt that an exhortation by the German monarch to protect the monastery would have been less offensive than one by Louis VII. Yet the letter itself clearly asserted the imperial right to admonish the Angevin to do his royal duty in the protection of the Church.[3] The language of imperial sovereignty reflects Barbarossa's political agenda of a "renewal of the empire" *[renovatio imperii]*, and Wibald of Corvey's voice can clearly be heard in the words of this letter.[4] There can be no doubt that the future archbishop of Cologne, Rainald of Dassel, left his own imprint on this letter, as he had been imperial archchancellor for about a year at this point.[5] It is just as instructive, however, to note that personal relationships were the basis on which this letter, purporting to assert such wideranging political authority, was initiated and transmitted.

Although this letter contained high-sounding rhetoric reflecting Bar-

---

2. *Die Kaiserurkunden des 10., 11. und 12. Jahrhunderts,* ed. Karl Friedrich Stumpf-Brentano (Innsbruck, 1865–83; reprint, Aalen, 1964), 2:331, no. 3769; *Wibaldi Epistolae,* in *Monumenta Corbiensa,* ed. Philip Jaffé, Bibliotheca Rerum Germanicarum, no. 1 (Berlin, 1864), 594, no. 461; *Böhmer,* 4, 2, pt. 1:142, no. 455. The latter is dated May 6, 1157.

3. Karl Leyser, "Frederick Barbarossa, Henry II, and the Hand of St. James," in *Medieval Germany and Its Neighbours (900–1250)* (London, 1982), 236: "It was not unusual in the twelfth century for the greater subjects of one ruler to enlist the good offices of another in dealings with their own king but a certain note of *hauteur* is unmistakable in Frederick's text."

4. Robert L. Benson, "Political *Renovatio:* Two Models," *Renaissance and Renewal in the Twelfth Century,* ed. Robert L. Benson and Giles Constable with Carol D. Lanham (Cambridge, MA, 1982), 339–86; Heinrich Appelt, *Die Kaiseridee Friedrich Barbarossas,* Österreichische Akademie der Wissenschaften, Philosophisch-Historische Klasse, Sitzungsberichte Band 252, Abhandlung 4 (Vienna, 1967); Otto Eberhard, "Friedrich Barbarossa in seinen Briefen," *DA* 5 (1942): 72–111.

5. *Die Urkunden der deutschen Könige und Kaiser: Die Urkunden Friedrichs I. Einleitung,* ed. Heinrich Appelt, MGH DD, vol. 10, pt. 5 (Hanover, 1990), 17.

barossa's intention to restore imperial leadership, the German court would soon learn that Henry II also sought to restore royal authority shattered during the civil war in England.[6] This important parallel between the two monarchs would set the tone for their early diplomatic encounters. The competing interests of protecting the *honor imperii* and the *honor regni* were present in this first exchange and would continue to characterize the political relationship between the two monarchs throughout the course of their respective reigns.

Such interests were the subtext behind the diplomacy initiated by a German embassy a few months before the dispatching of this letter. In late 1156 Henry II generously received the envoys, giving them twenty-five pounds and three shillings for their expenses and four gyrfalcons for the emperor's pleasure, yet just what the message they brought was remains unspecified in the Pipe Rolls.[7] In the following year the English king sent the clerics Herbert of Bosham and William to the German court at Würzburg with a letter bearing his official response.[8] In the letter delivered by Herbert and William, Henry thanks Frederick for the German embassy, acknowledging the letters and gifts that accompanied them. He then declares his "wish to obey" *[voluntas obsequendi]* the Staufer's "authority to command" *[auctoritas imperandi]*, rejoicing in the striking yet unspecified promise of Frederick to deal with the affairs of the English kingdom. The letter concludes with highlighting the accompanying gifts sent ("the most beautiful things that we have and such as would be pleasing to you") and mentioning curiously Barbarossa's request concerning a relic of the hand of St. James, about which Henry's envoys would explain the king's position more fully *viva voce*.

The purpose of the German embassy and the subsequent letter sent in response by Henry to Barbarossa—the so-called submissive letter—has

6. Leyser, "St. James," 238–39; W. L. Warren, *Henry II* (Berkeley, 1973; reprint, 1977), 54–64.

7. *The Great Roll of the Pipe for the Second, Third, and Fourth Years of the Reign of King Henry the Second, A.D. 1155–1158,* ed. Joseph Hunter (London, 1844), 112. Although the accounting for this expense occurs in the fourth year of Henry's reign, the expenses were actually accrued in the third year.

8. Otto of Freising and Rahewin, *Gesta Frederici,* 404–08. Herbert of Bosham was a clerk of Thomas Becket and eventually became cardinal archbishop of Benevento. See also *Böhmer,* 4, 2, part 1: 151–52, nos. 485–86. Several German scholars have sought to correlate the sending of this embassy with the first charter of trading privileges given to the Cologne merchants in England, using an 1157 date. This attribution is erroneous, as the charter could only have been issued during the years 1173–75.

elicited a great deal of commentary among historians, particularly those from Germany. Henry's letter has been cited numerous times as evidence for an imperial supremacy over Europe based on the Roman notion of *auctoritas*, which was supposedly recognized by the other western kings.[9] The emperor was to have exercised a universal patronage over other rulers and enjoyed political primacy. Yet none of these theoretical discussions dealt with the final clause of the letter, which holds the clue to the ultimate meaning of the missive.

Fritz Trautz was the first to attempt to understand the reference to the relic of St. James and its meaning for the letter.[10] He rejected the interpretation of the letter as "submissive" and surmised that the rhetorical posture taken by Henry II had something to do with the relic itself. Of course since the envoys were to discuss this matter orally, the letter left Trautz wondering about the details. A few years later Hans Eberhard Mayer traced the history of this relic (the hand of St. James) and discovered that the widow Matilda had brought it back with her to England along with many other treasures after the death of Emperor Henry V.[11] It was subsequently entrusted to the new royal abbey at Reading, where Henry I was buried shortly thereafter.[12] Mayer therefore concluded that this letter could not be used as evidence of an imperial *Weltherrschaft*.[13] It was rather an effusive blandishment for Henry's refusal to return the relic as Barbarossa must have requested.[14]

---

9. Foundational studies in this regard are Robert Holtzmann, *Der Weltherrschaftgedanke des mittelalterlichen Kaisertums und die Souveränität der europäischen Staaten* (Tübingen, 1953); Robert Folz, *The Concept of Empire in Western Europe from the Fifth to the Fourteenth Century*, trans. S. A. Ogilvie (London, 1969); Friedrich Kempf, "Das mittelalterliche Kaisertum," in *Das Königtum, seine geistigen und rechtlichen Grundlagen*, Vorträge und Forschungen, no. 3 (Konstanz, 1954; reprint, Lindau, 1969), 237f. Heinrich Appelt developed a similar concept built around the notion of *amicitia* in *Die Kaiseridee Friedrich Barbarossas*. See also Othmar Hageneder, "Weltherrschaft im Mittelalter," *MIÖG* 93 (1985): 257–78. For a full bibliography on the Staufen idea of empire see Horst Fuhrmann, "*Quis Teutonicos constituit iudices nationum?* The Trouble with Henry," *Speculum* 69, no. 2 (April 1994): 354–55.

10. Trautz, *Die Könige*, 65.

11. Hans Eberhard Mayer, "Staufische Weltherrschaft? Zum Brief Heinrichs II. von England an Friedrich Barbarossa von 1157," in *Festschrift Karl Pivec*, ed. Anton Haidacher and H. E. Mayer, Innsbrucker Beiträge zur Kulturwissenschaft, no. 12 (Innsbruck, 1966), 265–78 (reprinted in *Friedrich Barbarossa*, ed. G. Wolf, Wege der Forschung, no. 390 [Darmstadt, 1975], 184ff.).

12. Roger of Howden, *Chronica*, 1:181.

13. Mayer, "Weltherrschaft," 278.

14. Ibid., 276. Hans Kirfel (*Weltherrschaftsidee und Bündnispolitik: Untersuchungen zur Auswärtigen Politik der Staufer*, Bonner historische Forschungen, no. 12 [Bonn, 1959],

Frederick wanted the relic as part of his restoration of the *honor imperii*, since it had been part of the regalia of the imperial chapel. Indeed, the Bavarian annalist of St. Disibodenberg considered the missing relic as the cause for the recent internal conflicts in Germany.[15] Yet Henry II also saw the relic as part of his own heritage of royal prestige. His grandfather Henry I, the monarch whose royal prerogatives were so central to Henry II's vision of a restored kingship in England, was buried at Reading Abbey along with his second wife and eldest son, William. During the civil war Stephen had removed the hand to secure its benefits within his own private treasury. Henry II restored the relic to Reading Abbey immediately upon his own accession, and thus this act was understood not only as a useful means of drawing pilgrims to the royal abbey but also as one of many steps to be taken for the restoration of the *honor regni* in England. To lose the protection of the relic over his kin was unthinkable on both a dynastic and a personal level.

Several years after Mayer's study, Karl Leyser recounted this matter and added more details.[16] He showed that the use of the terms *auctoritas imperandi* and *voluntas obsequendi* had a long heritage, dating back to Einhard's *Vita Karoli Magni*.[17] Rahewin made deliberate use of Henry's letter, not only quoting it in his chronicle (while Barbarossa's original letter was not preserved), but also employing it again in his own glorious description of Frederick's relations with other western monarchs.[18] We have already seen Conrad III employ similar language of imperial suzerainty in the West, and through Rahewin this terminology reentered the imperial rhetoric. It will be called on again with specific application to England during the imprisonment of Richard I the Lionheart, at the royal election of Otto IV, and at the Fourth Lateran Council in 1215, as we shall see later. Hence, although the letter itself was intended to soften the refusal to return the relic of St. James—having done so would itself have been the best evidence for royal submission to imperial authority—it was preserved and used

---

178) asserts that the letter contained a formal offer of alliance from Barbarossa, but this cannot be confirmed by the text itself. Concerning the *honor imperii* see P. Rassow, *Honor Imperii: Die neue Politik Friedrich Barbarossas 1152–1159* (Munich, 1940).

15. The *Annales Sancti Disbodi* (23) express indignation at the loss of the relic, which was seen as a blow to the empire: "Mathildis regina in Angliam ad patrem proficiscitur, manum sancti Iacobi secum deferens; per quod irreparabile dampnum regno Francorum intulit." The use of *regnum Francorum* for Germany is an archaic form that was virtually gone by the twelfth century.

16. Leyser, "St. James."

17. Ibid., 234.

18. Otto of Freising and Rahewin, *Gesta Frederici*, 712.

within the imperial tradition as evidence for such submission on the part of other kings to the *auctoritas* of the emperor. Both royal courts used the relic to reassert their claims to sovereignty, yet the intended application of this sovereignty had its locus only *within* their respective realms. No actual or expected exercise of extraterritorial power ever occurred; in fact, the actual matter here was a personal desire for a relic rather than political hegemony in Europe. These medieval political figures were moved to act out of religious motives rather than out of the power politics of empire building.

Two final comments are needed in connection with this diplomacy. First, it is interesting in the light of later developments that the "submissive letter" was written in the chancery of Thomas Becket, who signed the letter and sent his secretary (Herbert of Bosham) as envoy.[19] It would not be long before Becket was writing rebukes to the two monarchs involved here. Perhaps his use of the terms *auctoritas imperandi* and *voluntas obsequendi* were a deliberate edge placed on the sword of refusal by Becket as an ironic response to Frederick's earlier imperious letter of May 6, 1157, and subsequent request for the relic, which had by this time been fully imbued with English royal prestige. The purpose of the "letter full of honeyed words" *[litteras mellito sermone plenas]* certainly did not escape the chronicler Rahewin. In any case this would not be the last time that Barbarossa found Henry II giving with one hand while taking back with the other. Nor would it be the last time that Frederick and his court claimed a kind of imperial sovereignty over the monarchs in Europe—an authority that also allowed the emperor to determine a suitable candidate for the papal throne.

Finally, attention must be drawn to the gift sent by Henry II, which is mentioned by Rahewin at the beginning of his account: it was a huge tent so large that winches were required to raise it. The gift duly impressed all who saw it. The tent was spacious enough for significant religious services, even a coronation, or accommodation suitable for a monarch while on campaign. Marjorie Chibnall has speculated that Henry's mother, Matilda, had suggested the tent as a gift to "sugar the pill" of rejection

---

19. Elsewhere Herbert of Bosham refused to dignify the German monarch with the imperial title and referred to him merely as *rex Alemannorum*. William Fitzstephen mentions Herbert's attitude in his *Vita Sancti Thomae*, ed. William Stubbs, RS, no. 67 (London, 1877), part 3. See also Beryl Smalley's chapter on Herbert of Bosham in *The Becket Controversy and the Schools* (Oxford, 1973).

concerning the relic.[20] Matilda surely recalled her own sojourns in Italy some forty years earlier and thus was probably one to consult on such matters. The tent must have seen much use during Frederick's numerous Italian campaigns. But perhaps most significant was the symbolic value of the gift. It ironically embodied Henry's diplomatic response to the emperor about the hand of St. James, as it was impressive and weighty in appearance but empty inside.

Rainald of Dassel and the Limits of Imperial Authority (1157–64)

The English envoys at Würzburg were most likely those who were also present, along with many other foreign embassies, at the famous diet of Besançon in the following month (October 1157). There they witnessed yet another impressive assertion of imperial authority,[21] for they observed firsthand the powerful performance of the imperial chancellor Rainald of Dassel. Rainald would not be elected archbishop of Cologne until 1159, yet his immediate predecessors in that office had been firmly in the Staufer's corner. Arnold II (1151–56) had been the imperial chancellor under Conrad III. A supporter of Barbarossa's election, he anointed and crowned the new king at Aachen on March 9, 1152,[22] and he served as host when the two celebrated Easter together in Cologne a few days later (March 30).[23] Arnold's short-lived successor, Frederick II of Berg (1156–58), was one of the most powerful ecclesiastical supporters of Barbarossa at Besançon.[24] As a result of a fall from his horse near Pavia on December 15, 1158, the archbishop died while accompanying Barbarossa on an Italian campaign as archchancellor of Italy.[25]

On hearing of Arnold's death Barbarossa immediately proposed Rainald of Dassel's candidacy for the office. Rainald's machinations at Besançon

---

20. Chibnall, *Matilda*, 165.
21. Otto of Freising and Rahewin, *Gesta Frederici*, 408.
22. *REK*, 2:88, no. 524. See also Heinz Wolter, *Arnold von Wied, Kanzler Konrads III. und Erzbischof von Köln*, Veröffentlichungen des Kölnischen Geschichtsvereins, no. 32 (Cologne, 1973); Friedrich Schneider, *Arnold II. Erzbischof von Cöln 1151–1156* (Ph.D. diss., Halle, 1884).
23. Ferdinand Opll, *Friedrich Barbarossa*, Gestalten des Mittelalters und der Renaissance (Darmstadt, 1990), 42ff.
24. Heinz Wolter, "Erzbischof Friedrich II von Köln (1156–1158)," *JKGV* 46 (1975): 1–50.
25. *REK*, 2:109, no. 674.

over the use of the term *beneficium* in a papal letter are well known and will not be discussed here in detail.[26] Suffice it to say that he was the foremost exponent of imperial *auctoritas* and a vitriolic opponent to papal counterclaims.[27] During Rainald's archiepiscopate (he was not ordained a priest and consecrated as archbishop until 1165, and thus he served six years of his eight-year pontificate as a nonclerical archbishop-elect) he became deeply involved in pressing foreign monarchs to support the imperial position against papal claims.[28] In this role, so clearly defined at Besançon, he eventually led negotiations with Henry II in an attempt to swing the Angevin kingdom against Pope Alexander III. This effort had much promise once Henry became embroiled in his own controversy with Thomas Becket in 1164 over the Constitutions of Clarendon, the centerpiece of Henry's own *renovatio regni* (to recoin a Staufen topos). From this point onward the potential inherent in the growing economic and political ties between Cologne and England would be tapped by Rainald.

The opportunity came to him at the death of Pope Hadrian IV in 1159,

---

26. See W. Heinemeyer, "*Beneficium—non feudum sed bonum factum:* Der Streit auf dem Reichstag zu Besançon 1157," *Archiv für Diplomatik* 15 (1969): 155–236; Walter Ullmann, "Cardinal Roland and Besançon," in *Sacerdozio e Regno da Gregorio VII a Bonifacio VIII,* ed. Friedrich Kempf, Miscellanea Historiae Pontificae, no. 18 (Rome, 1954), 107–26 (reprinted as chapter 4 in *The Papacy and Political Ideas in the Middle Ages* [London, 1976]). For studies on Rainald of Dassel see, in addition to those cited in nn. 27 and 28, Walther Föhl, "Studien zu Rainald von Dassel," *JKGV* 17 (1935): 234–63; 20 (1938): 238–60; Werner Grebe, "Studien zur geistigen Welt Rainalds von Dassel," *Annalen* 171 (1969): 5–44; Rainer Maria Herkenrath, *Rainald von Dassel: Reichskanzler und Erzbischof von Köln* (Ph.D. diss., Graz, 1963).

27. The debate continues over whether Rainald or Barbarossa was the architect of imperial policy. Arnold Stelzmann ("Rainald von Dassel und seine Reichspolitik," *JKGV* 25 [1960]: 60–82) argues that Rainald was the architect, while Werner Grebe ("Rainald von Dassel als Reichskanzler Friedrich Barbarossas (1156–1159)," *JKGV* 49 [1978]: 49–74) rejects this view. While determining pride of place in this matter is unnecessary for our purposes, it is clear that Rainald's politics as archbishop of Cologne cannot be distinguished from imperial policy. If Barbarossa himself set the agenda it is clear that Rainald often took the lead in determining the best means of achieving it, as we shall see. As one who should know, Heinrich Appelt has concluded, "None of the statesmen of Frederick I exercised stronger political influence than Rainald" (*Die Urkunden Friedrichs I.: Einleitung,* 18). See also Opll, *Friedrich Barbarossa,* 304–5; Johannes Laudage, *Alexander III. und Friedrich Barbarossa,* Forschungen zur Kaiser- und Papstgeschichte des Mittelalters, Beihefte zu J. F. Böhmer, Regesta Imperii, no. 16 (Cologne, Weimar, and Vienna, 1997), 89–94.

28. He was ordained a priest in Würzburg on May 29, 1165, and consecrated archbishop in Cologne on October 2, 1165, in the presence of Barbarossa and his wife: see *REK,* 2:138, nos. 819 and 822. For the canonical issues surrounding the bishop-elect see Robert L. Benson, *The Bishop-Elect: A Study of Medieval Ecclesiastical Office* (Princeton, 1968).

which resulted in a disputed papal election wherein the majority chose the imperial archenemy at Besançon, Cardinal Roland Bandinelli (Alexander III), while a minority of two cardinals elected Barbarossa's friend Cardinal Octavian (Victor IV). Barbarossa then claimed the imperial authority to convene a council at Pavia to resolve the conflict, and imperial letters were issued throughout Europe calling on all parties to come to the council. In these letters the assertion of imperial *auctoritas* to protect the Church appeared once again—the emperor even called Alexander III to be present.[29]

Behind Barbarossa's claims to universal sovereignty in Christendom lay not so much the realization of hegemony over the other western monarchs but rather an interest in extending the *honor imperii* into Italy. Since of his three kingdoms Italy was the one most central to his identity as Roman emperor, the reassertion of imperial power there—especially in the eternal city of the emperors—became the centerpiece of his diplomacy. During this thirty-eight-year kingship he conducted no less than six Italian campaigns and spent sixteen years there (some 42 percent of his reign).

The epitome of Barbarossa's political ideology occurred at the imperial diet of Roncaglia (November 1158) during his second Italian campaign. Here Roman law, complete with its lofty assertions of imperial power, was invoked for the pragmatic purpose of regaining regalian rights in Lombardy. The income derived from these rights amounted to around one hundred thousand pounds of silver a year, the recovery of which would have made Barbarossa one of the richest rulers in the West.[30] We must keep in mind, therefore, that the revival of exalted classical imperial claims to "preeminence over the provinces" was designed for internal

---

29. MGH Const., 1:255–56, no. 184; *Die Urkunden Friedrichs I. 1158–1167*, ed. Heinrich Appelt, MGH DD, no. 10 (Hanover, 1979), 2:96–98: "... evocamus totius imperii nostri et aliorum regnorum, scilicet Angliae, Franciae, Ungariae, Daciae, archiepiscopos, episcopos, abbates, et viros religiosos. ..." Similar language appears in letters to Archbishop Eberhard of Salzburg (MGH Const., 1:252, no. 181; *Die Urkunden Friedrichs I. 1158–1167*, 92–93; *Die Admonter Briefsammlung*, ed. Günter Hödl and Peter Classen, MGH Epistolae: Die Briefe der Deutschen Kaiserzeit, no. 6 [Munich, 1983], 76–78, no. 30) and Bishop Hartmann of Brixen (MGH Const., 1:253–54, no. 183; Appelt, ed., *Die Urkunden Friedrichs I. 1158–1167*, 95–96; Otto of Freising and Rahewin, *Gesta Frederici*, 648). See also Timothy Reuter, "The Papal Schism of 1159–1169, the Empire, and the West" (D. Phil. diss., Oxford University, 1975).

30. See Benson, "Political *Renovatio*," and Horst Fuhrmann, *Germany in the High Middle Ages (c. 1050–1200)*, trans. Timothy Reuter (Cambridge, 1986), 148.

consumption *within* the empire (i.e., the provinces of Germany, Burgundy, and Italy) to reassert *lost* royal authority, not as a concerted campaign to widen the emperor's hegemony *beyond* the borders of his already far-flung and thus unwieldy kingdoms. To impute an imperialist plan of European expansion to Barbarossa and his court is to expect medieval political conditions to resemble modern geopolitical realities and the dictates of modern statecraft. Frederick had his hands full within his territories; to have reached further was not only beyond his intentions but also clearly beyond his means.

Such Staufen imperial rhetoric may have carried some weight within the empire (though it was resisted there as well), but it found little resonance beyond its boundaries. It is instructive to note, for example, that the letter sent to Henry II announcing the Pavian council was not as authoritative in tone as those dispatched within the empire.[31] The letter bound for England was also ineffective and only imperial bishops attended the council, which not surprisingly selected Victor IV. Both Louis VII and Henry II rejected the imperial claim of *auctoritas* to decide the legality of a papal election or to convene an ecclesiastical council. They both needed to avoid antagonizing their own clergy at home. Henry II's position in the schism was even more complicated in that he had both French and English clergy to consider in his lands. Were he even to bring the English clergy to support the antipope, he would have unleashed great difficulties in his French territories, where the clergy consistently stood by Alexander III. Such a breach could be used by Louis VII to declare Henry II forfeit of his continental holdings. Therefore, once again regional and internal concerns overrode any extraterritorial matters, even if they concerned the legitimacy of a pope.[32]

Bishop Eberhard of Bamberg wrote to Archbishop Eberhard of Salzburg after the Pavian council to inform him of the events there, and he tells of the positions taken by the French and English kings as expressed by envoys.[33] The ambiguous posture of the embassies was surely the result of the two monarchs' interest in maintaining good relations with

31. MGH Const., 1:254–55, no. 183; *Die Kaiserurkunden des 10., 11. und 12. Jahrhunderts*, 2:341, no. 3870.

32. Frank Barlow, "The English, French, and Norman Councils Called to Deal with the Papal Schism of 1159," *EHR* 51 (1936): 264–68.

33. Otto of Freising and Rahewin, *Gesta Frederici*, 696–98; "Nuntius regis Francorum promisit pro eo neutrum se recepturum, usque dum nuntios domini imperatoris recipiat. Nuntius regis Anglorum idem velle et idem nolle promisit tam in his quam in aliis" (698).

the Staufen court, as they were enmeshed at the time in difficulties surrounding Henry II's marriage to Eleanor of Aquitaine.[34] This marriage
had decisively shifted the balance of feudal power in France and Louis
continued to dispute Henry's rights over the lands inherited by Eleanor.
In the same year as the Pavian council both Louis and Henry had sent
envoys to the emperor in northern Italy (early February 1159) hoping to
gain his diplomatic support in their quarrel.[35] At the time, the two western monarchs were especially engaged in a dispute over the city of
Toulouse, which was part of Eleanor's inheritance.[36]

Once again Rahewin mentions the imperial *auctoritas* and presents the
envoys' diplomacy with Barbarossa as that of two lesser parties who appealed to a superior authority to mediate the conflict. Setting Rahewin's
imperial propaganda aside, the appeal to the emperor was rather the action
of two kings who realized the value of having Barbarossa as an ally and an
alternate channel for negotiations. Rahewin's intentions become clearer
when, despite the earlier mention of the English ambivalence at Pavia, he
includes Henry II among those who consented to the decision for Victor IV,
which is a complete fabrication.[37] Barbarossa did send Bishop Peter of
Pavia (the very bishop whose see hosted the imperial council) to France in
the autumn of 1159 both to intercede in the dispute and to draw both
western monarchs to the candidacy of Victor IV. It appears unlikely that
this embassy made any appreciable difference in achieving consensus on
either the Capetian-Angevin territorial dispute or the papal schism.[38] A

---

34. In addition the two kings had agreed in their peace negotiations of May 1160 to
work in concert to resolve the schism: see Ralph de Diceto, *Ymagines historiarum,* ed.
William Stubbs, RS, no. 68 (London, 1876; reprint, 1964), 1:303; Robert of Torigni,
Chronica, 207; Frank Barlow, ed., *The Letters of Arnulf of Lisieux,* Camden Society, 3d
ser., no. 61 (London, 1939), 36, no. 27.

35. Otto of Freising and Rahewin, *Gesta Frederici,* 568–70. That Louis would still be
feuding over the marriage, which took place in 1152, says a great deal about the irritation at
the French court about it. See Warren, *Henry II,* 42–44.

36. Robert William Eyton, *Court, Household, and Itinerary of King Henry II* (London,
1878; reprint, 1974), 45–47; Warren, *Henry II,* 87–88.

37. MGH Const., 1:270, no. 183, from Otto of Freising and Rahewin, *Gesta Frederici,*
686–94. In a list of those consenting to the decision of Pavia, of which Rainald of Dassel is
at the head, the following appears: "Heinricus rex Anglorum per litteras et legatos suos
consensit." Peter Munz (*Frederick Barbarossa* [Ithaca, 1969], 216) unfortunately takes this
report by Rahewin as accurate. Formal French and English recognition of Alexander III
came at the councils of Beauvais (July 1160) and London (1160).

38. Robert of Torigni, *Chronica,* 206; Eyton, *Itinerary,* 48; Marcel Pacaut, *Louis VII et
son royaume* (Paris, 1964); Warren, *Henry II,* 88.

temporary truce was achieved in October—it was to last only until May 22 (a suitable respite for the winter months)—but the schism continued unresolved. The imperial court must have realized at this point that the local and regional contests fueled by the personal feud between Henry II and Louis VII were a major obstacle to developing any consensus for resolving the papal schism in the imperial favor. Once again, interregional diplomacy was driven by local, feudal interests; the imperial effort to interregionalize the issue of the papacy found little resonance amid local and regional conflicts.

Imperial envoys were also sent to the other kings of Europe and the Byzantine emperor to elicit their support for the Pavian decision.[39] Rainald of Dassel, the archbishop-elect of Cologne, went personally to the French and English courts in hopes of achieving what the bishop of Pavia could not.[40] No doubt Rainald had expected that his French education would serve him well on this diplomatic mission.[41] Arriving in France sometime in February 1160, he was unable to gain the support of Louis VII, and he hurriedly moved on to Rouen.[42] Here too he only achieved a limited measure of success. Rainald merely secured a promise from Henry II to delay his decision concerning the schism. The excommunication of the imperial party by Alexander III certainly interfered with these negotiations.

Rainald's hope of victory in the schism and of a vindication of imperial ideology was not fulfilled. The Alexandrine party's efforts were successful at preventing the western monarchs from supporting Victor IV, in no small measure because of widespread western ecclesiastical support for Alexander III.[43] The archbishop-elect's attempt at reviving English interest by another legation sent to England in December 1161 failed, and an

---

39. Otto of Freising and Rahewin, *Gesta Frederici*, 704.

40. *REK*, 2:117, nos. 700–701.

41. See J. Ehlers, "Deutsche Scholaren in Frankreich während des 12. Jahrhunderts," in *Schulen und Studium im sozialen Wandel des hohen und späten Mittelalters*, ed. Johannes Fried, Vorträge und Forschungen, no. 30 (Sigmaringen, 1986), 97–120; Keller, *Zwischen regionaler Begrenzung und universalem Horizont*, 308.

42. Rainald was joined in this trip by his relative Count Adolph II of Schauenburg (Holstein), according to Helmold of Bosau (*Slawenchronik*, 306). Rainald's mother was from the family of the counts of Schauenburg: see Helmuth Kluger and Edgar Pack, eds., *Series episcoporum ecclesiae catholicae occidentalis ab initio usque ad annum MCXCVIII*. Series 5, *Germania*, vol. 1, *Archiepiscopatus Coloniensis* (Stuttgart, 1982), 36.

43. The Cologne chronicle reports that the Alexandrine party, with the support of the Greek emperor, had been telling other kings of Barbarossa's ultimate plan to conquer their kingdoms once he destroyed Milan (*CRC*, 108).

even greater setback occurred when a meeting proposed for August 29, 1162, with Louis VII at St. Jean-de-Losne (on the river Saône at the border between the two kingdoms) never materialized. The conference was designed to settle the schism and Louis VII showed initial willingness to attend. Alexander III, however, refused to participate on the grounds that the pope was to be judged by no one. Subsequently Louis realized the difficulties he faced at home with a French clergy that offered strong resistance to the conference.

Confounded by yet another failed effort at diplomacy with a western monarch, Rainald let loose his famous complaint—with the usual imperial rhetorical flourish—that the *reguli* (kings of the provinces) arrogantly claimed for themselves the authority of the Roman emperor to adjudicate the papal schism.[44] This comment of the Cologne archbishop-elect only isolated his party more, as those he had hoped to draw to the Staufen side reacted in much the same vein as that represented in the famous statement of biblical proportions made by John of Salisbury after the council of Pavia in 1160:[45] "Who has made the Germans to be judges over the peoples? Who has given this crude and violent race the right arbitrarily to choose a lord over the children of man?"[46] Rainald's

---

44. See Opll, *Friedrich Barbarossa*, 76, 81–84; Walter Heinemeyer, "Die Verhandlungen an der Sâone im Sommer 1162," *DA* 20 (1964): 155–89; Franz Josef Schmale, "Friedrich I. und Ludwig VII. im Sommer des Jahres 1162," *Zeitschrift für Bayrische Landesgeschichte* 31 (1968): 315–68; Kienast, *Deutschland und Frankreich*, 1:203–10; Reuter, *Papal Schism*, 80–101; Laudage, *Alexander III. und Friedrich Barbarossa*, 145–49.

45. John of Salisbury maintained close contact with activities in Cologne by correspondence with his fellow student and good friend Gerard Pucelle (for their correspondence see *The Letters of John of Salisbury*, vol. 2, *The Later Letters (1163–1180)*, ed. W. J. Millor and Christopher N. L. Brooke [Oxford, 1979], 70, no. 158; 98, no. 167; 216, no. 184; 396, no. 226). Much to the chagrin of Thomas Becket, Gerard left the exiled *familia* of Becket and had taken a teaching position as *scholasticus* in canon law at Cologne—the heart of schismatic territory—during the Alexandrine schism. See Johannes Fried, "Gerard Pucelle und Köln," *ZRG kan. Abt.* 68 99 (1982): 125–35; Stephan Kuttner and Eleanor Rathbone, "Anglo-Norman Canonists of the Twelfth Century," *Traditio* 7 (1949–51): 296–303. Here we have yet another significant Anglo-Cologne connection amid the fabric of interregional contacts between the Rhineland and England.

46. *The Letters of John of Salisbury*, vol. 1, *1153–1161*, ed. W. J. Millor and H. E. Butler, revised by Christopher N. L. Brooke, Oxford Medieval Texts (Oxford, 1986), no. 124. The translation is from Fuhrmann, *Germany in the High Middle Ages*, 156. John of Salisbury's comment was not made so much out of loyalty to England as out of loyalty to the pontificate of Alexander III: see Timothy Reuter, "John of Salisbury and the Germans," in *The World of John of Salisbury*, ed. Michael Wilks, Studies in Church History, Subsidia, no. 3 (Oxford, 1984), 415–25; Johannes Spörl, "Rainald von Dassel auf dem Konzil von Reims 1148 und sein Verhältnis zu Johannes von Salisbury," *Historisches Jahrbuch* 60

imperious rhetoric was therefore matched by the Alexandrine party and hardly served the emperor's goals of asserting imperial prerogatives. The message was clear: implementing classical Roman ideals of emperorship did not fit the medieval political realities. Alexander had safely removed himself to the French territories of Henry II (Déols) as the planned meeting between the German and French monarchs drew near, and Louis VII knew he ran the risk not only of alienating his clergy but also of military engagement with Henry should the Capetian side with Victor IV.[47] Here again local and regional circumstances caused Louis to back out of the proposed conference. By 1164, with Barbarossa involved in another unsuccessful Italian campaign, the emperor was politically isolated by the schism and mired in such regional and local affairs in northern Italy as the growing conflict between Genoa and Pisa.

Even the German episcopate began to waver in their support of the antipope, as an exchange of letters between Archbishop Eberhard of Salzburg and Archbishop Henry of Reims in the summer of 1162 indicates.[48] Eberhard, a supporter of Alexander III, wrote first to Henry asking about the position of France in the schism, because rumors swirled that the Gallican church would soon retract their allegiance to Alexander. Henry replied that the Gallican church and Louis VII recognized Alexander III without reservation. Such correspondence between French and German ecclesiastics reveals an effort to shore up support for Alexander, in direct contradiction to the stated policy of the emperor.

Failed imperial diplomacy had reached such a pass that in April 1164 an Alexandrine cardinal could write with confidence to Thomas Becket to notify him of Archbishop Conrad of Mainz's defection to Alexander III. This left only Rainald of Dassel and the emperor's cousin Duke Henry

---

(1940): 250–57. Horst Fuhrmann has recently given a thought-provoking reply to John of Salisbury in "*Quis Teutonicos constituit iudices nationum?* The Trouble with Henry," *Speculum* 60: 2 (April 1994): 344–58.

47. Boso, *Vita Adriani IV et Alexandri III*, in *Le Liber Pontificalis: Introduction et Commentaire*, ed. L. Duchesne, Bibliothèque des écoles françaises d'Athènes et de Rome, 2d ser. (Paris, 1892; reprint, 1955), 407. See also Wilhelm Janssen, *Die päpstlichen Legaten in Frankreich vom Schisma Anaklets II. bis zum Tode Coelestins III.*, Kölner historische Abhandlungen, no. 6 (Cologne, 1961), 77 n. 90; Wolfgang Georgi, *Friedrich Barbarossa und die auswärtigen Mächte: Studien zur Außenpolitik 1159–1180*, Europäische Hochschulschriften, 3d ser., no. 442 (Frankfurt am Main, 1990), 64–79.

48. *Die Admonter Briefsammlung*, 139–140, nos. 81–82. Eberhard's question no doubt referred to the planned French-imperial council at St. Jean-de-Losne in August, which never transpired.

the Lion of Saxony/Bavaria among the major princes on the side of the imperial antipope.[49] To date, Barbarossa's policy of reasserting imperial authority even *within* his kingdoms was proving extremely difficult, and all efforts at creating extraterritorial political coalitions to assist him were even less successful. The reasons for this failure at obtaining extraterritorial alliances can be partly attributed to the religious nature of the schism. Since Barbarossa and his supporters had been excommunicated by Alexander III, those who joined his cause risked the same fate. In the final analysis, therefore, it was the pope, not the emperor, who successfully asserted a position of preeminence in Christendom that extended into all kingdoms of the West. If any force was succeeding in forming a truly European coalition it was a religious rather than a secular one. The ideals of the Roman church were more influential in Europe than those of the Roman Empire.

Also the basic nature of medieval political life worked against the emperor. The local and regional preoccupations of the English and French kings—not to mention their own personal feuding—restricted his diplomatic success, and his own internal preoccupation in reasserting royal prerogatives proved just as problematic. Ironically, the Staufer's diplomatic strategy of extending claims of imperial sovereignty beyond the borders of the empire was designed to obtain the support of other western monarchs, and yet this very rhetoric of hegemonic leadership undermined his position of authority both within and without his empire. It was a diplomacy that failed because it overlooked the realities of medieval political life. Those modern historians who have been seduced by Staufen rhetorical claims to European sovereignty have also overlooked the impossibility of translating the political theory of classical Roman emperors into medieval society.

Hence Barbarossa's early search for joint action among the Christian monarchs of Europe for the sake of reasserting their royal authority proved unrealized. The ideology of an imperial *renovatio,* led so energetically by the archbishop-elect of Cologne, met not only with resistance in Italy by the pope and the Lombard cities but also with general lack of interest elsewhere in Europe because of the other monarchs' own preoccupations with a *renovatio* of royal power within their respective realms.

---

49. *REK,* 2:135, no. 813; *Materials for the History of Thomas Becket, Archbishop of Canterbury,* ed. James C. Robertson, RS, no. 67 (London, 1875–85; reprint, 1965), 5:159, no. 84.

The result of this failed diplomacy was Barbarossa's political isolation in Europe and a weakened position within his own kingdoms.

Religious Politics, Marriage Alliances, and Regionalism:
A Second Try at *Renovatio* (1164–67)

The actions of three men—Rainald of Dassel, Thomas Becket, and Henry the Lion—during the years 1164–67 would breathe new life into the political machinations of the papal schism and unexpectedly revitalize both Anglo-imperial and Anglo-Cologne diplomatic relations in a way that redefined the political landscape of Germany and England for the next half century. Barbarossa's politely ignored clarion call to accept imperial authority was now to be coupled with a more traditional device for uniting the English and German ruling houses: a marriage union. What classical political ideology could not accomplish, the good old social dynamics of kinship and dynastic marriage ties did. The inventiveness of Rainald, the willing participation of Henry the Lion, and the resistance of Thomas Becket combined to make this a reality, and the Angevin-Staufen-Cologne-Welf matrix of interests would thereby finally be drawn together.

Victor IV died on April 20, 1164, and the hope of a reconciliation between Alexander III and Barbarossa was thereby rekindled. Yet Rainald of Dassel embarked on an even more ambitious program of asserting imperial sovereignty. First, he had a successor (Paschal III) elected at Lucca without notifying the emperor.[50] In fact the election took place even before the funeral ceremony for Victor had been completed. Rainald took a second step to bolster the failing imperial cause by removing the bones of the Three Kings (Magi) from the recently conquered city of Milan to his archiepiscopal city. He arrived in Cologne on July 23 and solemnly installed the relics as the new centerpiece of the cathedral.[51] Removing the Three

---

50. *REK,* 2:129, no. 791.

51. *REK,* 2:132–33, no. 804; *CRC,* 115. This was only one of three times that Rainald ever came to Cologne, the other two being a brief stop in 1159 to raise troops for the Italian campaigns (*REK,* 2:138, no. 822). See Odilo Engels, "Die Reliquien der Heiligen Drei Könige in der Reichspolitik der Staufer," and Hugo Stehkämper, "Könige und Heilige Drei Könige," in *Die Heiligen Drei Könige-Darstellung und Verehrung: Katalog zur Ausstellung des Wallraf-Richartz Museums* (Cologne, 1982), 33–50; Hans Hoffmann, *Die Heiligen Drei Könige: Zur Heiligenverehrung im kirchlichen, gesellschaftlichen und politischen Leben des Mittelalters,* Rheinisches Archiv, no. 94 (Bonn, 1975); and *Der Meister des*

Kings from Italy to Cologne was an effort calculated to strengthen Barbarossa's kingship. The sanctifying connection of such kings with Staufen rulership was a valuable ideological and spiritual support in the midst of the papal schism. Royal patron saints (no less than three of them) were a needed counterbalance to a Staufen kingship under papal excommunication. One had to fight spiritual fire with spiritual fire, since the secular sword of Roman imperial ideology had proven too rusty to rally support.

News of this great event spread quickly to England, and Robert of Torigni provides intimate details about the relics, which he says he learned from an eyewitness.

> Rainald, bishop-elect of Cologne, chancellor of Frederick, emperor of the Germans, transferred the bodies of the three Magi of Milan to Cologne. Their outer bodies remained intact so far as the skin and hair because they had been buried with balsam and other unguents. The first of the Magi, as was told to me by one who asserted that he had seen them, appeared (as far as could be determined from their outward appearance and hair) to be fifteen years old, the second thirty, and the third sixty.[52]

The relics of the Three Kings did less to renew relations between the Staufen and Angevin monarchs than other events in the same year of their *translatio*. While such efforts were being made in Germany to strengthen the monarch's hand, Henry II was facing the political fallout from the Constitutions of Clarendon, which he issued throughout England in 1164. Becket had already disappointed the king when he resigned the chancellorship upon his accession to the archbishopric of Canterbury. Henry had hoped for a beneficial relationship between himself and a trusted chancellor-archbishop, such as the emperor enjoyed with the archbishop of Cologne.[53] Becket's rejection of the constitutions and his flight

---

Dreikönigen-Schreins: Ausstellung im Erzbischöflichen Diözesan-Museum in Köln, 11. Juli bis 23. August 1964 (Cologne, 1964). Patrick Geary ("The Magi and Milan," *Living with the Dead in the Middle Ages* [Ithaca, 1994], 242–56) has asserted that these relics were actually the invention of Archbishop Rainald of Dassel. See also Bernard Hamilton, "Prester John and the Three Kings of Cologne," in *Studies in Medieval History Presented to R. H. C. Davis*, ed. Henry Mayr-Harting and R. I. Moore (London, 1985), 177–91.

52. Robert of Torigni, *Chronica*, 4:220–21.
53. Ralph de Diceto, *Ymagines historiarum*, 1:308.

into the waiting arms of Louis VII had only complicated the matter for the Angevin.[54]

Before then, Henry II had no real cause to repudiate Alexander III, but now he appears to have felt he needed some means to apply pressure on the pope to yield in the Becket affair. Perhaps he thought that threatening Louis VII with isolation by surrounding Louis's royal demesne with antipapal allies in Angevin France and the Staufen empire might put pressure on both Louis VII and Alexander III to resolve the matter in his favor. Of course, there was nothing in this scheme expressly intended to benefit Barbarossa, yet the emperor's unfortunate position might also have been the incentive needed to forge a coalition of convenience. For the first time both monarchs were chafing under the strictures of ecclesiastical resistance to their reassertion of royal authority and could now find common cause. Frederick Barbarossa and Henry II were in similar positions by 1164: each had inherited a territorial lordship on the continent and that extended beyond his main kingdom. The schism was complicating their efforts at reasserting royal prerogatives. The end of the schism, therefore, became a common interest of the kings. Yet it must be stressed again that this interest was understood in separate ways, that is, as an issue of the assertion of royal rights *within* their own individual and separate realms and not as a common cause for royal authority or of state sovereignty.[55]

When Becket fled England for Flanders in November 1164 Henry II sent John Cumin to the imperial court.[56] Whether this was an initial contact is unclear, yet Barbarossa no doubt saw the opportunity that the Becket controversy created for undermining the English king's support for Alexander III. Frederick sought a second time to achieve diplomatic cooperation with a western kingdom after the failed attempt with the French king at St. Jean-de-Losne in 1162. Cumin likely met the imperial court at the Reichstag in Bamberg, but we know nothing more of this early embassy. If the Bamberg diet was the meeting place, Duke Henry the Lion and Rainald of Dassel were surely present.

---

54. Becket's refusal to be tried by the king and his appeal to the pope had broken two crucial statutes in the Constitutions of Clarendon.

55. Fuhrmann, *Germany in the High Middle Ages,* 157.

56. *Materials,* 5:59, no. 36, where a nuncio writes to Becket of, among other things, Cumin's presence at the imperial court. John Cumin was the archdeacon of Bath and later the archbishop of Dublin. He may have been at the imperial court as early as 1163: see Timothy Reuter, *Papal Schism,* 252–53; Eyton, *Itinerary,* 75.

It was not until April 1165, however, that Henry II rejected overtures from Louis and Alexander III at Gisors, during a meeting that his mother, Matilda, had sought. Wearied by Becket's intransigence (Becket was now safely protected in Soissons) and angered by the papal and French support given to the errant archbishop, the English king instead received an impressive embassy at Rouen led by none other than Rainald of Dassel. The ensuing negotiations lasted three days and included discussion of many affairs concerning Christendom, from the schism to a crusade.[57] Such a short period of negotiations suggests that Henry II's frustrations had moved him to take some immediate and concrete steps to pressure the Alexandrine party. The result of these discussions was an Angevin-Staufen affinity of undeclared purpose to be established by a proposed double marriage. Henry II's daughter Matilda was to marry the Welf Henry the Lion; his other daughter, Eleanor, was to marry Barbarossa's young son and namesake, Frederick of Swabia. Since Eleanor was only three years old and Frederick was not even one year old (and was quite sickly at that), the marriage between Henry the Lion and Matilda was the main security for the long-term stability of Angevin-Staufen relations.[58]

The origin of this Welf-Angevin dynastic affinity must be understood only *within* the larger context of Staufen-Angevin diplomacy. It did not emerge as an anti-Staufen conspiracy but rather served as the foundation of the new coalition with the support and participation of the emperor himself.[59] With the loss of so many supporters in the empire, Henry the Lion was, next to Archbishop-elect Rainald, Barbarossa's greatest ally and advisor. The two men were cousins after all. The marriage between the Welf duke of Saxony/Bavaria and Matilda benefited the emperor by ending his political isolation while also tying Henry the Lion even closer to his own policies.

As far as Henry II was concerned, the dynastic tie of immediate importance was with the Welf house; hence he would deal with the Angevin-

---

57. *REK,* 2:135–36, no. 816.

58. Ahlers, *Die Welfen,* 24.

59. Hardegen, *Imperialpolitik*; Alexander Cartellieri ("Die Machtstellung Heinrichs II. von England," *Neue Heidelberger Jahrbücher* 8 [1898]: 269–83) and Editha Gronen (*Die Machtpolitik Heinrichs des Löwen,* Historische Studien, no. 139 [Berlin, 1919]), for example, portray Henry II as an imperialist competitor to Barbarossa and as joined by his son-in-law Henry the Lion as "enemies of the empire" *(Reichsfeinde).* These interpretations reflect the political conditions of the authors' modern world rather than those of the original medieval context.

Staufen marriage at a suitably later date. It was, in essence, a diplomatic compromise designed to put pressure on the papacy while not obliging the English king to repudiate Alexander III. Henry still had the domestic issue of the Alexandrine clergy in his domains to deal with and he could not lightly overlook this. Thus the marriage scheme seemed an attractive proposition for the Angevin monarch: it held out the prestige of a dynastic link to such a widely known imperial prince as the Welf and, although it did not signal a decisive break with the Alexandrine party, would exert enormous pressure to resolve the Becket controversy in his favor.[60]

The marriage was also in the interest of the duke, who was without a wife or male heir since his divorce of Clementia of Zähringen in November 1162 at the emperor's insistence.[61] Marriage to the eldest daughter of the English king offered a large dowry and an impressive increase in prestige by linking his dynasty to yet another royal house. Furthermore, it would secure Staufen support in his increasing difficulties with the Saxon nobles; Henry the Lion fashioned himself as a quasi-regal prince in his own right and was thus experiencing regional resistance to his extension of ducal authority in Saxony and parts further east. The marriage was a personal triumph for the duke; it was not the formation of a complex political constellation designed to shift the "balance of European power" away from Capetian France, though this has often been asserted.

No better evidence of this can be found than a letter the duke himself sent to King Louis VII around this time.[62] The letter dates from the period after the duke had divorced Clementia at Barbarossa's command because her brother Berthold had offered the French king his support in the schism. Nevertheless, Henry dispatched a most cordial letter to Louis, in which he thanked the king for receiving the son of one of his vassals and

60. Gerald of Wales included Rainald's embassy and its results among the "notabiles in Anglia nostri tempore eventus": see *Giraldi Cambrensis opera,* ed. J. S. Brewer, J. F. Dimock, and G. F. Warner, RS, no. 21 (London, 1861–91), 5:215.

61. *Annales Marbacenses,* 47–48. He had divorced Clementia after her brother Berthold had offered Louis VII his support in 1162: see Ahlers, *Die Welfen,* 43; Karl Jordan, *Henry the Lion,* trans. P. S. Falla (Oxford, 1986), 64–65. For Henry the Lion's role in Barbarossa's election see Heinrich Appelt, "Heinrich der Löwe und die Wahl Friedrich Barbarossas," in *Festschrift für Hermann Wiesflecker zum sechzigsten Geburtstag,* ed. Alexander Novotny and Othmar Pickl (Graz, 1973), 39–48.

62. *Recueil des historiens des Gaules et de la France,* ed. Léopold Delisle, 2d ed., Académie des Inscriptions et Belles-Lettres (Paris, 1878), 16:42, no. 137; *Die Urkunden Heinrichs des Löwen Herzogs von Sachsen und Bayern,* ed. Karl Jordan, MGH Diplomata: Laienfürsten- und Dynastenurkunden der Kaiserzeit (Weimar, 1949), 173–74, no. 117.

requested that the son now be returned home. Furthermore, he asked Louis to send eastward French students who wished to learn of his land and language. Now one might see in this letter some political intrigue on the duke's part, some sort of circumvention of the imperial will that had sent his wife away. But this would sound more modern than medieval. Nowhere in the letter does Henry even mention the papal schism, and there is no evidence that the French king took this as an opening for an alliance. Rather, it was a typical "cultural exchange program," so to speak, wherein German students were going in increasing numbers to gain an education in France (as did several archbishops of Cologne). Henry's offer to support a reciprocal program likely met with little enthusiasm among French students, yet the whole matter should remind us of the growing integration of the German territories into the cultural life of western Europe during the Central Middle Ages rather than of some initiative for secret geopolitical negotiations designed to undermine imperial power. The letter is archetypically medieval, revealing the personal nature of politics and the role of patronage in medieval society. We must accept that, in the complex web of personal ties in feudal society, there was no apparent contradiction for the duke to support Barbarossa on the matter of the schism and yet exercise his personal authority in the affairs of his own vassals, even if that entailed relations with the pro-Alexandrine king of France. His marriage to a daughter of another pro-Alexandrine king (Henry II) should not be seen in any other light.

According to Robert of Torigni, Rainald's imperial embassy arrived just after Henry II had concluded the conference with Louis VII on April 11 at Gisors, with the mediation of Count Philip of Flanders. Count Philip remained with Henry after this meeting and thus was present when the imperial embassy arrived.[63] Having made the appropriate oaths regarding the marriage pact, Henry sent envoys back with Rainald to Germany to obtain similar oaths from the emperor and the German princes. But it appears that before Rainald returned with the envoys, he crossed over to England to meet with the English nobles concerning these negotiations. Numerous English chronicles report that not all the nobles were pleased by such a visit. The justiciar, Count Robert of Leicester, would not greet the archbishop-elect, since the latter was a schismatic and an excommunicate.[64]

---

63. Robert of Torigni, *Chronica*, 4:224.
64. Roger of Wendover, *Flores historiarum*, ed. Henry Hewlett, RS, no. 84 (London, 1886–89; reprint, 1965), 1:39–40; Ralph de Diceto, *Ymagines historiarum*, 1:318;

Indeed, the English chronicles express an aversion to Rainald so strong that they claim all altars on which he performed the Mass in England were destroyed. This is clearly exaggeration, since Rainald was still archbishop-elect and had not yet received priestly ordination. Despite this pro-Alexandrine clerical attitude in the English chronicles, Pipe Roll entries show that Henry II paid for Rainald's passage across the English Channel. Rainald may even have paid a visit to Queen Eleanor's court in Hampshire, perhaps to meet the princesses.[65] Both Jens Ahlers and W. L. Warren accept Rainald's presence in England, while such German scholars as Richard Knipping question it.[66] Yet the evidence supports the archbishop-elect's visit. Certainly it would have been proper for Henry II to gain the counsel of his English barons before making such a major decision about ties to the schismatics.[67] The narrative accounts emphasize, though, just how difficult it would be to alter the almost absolute lack of support for the anti-pope Paschal III in England, let alone in the continental Angevin territories. Indeed, the best evidence for this resistance to Rainald's machinations is the response of Matilda, the widow of Emperor Henry V and thus likely to be sympathetic to the Staufen cause. She refused to receive the imperial legation in Rouen, because of their excommunicate status.[68] This measure of resistance must be kept in mind as we consider Rainald's next dramatic step at the diet of Würzburg.

Rainald declined to meet thereafter with the French king, citing his need to return to the imperial diet, to which he hastened with the English envoys John of Oxford and Richard of Ilchester.[69] Perhaps Rainald had

---

MPHA, 1:336; *MPCM*, 2:233; *Annales de Dunstaplia*, 3:19; Gervase of Canterbury, *Chronicle of the Reigns of Stephen, Henry II, and Richard I*, ed. William Stubbs, RS, no. 73 (London, 1879; reprint, 1965), 1:204.

65. *Pipe Roll 11 Henry II*, PR, 8:77 reads, "Et in corredio Nuntiorum Imperatoris per Johannem de Oxineford £23 per brevem regis," and at 108 King Henry authorized £69, 16s., 3d. "in passagiis et in corredio Archiepiscopi Coloniae." See also Eyton, *Itinerary*, 78 n. 4. John of Oxford was one of the English envoys who accompanied Rainald back to Germany.

66. Ahlers, *Die Welfen*, 45 n. 202; Warren, *Henry II*, 492; *REK*, 2:135, no. 816.

67. Peter Munz (*Frederick Barbarossa*, 241 n. 1) asserts: "G. Rill's speculation about Rainald's visit to London [in 'Zur Geschichte der Würzburger Eide von 1165,' *Würzburger Diözesan-Geschichtsblätter* 22 (1960): 7–19] is without foundation. It is improbable that such a visit should have gone completely unrecorded in England." This statement is remarkable in its lack of awareness of the English sources themselves, whether from the Pipe Rolls or from the narrative sources.

68. Chibnall, *Matilda*, 165–66.

69. *REK*, 2:136, no. 817.

avoided Louis VII since a meeting would have entailed discussions of reconciliation between the imperial and papal parties, which was the farthest thing from his mind at the time. His letter of apology to Louis VII mentions that the agenda of the talks were to have been plans for a settlement of the schism and for a possible crusade; neither a settlement nor a crusade could be achieved without compromise.[70] Rainald arrived at Würzburg on May 24 and, according to an eyewitness account, took the diet by storm.[71] Barbarossa had summoned the court to discuss with the princes what should be done about the schism. He had become so politically isolated both in Europe and within the empire itself that many German princes had fallen away from Paschal. He seems also to have been genuinely sincere about reaching a settlement with Alexander III. Rainald therefore arrived after discussions along these lines had been going on for two days. His late arrival explains the haste of his departure from Rouen and avoidance of the French king.

The Cologne archbishop-elect, in a dramatic attempt to reverse the direction of the proceedings, declared that he had won Henry II and more than fifty English bishops over to Paschal's side and that a marriage pact had solidified the agreement; he produced the two English envoys as proof. No doubt the number of fifty English bishops was used to counterbalance those imperial bishops who had sided with Alexander III. Rainald then took the opportunity to call on the emperor and all his vassals to swear an oath never to support Alexander III. This abrupt shift in the proceedings angered Frederick, as it caused a rather awkward situation. Aside from the improprieties of asking the emperor to take an oath, efforts at a reconciliation with Alexander III now seemed confounded in the face of possible widespread support by the English for Paschal, whom, after all, Frederick had already recognized.

With none of the bishops or princes able to produce a reason for withdrawing from Paschal, Archbishop Wichmann of Magdeburg spoke up and vented his frustration at Rainald's intervention. Wichmann declared that he would not take the oath until the Cologne archbishop-elect did so

---

70. *Recueil des historiens des Gaules et de la France*, 16:120, no. 369.

71. *Materials*, 5:184–88, no. 98 is a letter by an anonymous friend present at the diet to Alexander III informing the pope of its events. Julius Ficker (*Reinald von Dassel* [Cologne, 1850], 131) believed that this letter was written by Archbishop Conrad of Mainz. Gervase of Canterbury (*Chronicle*, 1:206) used this letter as the basis of his account, and Ralph de Diceto (*Ymagines historiarum*, 1:331) followed Gervase. A second, shorter version of the letter appears also in Robertson, *Materials*, 5:188–91, no. 99.

and was finally consecrated archbishop of his see. This was a frontal assault on Rainald, who, although elected six years earlier, had been unwilling to be consecrated as long as the fate of the schism was in doubt.[72] He likely wished to avoid being consecrated by the loser of the struggle and thus jeopardizing his own archiepiscopate. According to the eyewitness account already cited, when Rainald refused to accept Wichmann's challenge, the emperor lost his temper.

> "Behold," he said, "it is manifestly apparent that, unbeknownst to me, you presided in judgment over my pope like a traitor and deceiver, when just before the reception of my instructions that you not conduct an election of a substitute pontiff you immediately elected for me a new pope [i.e., Paschal III] with *Te Deum Laudamus* and according to your own good pleasure. This made you more of a traitor to me than the archbishop-elect of Mainz, whom you accused as the defendant of this crime—especially since he gave me useful counsel, namely, that God freed me from that trial in earlier times [i.e., with the death of the antipope Victor IV] so that I might in no way make myself subject to a successor [i.e., Paschal III]. Now, therefore, by necessity you recognize that you are compelled to run into the trap that you first prepared. And with others refusing to do it, you alone must undergo the trial that in your cunning you prepared for others."

Apart from the probable Alexandrine propaganda in this account (as well as the self-serving reference to Archbishop Conrad of Mainz, who might be the author of this letter) we find a believable anger over Rainald's independent election of Paschal and a sense of the emperor's weariness over the schism. He calls Rainald a traitor and deceiver, worse than the archbishop of Mainz, who had switched to the Alexandrine party. These are very strong words and are all the more remarkable when

---

72. John of Salisbury speculated in a letter to Ralph of Sarre (June/July 1160) concerning Rainald's unwillingness to be consecrated during the schism: "Raginaldus enim cancellarius imperatoris *[sic]* se Coloniensem gessit archiepiscopum, cum certum sit electionem eius a Romano pontifice Adriano fuisse dampnatam. Nec video quare, cum episcopatum ambiat, a Victore suo distulerit consecrari, nisi quia imminentem ruinam timet" (*Letters of John of Salisbury*, 1: no. 124). Ficker (*Reinald von Dassel*, 83) and Rill ("Würzburger Eide," 11 n. 29) accept John of Salisbury's reasoning, while C. Schambach ("Das Verhalten Rainalds von Dassel zum Empfang der höchsten Weihen," *Zeitschrift des Historischen Vereins für Niedersachsen* 80 [1915]: 173–95) and Herkenrath (*Rainald von Dassel*, 292) point out that Rainald would have had to renounce certain prebends to be consecrated.

set beside the emperor's characterization of the antipope as "meum papam."

Rainald was pushed into a corner and therefore took the oath and promised to be consecrated.[73] Thus use of the English envoys was effective, and Rainald's plan was accepted by the diet. Frederick took the "unusual oath" *[insolita sacramenta]* with his own hand and so did some of the secular princes; even the English envoys were said to have taken the oath in the name of their king.[74] Yet several princes, especially the bishops, were hesitant to take the oath and eventually circumvented the process either by secretly leaving the diet, giving conditional oaths, or obtaining delays in the taking of the oath. In the end only Rainald and his emperor were the leaders of the renewed support of Paschal, with several imperial princes refusing to participate in the scheme. In fact, even the English support so highly touted by the Cologne archbishop-elect would not be forthcoming. Thus the Würzburg diet's dramatics did little to change the course of the schism except to prolong it.

Historians have disagreed about whether Henry II had given his envoys either clear or tacit approval to take the "Würzburg oath" in his name. German scholars have traditionally believed that Henry did indeed participate in Rainald's plan and promised to change his allegiance to Paschal.[75] Julius Ficker blamed the failure of the strategy on Henry's "fickle character,"[76] and Arnold Stelzmann could even declare that "the national jealousy of England as well as that of France about the flourishing power of the Staufer bore the responsibility for this [failure]."[77] In opposition, Esser has argued that Henry knew nothing of the envoys' participation and had

---

73. He was made a priest five days later at Würzburg (*REK*, 2:138, no. 819) and consecrated archbishop by Bishop Philip of Osnabrück in the presence of the emperor and his wife in Cologne on October 2 of the same year (*REK*, 2:138–39, no. 822). Laudage (*Alexander III. und Friedrich Barbarossa*, 161–65) rejects the longer version of this eyewitness account as untrustworthy and limits his credence to the shorter version, which frames the dispute as solely about Rainald's hesitation to be consecrated.

74. *Letters of John of Salisbury*, 2:183–85, no. 177, contains a letter of John to the bishop of Poitiers citing evidence from a letter of Barbarossa to Count Henry of Champagne that John of Oxford took the oath with full knowledge of its meaning.

75. Gertude Maria Esser (*England, Frankreich und die römische Kurie in der Vorbereitung des Dritten Kreuzzuges* [Ph.D. diss., Cologne, 1953], 55) gives a summary of scholars who held this view. See also Georgi, *Friedrich Barbarossa*, 121–29, 136–40.

76. Ficker, *Reinald von Dassel*, 73: ". . . schwankenden Charakter . . ."

77. Stelzmann, "Rainald von Dassel und seine Reichspolitik," 75: ". . . die nationale Eifersucht Englands sowohl wie auch Frankreichs gegen die aufblühende Macht der Staufer trug die Schuld daran."

not authorized it; they were only to receive oaths concerning the marriage agreement, as Robert of Torigni's account states.[78] W. L. Warren has reversed the criticism, asserting that the envoys were sent concerning the marriages and with some intention to consider the issues of the schism in an attempt to put further pressure on the French king and Pope Alexander III and that they were exploited by the "devious" Rainald and drawn into taking the oath.[79] Yet, as Rill has pointed out, such experienced diplomats like John of Oxford and Richard of Ilchester were not easily deceived and maneuvered into decisions expressly against their mandate.[80] The Würzburg diet's confused proceedings have only served to keep modern historians muddled about its significance. Who, then, was more "devious," King Henry or Archbishop-elect Rainald? It seems that historians have based their answers to this question more on modern nationalist commitments than on medieval possibilities.

Henry II never really intended to move away from recognition of Alexander III. He actually benefited from a policy that was unclear and that played both ends against the middle. His true goal, which was not one of international intrigue and alliances but rather always focused on the internal conflict within his own lands, was to resolve the Becket controversy with a resolution in his favor.[81] So he attempted to put pressure on Alexander III and Louis VII through further developing ties to the schismatics. There was really little possibility that he could turn the episcopate in his territories against Alexander in any case,[82] and even his own influential mother was opposed to the venture. Thus Rainald's triumphant declaration of English support at Würzburg resulted from his misplaced confidence in the ambiguity of Henry II's intentions beyond the marriage agreement[83] and was the desperate act of a man whose anti-Alexandrine policy

---

78. Esser, *England, Frankreich,* 48–61.

79. Warren, *Henry II,* 492.

80. Rill, "Würzburger Eide," 12. See also Ahlers, *Die Welfen,* 48; Johannes Haller, *Das Papsttum: Idee und Wirklichkeit* (Basel, 1951–53; reprint, Esslingen am Neckar, 1962), 3:191f. For Richard of Ilchester's career see Charles Duggan, "Richard of Ilchester, Royal Servant and Bishop," *TRHS,* 5th ser., 16 (1996): 1–21. He was archdeacon of Poitiers at the time and eventually became bishop of Winchester. John of Oxford eventually became dean of Salisbury and then bishop of Norwich.

81. Berg, "Imperium und Regna," 23 n. 48; Opll, *Friedrich Barbarossa,* 28; Kienast, *Deutschland und Frankreich,* 1:221.

82. Gervase of Canterbury (*Chronicle,* 1:207) assures us that the English clergy would not support the Würzburg oath.

83. In a letter to Alexander III (*Materials,* 5:285, no. 156) Herbert of Bosham says that the emperor must have felt himself fooled by Henry II. Here we find evidence of Henry's

was crumbling.[84] Clearly Rainald's demand for an oath—even from the emperor himself—was an unexpected novelty introduced at the diet, and for this much gamesmanship we must give him credit. No such anti-Alexandrine oath was demanded of or given by the Angevin king. It is instructive to note that nowhere does Rainald mention the double-marriage proposal in these proceedings. Perhaps at no other moment than the Würzburg diet do we find Rainald at his finest and yet weakest as a politician: the attempt to impose his dream of a renewed Roman empire led him to such remarkable political machinations as these, and yet the dream's classical ideology fell so far afield of the medieval political realities that it was doomed to fail. Even mustering all of his legendary resourcefulness he still could not force a square peg into a round hole.

For his part Henry II only benefited from the ambiguity created at Würzburg. This ambiguity is consonant with that of the recent marriage agreement: the Angevin was committed to a degree of affinity that might or might not signal a reversal of his policy toward Pope Alexander III. Henry cannot be seen as a traitor to the imperial cause, since his allegiance had been at home and not with the emperor in the first place. His diplomacy was decidedly more anti-Becket than pro-Paschal and therefore was ambiguous from the start of Rainald's initiative. Henry's ability to get more out of maneuvering an ambiguous policy than with direct confrontation has been well documented.[85] Some might call him a deceiver; some might call him a judicious politician playing the many political forces in feudal society very well. In any case, it is clear that Henry II was never asked to take an oath of loyalty to Paschal as was Barbarossa. Surely worries over his errant archbishop and a brewing war in Wales, both internal affairs of his kingdom, kept his attention far more than did the overtures of the German court.[86]

---

focus on internal matters (i.e., Wales). Furthermore, Herbert, a supporter of Becket, was familiar with the Germans since it was he who delivered the so-called submissive letter of Henry II. His negative view of the king reflects the consternation caused in both the imperial and Alexandrine camps over Henry II's unclear intentions.

84. Friedrich Wilhelm Oediger, *Das Bistum Köln von den Änfangen bis zum Ende des 12. Jahrhunderts*, 2d ed., Geschichte der Erzbistums Köln, no. 1 (Cologne, 1972), 154.

85. H. Mayr-Harting ("Henry II and the Papacy, 1170–1189," *Journal of Ecclesiastical History* 16 [1965]: 53) has noted the careful nature of the king's politics, particularly during the Becket controversy and after Becket's assassination.

86. Herbert of Bosham's letter to Alexander III in 1165 (see n. 83) explains the English king's reticence to side with Barbarossa as a result of attention to a campaign against the Welsh.

Barbarossa had also used Würzburg to attend to his own domestic problems.[87] He sought to establish a pope who was accepted throughout Germany, since he needed such unity as a basis for his Italian operations. Hence both monarchs had a decidedly domestic focus to their policies and involved each other in their separate schemes only generally and as a means of applying pressure at common points of tension. There was no close union between the imperial and Angevin causes at this time. The archbishop-elect of Cologne made more out of the connection at Würzburg than had actually existed. Modern historians often seem to have been convinced more by Rainald's rhetoric than by the actual political realities behind it, thereby choosing to make more out of this event than really materialized.

Imperial propaganda continued to make use of the claim to English support, with the chancery issuing letters telling of the envoys' oaths.[88] In fact letters sent to the bishop of Passau and Abbot Erlebold of Stavelot (Stablo) include a remarkable yet clearly spurious statement that the oath of the English envoys was taken not only on behalf of the king but also on behalf of the English barons.[89] Six months later the crowning touch was added to Rainald's second attempt at achieving a victory in the papal schism: during Frederick Barbarossa's Christmas celebration at Aachen the bones of Charlemagne were solemnly raised to the altar and the Carolingian emperor was canonized by the antipope Paschal III (December 29, 1165).

In Frederick's diploma confirming the city of Aachen's privileges on this occasion (which contained the city's forged grant of liberties by

---

87. Laudage (*Alexander III. und Friedrich Barbarossa,* 165–66) concludes that Barbarossa and Rainald had together achieved a victory at Würzburg by obtaining general obedience to Paschal III. The significance of the Würzburg diet apparently played differently in England, as rumors spread throughout the kingdom that several German princes had sworn to elect an antiking who supported Alexander III: see U. Schmidt, *Königswahl und Thronfolge im 12. Jahrhundert,* Forschungen zur Kaiser- und Papstgeschichte des Mittelalters, Beiheft zu J. F. Böhmer, Regesta Imperii, no. 7 (Cologne and Vienna, 1987), 170; Opll, *Friedrich Barbarossa,* 92.

88. On June 1 an encyclical letter sent throughout the empire declared the decision of Würzburg and the role played by the English clergy. See *Die Urkunden Friedrichs I. 1158–1167,* 395–97, no. 480; MGH Const., 1:315–16, no. 223; *Materials,* 5:191–94, no. 100. This passage is also included in the imperial announcement of the required oath: see *Die Urkunden Friedrichs I. 1158–1167,* 398–99, no. 481; MGH Const., 1:316–18, no. 224.

89. *Die Urkunden Friedrichs I. 1158–1167,* 400–401, no. 400; *Die Admonter Briefsammlung,* 151–52, no. 1, and 401–2, no. 483; MGH Const., 1:319–20, no. 225; *Materials,* 5:182–84, no. 97.

Charlemagne) he declares that the decision to canonize Charlemagne was initiated "by the zealous petition of our dearest friend Henry, the illustrious king of England."[90] This reference must go back to the negotiations at Rouen between Henry II and Rainald, but nothing more is said about this in the document.[91] There was certainly some connection, however, between this 1165 translation of Charlemagne's bones and the 1161 translation of the body of Edward the Confessor in Westminster by Henry II.[92] Whereas Henry II had appropriated Edward's sanctity for the Angevin dynasty four years earlier in the midst of growing tension between *regnum* and *sacerdotium* in England, so too the Staufen dynasty was appropriating the legendary royal authority and sanctity of the first medieval emperor during the bitter papal schism. It is likely therefore that the imperial chancery closely read Henry II's papal certificate for the canonization of Edward the Confessor in 1161 and used it as their exemplar for Charlemagne's elevation to sainthood. This would explain the nature of Henry II's involvement in the affair.

The value for Henry in the canonization of Charlemagne, other than a snubbing of the Capetian claim to Carolingian heritage,[93] would have been a general glorification of royal power and a harkening back to their predecessor's dominant role in church affairs; perhaps the idea came up in the course of the Rouen negotiations. The canonization would of course benefit an emperor more, and during the proceedings the glory of

---

90. *Die Urkunden Friedrichs I. 1158–1167*, 430–34: "... sedula petitione karissimi amici nostri Heinrici illustris regis Anglie. ...." Concerning the forged privileges see Manfred Groten, "Studien zum Aachener Karlssiegel und zum gefälschten Dekret Karls des Großen," *Zeitschrift des Aachener Geschichtsvereins* 93 (1986): 15–29.

91. Gerhard Rauschen, *Die Legende Karls des Großen im 11. und 12 Jahrhundert*, PGRG, no. 7 (Leipzig, 1890), 132. Robert Folz (*Le souvenir et la légende de Charlemagne dans l'empire germanique médiéval* [Geneva, 1973], 203–7) believes that Rainald got the idea from Henry II, who would have benefited in prestige during his struggle with Becket and would have enjoyed the blow against Louis VII. Yet Folz overplays the "idee impériale" in Henry II's kingship.

92. Keller, *Zwischen regionaler Begrenzung und universalem Horizont*, 367–68; Jürgen Petersohn, "Saint Denis–Westminster–Aachen: Die Karls-Translatio von 1165 und ihre Vorbilder," *DA* 31 (1975): 420–54; idem, "Die päpstliche Kanonisationsdelegation des 11. und 12. Jahrhunderts und die Heiligsprechung Karls des Großen," in *Proceedings of the Fourth International Congress of Medieval Canon Law*, ed. Stefan Kuttner, Monumenta Iuris Canonici, ser. C, Subsidia, no. 5 (Vatican City, 1976), 163–206; Opll, *Friedrich Barbarossa*, 93; Odilo Engels, "Des Reiches heiliger Gründer: Die Kanonisation Karls des Großen und ihre Beweggründe," in *Karl der Große und sein Schrein in Aachen: Ein Festschrift*, ed. Hans Müllejans (Aachen and Mönchengladbach, 1988), 37–46.

93. Kienast, *Deutschland und Frankreich*, 1:221.

Charlemagne was certainly directed toward Barbarossa and not at Henry. In any case this reference to the English king must have come from Rainald of Dassel and was a further attempt to bolster royal authority in general and make use of the claimed Angevin support for Paschal in particular. Rainald was deeply involved in the canonization activity.[94] Not only was he a leader in imperial policy at this time, but the event occurred within his own archdiocese. With the coronation city of Aachen turned into a holy shrine of kingship and the Three Kings (Magi) residing in the Cologne cathedral, Rainald had created a center of holy kingship on the shores of the Rhine, at the heart of his archiepiscopal see.

Rainald of Dassel's extremely elevated assertions of both the spiritual authority of imperial power and the allegiance of the English monarch, while powerful in ideology, were less than realistic given the political events of the subsequent months. From the English side came denials that Henry II had ever instructed his envoys to take the anti-Alexandrine oath. Archbishop Rotrudus of Rouen, a mediating force in the Becket controversy, assured a cardinal priest that the only matter agreed on during the three-day conference in his episcopal city was the double-marriage proposal. And he guaranteed that Henry had accepted the marriage agreements only if they would not affect his spiritual allegiance to Alexander III and his feudal obligations to Louis VII. The archbishop also tells of the role of Matilda, the widowed wife of Emperor Henry V, who refused to meet with the schismatics "propter episcopos." Rotrudus says that Rainald's claim of the support of fifty English bishops shows his deception, since the English king did not even have that many bishops.[95] These references remind us of the impossibility of Henry's drawing the Angevin episcopate away from Alexander III and raise doubts about Rainald's subsequent actions at Würzburg.

Furthermore, Bishop Gilbert of London wrote directly to the pope and protested the innocence of his king.[96] Gilbert declared that Henry knew the emperor was a schismatic but did not know that he had been excommunicated. The bishop assured the pope that Henry was willing to accept the counsel and correction of the English church if he had entered into an

---

94. *REK*, 2:140, no. 829.

95. *Materials* (5:194–95) contains an account in Archbishop Rotrudus of Rouen's letter to Cardinal Priest Henry contradicting any willing involvement by Henry II at Würzburg.

96. Ibid., 5:203–9.

illicit marriage union. Certainly the English royal court knew of Rainald's excommunication and still, with the exceptions of Matilda and Robert of Leicester, received him. Yet these pro-Alexandrine members of the Angevin episcopacy defended Henry II and claimed that he had not thereby abandoned the pope.

Henry II himself, in a letter written in the following year and addressed to the cardinals, argued that he had shown no impropriety in contracting marriages within the empire. He protested again, perhaps unconvincingly, that he had not been told by Alexander III of Barbarossa's excommunicate status. In a thinly veiled reference to his goal of reestablishing the royal prerogatives of Henry I through the Constitutions of Clarendon, the Angevin king declared that he had only acted in the same manner as his grandfather when the marriage between Matilda and Emperor Henry V was contracted.[97] Here we see the English king's real strategy: to use the marriage agreement as leverage to gain a victory over Becket and a papal confirmation of the constitutions. However we distribute responsibilities for the machinations converging at Würzburg, the English king's goal did not change. He was pursuing his own *renovatio regni* and therefore had no intention of either assisting or undermining Barbarossa's *renovatio imperii*.

Henry II's personal relations with Barbarossa and Rainald of Dassel are not so different from other diplomatic ties he sought to cultivate during the latter years of the 1160s and early 1170s. His marriage negotiations with the kings of Castile and Aragon and the count of Savoy were directed either at furthering his standing in France through marriage unions for his children with suitable princely houses or at putting further pressure on Louis VII and Alexander III.[98] This form of diplomacy was a traditional means of securing cooperation and influence through personal advantage rather than geopolitical intrigue. The eventual marriage secured between William II of Sicily and Henry's daughter Joanna and the concurrent offer of English subsidies to the Italian cities of Parma, Cremona, Bologna, Pavia, and Milan in the late 1160s were not efforts designed to undermine Staufen power, as has often been argued.[99]

---

97. Ibid., 6:79–80.
98. Trautz, *Die Könige*, 73.
99. As Hardegen argues in *Imperialpolitik*. Fuhrmann *(Germany in the High Middle Ages)* also accepts a concerted effort on Henry II's part to spin "a wide network of alliances to encircle Staufer and Capetians" (168).

Rather, they were Henry's attempts to gain influence at the papal court through the Lombard allies of the pope.[100] The Angevin king was exploring all avenues to achieve his ultimate goal: the resolution of the Becket controversy, not the destruction of the Staufen dynasty.

In this vein the marriage of Matilda to Henry the Lion was also part and parcel of the same policy and not part of a carefully conceived and carried out anti-Staufen scheme. Although some of these moves might have hindered Frederick's successes, they were not specifically designed to do so, and therefore both modern historians' speculation about Henry's plotting an "Angevin Empire" to surround the Staufer and their casting of blame on the English king for neglecting his commitments to the emperor are simply misplaced and reflect political expectations that are more modern than medieval. Indeed, if Henry II had concocted any sort of encirclement strategy it would most certainly have been directed against the Capetian monarchy, not the empire. Consolidation, not conquest, was the basis of his diplomacy.

Henry II was to return to the same strategy when Becket, now a papal legate, excommunicated the English envoys to the Würzburg diet and annulled the Constitutions of Clarendon at Vézelay in June 1166.[101] The exiled archbishop charged Richard of Ilchester and John of Oxford with having in fact taken the oath. Does this suggest some real English collusion at Würzburg? Given that Alexander III would later absolve John upon his vow that he had not taken the oath—and that Alexander even confirmed John in the deaconry of Salisbury for his service to the imperial court—Becket's charge seems still based on rumor.[102] Becket even threatened Henry II himself with excommunication.

Roger of Wendover has preserved the king's response to these harsher measures.[103] Henry wrote to Archbishop Rainald and declared that he

---

100. Berg, "Imperium und Regna," 23–24; Trautz, *Die Könige,* 72–73.

101. Roger of Howden, *Chronica,* 1:238–39; this text is repeated in Becket's letter to Pope Alexander III (ibid., 1:254–55). *Materials* (5:389–91, no. 196) contains the letter of Thomas to Archbishop Conrad of Mainz, Bishop Sabinus, and Cardinals Jacinctus and Henricus wherein he tells of the excommunication of John of Oxford and Richard of Ilchester; this also appears in 5:395 as a letter from Becket to all his bishops in the province of Canterbury.

102. John of Salisbury was most disconcerted by this act of Alexander III: see *Letters of John of Salisbury,* 2:354, no. 214 (dated early 1167).

103. Roger of Wendover, *Flores historiarum,* 1:48–49. Roger includes at the end of this account an anecdote in a clearly pro-Becket tone about Bishop Gilbert Foliot of London, an opponent of Becket. The letter is also found in *MPHA,* 1:345; *MPCM,* 2:239–40; *Materi-*

had finally found occasion to break with Alexander (implying that hitherto he had not felt sufficiently driven to such a step). The king intended
to send to Rome a large embassy—which was to include the recently
excommunicated John of Oxford and the veteran of Anglo-German diplomacy John Cumin—to threaten the pope that unless he replaced Becket
and confirmed the Constitutions of Clarendon he would face repudiation
in England. Henry therefore asked for Rainald's assistance in providing
safe passage for the embassy to Rome. Sometime shortly thereafter the
king wrote Rainald again to warn him that the papal legates Henry of
Pisa and William of Pavia had come to France to raise money for the
support of Alexander.[104]

Becket's drastic actions had raised the conflict to a new level and
forced movement on the issue. Now Henry II was using the imperial connection forged by the double-marriage agreement to confront the pope
directly and in no uncertain terms. Alexander III was genuinely alarmed
at this move, since this time there was no ambiguity in Henry's declaration. The pope had recently returned to Rome from his French exile but
could only be maintained there through the defense of the north Italian
cities and the financial support of the Normans in Sicily. By autumn of the
same year, however, Barbarossa had marched into Italy and papal funds
were running low (as is suggested by the efforts of the aforementioned
legates in France). Furthermore, William I of Sicily had died in early 1166
and left only a minor under a regency. Hence in December 1166 Alexander reacted to the deteriorating situation and told Becket to cease his
actions. The pope also sent legates to make peace between archbishop
and king. Although no permanent resolution came about, the negotiations kept Becket in check for several months and kept the pope from any
punitive moves against the king. In this Henry had achieved his goal.[105]
He never desired to carry out the threat, which in itself was effective
enough in the light of Alexander III's weakened position.[106]

---

als, 5:428–29, no. 213. John of Salisbury gave to Count Henry of Champagne a copy of
this letter "sent me from Cologne" in which Henry II asked safe conduct for his messengers
going to Rome. John of Oxford would also seek absolution from the sentence of excommunication that Becket had pronounced against him. See also *Letters of John of Salisbury,*
2:185; *REK,* 2:148, no. 853.

104. *REK,* 2:149, no. 855.

105. Warren, *Henry II,* 495.

106. Esser, *England, Frankreich,* 64; Ahlers, *Die Welfen,* 51; Wissowa, *Politische
Beziehungen,* 28–29; Karl Hampe, *Germany under the Salian and Hohenstaufen Emperors,* trans. Ralph Bennet (Oxford, 1973), 184.

If he ever intended to repudiate Alexander III and join the imperial side, now appeared the time to do so. The papacy was in a vulnerable position and the emperor was making advances toward Rome. Rainald conquered Tusculum in late May 1167 and the imperial army marched into Rome later that summer. At what seemed the height of imperial power, Paschal III crowned Barbarossa and Beatrice at St. Peter's on August 1, 1167. Yet at his weakest moment in the struggle with the Staufer, Alexander III never lost the allegiance of the Angevin king or clergy. If Henry were truly an opportunist who secretly supported Paschal III, he should have shown his colors at this point, but he did not do so. Although Alexander lost Rome he did not lose Angevin loyalty.

What human political pressure could not resolve, nature—or, according to some, the hand of God—did. Tragedy struck at the moment of Staufen triumph in Rome, when an outbreak of malaria carried away over two thousand knights and Frederick's victory with them. Among the dead was Archbishop Rainald of Dassel. His death was seen by English chroniclers, as well as by the Alexandrine party in general, as divine judgment. Roger of Howden called the archbishop of Cologne "the head of the whole schism" *[totius schismatis caput]*.[107] These views only underscore the fact that Henry II was never in a position to repudiate the pope. Clerical sentiment in England and in Angevin continental territories was always in favor of Alexander III, and the Germans were seen as schismatics. In fact, taken as a whole, Henry II's actions were always in an Alexandrine context and never crossed over the line of the schism to Barbarossa's side. Although Rainald of Dassel had plucked the anti-Alexandrine chord loudly before Henry II, there was no resonance in England.

If the loose diplomatic association between Barbarossa and Henry II was intended finally to resolve both the schism and the Becket conflict, the plan failed on both counts.[108] But if it was designed to apply pressure on the Alexandrine party for entirely different purposes, the arrangement had moderate success. It enabled Frederick to stem the tide of defections to the Alexandrine party in Germany for a time, and Henry II was successful in getting Alexander to put Becket on ice at a crucial point.

---

107. Robert of Torigni, *Chronica,* 230–31; Roger of Howden, *Chronica,* 1:253. John of Salisbury wrote to a certain Petrus Scriptor and mentioned the pestilence at Rome as a divine effort of grace ending the "Teutonicum tyrannum" (*Materials,* 6:233–36 [quote from 235], no. 325).

108. Ahlers, *Die Welfen,* 52.

In essence time was bought with these maneuvers, but what changes time can bring. With the pestilence in Rome the second grand attempt of Rainald of Dassel to achieve victory in the schism was shattered. Frederick's hopes of reasserting royal prerogatives in his kingdom of Italy were now as lifeless as the body of his late archbishop, and once again local, regional, religious, and natural forces successfully resisted the imaginative yet impossible imperial ideology of Archbishop Rainald. The only element of the supposed "Staufen-Angevin alliance" actually realized was the social and religious act of marriage between Matilda and Duke Henry the Lion, which was celebrated just six months after the Roman plague destroyed the imperial army. From this union would emerge new dynamics that radically reformulated Anglo-German diplomatic relations in general and Anglo-Cologne relations in particular. The remarkably energetic mind and intense ideological dreams of the late Cologne archbishop died along with him, and a new era of European diplomacy was born.

3

Philip of Heinsberg, Henry the Lion, and Anglo-German Relations: Cooperation and Regionalism

The last twenty years of Barbarossa's long reign were crucial in the transformation of internal political order in Germany. During this period Frederick would have serious personal struggles with, among others, two of his hitherto most loyal princes—Duke Henry the Lion and the archbishop of Cologne. These personal struggles also signaled profound changes occurring in Germany from the twelfth century onward: a growing urban economy further integrating the German territories into the larger European trading network, and concurrently the emergence of territorial principalities in place of the old tribal stem-duchies. In essence, Barbarossa's troubles with the Italian cities during the papal schism would be replicated by a similar drive for regional independence on the part of German princes. The Staufen dream of a *renovatio imperii* in Italy and papal Rome under the guidance of Rainald of Dassel had brought only political isolation and continued frustration. Barbarossa would find a similar result in his German realm, which was being transformed by the same forces as those in his Italian kingdom. Since the Welf duke and archbishop of Cologne would be directly involved in this political transformation of Germany and thereby at odds with the emperor, Anglo-German diplomacy would naturally be reconfigured. Once again, however, the Staufer's "foreign policy" with England would be frustrated by personal and regional interests—this time by those of his two leading diplomats to England: Philip of Heinsberg and Henry the Lion.

The Loosening of Angevin-Cologne-Staufen Ties

The remainder of the year 1167 saw two other events of note: the death of the widowed empress Matilda and the first steps toward consummation of the marriage between Henry the Lion and Matilda's granddaughter and namesake. The death of the elderly empress—mother of Henry II and great-aunt of Frederick Barbarossa—ended the Angevin ruling house's dynastic tie to the Staufer and may have weakened relations between the two to some extent.[1] It also signaled the end of a generation that saw close diplomatic contact established between the regions. The marriage of the Welf to Henry II's daughter signaled the beginning of a new era of personal politics in which English relations with the Staufen house would change drastically as a result of growing Welf-Staufen animosity.

During the months leading up to Barbarossa's disaster in Rome the English king succeeded in obtaining some measure of satisfaction through his threatened defection to the imperial side. Pope Alexander had forbidden Becket to issue any excommunications or interdicts, and John of Oxford was absolved of his excommunication.[2] Since such renewed contacts with the Germans proved effective, Henry II drew on the German connection again by carrying out the promised marriage between his daughter Matilda and Duke Henry the Lion of Saxony/Bavaria in the autumn of 1167. A Saxon embassy came and took Matilda to Germany shortly before Michaelmas, and they were married in Minden Cathedral on February 1, 1168.[3] The marriage had the blessing of Barbarossa since direct conflict between the Welf and the emperor would not develop until 1176.[4] Indeed, with the death of Rainald of Dassel the emperor's

---

1. Kienast, *Deutschland und Frankreich*, 1:221; Trautz, *Die Könige*, 71. Matthew Paris (*MPCM*, 2:324–25) gave her an epitaph which befits her many connections in the histories of England and the empire: "Ortu magna, viro major, sed maxima partu, Hic jacet Henrici filia, sponsa, parens."

2. *Materials*, 6: no. 395.

3. Ahlers, *Die Welfen*, 54. English chroniclers mention this event, with Robert of Torigni being careful to delineate the Welf's prestigious heritage and wealth in his *Chronica* (4:234, 303). Gervase of Canterbury (*Chronicle of the Reigns of Stephen, Henry II, and Richard I*, 1:205), Roger of Howden (*Chronica*, 1:220), and Ralph de Diceto (*Ymagines historiarum*, 1:330) mention that the counts of Arundel and Schwerin accompanied Matilda. *CRC* (123) also records the event. The amount of the dowry is never specified, though it was "infinita pecunia" according to Robert of Torigni. For English chroniclers' views on Henry the Lion see Herbert W. Wurster, "Das Bild Heinrichs des Löwen in der mittelalterlichen Chronistik Deutschlands und Englands," in *Heinrich der Löwe*, ed. W. D. Mohrmann (Göttingen, 1980), 407–39.

4. *Annales Palidenses*, ed. G. Pertz, MGH SS, no. 16 (Hanover, 1859), 94: "Heinricus dux dismissa uxore priore, Bertoldi ducis de Zaringe sorore, duxit filiam regis Anglorum; et hoc factum est instinctu et voluntate imperatoris." In fact a passage in the appendix (p. 350) of G. Waitz's edition of the *Gesta Frederici* MGH SS rer. Germ., no. 46 [Hanover, 1912; reprint, 1978]) claims that the success of imperial mediation for a peace between France and

maneuvering room in the schism had expanded considerably, and his approval of the Angevin-Welf marriage was a first step toward extricating himself from political isolation.

A new archbishop of Cologne appeared on the scene as well—Philip of Heinsberg, who would himself alter traditional Anglo-German diplomatic relations even more than would the Angevin-Welf marriage. While still continuing in his predecessors' role as a personal liaison between the English and German courts, this archbishop immensely complicated Anglo-German diplomacy through his own independent *Territorialpolitik*, which would eventually lead to alienation from *both* the Staufen and Welf dynasties.[5] Thus English diplomacy would become increasingly complex as traditional Welf-Staufen-Cologne cooperation broke down after the death of Rainald of Dassel.

Philip began his career as a partisan ally of the emperor. He rose through the ranks of the imperial chancery after an education in France and then served in Italy as Barbarossa's imperial chancellor at the suggestion of Rainald. He had even led imperial forces in central Italy after the pestilence in Rome.[6] Philip only left the Italian campaign and made his way to Cologne after being chosen by the emperor as Rainald's successor in June 1168. Following a route through Burgundian territories, Philip reached Cologne on August 15 and was consecrated there by Bishop Godfrey of Utrecht on September 29.[7] Unlike his predecessor, he obtained episcopal consecration very quickly.

Philip returned to Cologne with more than his consecration in mind, however, as he was underway within days thereafter to Rouen for a meeting with both Henry II and Louis VII.[8] The emperor had assembled a very prestigious embassy to the monarchs, as Philip was joined by Henry the Lion and Archbishop Christian of Mainz. Barbarossa had in fact sent to Normandy the two most powerful ecclesiastical princes and the most powerful secular prince of his German realm. The presence of the Welf

---

England was based on good relations between the emperor and English king as a result of this marriage.

5. Hugo Stehkämper, "Der Reichsbischof und Territorialfürst (12. und 13. Jahrhundert)," in *Der Bischof in seiner Zeit, Bischofstypus und Bischofsideal im Spiegel der Kölner Kirche: Festgabe für Joseph Kardinal Höffner, Erzbischof von Köln*, ed. P. Berglar and Odilo Engels (Cologne, 1986), 95–184.

6. *REK*, 2:163, no. 906.

7. *CRC*, 120: *REK*, 2:165–66, nos. 909–13.

8. *CRC*, 120; *REK*, 2:166–67, no. 915. The Cologne chronicle does not mention any participation by the French king.

prince and Archbishop Philip in particular was a sign of the seriousness of Barbarossa's diplomacy, for they embodied the strongest Anglo-German ties existing at the time.[9] Clearly Barbarossa had hoped to capitalize on the recent Welf-Angevin marriage union as a diplomatic channel for finally settling the schism. The princes were escorted on the first leg of the journey by Bishop-elect Peter of Cambrai, who had come to Cologne on his way to receive the imperial investiture from Barbarossa but was told to accompany them back to Cambrai, where they were festively received on October 14. There they were joined by Count Philip of Flanders, who relieved the bishop and escorted the party to Rouen.[10]

As the Cologne chronicle states, the details and results of this clearly important conference remain unclear. Robert of Torigni reports only that Henry the Lion left the meeting richly rewarded with gifts,[11] and Gervase of Canterbury says the meeting was intended to form a coalition against the French in return for a settlement on the papal schism.[12] Gervase's assertion seems unlikely since Barbarossa was in no position to give Henry II armed assistance against France. The empire was still divided over the schism, and the drastic setback suffered in Italy the previous year would have prevented such support. The offer seems most absurd if, as the annals of Cambrai assert, Louis VII took part in the negotiations. These annals, written where the embassy had sojourned en route and thus a more reliable source, say that the negotiations were in general about a peace between France and England as well as a final settlement of the schism.[13]

Whatever its purpose, nothing concrete came of this high-powered conference. Another imperial attempt at diplomacy with the western monarchs

---

9. Arnold Peters, *Die Reichspolitik des Erzbischofs Philip von Köln (1167–1191)* (Ph.D. diss., Marburg, 1899), 19–20.

10. *REK*, 2:167, no. 916.

11. Robert of Torigni, *Chronica*, 239.

12. Gervase of Canterbury, *Chronicle*, 1:205. Kienast (*Deutschland und Frankreich*, 1:222–24), Eyton (*Itinerary*, 116), Marcel Pacaut ("Louis VII et Alexandre III (1159–1180)," *Revue d'Histoire de l'Eglise de France* 39 [1953]: 197), and J. H. Ramsay (*The Angevin Empire or the Three Reigns of Henry II, Richard I, and John* [London 1903], 98) all accept Gervase's account of the conference's purpose. Yet inconsistencies, such as Gervase's errant inclusion of the bishop of Liège in the embassy and reference to Archbishop Philip as still "electus," make it clear that he is confusing this Rouen parley with that by Rainald of Dassel in 1165 and thus that his account is untrustworthy.

13. *Annales Cameracenses*, ed. G. Pertz, MGH SS, no. 16 (Hanover, 1859; reprint 1994), 545. Haller (*Das Papsttum*, 3:226), Munz (*Frederick Barbarossa*, 394), Warren (*Henry II*, 497), and Reuter (*Papal Schism*, 151) take the chronicle as an accurate depiction of the meeting.

must have proven unattractive to the English since Paschal III had just died (September 20, 1168) and his successor Calixtus III had little support even in the empire; thus he was not much of an alternative to Alexander III.[14] Louis VII, moreover, was wary of imperial intentions because of the "fedus et amicicia" between the emperor and Henry II as a result of the recent Welf-Angevin marriage union.[15] Louis VII may well have met with the German embassy separately from Henry II. Thus the German embassy had little bargaining power either to effect an end to the schism or to assist in a peace between the French and English kings.

Frederick's hopes for a Staufen-Cologne-Welf-Angevin coalition based on Henry the Lion's marriage and on the appointment of the new archbishop of Cologne began to fade as early as the close of this ineffective conference. Indeed, based on his actions after the meeting, one doubts that Archbishop Philip worked as hard at Rouen for the imperial goals as he did subsequently for his own personal objectives. While the duke of Saxony and the archbishop of Mainz returned to Barbarossa with Bishop-elect Peter via Cambrai, Archbishop Philip showed his independent agenda by returning separately via Cologne to hastily attend to a pressing personal matter.

Philip showed early on that his interests would always revolve around his own regional politics *(Territorialpolitik)* rather than around imperial politics *(Reichspolitik)*,[16] and this was a radical shift in the policy of the archbishops of Cologne. Under the era of Rainald of Dassel there was no distinction between *Reichspolitik* and Cologne regional policy; however, from the pontificate of Philip of Heinsberg onward the archbishops of Cologne strove to expand their territorial power and gain complete independence from imperial control. This would have a major impact not only on German constitutional development but also on German diplomacy with England.

As the archbishops of Cologne increasingly resisted imperial encroachments on their regional power in northwest Germany they would often look to England as an ally—much in the way that Henry II looked to the Germans to offset his own sovereign's (i.e., the French king's) encroachments in his continental lands. Archbishop Philip and his successors would prove even more adept at playing the English kings to their advan-

---

14. Ahlers, *Die Welfen*, 62.
15. Otto of Freising and Rahewin, *Gesta Frederici*, 350 (appendix).
16. Wand, "Die Englandpolitik der Stadt Köln," 79.

tage than Henry II was with Barbarossa. While it may be said that Henry II got the better result in diplomacy with Rainald of Dassel, the archbishop's successors would more than reverse the trend.

Much has been written about the independent-minded *Territorialpolitik* of Duke Henry the Lion and his resulting conflicts with the emperor, yet the archbishops of Cologne after Rainald of Dassel should be seen in the same vein as those German princes who set the development of their territorial power above that of imperial interests—the expansion of Archbishop Philip of Heinsberg's regional principality occurred even at the expense of the Welf territories in Westphalia, as we shall see. When all was said and done, the archiepiscopal principality of Cologne would still be standing after both the Staufen and Welf dynasties collapsed. The archbishops themselves had not a little to do with the demise of these two dynasties as well.

Let us return to Philip's solo departure from Rouen. The cause of his independent trip back to the emperor was this: while still in Italy during the month of February 1168 as archbishop-elect of Cologne, the crafty Philip had obtained from Paschal III a charter confirming the transfer of the bishopric of Cambrai from the metropolitan jurisdiction of Archbishop Henry of Reims—an avowed supporter of Alexander III—to the jurisdiction of the archbishopric of Cologne.[17] This of course was disputed from the start, on canonical grounds as well as because both Reims and Cambrai recognized Alexander as pope. Thus it was no coincidence that Bishop-elect Peter of Cambrai was imposed on to accompany the embassy back to Cambrai before making his way to Barbarossa for investiture. There can be no doubt that on their way to Cambrai the members of the embassy held discussions concerning this conflict.

Bishop Peter was in a difficult position, since Cambrai was in the duchy of Brabant and therefore just inside the borders of the empire; however, its ecclesiastical jurisdiction fell to the archbishop of Reims, a French prelate. One can imagine the impatience Philip of Heinsberg must have felt in knowing that Peter was on his way to the emperor while he was in Rouen. The upshot of the whole affair was that Peter, although a supporter of Alexander, was invested by Frederick after taking an oath of loyalty. In return the emperor decided that the archbishop of Reims, rather than Archbishop Philip, should receive the submission of the bishopric of Cambrai, although Philip had requested this privilege upon his arrival at

17. *REK*, 2:164–65, no. 908.

the imperial court. We learn also that a decisive factor in the emperor's decision was the support for Peter not only by the empress but also by Henry the Lion and Archbishop Christian of Mainz, the two sojourners with Philip to Rouen.[18] This would explain why Philip did not return from Rouen with these two princes, and it perhaps helps to explain the barren nature of the Rouen parley—apparently there had been a falling out within the German embassy over the issue of Cambrai. Perhaps Philip even went his own way to assure a meeting with Louis VII to plead his case for jurisdiction over the diocese of Cambrai.[19] Again, regional and local ambitions—this time the personal interests of the emperor's own ambassadors—overshadowed Barbarossa's grand plans involving the monarchs of Christendom.

The conflict over Cambrai, wherein Philip's growing regional interests are revealed, was the beginning of a gradual estrangement of the archbishop both from Barbarossa and from Henry the Lion, whose own territorial interests in Saxony could not abide an expansion of Philip's power in the region.[20] This new dynamic, coupled with the newly established dynastic tie between the Welfs and the Angevins, would make Anglo-German relations much more complex and difficult to manage for all parties involved.

Since imperial influence proved no longer effective in Henry II's continuing conflicts with Louis VII and Thomas Becket, the English king began to search elsewhere for assistance in the late 1160s. He attempted to buy outright influence at the papal court through subsidies to the Italian cities of Milan, Cremona, Parma, and Bologna and even made efforts to bribe the pope directly. He then betrothed his daughter Joanna to the young William II of Sicily in a further attempt to draw support from those who had influence with the papal curia. There were also negotiations for marriage ties with princes from Navarre, Aragon, and Savoy at this time, to secure Angevin influence around his territories in southern France.[21] These efforts were not directed against the emperor,

---

18. *Annales Cameracenses,* 546.

19. Georgi (*Friedrich Barbarossa,* 267–68) suggests this to explain the disappearance of Archbishop Philip after the failed negotiations.

20. Peters, *Die Reichspolitik,* 21.

21. King Henry II sought unions for his children: a Savoyard princess for John, a Spanish princess for Richard, and a Spanish king for Eleanor. Only the marriage of Eleanor to Alfonso VIII of Castile resulted from these negotiations. Richard would marry Berengaria of Navarre several years later after a new round of negotiations was initiated.

although Henry risked his tenuous ties to Barbarossa by such actions. Yet we find no evidence that Frederick took these actions as aggressive moves against him.[22]

Perhaps Henry's decision to promise Joanna to William II of Sicily reflected some disappointment over Barbarossa's choice of the imperial son Henry (VI) as heir to the royal throne instead of the eldest, yet quite sickly, imperial son Frederick of Swabia, to whom the English king's daughter Eleanor had been betrothed in 1165.[23] When young Frederick died soon thereafter (in 1170) at the age of seven the last personal Angevin-Staufen tie to the 1165 agreement had been broken; Eleanor was then betrothed to King Alfonso VIII of Castile.[24] These diplomatic moves in any case show a lack of consideration for the emperor's position and signal an end to Angevin efforts at working through imperial channels. Angevin kinship ties to Saxony and growing economic ties to Cologne were now stronger than any political commitments to the Staufen dynasty.

The English king may well have found benefit through the Welf family connection early on. There is some evidence that Henry the Lion was personally involved in the peace finally reached between Henry II and Louis VII at Montmirail in January 1169,[25] which may have had some connection to the parley at Rouen in October 1168.[26] If so, kinship ties did more to give Henry II leverage than any geopolitical gamesmanship with leaders of foreign governments. No settlement on the schism including the emperor appears in the Montmirail negotiations; thus Henry the Lion's intercession was directed at the interests of his father-in-law rather than at those of his imperial lord.

In July 1170 Henry had even reached an unsteady peace with Becket, and so the English king's two major problems had been resolved for the time being—at least he had a truce with the French king and his own archbishop. Henry's need for imperial leverage was thus greatly lessened and he married his daughter Eleanor to Alfonso VIII of Castile rather than

---

22. Alhers, *Die Welfen*, 61; Jordan, *Henry the Lion*, 149: "However, this [i.e., the marriage of Eleanor to Alfonso of Castile] and other marriages planned for Henry II's children should not, as is sometimes suggested, be regarded as proof that the Angevin king was, from the early 1170s onwards, pursuing 'imperial' ambitions against Barbarossa, in which he sought to involve his son-in-law Henry the Lion."

23. Ahlers, *Die Welfen*, 61; Jordan, *Henry the Lion*, 149.

24. See E. Assmann, "Friedrich Barbarossas Kinder," *DA* 33 (1977): 435–72.

25. His role in the negotiations, however, remains uncertain: see Jordan, *Henry the Lion*, 148.

26. Peters, *Die Reichspolitik*, 20.

betrothing her to another German prince.[27] Meanwhile Barbarossa's renewed negotiations with Alexander had bogged down because of a papal attempt to include the Lombard cities in the discussions.[28] Regional and personal conflicts continued to hold the respective monarchs' attention.

The conflicts that had caused Henry II to dabble with ties to the imperial court had receded for the time being and so the intensity of diplomatic relations between the two began to wane. Even the sensational murder of Becket, which isolated the English king for a time, only served to draw him closer to the Alexandrine papacy, as his absolution of May 1172 shows. One might have thought that Henry would join Barbarossa at this point, for each had experienced a horrific setback in their disputes with the Church (Becket's murder in 1170 and the Roman plague of 1167). Yet the English king found compromise with Alexander III sooner than did the German emperor, and though having achieved success through compromise with the Church, he was thereafter busied with the internal instability caused by his rebellious sons for a number of years thereafter.[29] There would be no close interregional diplomatic ties with the emperor under such changed regional and personal circumstances.

As a result of this Angevin rapprochement with the papacy, Louis VII saw the advantage of closer relations with Barbarossa to place pressure on the pope as Henry II had previously done. The emperor, for his part, needed an ally to replace the generally limited and now rather lifeless English diplomatic channel, especially since the continuance of the schism prevented papal recognition of his son Henry (VI) as heir to the imperial throne. Rarely, if ever, has Louis VII been criticized for his diplomacy with Barbarossa at this time, and his ultimate loyalty to Alexander III has not been questioned, though he now pursued the same strategy as had Henry II in developing imperial ties to pressure the pope to intervene on his behalf—in this case *against* the Angevin king and in favor of Thomas Becket. Becket's murder and renewed skirmishes over control of the Auvergne in late 1170 only increased Louis's incentive to parley with Barbarossa, especially in view of the new Angevin ties to Aragon and Castile.

The two monarchs met in Maxey-sur-Vaise (between Toul and Vaucouleurs) on February 14, 1171, but the only issue they then resolved

---

27. Robert of Torigni, *Chronica*, 247.

28. Haller, *Das Papsttum*, 3:226–28; Georgi, *Friedrich Barbarossa*, 269–73.

29. The Treaty of Avranches reached by a papal legate and Henry II (May 21, 1172) settled the issues resulting from the Becket murder. See Warren, *Henry II*, 530–36.

surrounded border disputes.[30] An offered Staufen-Capetian marriage union went nowhere because of the resistance of Alexander III, yet the offer had the immediate effect of stirring the anxiety of the pope in the same way that the Angevin-Welf marriage had done in 1165.[31] Although little concrete emerged from this meeting, it proved to be momentous: it was the diplomatic opening Barbarossa sought in vain almost a decade before at St. Jean-de-Losne in August 1162. At Maxey-sur-Vaise the groundwork was laid for a Staufen-Capetian diplomacy that would last well into the thirteenth century and radically alter diplomatic relations between the English and imperial courts for the remainder of the Central Middle Ages. Two years later marriage negotiations between the Capetian and Staufen houses began again amid renewed fighting between Louis VII and Henry II.[32]

The discussions between Louis VII and Barbarossa ultimately led neither to a dynastic union nor to a resolution of the schism; however, the negotiations as a whole represent on the part of the Staufer emperor a major policy shift that effectively ended the era of ambiguous yet cooperative Staufen-Angevin diplomatic relations. Although Louis intended to use these contacts to pressure the pope, Frederick's rapprochement with France would have important repercussions for the future relationship of the Staufer rulers to both the Welfs and the English monarchs.[33] Henry II, for his part, had turned to Spanish monarchs and the Welf ducal house for multiple new diplomatic channels to Paris and Rome via southern France and northern Germany.[34] In particular we begin to see the outline

---

30. *Materials*, 1:436, 7:445.

31. The marriage was probably suggested between Frederick's son Henry (VI) and Louis's daughter Agnes. See *PL*, 200:783, no. 872; Keinast, *Deutschland und Frankreich*, 1:224; Ahlers, *Die Welfen*, 64; Laudage, *Alexander III. und Friedrich Barbarossa*, 191. Alexander III resisted the union and recommended rather that Agnes marry the Byzantine heir to the throne Alexius III Comnenus, which she did in 1180.

32. *CRC* (125) mentions this warfare and includes a reference to the murder of Becket: "Ipso anno Ludewicus rex Franciae et filius regis Angliae et comes Flandrensis Heinricum seniorem regem Angliae bello petierunt. Set rex Anglorum primo penitentiam agens de occisione martiris sancti Thomae, victoriam adeptus est, plurimis de Flandria captis vel fugatis." Henry thus gained the victory because of his penitence for Becket's death.

33. Ahlers, *Die Welfen*, 65; Opll, *Friedrich Barbarossa*, 108.

34. To apply diplomatic pressure on the papal curia to resolve the Becket controversy Henry II even went so far as to cultivate Byzantine ties to Emperor Manuel I through his payments to Lombard cities during these years. See *Materials*, 7:299, no. 668; Haller, *Das Papsttum*, 3:228, 571; Frank Barlow, *Thomas Becket* (London, 1987), 199. For diplomatic relations between Henry II and Manuel I see A. Vasiliev, "Manuel Comnenus und Henry Plantagenet," *Byzantinische Zeitschrift* 29 (1929–30): 233–44.

of a Staufen-Capetian versus Welf-Angevin alignment, within which the archbishops of Cologne would play an independent mediating role for the next fifty years. It is ironic that the personal feuding between the English and French kings over regional issues proved to be the avenue for Frederick Barbarossa's emergence from his long diplomatic isolation in western Europe as well as that for the archbishop of Cologne's emerging independence from imperial control.

Henry II continued to exchange embassies with the imperial court[35] but felt so little a threat from the cooperative Capetian-Staufen diplomacy that he could leave the continent in August 1171 to begin the conquest of Ireland.[36] His optimism was shattered, however, when an internal revolt within his own family broke out with the full support of Louis VII. Henry (III), Richard, and John all joined against their royal father with the support of their mother, Eleanor of Aquitaine. The French king had the leverage now, and papal fear of losing Louis to the Staufen court resulted in the dispatching of legates several times to resolve the conflict. With Louis entertaining alternatives, Alexander could not afford to lose Henry II's support. In a remarkable balancing act, the pope managed to negotiate a settlement between Henry II, his rebellious sons, and their French royal patron.[37]

This skirmish, a brief yet very dangerous chapter for Henry II, tells the same story as the one we have just reviewed, with the players only changing their respective positions. We have a monarch who plays the trump card of closer relations with the schismatic emperor to get papal movement on long-standing disputes with another western monarch. This time it was the French king instead of the English. In both cases the papacy followed a delicate diplomatic dance and the German emperor remained isolated from the actual points of conflict; the regional conflicts tended to overshadow his interregional agenda of resolving the papal schism. Barbarossa's policy remained consistent also. He sought some means of extracting himself from diplomatic isolation caused by the schism and focused his own attentions on private and regional concerns, never intending to actually intervene in western affairs. In this case he was busy planning his fifth Italian campaign. Nowhere can we discern either a sort

---

35. Eyton, *Itinerary,* 139; *Materials,* 7:475, no. 750.

36. Eyton, *Itinerary,* 160–63; Ramsay, *Angevin Empire,* 151–57; Warren, *Henry II,* 193–206.

37. A truce that ended the siege of Rouen was concluded on September 8, 1174, and a peace was achieved at Montlouis on September 30.

of geopolitical *Realpolitik* on the part of the western monarchs to extend their hegemony or the exercise of *Weltherrschaft* by the emperor; rather, we find continued, consistent attention to personal, local, and regional political affairs on all sides.[38]

In particular, there was no expansionist plan for an "Angevin Empire" at the expense of either France or Germany. A single remarkable cleric (Thomas Becket) did more to shape Angevin politics than did any master plan of Henry II. The same can be said of Barbarossa with regard to Rainald of Dassel, Alexander III, and the papal schism. The politics of each monarch emerged in response to a troublesome churchman—be it archbishop or pope—who raised issues that had a direct impact on the assertion of royal prerogatives and authority *within* the respective royal lands. The religious convictions of this age—rather than the political interests of another age—shaped its politics. External diplomatic leverage was sought to resolve an internal conflict, not to extend political control beyond traditional boundaries. The lack of real depth to these attempted interregional constellations of cooperation appears clearly in the series of false starts and in the ephemeral consequences when they were actually carried out. Perhaps nowhere better is this pattern reiterated than in the clash between Frederick Barbarossa and Henry the Lion in the aftermath of the emperor's disastrous fifth Italian campaign.

The Fall of the Lion and the Rise of Prince Philip

The decade of the 1170s saw the testing of imperial authority in the kingdom of Germany, which finally resulted in the fall of Henry the Lion and his exile in Angevin territories and in the rise of Archbishop Philip of Heinsberg as a territorial prince. Archbishop Philip was instrumental in both Henry's fall and the duke's eventual restoration, and in many ways he replaced the duke as the leading exponent of princely power in northern Germany.

In 1177 Frederick Barbarossa had suffered a devastating defeat at Legnano, blamed in part by historians on the Welf's refusal at Chiavenna to send troops, and the emperor finally signed an armistice at Venice with the Lombard League. Barbarossa's inability to enforce his will over all Italy after five massive campaigns finally brought him to a reconciliation with Alexander III. Henry the Lion had placed his own territorial interests

---

38. Opll, *Friedrich Barbarossa*, 273.

above the call to serve the emperor in Italy, and much has been made of this by modern historians. Yet the Welf had not participated in such campaigns since 1161, and there is no evidence of hostile relations between the two men upon Barbarossa's return to Germany. Hostilities did emerge, however, between Henry the Lion and his Saxon princes; indeed, the point of tension was embedded in the Treaty of Venice itself, which provided for the reinstatement of Bishop Ulrich of Halberstadt. Ulrich had been deposed by the duke and his restoration would inevitably lead to conflict in Saxony.[39] Frederick was obliged to enforce the treaty, and since by this point his ducal cousin had become less integral to imperial politics, he had no incentive to provide unqualified support should hostilities break out. Barbarossa was in this instance to play the royal role as neutral protector of the peace in his German kingdom.

When in autumn of 1177 Ulrich demanded the restoration of church lands that had been seized during his exile, the Welf refused and was duly excommunicated by the bishop. Henry then retaliated by destroying the episcopal castle at Nornburg. Warfare also broke out in Westphalia, in which Archbishop Philip of Cologne took part against the duke of Saxony. Philip's justification for his involvement was a claim to the inheritance of lands that had been held by his nephew and that Henry the Lion had expropriated at the nephews' death. Hence the combination of kinship and ecclesiastical motives forged a coalition between Ulrich and Philip in early summer of 1178, and military incursions by Philip into Westphalia continued until Archbishop Wichmann of Magdeburg and Bishop Eberhard of Merseburg negotiated an armistice.[40] The Welf, however, did not observe the armistice, and skirmishes continued.

This conflict was also a result of the archbishop's expanding *Territorialpolitik* in western Saxony. By the mid–twelfth century the archbishopric of Cologne already exercised a de facto ducal authority in Westphalia, which had been gradually built up through an aggressive policy of land purchases. Both Rainald of Dassel and Philip of Heinsberg acquired entire dynastic allodial holdings (e.g., from the counts of Arnsberg), which extended their common-law lordship into the region of Henry the Lion's

---

39. Jordan, *Henry the Lion*, 167–68.

40. *REK*, 2:206–7, no. 1106; *CRC*, 129. For the text of the 1178 treaty of alliance between Archbishop Philip and Bishop Ulrich see *Urkundenbuch des Hochstifts Halberstadt und seiner Bischöfe*, ed. G. Schmidt, Publicationen aus den königlichen preussischen Staatsarchiven, no. 17 (Leipzig, 1883), 1:246–47, no. 283.

feudal lordship. Growing hostilities about such encroachments and juris-dictional confusion, when added to the internal politics of Saxony, pro-duced a civil war in the region.[41]

As a result, at the imperial assembly of Speyer in November 1178 both Archbishop Philip and Henry the Lion brought charges against each other for breaches in the peace of the land, a matter clearly in the tradi-tional purview of the emperor.[42] In an effort to restore the peace in Saxony Barbarossa called his cousin to answer the charges.[43] We shall not cover the details of the trial, as this has been done thoroughly else-where.[44] Henry the Lion's repeated refusals to appear at court to defend himself from the charges finally resulted in his condemnation as an out-law and in the forfeiture of his feudal lands by imperial decree.

The emperor's decision, however, took two years to enforce, because of the duke's regional power and continued recalcitrance. Warfare in Saxony persisted throughout this period, with Archbishop Philip's armies heavily involved.[45] By 1182 Duke Henry stood defeated and exiled, while Archbishop Philip had benefited tremendously from his participation in the conflict. At the imperial diet of Gelnhausen on April 13, 1180, Freder-ick Barbarossa, not following the custom of waiting until a year and a day after their escheat to regrant fiefs, gave the archbishopric of Cologne

---

41. *CRC* (129) records a "dissensio inter episcopum Coloniensem et ducem Saxonie" in 1170. See Stefan Weinfurter, "Erzbischof Philipp von Köln und der Sturz Heinrichs des Löwen," in *Köln, Stadt und Bistum in Kirche und Reich des Mittelalters: Festschrift für Odilo Engels zum 65. Geburtstag,* ed. Hanna Vollrath and Stefan Weinfurter, Kölner historische Abhandlungen, no. 39 (Cologne, 1993), 471–73.

42. *REK*, 2:207, no. 1107. Emperors since Henry IV had made use of the imperial right to uphold peace *(Reichslandfrieden)* as a weapon against the unlimited use of blood feud by the aristocracy. Haverkamp *(Medieval Germany,* 164) concludes, "In spite of . . . failures, the imperial public peaces gave new substance to the monarchy, and also opened up real possibilities for empire-wide policies."

43. Jordan, *Henry the Lion,* 168.

44. See, for example, Jordan, *Henry the Lion,* 168–82; Ahlers, *Die Welfen,* 82–111; Odilo Engels, "Zur Entmachtung Heinrichs des Löwen," in *Festschrift für Andreas Kraus zum 60. Geburtstag,* ed. Pankraz Fried and Walter Ziegler, Münchener historische Studien: Abteilung Bayerische Geschichte, no. 10 (Kallmünz, 1982), 45–59; Ferdinand Güterbock, *Die Gelnhäuser Urkunde und der Prozeß Heinrichs des Löwen,* Quellen und Darstellungen zur Geschichte Niedersachsens, no. 33 (Leipzig, 1920); Carl Erdmann, "Der Prozeß Hein-richs des Löwen," in *Kaisertum und Herzogsgewalt: Studien zur politischen und Verfas-sungsgeschichte des hohen Mittelalters,* ed. Theodor Mayer, Konrad Heilig, and Carl Erdmann, MGH Schriften, no. 9 (Stuttgart, 1944), 273–364; Opll, *Friedrich Barbarossa,* 124–42.

45. *REK*, 2:211, no. 1127; 2:213–14, no. 1137; 2:224, no. 1167.

the ducal title for the lands of Westphalia (in the dioceses of Cologne and Paderborn), with full ducal rights.[46] This grant encompassed territories reaching east clear to the Weser River and was issued as an imperial gift rather than as an imperial fief. The archbishops of Cologne had already enjoyed ducal rights west of the Rhine since the reign of Conrad III, so they were now in possession of what amounted to a double duchy.[47]

The results of this momentous shift in power in northern Germany were of great significance for Anglo-German relations. With an enormous increase in power as a result of the Gelnhausen charter, Archbishop Philip was unquestionably the leading prince in northern Germany, and thereafter the archbishops of Cologne would dominate affairs in the lower Rhine. Therefore their attention was drawn increasingly toward lower Rhenish territorial politics and away from imperial affairs, in much the same way that Henry the Lion had been drawn to activity in northeast Germany. Archbishop Philip was so proud of his achievements in building this territorial principality that his tomb was laden with the following remarkable inscription: "Receive, O Peter, the duchy I present to you, which I have purchased for you for fifty thousand marks." This statement rivals any gesture made by Henry the Lion to express his princely pretensions.[48] Such an independent *Territorialpolitik* would of course result in friction with the emperor, as it had in the case of the Welf, and would further complicate English diplomacy with the empire. The Angevin court had now not only to manage broken relations between the emperor and the Welf Henry the Lion, who now came there as an exile, but also to cultivate ties with the episcopal prince in Cologne, whose rising influence made him indispensable in Anglo-German diplomacy with an eye toward

---

46. *REK*, 2:216–17, no. 1145; *UGN*, 1:331–32, no. 472: "cum omni iure et iurisdictione, videlicet cum comitatibus, cum advocatiis, cum conductibus, cum mansis, cum curtibus, cum beneficiis, cum minsterialibus, cum mancipiis et cum omnibus ad eundem ducatum pertinentibus."

47. Jordan, *Henry the Lion*, 173.

48. St. Peter was the patron saint of the cathedral in Cologne. See Oediger, *Das Bistum Köln*, 161. In addition to the duchy of Westphalia, Philip had purchased extensive holdings within the region surrounding Cologne—*REK* (2:277–82, no. 1386) contains a list of one hundred and two separate parcels of property that he added to the archiepiscopal demesne. Hans Patze ("Die Welfen in der mittelalterlichen Geschichte Europas," *Blätter für deutsche Landesgeschichte* 117 [1981]: 153) has even argued concerning the grant of the duchy of Westphalia at Gelnhausen: "We cannot exclude the possibility that Archbishop Philip of Cologne influenced Barbarossa with money and expedited the court proceedings which lead to the day of Gelnhausen." See also Gerhard Kallen, "Das Kölner Erzstift und der 'ducatus Westfalie et Angarie' (1180)," *JKGV* 31/32 (1956/57): 78–107.

France. Before long the archbishops of Cologne would prove more important to English politics than were the Welfs or the German monarchs.

Before considering the policies of Archbishop Philip in detail, we must address the exile of the Welf family in England. This is necessary to reiterate that there had not been an anti-Staufen conspiracy between the Welfs and the Angevins before 1198, though several historians have suggested one, even erroneously implicating Archbishop Philip of Heinsberg in such a conspiracy. It is tempting to see Henry II's marriage negotiations with Sicily and Savoy, as well as his subsidies to the Italian cities in connection with his intercession for the Welf during Henry the Lion's exile, as part of a comprehensive anti-Staufen policy,[49] which was then continued by Richard I in his treaty with Tancred of Sicily and alleged support of Henry the Lion's fight to regain his lands (1189–94). This alleged collusion was supposed to have reached its ultimate fulfillment in the German kingship of Otto IV in 1198. Since the archbishops of Cologne subsequently become deeply involved in efforts to reconcile the exiled Henry the Lion to Barbarossa, in the negotiations for Richard the Lionheart's release from imperial imprisonment, and in the 1198 election of Otto IV, they too have been made accomplices in this so-called Welf-Angevin-Cologne conspiracy against the Staufen dynasty.

Yet such an interpretation is incorrect, viewing affairs as it does retrospectively from the coming Welf-Staufen dynastic conflict of 1198–1216 for the German throne *(Thronstreit)*. We have already seen that Henry II's marriage negotiations with Savoy and Sicily, as well as his subsidies to Italian cities, had no imperialistic basis but rather were means to pressure both Louis VII and Alexander III to be more amenable in the Becket controversy and in southern France. Furthermore, the marriage between Matilda and Henry the Lion was part of a Staufen plan to establish ties with the Angevins and was not inspired by anti-Staufen intentions. Until 1176 Henry the Lion was always in the service of the emperor. It was rather Barbarossa himself who altered the Staufen-Welf-Angevin relationship by his own rapprochement with France, while the Welfs remained tied to the original policy of the marriage union. The erroneous interpretation of a growing "Welf-Staufen dynastic conflict," until recently widely accepted, was the result of historians taking at face value later chronicles that read the Welf-Staufen civil war after Barbarossa's death as the direct

---

49. Opll (*Friedrich Barbarossa*, 296) refers to England during Henry the Lion's exile as "a focal point of the anti-Staufen politics of this year."

result of Henry the Lion's fall at the hands of the emperor.[50] This created a teleological history of an animosity that existed between the two dynasties throughout the twelfth century and that supposedly reached its logical conclusion in the *Thronstreit* of 1198–1216. Contemporary evidence, however, does not support such a teleology.[51]

Thus the subsequent conflict between Henry the Lion and Barbarossa was not part of some sort of conspiracy involving the Angevins. There had never been any geographical overlapping of Staufen/Angevin territorial interests, and Henry II never took advantage of Barbarossa's weakened position after the pestilence in Rome. His focus was always on the reestablishment of royal power in his own territories after the anarchy of Stephan's reign. Although the primary source evidence militates against it, echoes of such an anti-Staufen encirclement policy *(Einkreisungspolitik)* by a Welf-Angevin conspiracy still resound in German scholarship.[52]

There is little surviving evidence of close contact between Saxony and

---

50. Werner Hechberger, *Staufer und Welfen, 1125–1190: Zur Verwendung von Theorien in der Geschichtswissenschaft*, Passauer historische Forschungen, no. 10 (Cologne, Weimar, and Vienna, 1996), 330–47.

51. Ibid., 330–31: "The theory of a Staufer-Welf antagonism, which broke out anew between 1176 and 1181, can contribute nothing to illuminate the events. On the contrary: the assumptions that arise from the use of this notion are all hardly convincing. An old, long smouldering conflict has not been rekindled here nor can the conflict be understood as a collision of two differing personalities or even of two opposing political concepts. . . . The power of Henry has actually been long overvalued. To describe him as a 'competing emperor' (Nebenkaiser) and to speak of a 'government of two men' (Zweimännerregierung) in the empire is certainly exaggerated, and whether the duke actually had ambitions for royal status is at least disputed. But in any case the oft-cited notion of Mitteis that since 1138 a 'latent Welf anti-kingship' existed leads one astray." Indeed, Hechberger argues that even the very notion of Welf and Staufen dynasties is a modern paradigm that the medieval sources do not support.

52. Ahlers (*Die Welfen*, 76–84) reviews the *Einkreisungspolitik* thesis against Staufen power by a Welf-Angevin alliance in the scholarship of Gronen, Treu, Hampe, Engels, Fuhrmann, Hiller, Mitteis, Güterbock, Brackmann, Schmidt, Drögereit, and Hiller and correctly concludes, "The concern of Henry II was not conquest, but consolidation of his lordship" (81). Alexander Cartellieri ("Die Machtstellung Heinrichs II. von England," *Neue Heidelberger Jahrbücher* 8 (1898): 278) and Friedrich Hardegen (*Imperialpolitik,* 20–27) initiated the *Einkreisungspolitik* thesis, reflecting their contemporary political world of *Realpolitik* rather than the original medieval social context. Only recently, however, have German scholars like Ahlers and Werner Hechberger questioned this interpretation. Hechberger (*Staufer und Welfen,* 306–7) concludes about the relationship between Barbarossa and Henry the Lion prior to 1176: "It becomes discernible that Barbarossa never once considered his cousin as a potential enemy, but rather saw in him a clearly important, perhaps even the most important, pillar of his politics in the ranks of the secular princes. This cooperation was established for a long time and obviously an expression of a close, personal bond."

the English court after the marriage of Matilda and Henry the Lion.[53] Only during the trial of Henry the Lion do embassies seem to have passed with some regularity.[54] The Welf could, however, expect little help from Henry II, who was said to have been greatly distressed both by the trial and by the distance that prevented him from assistance.[55] Henry the Lion turned for help rather to King Valdemar of Denmark, whose son and heir Cnut VI had been engaged to the Welf's daughter Gertrud sometime during the years 1171–76.[56] Clearly the Welf expected better results from his Danish royal relatives than he had received from his English kin. No English help was forthcoming throughout the fall of Duke Henry the Lion, although King Henry II was at the height of his power in 1180–81. It was only during the Welf's exile in Angevin territories that close ties were established. Archbishop Philip of Heinsberg, for his part, had only benefited from the fall of the duke and had little incentive to support him.[57] It was not until the *Thronstreit* of 1198–1216, in the generation after Henry II and Frederick Barbarossa, that a true Welf-Plantangenet-Cologne anti-Staufen coalition was formed, and even then it was shaky at best, as we shall see.

Our attention to the details of the time spent by the Welf family in exile (from the first exile in July 1182 to April 1185) will be restricted to the point at which Philip of Heinsberg enters the picture, since the Welf sojourn in Angevin lands has been ably detailed elsewhere.[58] Henry II

---

53. Jordan, *Henry the Lion*, 149.

54. Ahlers, *Die Welfen*, 99.

55. Roger of Howden, *Gesta regis Henrici secundi Benedicti abbatis*, ed. William Stubbs, RS, no. 49 (London, 1867; reprint, 1965), 1:249: "Quod cum nunciatum esset domino regi Angliae, cujus filiam primogenitam idem dux Saxoniae in conjugem duxerat, doluit vehementer de inquietatione generis sui, eo quod pro voluntate sua ei auxiliari non potuit propter locorum distantias." For a consideration of the authorship of the *Gesta regis Henrici secundi* see Antonia Gransden, *Historical Writing in England, c. 550 to c. 1307* (Ithaca, 1974), 226–30.

56. Jordan, *Henry the Lion*, 174.

57. Roger of Howden (*Chronica*, 2:199–201) has a rather detailed account of the fall of Henry the Lion, which includes the role played by Philip of Heinsberg. Where the apocryphal information in this account about defense of the city of Cologne came from is uncertain. Gervase of Canterbury (*Chronicle of the Reigns of Stephen, Henry II, and Richard I*, 311–12) also emphasizes the central role played by Archbishop Philip in the fall of Henry the Lion. We learn here also that the Welf made a pilgrimage to St. Thomas at Canterbury.

58. For this see A. L. Poole, "Die Welfen in der Verbannung," *Deutsches Archiv für Geschichte des Mittelalters* 2 (1938): 129–48, which makes extensive use of the Pipe Rolls for the expenses accrued by the Welfs; Ahlers, *Die Welfen*, 112–38; Jordan, *Henry the Lion*,

could gain little value from an exiled son-in-law[59]—indeed Poole estimates that the Welf stay at the English court cost the royal exchequer over eight hundred pounds.[60] So he began to intercede before Barbarossa on behalf of the Welf.[61] The English envoy was unable to obtain a pardon for the duke, but he did gain some concessions. Frederick allowed all those who had gone in exile with the duke the right to return to Saxony, and "pro amore regis Angliae" the emperor granted Matilda her dowry from the German lands. The author of the *Gesta regis Henrici secundi* says that the French king and the count of Flanders also interceded with Henry II, and thereby six years were removed from the sentence of exile.[62] Only after the duke's sentence of deposition and exile, therefore, did the English monarch move to assist him, and then in concert with other European princes. With this slight softening of the judgment, the duke's family went to Normandy, while he went to Santiago de Compostela as penance for his excommunication.[63]

The chosen punishment for the Welf's crime of resisting royal power was a spiritual one—hardly a result that a modern political analyst would expect for someone convicted of fomenting rebellion and international conspiracies against the state. But, then again, there was no modern state or international conspiracies designed to destroy such a state here. Rather we have a powerful prince who resisted the greater royal power of his cousin so that he might assert his jealously guarded rank in society, and who, after seizing land from (among others) the archbishop of Cologne's

---

182–88. English chroniclers recorded Henry's exile in detail: see Robert of Torigni, *Chronica*, 4:234; Roger of Wendover, *Flores historiarum*, 1:129; *MPHA*, 1:424; *MPCM*, 2:318. Ralph de Diceto (*Ymagines historiarum*, 2:12–13) includes the archbishop of Cologne in his account: "Henricus dux Saxonum, Matildem filiam regis Anglorum primogenitam habens in conjugem, insurrexit in Philippum Coloniensem archiepiscopum, et eum enormibus damnis affecit. Archiepiscopus copiis undique congregatis viriliter duci restitit, imperatoris auxilium adeptus et gratiam. Res tandem eo processit, ut principum totius imperii calculo sententiali prolato, dux exilium cogeretur subire. Qui veniens in Normanniam ad socerum suum, habens secum ducissam, habens et duos filios Henricum et Ottonem, habens et filiam nubilem,—tertius namque filius Lotharius nomine [he died at Augsburg in 1190] remanserat in Teutonica,—receptus est honorifice, plusquam per tres annos continuos abundanter exhibitus profusioribus epulis et regali munificentia." *CRC* (132) of course also mentions it.

59. Frank Barlow, *The Feudal Kingdom of England, 1042–1216*, 4th ed. (New York, 1988), 347: "Little profit accrued to Henry from the Welf connexion."

60. Poole, "Die Welfen in der Verbannung," 142.

61. Roger of Howden, *Chronica*, 2:269–70.

62. Roger of Howden, *Gesta regis Henrici secundi*, 1:287–88.

63. Engels, "Entmachtung," 48–49.

family, was given a pilgrimage of spiritual penance while his own family went into exile to live with kin. The facts are less glamorous than international intrigue and empire building perhaps, but a medieval, rather than modern, social and political context is operative here.

The Consolidation of the Archbishop of Cologne's *Territorialpolitik*

The personal reconciliation between emperor and duke that allowed the Welf's return to Saxony in 1185 was preceded by the reconciliation between Philip of Heinsberg and the duke. The archbishop, accompanied by Count Philip of Flanders, came to England in September 1184[64] ostensibly on a pilgrimage to St. Thomas at Canterbury; however, it is clear that the two had come on a diplomatic mission.[65] We do not know if this pilgrimage to the tomb of Thomas (who was murdered fourteen years earlier, in Henry II's reign) suggested any political implications regarding proper relations between *regnum* and *sacerdotium*. In any case the English king met the alleged pilgrims at Dover and, after their pilgrimage to Canterbury, brought them to London, where they celebrated Mass at St. Paul's Cathedral and then were received in splendor at Westminster. They remained there for five days of negotiations.

Archbishop Philip had come to ask for a marriage between Henry II's son and heir Richard and Barbarossa's daughter Agnes—this was no

---

64. Ralph de Diceto, as the dean of St. Paul's, was certainly a participant in the reception of Philip in London. Hence his account is of great use to us. He writes (*Ymagines historiarum*, 2:31–32): "Philippus Coloniensis archiepiscopus, habens solacium in itinere Philippum comitem Flandriae, venit in Angliam, beato Thomae vota soluturus orationum. Archiepiscopo rex occurens et comiti, petiit ab eis ut transitum facerent usque Lundoniam. In eorum adventu, quod ante non vidimus, civitas coronata fuit, gaudium, honor et tripudium per omnes civitatis plateas. Archiepiscopus sollenni processione receptus est in ecclesia doctoris gentium Pauli. Susceptus est etiam apud Westmonasterium ipsa die sollenni processione sumptibus regiis, expensis effusioribus, lautioribus cibis omnem ultra sufficientiam abundantibus, per quinque dies infra regis palatium hospitatus. Sed an recesserit donatus multis muneribus est superfluum quaerere." See also Roger of Wendover, *Flores historiarum*, 1:131; Roger of Howden, *Gesta regis Henrici secundi*, 1:318–19; idem, *Chronica*, 2:288; *MPHA*, 1:427; *MPCM*, 2:319–20; *REK*, 2:238–39, no. 1232.

65. The Pipe Rolls show that Henry II was expecting the arrival of the archbishop and count. *Pipe Roll 13 Henry II*, PR, no. 33, 136 reads "Et pro xii tonellis vini emptis ad opus Regis contra adventum archiepiscopi Colonie et comitis Flandrie xxii li. et xiii s. et iiii d. per breve Regis," and 145 reads, "Et Johanni de Morewic et Willelmo de Rudes servientibus Regis xxv li. et vi s. et iiii d. ad inveniendum quod necessarium fuerit in hospito Regis quando occurrit archiepiscopo Colonie et comiti Flandrie per breve Regis."

doubt an attempt by the imperial court to revive the 1165 Staufen-Angevin marriage union agreement that had failed to materialize. The author of the *Gesta regis Henrici secundi* says, on the one hand, that Philip suggested this "ex parte domini sui Friderici," while Roger of Howden asserts, on the other, that the offer was made "ad petitionem regis Angliae." Roger admits though that "Sciebat [i.e., Archbishop Philip] enim ipsum imperatorum hoc velle, et plurimum desiderasse." The English monarchy agreed to the marriage union, but only under the condition that the archbishop be reconciled to Henry the Lion. This request placed the archbishop in a difficult position, since he could ill afford the restoration of the Welf in Saxony after his archbishopric had gained the lands of Westphalia. But it appears that he did receive Duke Henry back into his favor, although one account suggests that he did so only grudgingly.[66] There was an added benefit of this reconciliation: it allowed the emperor to consider restoring the Welf to some extent in Germany. This was so because Barbarossa had taken an oath *per thronum regne sui* in November 1181 never to restore Henry the Lion to his *gradum pristinum* without the approval of the imperial princes. Such a public reconciliation with his greatest nemesis opened the door to returning to Saxony.[67]

The archbishop was unwilling, however, to intercede personally on behalf of the Welf and instead suggested that Henry II send envoys to the pope, asking him to serve as a mediator.[68] The envoys found Barbarossa in Milan on his sixth Italian campaign shortly thereafter and then passed on to Pope Lucius III at Verona in late October. The pope had gone there to meet with the emperor on November 4, 1184, for talks concerning Barbarossa's son Henry (VI), whom the emperor wanted crowned king of Italy at Milan and married to Constance of Sicily. Philip of Heinsberg knew of the planned meeting and suggested sending the envoys there as a convenient opportunity for negotiations on behalf of the Welf. Lucius III was successful in negotiations with the emperor—he released Henry the Lion from his oath of exile, and Barbarossa granted the duke the right to return to Saxony.[69]

66. Gervase of Canterbury, *Chronicle of the Reigns of Stephen, Henry II, and Richard I,* 1:313.

67. Weinfurter, "Erzbischof Philipp von Köln," 476.

68. Roger of Howden, *Gesta regis Henrici secundi,* 1:322–323; *Chronica,* 2:289.

69. Roger of Howden (*Gesta regis Henrici secundi,* 1:334) tells of the joy at the English court upon hearing the news.

Why would Archbishop Philip of Cologne have been willing to be reconciled with Henry the Lion and give at least some counsel about how to obtain his return to Saxony? Certainly there were great disadvantages for him in a renewal of Welf power in Saxony. Why would there have been an interest in establishing a Staufen-Angevin marriage union in the first place? Odilo Engels has argued that Henry the Lion served as a negotiator himself for an anti-Capetian coalition between the German and English monarchs.[70] According to this interpretation the duke's earlier trip to the Mainz court in March of 1184 was not solely to request a release from exile but also to serve as an envoy of Henry II to establish the coalition. These alleged negotiations are said then to have been completed during Archbishop Philip's visit to England in September, which was sealed with the marriage agreement and a reconciliation between Philip and Henry the Lion. Count Philip of Flanders was supposedly involved because both English and imperial worry over Capetian encroachments in Flanders was the common interest that established the coalition. Engels even argues that Frederick's son Henry (VI) had gathered an army and was prepared to invade France, except that the count of Hainault refused to allow passage of the troops through his territory. With such a view the restoration of Henry the Lion would have been closely linked to French-Flemish affairs.

This theory, however, has problems, not the least of which is Engels's assertion that, while Henry II was the initiator of the coalition, the German side planned an invasion of France desiring that the English remain neutral.[71] How does one explain away the unexpected request that Archbishop Philip be reconciled with his Welf enemy if his visit were only one piece of ongoing negotiations that included the Welf? There is no evidence that Henry II sought a military confrontation with his French feudal lord at this time. Furthermore, the author of the *Gesta regis Henrici secundi* indicates that it was the death of the Wittelsbach recipient of Henry's ancestral lands in Bavaria that prompted his unexpected

---

70. Engels, "Entmachtung," 53–59; *Der Niederrhein und das Reich im 12. Jahrhundert,* Gesellschaft für Rheinische Geschichtskunde Vorträge, no. 23 (Cologne, 1983), 16–23 (these pages originally published in *Königtum und Reichsgewalt am Niederrhein,* Klever Archiv, no. 4 [Kleve, 1983], 93–96]. Opll (*Friedrich Barbarossa,* 291–92) follows this line as well, declaring the negotiations "doubtless an important success of Staufen diplomacy" (291).

71. Engels, *Der Niederrhein und das Reich,* 18 n. 77.

(and illegal) voyage to the imperial court in March 1184 in false hopes of recovering the duchy.[72]

Rather it seems more likely that the marriage negotiations were an effort on Barbarossa's behalf to gain English influence in Rome and Palermo with regard to his ongoing negotiations with the pope about the Sicilian kingdom.[73] The English envoys who not coincidentally found Barbarossa and Lucius III at Verona must have had more on their minds than the Welf's restoration, and Archbishop Philip of Heinsberg's suggestion to send envoys to Verona also included imperial concerns over Sicily.[74]

Archbishop Philip's own involvement and personal interests in the London embassy can be understood only with reference to his traveling companion, the count of Flanders. The archbishop's territorial interests had been disturbed by recent events in lower Lotharingia that involved Flanders. In August 1184 (a month before the embassy to England) tensions between Count Baldwin V of Hainault and Duke Godfrey of Brabant, which had been held in check by an uneasy truce since January 1183, broke out into renewed warfare.[75] The archbishop of Cologne, along with the count of Flanders, had used family and feudal ties to pressure the two warring factions to accept the earlier truce,[76] but Count Baldwin would no longer remain at peace. He demanded that Count Philip of Flanders, his brother-in-law and ally, support him in an attack on Brabant, but Philip refused and even sent two hundred Flemish knights to the Brabantine army. Count Baldwin, thus realizing his isola-

---

72. Roger of Howden (*Gesta regis Henrici secundi*, 1:310) tells only of Henry the Lion's dashed hopes of returning to Germany after the death of Otto of Wittelsbach, to whom the duchy of Bavaria had been given at Gelnhausen in 1180. Thus Henry II's urging of the Welf to go to Mainz was made in regard to recovering his lands, with no mention of either an anti-Staufen or anti-French activity.

73. Ahlers, *Die Welfen*, 121–22.

74. Engels ("Entmachtung," 53) suggests that Barbarossa made his trip to Verona via Milan in order to meet with the English embassy and learn of the results of the London negotiations before meeting with the pope.

75. For the Hainault-Brabant war see Kienast, "Die Deutschen Fürsten," 10:106–19.

76. Count Philip of Flanders was the brother-in-law of Count Baldwin V of Hainault, who was the father-in-law of the French king Philip II Augustus. Both the duke of Brabant (sometimes referred to as the duke of Lotharingia or the duke of Louvain) and the count of Flanders held fiefs of the archbishop of Cologne (*REK*, 2:28, no. 183; 2:281, no. 1386), and they joined the archbishop in the battles against Henry the Lion in 1170–80 (*REK*, 2:213–14, no. 1137; 2:219, no. 1149). The archbishop of Cologne looked with misgivings at the potential power of Baldwin of Hainault, who stood to inherit both the counties of Flanders and Namur. The truce was negotiated in Brussels: see *REK*, 2:231, no. 1203.

tion, went to Paris in September 1184 and concluded an alliance with his son-in-law and the new French king (Philip II Augustus) against Flanders. This tipped the balance of power in the region and threatened not only to bring chaos to lower Lotharingia but also to open the door for the expansion of Capetian influence very close to Cologne.

The Capetian willingness to join a coalition against Flanders was the result of both Count Philip's rapprochement with Henry II and inheritance claims. In the last months of 1183 Count Philip was engaged to the princess Matilda of Portugal as a result of the diplomatic assistance of the English king. Henry II had even paid to have Matilda brought to Philip on the king's own royal ship.[77] The marriage eventually took place in August 1184, the same month that the count of Hainault renewed hostilities with Brabant. This was not coincidental, since Count Baldwin would forfeit his expected inheritance of Flanders if Matilda should bear children to Philip. To complicate the matter even more, the dowry given to Matilda by Philip included St. Omer and Aire, which the count had already promised to Isabella of Hainault, the daughter of Count Baldwin, as part of her dowry for marriage to Philip II Augustus.[78] Thus the quite entangled dynastic relations between the noble houses of the Low Countries had drawn in the interests of rulers from England and France. German princes were not to be excluded either, especially the archbishop of Cologne.

Count Philip of Flanders, fearing the escalation that resulted in a Capetian-Hainault coalition directed against him, had already sent envoys to the imperial court at Mainz—the same one that Henry the Lion had visited without success in May of that year—to seek German support. He could expect such support because he had good relations with the archbishop of Cologne and was also an imperial vassal for some of his lands in Flanders. Young King Henry (VI), Duke Frederick of Swabia, and Archbishop Philip of Cologne all promised to support the count of

---

77. *Pipe Roll 30 Henry II*, PR, 33:xxv gives a summary of the expenses paid by the king for Matilda's trip.

78. The marriage of Philip II Augustus and Isabella, daughter of Count Baldwin V of Hainault and niece of Count Philip of Flanders, took place on April 28, 1180. Count Philip had arranged the marriage and given Artois, St. Omer, Aire, and Hesdin to Isabella for her dowry, saving the income for himself during his lifetime. Therefore part of the conflict between France and Flanders was over the inheritance of Picardy. See Robert Fawtier, *The Capetian Kings of France*, trans. Lionel Butler and R. J. Adam (London, 1960), 111–13; Jean Dunbabin, *France in the Making, 843–1180* (Oxford, 1985), 322, 354.

Flanders, while Barbarossa declined direct involvement, as he was busied with Italian affairs.[79] Yet again we see Frederick's consistent policy of attending to *internal* affairs—in this case the coronation and marriage of his son and heir Henry (VI)—rather than risking foreign involvement. In a clear refusal to participate, he declared that he would not cross over the boundaries of his kingdom.[80] Another truce was arranged in May through Henry II's mediation with King Philip II—perhaps out of Capetian fear of German involvement; however, the intrigues continued throughout the next few months.

The embassy of Archbishop Philip of Cologne to Henry II in September of this year must be seen in the context of these events as well as in the context of Barbarossa's negotiations in Verona. Philip had come not only to do the emperor's bidding and obtain English support but also to attend to affairs within his own territorial sphere of influence. He could ill afford an expansion of Capetian power in the lower Rhine territories. The presence of Count Philip of Flanders on this trip is self-evident. He sought to coordinate plans with his feudal lords[81] and maintain their support in his ongoing dynastic struggles with the French and Hainault nobility. The participation of the count of Flanders in this embassy is certain evidence that the archbishop of Cologne was negotiating concerning matters involving his own territorial interests in addition to those of the emperor.

With this agenda the embassy came to London under the guise of a pilgrimage—perhaps a subterfuge to avoid raising tensions further in the Capetian-Hainault camp during their absence. Archbishop Philip's reconciliation with Henry the Lion must therefore have been the result of Henry II's masterful diplomacy. He too had an agenda item, the restoration of his son-in-law, and he therefore exploited to his advantage the opportunities presented him by Barbarossa's Italian ambitions and the tensions involving Flanders. The price of the Angevin king's further involvement in these two matters depended on the reconciliation of Henry the Lion with Archbishop Philip and on efforts at his restoration in Saxony.

The Cologne archbishop was obviously caught in the middle, as he did

---

79. *REK*, 2:236, no. 1226.

80. Kienast, *Deutschland und Frankreich*, 1:233f.

81. Count Philip of Flanders was a vassal of the English king by virtue of a money fief, which he received "quamdiu regi placuerit" (*Pipe Roll 30 Henry II*, PR, 33:14, 69, 95). Philip would continue to receive this subsidy in subsequent years.

not want to see the Welf back in Saxony and yet needed English support on two fronts. But the specter of Capetian expansion into his sphere of power west of Cologne was more dangerous than the return of Henry the Lion (who would return with only his allodial lands intact) in Saxony to the east. Thus he made the only choice that would allow him to achieve the objectives of both the emperor and himself. He was careful, however, not to speak on behalf of the emperor in regard to the restoration of Henry (a separate issue from his own personal reconciliation with him) and rather directed the matter to Verona. Surely Barbarossa's desire for English support at Verona, along with papal support for Henry's restoration, did much to move the emperor in this direction. Thus Archbishop Philip's reconciliation with the Welf should be seen as not an anti-Staufen move designed to undermine imperial authority but rather a concession for the furtherance of the emperor's interests, as well as Philip's attention to his own city's interests in England.[82] This is verified by the fact that Barbarossa himself did not see the reconciliation as treacherous and agreed to the Welf's restoration shortly thereafter. The collage of conflicts all sought the same social solution: familial and personal reconciliation rather than strategic political alliances.

Archbishop Philip's independence from imperial interests were expressed rather in his efforts concerning Flanders and France. At this point there was no divergence between imperial policy and his own *Territorialpolitik*. His efforts were clearly directed against Capetian France, as evidenced by the choice of Richard of Poitou as the bridegroom for the imperial princess. Richard, heir to the English throne, had been engaged for years to Alice, a half sister of Philip II Augustus—indeed she had even been living at the English court.[83] Thus the change must have struck a strong personal blow to the French king. The marriage never occurred, however, since Agnes died later that same year. The London embassy of September 1184 therefore failed again to forge an Angevin-Staufen union, but it was the beginning of a constructive cooperation among the Cologne-Angevin-Welf triad—one that did not have an anti-Staufen policy at this point but that would soon serve as the foundation for Otto IV's kingship.

82. Gerhard Kallen, "Philip von Heinsberg, Erzbischof von Köln (1167–1191)," in *Im Schatten von St. Gereon*, Veröffentlichungen des Kölnischen Geschichtsvereins, no. 25 (Cologne, 1960), 196.

83. Kienast, "Die Deutschen Fürsten," 10:111.

Archbishop Philip's activity immediately following the London embassy further shows the focus of his own attention at this juncture. Philip of Flanders was forced to rush back from London to Flanders upon reports of an invasion by Baldwin of Hainault into his county and of the establishment of the French-Hainault military coalition. Archbishop Philip returned with him and armed for conflict. Then, in early November 1184, the archbishop, along with Duke Godfrey of Brabant (a vassal of the archbishop), his son Henry of Brabant, and the count of Flanders, attacked the county of Hainault.[84] The archbishop brought thirteen hundred knights and many other armed soldiers to the invasion. Philip II Augustus, however, remained distant and never delivered the promised troops. After quickly meeting with Count Baldwin, yet another truce was set, and Archbishop Philip's coalition proved victorious. Henry II and Barbarossa did not involve themselves directly in the hostilities, as they were intent on the negotiations at Verona.

Archbishop Philip of Cologne continued to involve himself in the dynastic and territorial affairs of lower Lotharingia in the following years. While Frederick Barbarossa was busied with Italian affairs the archbishop met at Liège in September 1185 with the emperor's son Henry (VI), the count of Flanders, and the duke of Brabant in an attempt to get the king to provide the military assistance he had promised at Mainz for Count Philip against the French king.[85] They also hoped Henry would force Count Baldwin V of Hainault to forgo his alliance with Philip II of France and allow their armies to pass through Hainault and into France. Clearly, then, Archbishop Philip of Cologne and Count Philip of Flanders (the two members of the London embassy in the prior year) had been the architects of this plan. The Welf Henry the Lion, whom Engels has postulated as the architect, was nowhere to be found.

Baldwin refused to appear before the German king, since he feared foul play, so Henry (VI) sent Archbishop Philip, Bishop Rudolf of Liège, Duke Henry of Limburg, and other princes to provide safe conduct. The count of Hainault finally came, but he rejected the allies' demands and returned to his lands to prepare for war. At the last minute Barbarossa forbade his son to give military aid to the Count of Flanders and the venture was called off. Archbishop Philip's enlistment of the young King

84. Ralph de Diceto, *Ymagines historiarum*, 2:32; Roger of Howden, *Gesta regis Henrici secundi*, 1:322; idem, *Chronica*, 2:288; *REK*, 2:239–40, no. 1234.

85. *REK*, 2:243–44, no. 1244.

Henry (VI), although a false start militarily, must have given much impetus to a settlement. For only two months later (November 7) a firmer armistice was established between the Capetian and Flemish houses at Aumale in Normandy.[86] The leading negotiators present at this meeting were the kings of England and France, the archbishops of Cologne and Reims, and the Count of Flanders. Final agreement was hammered out four months later at Amiens.[87] Little more need be said about who represented German power and influence in affairs that involved France, England, and lower Lotharingia.[88] Also in the autumn of 1185, Archbishop Philip, along with the count of Flanders and the duke of Brabant, forced the count of Namur to take back his wife Agnes, the daughter of Count Henry of Guelders, whom he had put aside some fifteen years earlier. This was done so that he might have heirs and thus prevent Count Baldwin V from inheriting Namur.[89] Such intimate involvement by the archbishop in the dynastic and territorial affairs of this region is solid evidence for his own independent-minded *Territorialpolitik*.

Thus far one cannot speak of a Cologne-Angevin-Welf coalition against Staufen power, including either Henry the Lion or Archbishop Philip of Heinsberg, the latter of whom maintained cooperative relations with Barbarossa and Henry (VI).[90] Yet Philip's territorial interests were

---

86. *REK*, 2:244, no. 1249.

87. Fawtier, *The Capetian Kings of France*, 113. Count Philip of Flanders was thereafter an ally of the French king and was at Ptolemais on June 1, 1191, while on the Third Crusade.

88. Ralph de Diceto (*Ymagines historiarum*, 2:38) states that the Aumale settlement was established subject to the approval of the emperor, thus Archbishop Philip must have represented imperial interests. See Kienast, "Die Deutschen Fürsten," 10:117–18. Count Philip of Flanders and King Henry (VI) made their way to Italy to gain Barbarossa's approval for the settlement. The emperor gave his consent after celebrating the marriage of Henry (VI) to Constance of Sicily on January 27, 1186. Count Philip then met with King Philip II, King Henry II, and Count Baldwin of Hainault near Gisors upon his return north, and the treaty of Amiens was there concluded. Clearly Henry the Lion was not a participant in these affairs.

89. *REK*, 2:244, no. 1248.

90. Arnold of Lübeck (*Chronica Slavorum*, ed. J. M. Lappenberg and G. Pertz, MGH SS rer. Germ., no. 14 [Hanover, 1868]), 97–98) asserts that a conflict arose between Archbishop Philip and King Henry (VI) at the beginning of this year over Duisburg, but such a conflict is highly unlikely, especially based on their later cooperation at Liège. W. von Giesebrecht (*Geschichte der deutschen Kaiserzeit* [Leipzig, 1881–95] 6:83f., 614ff.) argues persuasively that the archbishop was not at this point at odds with royal authority and thus that the report of Arnold is not credible. Peters (*Die Reichspolitik*, 74), however, accepts the account and prematurely dates the beginning of the era of conflict between archbishop and emperor. *REK* (2:241, no. 1236) and Oediger (*Das Bistum Köln*, 164) follow Giesebrecht.

expanding rapidly, particularly after he gained the duchy of Westphalia, and there had been earlier friction over the jurisdiction of the bishopric of Cambrai. We have also seen cooperation between Cologne, the English court, and the Welfs during an era when the emperor was developing closer contacts with Capetian France. The Cologne archbishop's territorial policy at this time was clearly anti-Capetian, and it was this policy against Capetian expansion—not an anti-Staufen policy involving the Welfs—[91]that drew the archbishop of Cologne and the English king together. This realignment of interests would see its first friction in the remaining years before the Third Crusade.

Conflict with Cologne and Crusading: The Limits of Imperial Lordship

Relations between Archbishop Philip of Heinsberg and Barbarossa had been cooperative throughout the 1170s, although there had been points of friction along the way (as over the bishopric of Cambrai). As long as their personal and regional interests did not clash directly, there was little occasion for a confrontational relationship. But tension did result in an open breach during the years 1186–87 as a result of competing interests, in much the same way as the conflict between Henry the Lion and Barbarossa developed. This would in turn raise imperial worries over the archbishop's ties with England, whose dynastic link with the Welfs would become important again when Barbarossa prepared to leave the empire on the Third Crusade. Frederick grew ever more concerned about the growing regional power of the archbishop after the ducal grant at Gelnhausen. Had he, after bringing down the most powerful prince in

---

Alexander Cartellieri (*Philip II. August, König von Frankreich* [Leipzig, 1899–1922], 1:319) argues that Archbishop Philip attempted to establish a Cologne-France-England-Flanders-Welf anti-Staufen coalition at Aumale; however, this conclusion far exceeds the evidence. Wand ("Die Englandpolitik der Stadt Köln," 80) has followed Cartellieri, while Kienast ("Die Deutschen Fürsten," 10:118 n. 1) successfully opposes Cartellieri's view. It would seem at least inconsistent to assert that Philip was fomenting anti-Staufen action at a conference whose conclusion was accepted contingent on Staufen approval. These are attempts to find the anti-Staufen policy among the archbishops of Cologne at an earlier date than it actually developed—much in the same way that others have incorrectly seen an anti-Staufen policy within the Welf-Angevin dynastic tie before 1198.

91. Henry the Lion had little role in the affairs of lower Lotharingia that had brought the English court and Archbishop Philip to closer diplomatic relations. Henry the Lion was not in a position to provide any additional support or influence at this time.

northern Germany, created another powerful rival to his authority in the region?

The first point of conflict arose at the Mainz Reichstag of 1184, where both Henry the Lion and the count of Flanders had sought favor.[92] On the day of Pentecost a dispute broke out between the archbishop and Abbot Conrad of Fulda before the celebration of Mass. The abbot claimed that, according to ancient custom, during a general assembly in Mainz the abbot of Fulda had the right to be seated on the left hand of the emperor while the archbishop of Mainz was to be seated on the right hand. When Barbarossa asked Philip to accept this demand and thus avoid dissension the archbishop, his pride wounded at this affront to his rank, prepared to leave the assembly in anger. The count palatine of the Rhine (the emperor's half brother), the count of Nassau, the duke of Brabant, and other princes rose in support of Philip, and the heated situation calmed only through the intercession of young King Henry (VI), who is said to have fallen on the neck of the archbishop, and a promise of the emperor that he had intended no offense. The abbot eventually was persuaded to relinquish his claimed position of honor, and peace was restored. The residual effect of Barbarossa's slighting of Philip's archiepiscopal rank both at Mainz and concerning the bishopric of Cambrai placed an edge on the archbishop's actions in the following years.

By the beginning of 1186 relations between emperor and archbishop had soured and an open break resulted. The initial cause, however, was not either anti-Staufen or anti-Welf sentiment but rather relations with the papacy. The Cologne chronicle says that the reason Philip was no longer on good terms with Barbarossa was because Philip supported Pope Urban III.[93] The emperor had renewed conflict with the papacy as a result of the marriage of Henry (VI) to Constance of Sicily in January 1186. Constance was the heiress of Sicily and thus Barbarossa had united the Sicilian kingdom to the empire, effectively encircling the papal states. Archbishop Philip did not attend this marriage, but he did not stay away because, as Arnold of Lübeck alleges, he had received a warning from the archbishop of Mainz that his life would be endangered

---

92. *REK*, 2:236, no. 1224.
93. *CRC*, 136: "Non enim in gratia imperatoris admodum fuit, eo quod papae, qui imperatori infestus erat, magis videretur favere, et pro hac suspicione imperatoriae offensae fides de facili prestita fuit huic machinationi."

should he appear.[94] It is more likely that he stayed away because he supported the papal position on the marriage.

Archbishop Philip had been developing closer relations with the papacy in this year in an effort to advance his episcopal independence from imperial authority. This was the true heart of his conflict with the emperor. He had written a letter to the new pope, Urban III, in support of the papal appointment of Archbishop Folmar of Trier on June 1, 1186.[95] In making the appointment Urban III had claimed spiritual authority to fill vacant and disputed sees. Barbarossa of course had rejected this circumvention of his own authority to make episcopal appointments when disputed. Urban III quickly recognized the value of Philip's support in his conflict with the emperor, and later that year he made the archbishop a papal legate for his archdiocese.[96]

Philip's support of Urban III in the dispute over the see of Trier was only one facet of his effort to forge episcopal independence from imperial authority. His crowning achievement in this policy was gaining papal recognition for the canonization of his predecessor Anno II. Whereas his immediate predecessor, Rainald of Dassel, fashioned a patron saint of imperial authority in Charlemagne, Philip orchestrated the canonization of Anno II—an archbishop whose sanctity the citizens of Cologne themselves likely doubted—to create a patron saint of archiepiscopal authority. While the strategy was the same in both instances (i.e., canonization), the implications were radically different and reflect the changing conditions of political life in Germany during Barbarossa's reign. Also in the summer of 1186 Philip held a general synod at which an official declaration of both his appointment as papal legate and Anno's canonization was made.[97] The papal legates John of Anagni and Peter of Luna had already declared Anno's canonization in 1183, so Philip's coupling of these announcements was definitely timed to maximize his ecclesiastical status.[98]

---

94. Arnold of Lübeck, *Chronica Slavorum*, 101; *REK*, 2:246, no. 1255.

95. *REK*, 2:248, no. 1261.

96. *CRC*, 135; *REK*, 2:249, no. 1263.

97. *REK*, 2:249–50, no. 1264.

98. The Cologne archbishopric now had its own patron saint to compete with the royal saints, the Three Kings, and Charlemagne. Philip decreed that Anno II was to be revered not as a mere *fidelis defunctus* but rather as a *confessor sanctissimus*. The burghers of Cologne would certainly have caught the significance of using Anno II as a model for archiepiscopal rule in the city.

We have a report from Arnold of Lübeck that in late summer of the same year, Philip met with Emperor Frederick upon the latter's return from Lombardy. Frederick asked Philip whether or not he could count on the archbishop's support in his conflict with the pope, and the archbishop's answer is quite instructive.[99] After referring to his past record of allegiance to the emperor, he chose to speak for all bishops in the name of justice. Philip complained that the emperor was placing too heavy a burden on the bishops to pay for his ventures, and he also made reference to the Trier dispute by supporting the papal argument against allowing sees to remain vacant in order that the emperor could draw from its wealth for his own purposes.[100] Here we see why Philip was supporting the papacy and thereby incurring the wrath of Barbarossa. He was consistently working for the establishment of episcopal independence from imperial authority in an effort to strengthen his own territorial principality. His policy was therefore not so much anti-Staufen as it was pro-archiepiscopal, and it did not have Welf or English support. Archbishop Philip's agenda was not imperial but territorial.

Frederick of course responded that he would continue to exercise imperial rights and, according to Arnold, made Philip swear that he would not attend the upcoming Reichstag at Gelnhausen. Arnold was misinformed about this oath, as Philip did attend the Reichstag at the end of November 1186.[101] Here Barbarossa laid out his complaints against Urban III and sought to gain the support of all the ecclesiastical and secular princes. Archbishop Philip alone refused to support the emperor and is even said to have begun a conspiracy against him.[102]

The situation became even more tense when Philip gave asylum to Bishop Bertram of Metz.[103] Bertram, who had been a canon at St. Gereon in Cologne, was a supporter of Archbishop Folmar of Trier and thus was driven from his see by the emperor (Folmar had been exiled in France). On March 22, 1187, Philip convened a synod in Cologne that all his

---

99. Arnold of Lübeck, *Chronica Slavorum*, 105–6.

100. *REK* (2:251, no. 1270) states that this report of Arnold is "obviously a product of Arnold's imagination" and that "Philip had the least basis to complain about the right of spoils." But this complaint was made in regard to the Trier conflict, and the matters raised by Philip in Arnold's account do at least reflect the archbishop's policies.

101. *REK*, 2:252, no. 1275.

102. *Annales Pegavienses*, ed. G. Pertz, MGH SS, no. 16 (Hanover, 1859), 265; *Gesta Treverorum continuatio tertia*, ed. G. Waitz, MGH SS, no. 24 (Hanover, 1879; reprint, 1974), 387.

103. *CRC*, 135; *REK*, 2:254, no. 1284.

suffragan bishops and the princes of the land—even the count of Flanders and the landgrave of Thuringia—were said to have attended.[104] This was apparently a move to mobilize his vassals for war against imperial troops. Urban III gave Philip additional regional authority in an effort to bolster the archbishop's position.[105]

At this point Capetian and Staufen interests converged. The young Capetian monarch Philip II Augustus had been increasingly offended by the personal affronts of the Angevins toward him in his relations with them.[106] Territorially speaking he was troubled by Henry II's acquisitions in eastern Berry, in Auvergne, and in the Poitevin marches and angered by the English king's retention of the Norman Vexin (which had been the dowry for his half sister) after the death of Henry II's eldest son, Henry. But the most embarrassing problem was Henry II's long guardianship of Philip's other half sister, Alice, who had been promised but not yet married to Richard the Lionheart. Philip II apparently believed that she had been seduced by the English king, and we have already seen the affront caused by the short-lived betrothal of Richard to a daughter of the emperor while Alice languished at the English court. Until 1187 Philip II was not strong enough to fight and thus could only complain; however, he responded militarily in May of this year by crossing the river Cher with an army and laying siege to Châteauroux.

Barbarossa had his own problems with the archbishop of Cologne and the pope and needed a means to pressure Philip into submission. He had already isolated Philip at Gelnhausen and now sought to bring the issue to a conclusion. Who better to turn to than the French king, who had endured the machinations of the archbishop of Cologne against his father-in-law in Hainault three years earlier and certainly knew of his regional power and English diplomatic ties. The French king may also have wished to neutralize Frederick's son Henry (VI), whose involvement in the Flanders-Hainault conflict almost led to an invasion of France.[107] In any case the threat of imperial support against the Angevins would serve his purposes well.

Thus the two monarchs reached an alliance treaty at Toul on May 17, 1187.[108] The contents of the treaty are not available to us, but we know

---

104. *REK*, 2:253, no. 1281.
105. *CRC*, 135.
106. Barlow, *Feudal Kingdom of England*, 348.
107. Trautz, *Die Könige*, 78.
108. *REK*, 2:254, no. 1285.

that Philip Augustus promised to drive Archbishop Folmar of Trier from his kingdom and fight jointly against the archbishop of Cologne in return for similar support against the English.[109] For Philip II the coalition wound up having little practical use, as a month later (June 23) Henry II accepted a two-year truce before any real military engagement occurred. Not out of fear of the emperor, but rather because of the position taken by Henry's son Richard, the king felt compelled to reach a quick settlement.[110] Richard had reconciled with Philip II shortly before the French king began his invasion of the duchy of Berry.[111] The evident lack of any expectation of imperial aggression against England can be seen in Henry II's letter to Barbarossa after the settlement with Philip II, in which he tells the emperor that he has taken the cross.[112] Henry even asked the emperor for safe passage through his lands. Barbarossa's return letter is full of goodwill, and thus we cannot take seriously a real threat of imperial invasion of Angevin lands.[113]

Fear of the emperor's army did strike the citizens of Cologne, however, as they knew the military action was really directed against their region.[114] Barbarossa had gained Capetian support in driving out Folmar, who had earlier fled to France; thus added pressure was placed on those supporting the pope in the matter—principally Archbishop Philip. Cologne and its environs were quickly fortified and provisioned in preparation for a siege, and one probably unreliable report says that the Cologne burghers even went and destroyed the bridge built across the Moselle River for imperial crossing.[115] Reports of these actions increased the anger of the emperor and he ordered Philip to appear before an imperial diet at Worms.[116] Yet Frederick never brought his army to Cologne, instead remaining in Saarland and Hagenau during the months of June and July.

---

109. Keinast, "Die Deutschen Fürsten," 10:126, *Gesta Treverorum continuatio tertia,* 387.

110. *CRC,* 135–36: "Regis Angliae Heinrici filius Richardus, mari transmisso, terram regis Francorum Philippi cum copiis suis invasit, unde idem rex Francorum opem Friderici Romanorum augusti asciscit; pro cuius metu Anglicus, treugis datis, ab incepto desistit." Obviously the Cologne chronicle was ill informed in this matter, since Richard had joined the side of Philip II at this time. The chronicle, intended to glorify royal achievements, does an admirable, although false, job here.

111. Trautz, *Die Könige,* 78.

112. Ralph de Diceto, *Ymagines historiarum,* 2:51–52.

113. Ibid., 2:52.

114. *CRC,* 136.

115. *Chronicon Henrici de Hervordia,* ed. August Potthast (Göttingen, 1859), 169.

116. *REK,* 2:254–56, no. 1286.

To put further pressure on the archbishop and the city the emperor had the Rhine blocked from the north of Cologne.[117] This cut off the flow of grain and wine and effectively ceased the city's trading activity. The Reichstag was duly held at Worms on August 15, but Philip did not appear. This was an act of contumacy strikingly similar to Henry the Lion's earlier refusal to make account before the imperial court. Barbarossa interestingly enough charged both the archbishop and the citizens of Cologne with the crime of barring his passage through imperial territory and with accusing him shamefully of intending to destroy the city under the pretense of coming to the aid of the French king. Philip was called to answer again at the next diet in Strasbourg.[118] Although Philip did not appear at Worms, the cathedral deacon (and future archbishop of Cologne) Adolf of Altena was present and interceded on his behalf along with Philip's vassals the counts of Jülich, Sayn, and Arnsberg. Adolf was present also at the emperor's court at Überlingen in the month of September, suggesting that lengthy negotiations were pursued.[119]

The Third Crusade was preached at the diet of Strasbourg in early December, which added to the urgency of resolving the rebellion of Archbishop Philip. The conflict dragged on, however, and Philip did not appear at Strasbourg either.[120] Only on the emperor's third demand that he appear, at the Reichstag in Mainz (March 27, 1188), did Philip finally come. Likely remembering the fate of Henry the Lion after a third refusal to appear, he submitted himself unconditionally to Barbarossa and was taken back into the emperor's favor after the intercession of several imperial princes and the cardinal legate Henry of Albano. No doubt the resolution was encouraged under legatine influence because of the urgent need to launch the Third Crusade.

The conditions for reconciliation were as follows: Philip had to swear three oaths of purgation, one each for his absence at Worms and Strasbourg and the third for his levying monetary fines on certain Jews. The final charge was a reminder that such activity was still the right of the crown as part of its role as protector of the Jews *(Judenschutz)*. Furthermore, both archbishop and the city were to pay a fine of 2,000 marks to the emperor and 260 marks *"in curiam."* As a sign of submission the city's gate

117. *REK,* 2:257, no. 1297; *CRC,* 136.
118. *REK,* 2:259, no. 1303; *CRC,* 136.
119. *REK,* 2:259, no. 1304.
120. *REK,* 2:260, no. 1309.

had to be torn down and its moat was to be filled in at four locations. The equally independent-minded citizens of Cologne restored the gate and moat the following day.[121] These remedial steps were an open admission of rebellion against imperial authority, and Barbarossa had won this war of nerves and prestige. The emperor was now free to fulfill his vow to embark on crusade. Note that no mention is made of English or Welf involvement in this rebellion.[122] The French and English had observed a truce for almost a year by this point, Henry the Lion's sphere of influence was restricted to his allodial lands in Saxony, and Urban III had died on October 20, 1187, after a settlement had been reached concerning the Trier archbishopric. Philip had therefore gone this rebellion alone and held out until there was no use in continuing the struggle.

Philip thereafter remained loyal to the Staufen rulers. In March 1190 he participated with Archbishop Conrad of Mainz in settling an imperial dispute with the Welfs in Saxony[123] while continuing his territorial intrigues in the Low Counties.[124] He was always on good terms with King Henry (VI) and was often in his company; it appears that King Henry even attempted to reconcile Philip with Barbarossa shortly before the Mainz council.[125] Henry rewarded Philip for his efforts at reaching a settlement with the Welf by granting him minting and toll privileges on March 25, 1190.[126] In November of the same year, Philip went to Italy in the service of King Henry to negotiate for his imperial coronation. While on this mission, he died suddenly of the plague on August 13, 1191, near Naples, and his bones were brought to Cologne and laid in the cathedral beside those of Rainald of Dassel.[127] This was a most appropriate resting place for an

---

121. *REK,* 2:261, no. 1317; *CRC,* 139.

122. In fact the *Annales Marbacenses* (59) tell of the reconciliation between Archbishop Philip and Barbarossa at Mainz and then of the taking of the cross by the emperor and the kings of France and England as a common cause.

123. *REK,* 2:269, no. 1350.

124. Archbishop Philip joined Philip of Flanders in a three-day conference near Brussels in October 1189 to achieve peace again between Duke Henry of Brabant and Count Baldwin of Hainault (*REK,* 2:268–69, no. 1344) and negotiated a further peace in July 1190 between Baldwin of Hainault and his uncle Count Henry of Namur, whereby Baldwin would inherit the county of Namur (*REK,* 2:270–71, no. 1353).

125. *REK,* 2:260–61, no. 1314, although the authenticity of this letter from Emperor Frederick to his son, in which the emperor rebuked his son for being deceived by the machinations of the archbishop, is in doubt.

126. *REK,* 2:269–70, no. 1351. The Cologne chronicler indicates King Henry's intention in this grant: "Nitebatur enim modis omnibus eum sibi allicere, eo quod vir strennuus et victoriosus esset" (*CRC,* 147).

127. *REK,* 2:284, nos. 1423–24.

archbishop who was every bit the equal of his predecessor in skill, creativity, and drive, though their personal goals were quite divergent.

Meanwhile Barbarossa, having exiled Henry the Lion once again and departed for the Holy Land, had drowned in the river Saleph on June 10, 1190, at the start of his crusade. Henry II of England had died already on July 6, 1189, after a humiliating defeat near Tours at the hand of his son Richard, who was supported by Philip II.[128] Hence we have the remarkable coincidence of the deaths of all the major political players, with the exception of Henry the Lion and the young king of France (Henry would die five years later; however, his wife Matilda died on July 13, 1189).[129] The Third Crusade was a watershed for relations between England and Germany. The subsequent generation would see a real Cologne-Angevin-Welf alignment against a Staufen-Capetian alliance, with the papacy as a shifting force between the two camps.

But it must be said again that until 1189 there was no such alliance constellation in operation, either overtly or tacitly. Henry II never gave direct support to Henry the Lion until his exile, and after the Welf's return the king was in no position to do so, as he faced the rebellion of his own sons. Although Henry welcomed the duke back during a brief second exile,[130] the king died soon thereafter, and there is no evidence that any English assistance was given to the duke when upon the death of Barbarossa he returned early to Saxony to regain his lands.[131] Richard was involved in the Third Crusade and showed no interest or intention to provide such aid. Archbishop Philip's actions had never been anti-Staufen—though some have tried to argue so[132]—but rather were

---

128. Barlow, *Feudal Kingdom of England,* 350.

129. *Böhmer* 5, 1:52, no. 185e.

130. Roger of Howden (*Gesta regis Henrici secundi,* 2:62) says that the duke accepted exile because he wished neither to participate in the crusade nor to have his eldest son go on crusade without the counsel of Henry II.

131. CRC (143) is overzealous in its charge that such a conspiracy existed between Richard and the Welf: "Heinricus quondam dux Saxonum, cognita imperatoris absentia, contra iuramentum de Anglia reversus, nativum solum expetit, astipulante sibi rege Richardo, cuius sororem habuit, et rege Datio, genero suo. Bellatur inter filium eiusdem ducis et regem Romanum." See Ahlers, *Die Welfen,* 131–33.

132. Although Peters (*Die Reichspolitik,* 81) makes a great deal out of the supposed anti-Staufen intentions in Philip's actions and considers an Angevin-Welf-Cologne alliance probable, he admits," Whether Philip had now actually concluded a formal alliance with England, Henry the Lion, and Knut of Denmark, a relative of Henry who had refused to perform feudal homage to the emperor, cannot be proven." One cannot prove it because there is no evidence for it.

attempts at both establishing a territorial principality independent of imperial authority and also avoiding Capetian expansion into lower Lotharingia. His friction with the Staufer resulted from his independence and assertion of personal rank as an imperial prince rather than from any conspiracy aimed at the Staufen house. As we have seen, he had been generally on good terms with King Henry (VI) throughout this period. The tensions between Welf and Cologne interests were too great to bring about a coalition between the two, even if Henry the Lion were in a position to support the Cologne rebellion against the emperor.

Finally, the Staufen-Capetian alliance signed at Toul was of virtually no real consequence, as each monarch pursued independent courses of action over separate concerns. Henry II showed no worry over imperial involvement in his conflict with Philip II, and Archbishop Philip and the Cologne burghers knew that their danger of being besieged did not come from France. The emperor, for his part, had little to fear from the English king during this conflict with the pope and archbishop of Cologne, since Henry II had already begun to fade politically; and Henry the Lion played no role in the rebellion. Rather the archbishop of Cologne stood alone against Barbarossa and had done so over issues of personal prestige, ecclesiastical independence, and territorial interests.

Those who have seen such a conspiracy during Barbarossa's reign have either viewed this period retrospectively through the future events of 1198–1216 or superimposed on Angevin-Staufen relations modern conceptions of power blocks and imperial competition. Yet these two perspectives misjudge the nature of twelfth-century political life. Both Barbarossa and Henry II focused their efforts consistently on domestic matters and showed little taste for power politics outside their kingdoms. They were the most powerful monarchs of their era, yet they were constantly beset with problems in the enforcement of their claims to traditional royal and imperial rights among their own subjects. As a result Barbarossa was beset by three internal political conflicts that dominated his reign: the papal schism, disputes with independent-minded Lombard cities, and disputes with independent-minded German princes, such as Henry the Lion and Archbishop Philip of Cologne.[133] Perhaps not so remarkably, Henry II of England faced identical types of challenges: papal and ecclesiastical resistance, rebellious nobles at home (even his own sons), and instability in his lands beyond the English

---

133. Opll, *Friedrich Barbarossa*, 305–7.

kingdom (often encouraged by the French king in the same way that the pope agitated against Barbarossa in Italy). These very similar political problems kept both monarchs busy with internal affairs, and neither had need or resources to confront the other in some sort of competition for the largest empire in Europe.[134]

Furthermore, the *Familienpolitik* of both monarchs reveals political behavior much more akin to that of their fellow nobles than to that of great state-builders presaging modernity. Better known perhaps is Henry II's conflicts with his sons over their inheritance of the Angevin territories, during the latter years of his reign. Karl Leyser has deftly shown, however, that after returning from the disastrous fourth Italian campaign Frederick Barbarossa busied himself with obtaining numerous territories in Swabia to consolidate a regional power base for his sons. The lands gathered were mostly taken from those members of his retinue who had died in the Roman plague![135] Here Barbarossa looks much more like his estate-building fellow nobles than like the state-building imperial ideologue he is most often made out to be.[136] Indeed, here Frederick used the Reich to strengthen the Staufen house, rather than the reverse. As Leyser rightly concludes, "Why then should we know better and father Grand Designs or state planning upon them? It was the house that mattered, not the reorganization of the state, whatever that meant."[137] The same can also be said for Henry II with regard to the "Angevin Empire." Both men were cut from medieval aristocratic cloth, and their ultimate affections were attached to securing their house's power rather than being spent on creating the foundations for the modern constitutional history of Europe.

In one of the most ironic moments of medieval history, the Third Crusade was probably the closest Frederick Barbarossa got to his chivalric dream of leading Christendom as the Christian emperor.[138] Yet his

---

134. Trautz, *Die Könige*, 80.

135. Karl Leyser, "Frederick Barbarossa and the Hohenstaufen Polity," *Viator* 19 (1988): 154–76 (reprinted in *Communications and Power in Medieval Europe: The Gregorian Revolution and Beyond*, ed. Timothy Reuter [London and Rio Grande, OH, 1994], 115–42).

136. Ibid., 160: ". . . there were no politics in the modern sense of the word focused on the growing apparatus of government. Instead, it was the age-old competition between houses for *honores* and inheritances which harnessed to itself the economic, demographic, and cultural developments we have outlined, rather than being transformed by them."

137. Ibid., 174.

138. Opll, *Friedrich Barbarossa*, 308: "For Barbarossa himself the crusade must have been in many respects the fulfillment of his knightly ideals of life."

accidental death away from the battlefield was an echo of earlier trage-
dies in his effort to assert a predominant position in Christendom for the
German emperor: the Roman plague in 1167 and the disastrous defeat at
Legnano in 1176. At his own death Henry II was reduced to resisting the
attacks of his own sons. In the end, these paragons of renewing royal
prerogative appear more like medieval kings trying to hold their own
against the centrifugal forces of the nobility and the church than like
precursors of modernity as either state or empire builders.

What we have witnessed thus far has been more of a social than a
geopolitical history of political communities, complete with marriages
and marriage proposals, personal relationships (even within families) being broken and reconciled, religious scruples being asserted and manipulated, and the frustrations of implementing abstract policies when the
independent interests of the powerful members involved so often di-
verged. Barbarossa's failure to realize a revived classical Roman empire
was not so much a story of defeat as a reminder of the possibilities of
medieval politics. The social realities of political life mattered more than
the institutional forms. The lesson of Frederick Barbarossa's reign might
well be the impossibility of wedging an institutional model into an unsuit-
able social context. This is a lesson for historians who evaluate the Middle Ages with modern expectations about the state and diplomacy.

The Third Crusade is a good point at which to stop and take stock of
Anglo-German diplomatic relations and the role played by the archbishops
of Cologne. By this time Europe had seen the emergence of the empire from
an original eastern and southern focus toward an involvement in the affairs
of the western powers. This development was the result of increasing
conflicts with the papacy, since the German monarchs sought to free themselves from the political isolation of schisms and antipopes. The English
response thus far has been one of reserved involvement with the German
monarch as well as with the imperial princes. The reservation of course
came from the same source that drove the Germans to seek western ties,
namely, the papal schisms and antipopes. It seems hardly likely that Henry
II would have been so reticent to commit himself to an imperial coalition if
the clergy in both his English and continental lands had supported the
imperial antipopes, especially within the crucible of the Becket controversy. Thus Anglo-German relations so far have been defined and dominated by the religious requirements of the day.

We have also seen the emergence of a powerful ecclesiastical principality under the control of the archbishops of Cologne, with the principal

architect being Philip of Heinsberg. Efforts directed at independence from imperial constraint and at consolidation of regional power had resulted in friction similar to that of Henry the Lion's policies in Saxony, yet in this instance the archbishop survived with his lands intact. The growing independence and regional power of the archbishops of Cologne was a major element in all subsequent Anglo-German relations during the thirteenth century.

We have also seen a growing interest in the Low Countries on the part of the monarchs of England and France as well as the archbishop of Cologne. They were interested in this region as much for economic reasons as for political advantage, because of the growing European trading nexus emerging there. The courting of the principalities in the Low Countries by all parties concerned would draw them deeply into the Anglo-French and Staufen-Welf conflicts of the next generation. Within this configuration of principalities on the lower Rhine River and the Meuse River the dominant political force was the archbishop of Cologne, who would have to be reckoned with in any constellation of power.

As imperial authority faded in northern Germany during the thirteenth century the archbishops of Cologne would become the power brokers of this region. As such the English court would continue to cultivate diplomatic relations because of the potential of Cologne as a flagship, among German principalities, for an anti-Capetian confederation. This anti-Capetian diplomatic project of Plantagenet monarchs during the thirteenth century will crash on the same rocks as Barbarossa's imperial dream of the twelfth century: namely, the regional independence of German princes and their territories.

4

Richard the Lionheart and Otto IV: Itinerant Kingship and the City of Cologne

The Third Crusade, a failure by all accounts in the Holy Land, had profound consequences for the political communities of western Europe. Not only did it signal the emergence of a new generation of political leaders, but the results of interregional cooperation and conflict during the crusade also went a long way toward shaping the nature of political possibilities in Europe during the thirteenth century. This was most certainly the case for Anglo-German diplomatic relations. The generation of the Alexandrine schism had passed away: already gone were Frederick Barbarossa, Henry II, Rainald of Dassel, Thomas Becket, and Alexander III; and by 1192 Philip of Heinsberg was gone as well. Therefore new possibilities existed for reshaping European diplomatic activity as the surviving crusaders returned to their homes. One of the returning crusaders in particular would redirect the thrust of European diplomatic discourse through an effort to elevate his nephew as an ally against his own feudal lord, with whom this paragon of crusading zeal was constantly at odds. The knight we speak of was the new English king, Richard I the Lionheart.

Richard the Lionheart as Crusader and Hostage of the German King: Anti-Staufen Conspirator or Knight Errant?

Because Richard I had close familial relations with the Welf dynasty and because he was later imprisoned by Barbarossa's son Henry VI a suspicion has lingered that he was a conspirator in yet another allegedly Angevin-led anti-Staufen conspiracy. This theory, however, is as lacking in hard evidence as the similar charge against his father. With regard to Henry the Lion in the first instance, the conflict in Saxony after the Welf's early return from his second exile cannot be linked in some conspiratorial way with Richard's actions during the Third Crusade.[1] Although from personal interest Richard probably hoped for a Welf restoration in Saxony, there is no evidence that he gave material support to Henry the Lion when the duke returned to Saxony upon the death of Barbarossa to reclaim his ducal lands. The Welf duke did send his own son Henry to Richard at La Réole (Gascony) in February 1190, no doubt to discuss affairs in Saxony, but Richard was in no position to assist his brother-in-law.[2] Amid preparations for the crusade no help could be expected from Richard.[3]

Furthermore, Henry VI was less troubled by Henry the Lion than his father had been.[4] While the Welf duke initially employed military means to force a settlement, the new German king was more inclined to seek a negotiated compromise. He was willing to conciliate in order to settle the conflict and thus be freed to concentrate on capturing the kingdom of Sicily from the upstart Count Tancred of Leece, the illegitimate son of Roger of Apulia. Archbishop Philip of Heinsberg participated in these negotiations with the Welf duke before his death, and the Peace of Fulda was finalized in July 1190.[5] The Angevins were of no help to the Welfs, then, in their struggle to gain reinstatement in Saxony, nor are they mentioned in the Peace of Fulda. Reinstatement in the family's lands of Saxony was only reached through the generosity of Henry VI, not via aid from the Angevin house.[6]

The second instance often tendered as evidence for an anti-Staufen conspiracy led by Richard I is his sojourn on the island of Sicily en route to Palestine in the winter of 1190–91. The "alliance" established between Richard and Tancred of Leece is quite often depicted as a pro-Welf

---

1. Ahlers, *Die Welfen*, 139–40.

2. Lionel Landon, *The Itinerary of King Richard I, with Studies on Certain Matters of Interest Connected with His Reign*, PR, NS, no. 13 (London, 1935), 25, where Henry appears among the witnesses to a charter to the Abbey of St. Sever.

3. Jordan (*Henry the Lion*, 191) even concludes: "The Welfs could have expected no help from the king of England at this time; it is more likely that Richard urged Henry the Lion to make his peace with King Henry."

4. Kienast, "Die Deutschen Fürsten," 10:135.

5. Jordan, *Henry the Lion*, 191–92. It is interesting to note that, as part of the peace settlement, Archbishop Hartwig II of Bremen was deposed and went into exile to England. Thus he followed the footsteps of his patron. The Peace of Fulda is mentioned in Roger Howden, *Chronica*, 3:73–74; *Gesta regis Henrici secundi*, 2:145.

6. Ahlers, *Die Welfen*, 147.

blow against Henry VI.[7] In fact, however, the circumstances and details surrounding this facet of Richard's supposedly "major hostile coalition, implicating the papacy and reaching from Sicily to England"[8] reveal a very different picture.

During Richard's sojourn on the island tensions grew between his troops and Sicilian citizens over rising food prices. This was a consequence of the shortages due to the presence of crusading soldiers. At one point a riot broke out in which the Angevin army seized the city of Messina. Richard, in addition to taking hostages from among the wealthier merchants, erected a wooden castle on a hill overlooking the city and named it "Mategriffon"—meaning "kill the Greeks."[9] From this vantage point the entire area, including the straits, could be controlled by Richard's crusaders. Richard was not only angry with the Sicilian merchants. He also resented Tancred's withholding of the dower of his sister Joanna, the widow of King William II (Tancred's half brother), and Tancred's refusal to pay a substantial legacy that the deceased Sicilian king had bequeathed to Henry II.[10] These conflicts were all *personal* in nature, since Richard demanded that Tancred fulfill obligations to his Angevin family and vassals. If he wished to regain the city, Tancred had little choice but to reach a settlement favorable to Richard. Tancred's position on the island was still shaky at best, and an attack by Henry VI seemed imminent. To make matters worse Tancred had already sought in vain an alliance with the French monarch Philip II, and so he had precious little room to maneuver.

Richard came away from the "alliance" agreement with handsome

---

7. See, for example, Zatschek, *England und das Reich,* 21; Lothar von Heinemann, *Heinrich von Braunschweig: Ein Beitrag zur Geschichte des staufischen Zeitalters* (Gotha, 1882), 17f.; Editha Gronen, *Die Machtpolitik Heinrichs des Löwen und sein Gegensatz gegen das Kaisertum,* Historische Studien, no. 139 (Berlin, 1919), 105; Thoedor Toeche, *Kaiser Heinrich VI.* (Leipzig, 1867), 156–59; Kate Norgate, *England under the Angevin Kings* (London, 1887), 2:319; Karl Hampe, *Deutsche Kaisergeschichte in der Zeit der Salier und Staufer,* ed. F. Baethgen (Heidelberg, 1969), 222; F. M. Powicke, *The Loss of Normandy,* 2d ed. (Manchester, 1961), 90; Heinrich Mitteis, *Der Staat des hohen Mittelalters,* 8th ed. (Weimar, 1968), 265; Evelyn Jamison, "Alliance of England and Sicily in the Second Half of the Twelfth Century," *Journal of the Warburg and Courtauld Institutes* 6 (1943): 31; Geoffrey Barraclough, *The Origins of Modern Germany* (Oxford, 1947), 195; Trautz, *Die Könige,* 81; John Gillingham, *Richard the Lionheart* (London, 1978), 154; Helmut Hiller, *Heinrich der Löwe: Herzog und Rebell* (Munich, 1978), 263.

8. Barraclough, *Origins of Modern Germany,* 195.

9. Gillingham, *Richard the Lionheart,* 153.

10. Ibid., 151.

funding for his crusade. Tancred paid twenty thousand ounces of gold in lieu of Joanna's dower and agreed to pay an additional twenty thousand ounces for the planned marriage between one of his daughters and Richard's nephew Arthur of Brittany, whom the Angevin king designated as his heir. In return Richard agreed to protect Tancred's claims to Sicily from outside intervention—*but only as long as Richard remained on the island.*[11] An eventual marriage union was many years away (if it was ever really contemplated), since Arthur was only three years old; and Richard was to leave the island when the winter had passed,[12] thus ending his obligation to defend Tancred. Perhaps these were face-saving gestures for Tancred in order to make the settlement more palatable. In essence Richard had found a creative way to fund his crusade; he even gave one-third of the forty thousand ounces of gold to Philip II,[13] which further undermines the notion that this agreement was directed against a Capetian-Staufen political bloc.

Tancred had purchased only an expensive peace with Richard and his rioting crusaders, rather than an alliance against Henry VI. In fact, the French king was able to stir up Tancred's continuing distrust of his new "ally" when Queen Eleanor appeared at Naples in February 1191 with a large following.[14] Eleanor, accompanied by Count Philip of Flanders, had come with Berengaria of Navarre as a bride for her royal son, yet Tancred feared the sizable number of retainers who had escorted her. Philip II had good reason to interfere, since Richard had been betrothed to his half sister Alice for years (at this point for some twenty years!) and she had been slighted already once before when Richard was promised to a daughter of Barbarossa. Now her honor was finally being destroyed and Philip's humiliated by this new marriage to a Spanish princess.

Tancred's fears increased when Eleanor met Henry VI in Lodi on January 20, 1191.[15] This meeting, at which no doubt Henry VI inquired

---

11. *Rymer,* 1:66–67: "Charta pacis factae inter Richardum Regem Angliae et Tancredum Regem Siciliae. . . . Hoc nihilominus addito, quod quamdiu in Regno vestro moram fecerimus, ad defensionem terrae vestrae ubicunque praesentes fuerimus, vobis auxilium praesentamus contra quemcunque qui vellet eam invadere, aut vobis bellum inferre."

12. The failure of Richard to mention the defensive alliance as part of the agreement in his letter to Pope Clement III suggests the priority he placed on the matter. See *Rymer,* 1:68.

13. Gillingham, *Richard the Lionheart,* 155.

14. Roger of Howden, *Gesta regis Henrici secundi,* 2:157–159; see also Gillingham, *Richard the Lionheart,* 158–60; Gillingham, "Richard I and Berengaria of Navarre," *Bulletin of the Institute of Historical Research* 53 (1980): 157–73.

15. *Böhmer,* 4, 3:51, no. 1191. "Lyenor regina Anglie" appears as a witness to a charter of Henry VI to the bishop and church of Trent.

about Richard's business on Sicily, gives us no indication that Henry VI perceived Richard I to be his enemy, despite his activities with Tancred. After all, the French king had also wintered on Sicily as part of the crusading flotilla rather than as an ally defending Tancred's interests against the German king. Assurances were given to Tancred by Richard, and Philip II's challenge to his marriage with Berengaria was bought off with ten thousand marks. This occurred, however, only after Richard protested that he could not marry Alice, because, he claimed, she had been the mistress of his father and had borne Henry a child. The personal animosity between Richard and Philip II became legendary even before they reached Palestine.

Certainly Henry VI was offended by Richard's agreement with Tancred. Richard had after all broken a pledge not to infringe on the German king's rights when passing through his lands, and Richard surely knew of Henry's claim to the kingdom of Sicily.[16] Richard's riotous capture of Messina and extortion of the Sicilian treasury, not to mention the de facto recognition of Tancred, certainly displeased the Staufer.[17] Yet Henry VI's plans were not affected by Richard's activities on the island, and his meeting with the elderly Eleanor does not suggest a hostile attitude.

In any case Richard's actions cannot be considered an attack on the Staufer. He rather sought his own personal and dynastic goals and typically managed in the process to offend the two leading monarchs of Christendom—Philip II and Henry VI. Richard would continue to offend others throughout the Third Crusade and thus fashion the grounds for his imprisonment and for the extortion of his own wealth. Perhaps Henry VI felt justified, or at least pleased, to hold Richard for a payment from the English king's treasury in response to the plundering of the Sicilian treasury in 1190. But when all is said and done, the "Sicilian Matter" looks much more like an intrafamily squabble than a geopolitical struggle. We

---

16. The *Annales Marbacenses* (61) blame Richard for breaking his promise to Henry VI not to infringe on the Staufer's rights in return for safe passage. Ralph of Coggeshall (*Chronicon Anglicanum,* ed. Joseph Stevenson, RS, no. 66 [London, 1875; reprint 1965], 58–59) includes this as one of the charges that Henry VI leveled against Richard upon his imprisonment.

17. Roger of Howden (*Chronica,* 3:186) says that the Austrians chose to capture Richard and hand him over to Henry VI. Yet it is important to note that Richard successfully defended himself from these charges (ibid., 3:199). Thus these passages indicate not that Richard actually provided Tancred any actual assistance but rather that the settlement reached at Messina was used as a pretext to hold Richard, along with the charge of murdering the marquis of Montferrat.

must remember that Henry VI's claim to Sicily was based on his wife Constance, who was the aunt and legitimate heiress of the deceased King William II and also the aunt of Tancred, while Richard's sister Joanna (daughter of Henry II) was the widow of King William II. Hence Richard's claims against Tancred were no less based on familial rights than Henry VI's and were in no way prejudicial to Henry's claims. Once again the social realities of the medieval political community loom larger than modern expectations for state and empire building.

The fall of Acre in 1191 was the site of Richard's next conflict that concerns us. The Angevin and Capetian monarchs were latecomers to the siege of the city, yet they raised their banners throughout its streets after capitulation, as a sign of their lordship. This did not sit well with those who had done most of the fighting, especially since the banners signaled a claim to the lion's share of the spoils. Duke Leopold V of Austria had been one of these disaffected warriors, and he sought to remedy the situation by hoisting his own banner beside those of the two western monarchs. Leopold V led the small German contingent that pressed on after the death of their emperor Frederick Barbarossa. Barbarossa's son Duke Frederick of Swabia fell at the gates of Acre, but from a fever rather than a sword. Hence Leopold V represented the Germans. Allowing his banner, then, would have admitted his share to the plunder as well as recognizing him as the leader of the Germans. These claims were simply too much to bear and his banner was torn down and destroyed by Richard's soldiers.[18] Richard not only managed to offend the Babenberger duke but continued arguing with Philip II over the plunder. The French king left for home shortly thereafter in disgust.

Richard had created enough personal enemies that when Marquis Conrad of Montferrat was murdered by two assassins of Rashid ed-Din Sinan (the "Old Man of the Mountain") the blame was laid at his feet.[19] The

---

18. Gillingham (*Richard the Lionheart*, 176–77) concludes, "For him to raise his standard in Acre was totally unrealistic." Albert Schreiber ("Drei Beiträge zur Geschichte des deutschen Gefangenschaft des Königs Richard Löwenherz," *Historische Vierteljahrschrift* 26 (1931): 268–74) suggests that Richard also held personal animosity against the Babenberger duke of Austria because there had been disputes between the Babenbergers and Welfs concerning the duchy of Bavaria and Styria in the preceding years. If so we have yet another familial motive for political action.

19. Gillingham, *Richard the Lionheart*, 203–7. German chronicles, especially the Cologne chronicle, show the acceptance of this charge against Richard, as well as the tension between the king and the duke of Austria. See *CRC*, 155–56; *Monumenta Welforum antiqua*, ed. G. Pertz, MGH SS rer. Germ., no. 43 (Hanover, 1869), 55, 58.

rumor of his involvement would become one of the charges leveled against him during his detention at the hands of Henry VI.[20] The marquis of Montferrat, an imperial vassal, had disputes with Richard in Palestine—eventually even causing them to negotiate separately with Saladin. Conrad was elected king of Jerusalem over Richard's candidate Guy de Lusignan (the Poitevin baron whom Richard then installed as king in Cyprus). Conrad's brother Boniface was one of Henry VI's most loyal supporters, therefore his murder caused great anger at the imperial court. Fused with general distrust and contempt for Richard at the imperial court after his episodes in Sicily and Acre, the convenient rumor of his participation in the murder of Conrad provided the pretext for detaining the king on his return home in 1192.

We shall not cover the details of Richard's attempted return from the crusade through Austria and the details of his capture, except to consider why he chose to pass through imperial territory.[21] It seems likely that he had intended to reach Bohemia and thereby travel through territory under the lordship of allies of his kinsman Henry the Lion, eventually reaching eastern Saxony. Thus he would have avoided passing through the lands of Philip II or the count of Toulouse. Unfortunately for Richard, this route necessitated crossing the territory of Duke Leopold V of Austria. It proved to be a most ironic twist as he was captured by the duke's men just outside Vienna and imprisoned in the castle of Dürnstein.[22] This was the ultimate personal revenge for the duke, who employed the age-old aristocratic practice of hostage taking to extort ransom. The origin of Richard's imprisonment in Germany was a *personal* grudge between two crusading knights rather than spy catching between political power blocs.

Richard was eventually sold to Henry VI and lengthy negotiations for his release ensued.[23] We have interest in these negotiations because of a

---

20. Roger of Wendover's *Flores historiarum* (1:225–26) contains a forged letter of the Old Man of the Mountain to Duke Leopold of Austria, in which the old man claims the innocence of Richard concerning the murder of Conrad of Montferrat. The letter also appears in *Rymer*, 1:71.

21. See Schreiber, "Gefangenschaft," 274–82; Gillingham, *Richard the Lionheart,* 217–40; John T. Appleby, *England without Richard, 1189–1199* (London, 1965), 107–69.

22. *Annales Marbacenses,* 63.

23. Roger of Howden (*Chronica,* 3:186–235), who may well have even accompanied Richard on this crusade and if so knew his itinerary personally, has the most complete and reliable account of Richard's imprisonment. For the possibility of Roger of Howden's presence in Richard's entourage see Antonia Gransden, *Historical Writing in England* (Ithaca, 1974), 227. Many of the details are repeated in Ralph of Coggeshall, *Chronicon*

simultaneous development in northern Germany that would have an impact on Richard's fate. In November 1192, as Henry VI was reaching a settlement with the once more rebellious Welfs in Saxony, the bishop-elect of Liège, Albert of Brabant (Louvain), was murdered.[24] In a remarkably similar accusation to that leveled against Richard concerning Conrad of Montferrat's death, rumor spread that Henry VI himself had instigated this murder. By the time that he met Duke Leopold V and the imprisoned Richard at Regensburg in January 1193,[25] a rebellion had emerged, led by the new archbishop of Cologne, Bruno III of Berg,[26] his vassals the duke of Brabant (brother of the murdered bishop) and the duke of Limburg (uncle of the murdered bishop), and other lesser nobles of the area.[27]

By late January 1193 the rebels had been joined by the landgraves of Thuringia and Meißen, King Ottokar of Bohemia, the archbishop of Mainz, and the Saxon Welf and Zähringer families. This revolt was directed as much against the imperial candidate for the bishopric of Liège, Lothar of Hochstaden (prior of Bonn and earlier candidate for the archbishopric of Cologne), as against Henry VI himself; Bruno III was deeply enmeshed therein because of his own dynastic ties to the parties involved.[28] The rebels even planned to dethrone Henry VI and replace him with Duke Henry of Brabant. No doubt the pope would have been willing to support such a move, and the involvement of other European powers in this conflict was assured by the imprisonment of the English king.

For Henry VI the capture of Richard could not have come at a better time, as he faced virtually half of the German princes in open revolt. The

---

Anglicanum, 52–62; *MPCM*, 2:394–98; Ralph de Diceto, *Ymagines historiarum*, 2:106–18; Roger of Wendover, *Flores historiarum*, 1:221–26. Roger of Wendover (op. cit., 1:221–22) tells of Duke Leopold of Austria's sale of Richard to Henry VI for sixty thousand pounds "ad pondus Coloniensium," and Roger of Howden (*Chronica*, 3:194) tells of Henry VI's letter to Philip II recounting the capture of Richard, in which he refers to him as "inimicus imperii nostri, et turbator regni tui, rex Angliae." This letter appears also in *Rymer*, 1:71–72; *Böhmer*, 4, 3:110–11, no. 271; *Die Kaiserurkunden*, 2:436, no. 4790.

24. Raymond H. Schmandt, "The Election and Assassination of Albert of Louvain, Bishop of Liège, 1191–1192," *Speculum* 42 (1967): 639–60.

25. *Böhmer* 4, 3:111, no. 271a (dated January 6, 1193).

26. The short pontificate of Bruno III (1191–93) followed Philip of Heinsberg's.

27. *REK*, 2:289, no. 1440.

28. Lothar of Hochstaden had originally been elected by the Cologne cathedral chapter to succeed Philip of Heinsberg, but he withdrew after threats from Bruno's powerful relatives—Bruno was the son of Count Adolf of Berg and was related to the duke of Brabant and the count of Flanders (*REK*, 2:285, no. 1429). So the conflict with the emperor had direct local implications in Cologne as well as regional implications.

English crusader was not a member of the rebellion (though some have argued so) but rather a means of resolving it.[29] The English king, whose realm had strong economic ties to the lower Rhine region, would serve as a valuable playing card in the following months. The use of Richard in negotiations with the princes, the pope, and the king of France created new possibilities for Henry at just the right time.

With Richard in a most disadvantageous position, an initial agreement for his release was reached at Würzburg on February 14, 1193. Duke Leopold V demanded that Richard work to obtain his release from papal excommunication[30] and that he restore Emperor Isaac of Cyprus and his daughter to their island kingdom. An enormous sum of one hundred thousand marks was to be paid as ransom[31] and Richard was to participate in the projected Sicilian campaign by providing the Staufer fifty galleys and two hundred knights for a year. Finally he was to give two hundred hostages as assurance for full payment.[32] Richard was then handed over to Henry VI on March 21, 1193, at Speyer. We have no evidence of any role played by the Welfs in these early negotiations, but if they participated their involvement was not significant.[33] Archbishop Bruno III of Berg, however, did send his cathedral prior Adolf of Altena (who had also interceded for Archbishop Philip at the Reichstag of Worms in 1187) to negotiate for the rebels with Henry VI in Speyer a week after Richard was handed over by Duke Leopold V.[34]

On April 19 in Hagenau Henry VI and Richard signed a friendship treaty of mutual support in the protection of their respective royal rights. This was of obvious benefit to Henry in the face of the Rhenish rebellion

---

29. Gillingham, *Richard the Lionheart,* 225. Richard was certainly in no position to give material support to this uprising, as he had been on crusade and then imprisoned. The thesis of Richard's supposed complicity in the rebellion is held by Martin Philippson (*Heinrich der Löwe, Herzog von Bayern und Sachsen, und seine Zeit,* 2d ed. [Leipzig, 1918], 498ff.), Karl Hampe ("Heinrich der Löwe," *Herrschergestalten des deutschen Mittelalters,* 7th ed. [Darmstadt, 1979], 194ff.), and Karl Jordan ("Investiturstreit und frühe Stauferzeit," *Gebhardts Handbuch der deutschen Geschichte,* 8th ed. [Stuttgart, 1954], 332). Trautz (*Die Könige,* 85) rejects this view.

30. The pope had excommunicated him for capturing Richard, who was a returning crusader under papal protection.

31. Note that the silver was to be paid "ad pondus Coloniensium" (Roger of Wendover, *Flores historiarum,* 1:221–22).

32. MGH Const., 1:502–4, no. 354; *Böhmer,* 4, 3:114–16; *Die Kaiserurkunden,* 2:438, no. 4800.

33. Ahlers, *Die Welfen,* 160.

34. *REK,* 2:290–91, no. 1445.

and to Richard as well in the face of the current machinations of his brother John and the French king. Henry furthermore agreed that he would release Richard as soon as the first seventy thousand marks were paid and hostages were handed over for the remainder.[35] Nevertheless, the Plantagenet king was still in a vulnerable position as he waited for his ransom to be raised. In May 1193 Philip II of France approached Henry VI seeking to become directly involved in the affair, and the German monarch arranged a meeting for June 25 at Vaucouleurs. The meeting was ostensibly arranged to make peace between the Capetian and Angevin monarchs, yet Richard realized the very real possibility that he could be handed over to a French prison, from whence there might be no return. With Capetian assistance Henry VI could also attack the lower Rhine from two sides and crush the rebels. This was likely a calculated move on the part of the German monarch to force a settlement with the rebels. He had already reached a settlement with Richard, and now he sought to use English connections to the lower Rhine to his favor. Under the circumstances Richard quickly became a diplomat.[36]

The imprisoned king eventually found creative means to move the Rhenish princes to reconciliation with Henry VI.[37] He offered generous financial rewards, as we shall see, and the threat of Capetian involvement provided additional incentive to the rebels. The Staufer eventually made individual settlements with each prince as the coalition fragmented, and a final peace was established at Koblenz in June. With the rebellion at an end Henry VI called off the planned meeting with Philip II; he was certainly pleased with the results of his French ploy. The Welfs, however, were expressly ignored in the Koblenz settlement. They did not submit to Henry VI as the coalition dissolved but rather sought the aid of the king of Denmark in the summer/autumn of the same year.[38] Richard was asked to intervene again in an effort to reconcile the Welfs to Henry VI.

---

35. Roger of Howden (*Chronica*, 3:211) includes a letter from Henry VI to the English magnates concerning this agreement; Henry encouraged them to show loyalty to Richard and assured them of his gratitude. The value of this alliance to Henry VI in regard to the collection of the ransom is obvious here. The letter also appears in *Böhmer*, 4, 3:119, no. 293, *Die Kaiserurkunden*, 2:438–39, no. 4809.

36. Gillingham, *Richard the Lionheart*, 233; Ahlers, *Die Welfen*, 161.

37. Roger of Howden, *Chronica*, 3:214. William of Newburgh's account of these events (*Historia rerum Anglicarum*, ed. Richard Howlett, RS, no. 82, [London, 1844; reprint, 1964] 1:398–99) makes plain the intention of Henry VI to hand Richard over to his French overlord.

38. Ahlers, *Die Welfen*, 162.

As evidence of this new mission, Richard reached a revised settlement with Henry VI and on June 29 the agreement was announced at Worms.[39] Involvement in the Sicilian campaign was commuted to an additional payment of fifty thousand marks of silver, which was due within seven months after Richard's release, and Eleanor of Brittany was to be sent to Austria to marry Duke Leopold V's son. The additional fifty thousand marks of silver could, however, be remitted, "if the lord king should fulfill the promise that he made to the lord emperor concerning Henry, formerly the duke of Saxony."[40]

What was this promise made by Richard in regard to Henry the Lion? Surely it had something to do with peace between the Welf and Henry VI. Yet there may be more behind this than at first meets the eye. It could not have been a promise to refuse aid to the Welfs, since the promise was to be fulfilled before he was released; nor could it have been a promise to get the Welfs to take Richard's place in the Sicilian campaign, since the Welfs could not provide military assistance equivalent to fifty thousand marks of silver. Rather, it was likely the prevention of a marriage between Henry of Brunswick (son of Henry the Lion and nephew of Richard I) and Agnes, daughter of Conrad of Staufen, the half brother of Barbarossa by his second wife, Agnes of Saarbrücken (thus he was the uncle of Henry VI), and count palatine of the Rhine since 1156.[41]

Henry VI wanted Agnes (who had been betrothed to Henry of Brunswick since childhood) to marry Duke Ludwig of Bavaria instead, so that Staufen control of the palatinate would not be lost into the hands of the

---

39. Roger of Howden, *Chronica,* 3:214–15. The charter follows (ibid., 3:215–16). (1) one hundred thousand marks of pure silver "ad pondus Coloniae" were to be delivered, with the king bearing the responsibility of transfer to the borders of the empire; (2) fifty thousand marks were to be paid to the duke of Austria, for which hostages were to be given ("scilicet, domino imperatori pro triginta millibus marcis sexaginta obsides; duci vero Austriae septem obsides pro viginti millibus marcis"); (3) there was to be a marriage between Richard's niece, the daughter of the Duke of Brittany, Eleanor, and a son of the duke of Austria within seven months of Richard's release; (4) there was to be safe conduct for Richard to the borders of the empire (June 25–29, 1193). See also *Rymer,* 1:84–85; *Böhmer,* 4, 3:123–25; MGH Const., 1:504–5, no. 355; *Die Kaiserurkunden,* 2:440, no. 4822.

40. Roger of Howden, *Chronica,* 3:216: "Si autem dominus rex solverit promissionem, quam domino imperatori de Henrico quondam duce Saxoniae fecerat."

41. Schreiber, "Gefangenschaft," 287–89. Ahlers (*Die Welfen,* 163) follows Schreiber's view. For Conrad's role in the Staufen family see H. Werle, "Staufische Hausmachtpolitik am Rhein im 12. Jahrhundert," *Zeitschrift für die Geschichte des Oberrheins* 110 (1962): 299–321.

Welfs. Philip II of France, who apparently knew of this dilemma facing Henry VI, had even sought the hand of Agnes in August 1193 as part of his intrigue against Richard. Agnes refused to marry the French king and secretly went through with the marriage to Henry of Brunswick.[42] The fifty thousand marks of silver were never remitted, which likely signaled Richard's failure to prevent this marriage between a branch of the Staufen house and his Welf nephew Henry of Brunswick. At any rate he failed to reconcile the Welfs and Henry VI and so was obliged to pay the full balance of the ransom. We should note here two crucial things. Firstly, Richard's mediation failed to reconcile the Welfs to the Staufen monarch, even though the English king was capable of reconciling the other German princes. This hardly bespeaks of Richard's anti-Staufen agenda taken as a whole. Secondly and more importantly, a Welf-Staufen dynastic union was the net result of failing to reconcile Henry VI to the Welfs! Such an apparently contradictory mixture of dynastic and diplomatic activity is surely a reminder to us that modern conceptions of politics do not fit medieval practices. It tells us that familial and dynastic goals drove medieval political and diplomatic activity more than did state diplomacy and institutionalized power structures as modernly conceived. Once again the social aspects of medieval politics get us closer to the center of the actual history than modern institutional categories allow.

After the largest portion of the enormous ransom had been delivered, Henry VI announced shortly before Christmas 1193 that Richard would be released on January 17, 1194.[43] This disturbed both Philip II and John, who then began to agitate again at the imperial court. In January they offered the German monarch 150,000 marks for Richard (the equivalent of the ransom) or 100,000 marks if he were at least detained until the autumn and 1,000 pounds for every month of additional detention.[44] In the face of these temptations, Henry VI learned of the secret marriage between Henry of Brunswick and the Staufer Agnes in mid-January, just days before Richard's release. It could have been that Richard was unprepared to come up with the additional fifty thousand marks needed as a

---

42. Roger of Howden, *Chronica*, 3:224–25; Ralph de Diceto, *Ymagines historiarum*, 2:113: "Circa dies istos Henricus, Henrici ducis Saxonici primogenitus, nepos Ricardi regis Anglorum, filiam unicam et haeredem Conradi palatini comitis duxit uxorem."
43. Roger of Howden, *Chronica*, 3:227 (Gelnhausen, December 20, 1193). It also appears in *Rymer*, 1:84; *Böhmer*, 4, 3:133–34, no. 328; *Die Kaiserurkunden*, 2:440, no. 4843.
44. Roger of Howden, *Chronica*, 3:229 (Mainz, February 2, 1194).

result of the marriage, and so his release was delayed. The younger sons of Henry the Lion, Otto and William (who both had grown up at the English court), were used as hostages, which might hint at Henry VI's distrust of the Welf after the secret marriage.[45] Alternatively it may have been simply that Henry was drawn to the French offer and delayed Richard's release pending an assembly at Mainz on February 2.[46]

The French offer was declared before the English and German nobles at Mainz, where Henry VI sought consideration of the matter. Yet two elements persuaded the German king to release Richard after two days of negotiations. First and foremost, the German princes, primarily those from the lower Rhine, including the archbishop of Cologne, had already stood as surety for the Worms agreement, and they pressured him into keeping the promise of Richard's release.[47] Second, Richard made an additional concession. At the suggestion of his mother, Eleanor, who had come to receive him, he offered to hold England as a fief of the emperor and pay Henry VI five thousand pounds a year as a vassal.[48] Henry finally relented under these face-saving conditions.

Richard's offer of feudal services for England corresponded well to the wishes of Henry VI, who had earlier promised to make Richard king of Arles (Burgundy)—a territory over which he actually had little real control.[49] Such a feudal arrangement would raise the prestige of the emperor and assure his influence in western European affairs. One wonders what the message might have been to the Capetian Philip II, who was Richard's feudal lord as well. In any case, such an act would allow Richard to go free. Thus both sides saw a benefit in this offer. No such obligation, however,

45. Victor Röhrich (*Adolf I. Erzbischof von Köln. I. Teil: Adolf als Reichsfürst* [Ph.D. diss., Könisberg, 1886]) believed that Henry VII's anger over the secret marriage delayed Richard's release.

46. Ahlers, *Die Welfen*, 164–65.

47. Roger of Howden, *Chronica*, 3:213–33. The Robert de Nunant mentioned here was the same man who had delivered John's bribe to Henry VI for keeping Richard imprisoned. Thus there were forces working against Richard at this very meeting, but the German princes prevailed. The justiciar Walter of Rouen wrote a letter to Ralph de Diceto (*Ymagines historiarum*, 2:112–13) that indicates the key role of the archbishop of Cologne in these negotiations.

48. Roger of Howden, *Chronica*, 3:202–3. There is no evidence that Richard ever paid this yearly sum.

49. Ibid., 3:225–26. Richard's sending for his mother and others is a sign that he expected to be set free soon. This grant also appears in *Böhmer*, 4, 3:134, no. 329. In both of these propositions, Henry VI was attempting to place a feudal dependence on Richard. For more on the plans for the kingdom of the Arelate see Trautz, *Die Könige*, 87.

was recognized by Richard after his release. Indeed he was recrowned to wash away the stain of his imprisonment and vassalage to the German monarch, and there is no subsequent history of imperial claims to feudal authority over England.[50] Hence what seemed to be a major event resulted in no real consequences.[51] Roger of Howden even declared that Henry released Richard from these obligations on his deathbed.[52]

It may appear that Richard had been taken advantage of in this new feudal relationship, yet looks are deceiving. On the same day of his release, February 4, Henry VI and the German princes issued a proclamation ordering Philip II and John to give back to Richard all the territories taken during his imprisonment and declared their support in Richard's efforts to regain his possessions. The impetus behind this was Richard's own procurement of vassals from among the German princes.[53]

Through liberal promises of money fiefs he was able to gain the vassalage of the archbishops of Cologne and Mainz; the bishop-elect of Liège; the dukes of Austria, Brabant (Louvain), Limburg, and Swabia (Henry VI's own brother); the marquis of Montferrat; the count palatine of the Rhine (another Staufer); the count of Holland, and the son of the count of Hainault, "salva fidelitate imperatoris." The Salzburg chronicle makes it clear that this was done with the approval of Henry VI, and the Burton annals state that the focus of this coalition was "contra regem Franciae." There can be no doubt that these were the princes with whom Richard had developed diplomatic ties during his imprisonment negotiations. Certainly the duke of Austria and the marquis of Montferrat are included in this list because their money fiefs were a means of satisfying claims against Richard.[54] Furthermore, payments to the duke of Swabia, the

---

50. Gervase of Canterbury, *Chronicle,* 1:524f.; Ralph of Coggeshall, *Chronicon Anglicanum,* 64. Cf. Appleby, *England without Richard,* 134–36.

51. Henry VI is said to have sent Richard a golden crown in July 1195 and to have commanded him to attack France, with the promise of imperial support. Cf. Kienast, "Die Deutschen Fürsten," 10:132–33; *Böhmer,* 4, 3:187, no. 461; *Die Kaiserurkunden,* 2:452, no. 4952.

52. For more on Richard's vassalage to Henry VI see Trautz, *Die Könige,* 87–89. Trautz concludes that the arrangement applied only to Richard personally and was not binding on his successors.

53. Roger of Howden, *Chronica,* 3:233–34; *Annales de Burtonensis,* ed. Henry Richards Luard, RS, no. 36 (London, 1864; reprint, 1965), 1:190–91; *Annalium Salisburgensium additamentum,* ed. W. Wattenbach, MGH SS, no. 13 (Hanover, 1881; reprint, 1985), 240.

54. Pope Celestine III sought to force the duke of Austria to pay back the money he received from Richard's ransom. On June 6, 1194, the pope ordered the bishop of Verona to

count palatine of the Rhine, and the archbishop of Mainz were made as a reward for their assistance in getting the English king released. Geographically speaking these five southern princes were not as affected by Angevin-Capetian conflicts as were their Lotharingian counterparts, so they were of little value against France. Since two of these three princes were directly related to Henry VI and since all German princes reserved their liege homage for the emperor, it is clear that their "alliance" with Richard was not directed against Henry VI.

The remainder of the new vassals are our principal interest here, as they all come from the lower Rhine region and were members of the uprising against Henry VI. As A. L. Poole has deftly shown, it was Richard himself who had interceded with these princes and managed a reconciliation with Henry; thus their payments probably reflect a promise on his part to reward them for making peace with their king and assisting in Richard's release from captivity. The English king, however, had smartly parlayed this arrangement of the rebellion into a coalition scheme against Capetian France. Richard is seldom given credit as a diplomat, yet this was a masterstroke that altered the Angevin-Capetian equation decisively in his favor. Perhaps concern over Capetian encroachment into the region allowed Henry VI's consent,[55] yet the arrangement would backfire on the Staufen house. It soon served as the foundation for the Welf kingship of Richard's nephew Otto. In any case we can surely say that Richard, although a hostage, was crafty enough to prevent himself from becoming a mere pawn in Henry VI's chess game.

---

have Leopold take an oath to do this (*Rymer*, 1:88). And in 1198 Innocent III wrote to the son of Leopold ordering him to return the money (*Rymer*, 1:102). The pope also wrote to the archbishop of Magdeburg ordering him to induce the duke of Swabia to do likewise (*Rymer*, 1:102–3). Roger of Wendover (*Flores historiarum*, 1:236–39) and Matthew Paris (*MPHA*, 2:52–54) both tell of Duke Leopold's excommunication and the placing of his lands under interdict. They then present the duke's fall from a horse and subsequent death from gangrene in gruesome detail as a just judgment from God for his treatment of Richard. Matthew Paris (2:58) reports that after seeing what befell the duke, Henry VI feared divine punishment for Richard's imprisonment. He then supposedly gave the ransom money to the Cistercians, an ironic twist since a year's worth of wool production, along with gold and silver plate, had been taken from the English Cistercians to pay Richard's ransom. This passage reflects Matthew's own monastic attitudes rather than the actual events.

55. Kienast, "Die Deutschen Fürsten," 10:136. A. L. Poole ("Richard the First's Alliances with the German Princes in 1194," in *Studies in Medieval History Presented to F. M. Powicke*, ed. R. W. Hunt, W. A. Pantin, and R. W. Southern [Oxford, 1948], 92) argues that Henry VI also wanted good relations between Richard and the princes of lower Lotharingia so that the ransom could be safely brought from England through these lands.

Simon, the sixteen-year-old bishop-elect of Liège and son of Duke Henry III of Limburg, was not destined to play a role in this coalition scheme. He was removed from office by Pope Celestine III in November 1194 and, remarkably, made a cardinal instead. Baldwin, the son of Count Baldwin V of Hainault and Flanders, initially followed his father's lead and sided with the Capetians upon his inheritance of the counties, but by 1197 he returned to the Angevin camp as a result of economic pressure.[56] After this point he received payments from his English fief.[57] Duke Henry of Limburg was always on good terms with the Angevin king and duly received his fief from Richard. Duke Henry I of Brabant eventually received the Honor of Eye in Suffolk by virtue of his marriage to its heiress, Matilda.[58] He, however, did not obtain legal claim to it until Easter 1198, just before his wife had betrothed their daughter Maria to the Welf Otto IV at his royal coronation.[59] Count Dietrich VII of Holland does not appear in the English accounts, yet he was present at Otto IV's coronation.[60]

The archbishop of Cologne received his pension immediately from the manors of Soham in Cambridgeshire and Brampton in Huntingdonshire. The rent of fifty-eight pounds a year appears consistently in the Pipe Rolls from 1194 to Easter 1200.[61] It was received on behalf of the archbishop often by his butler Adam and by a certain Lambert of Cologne and occasionally by the envoy Gilbert de Carenci. Lambert himself also received a yearly pension, no doubt in reward for his diplomatic service in the name of the archbishop. With some supplemental payments the total received by the archbishop and Lambert for these years was just over £434.

Richard's investment in the archbishop of Cologne proved worthwhile

---

56. Poole, "Alliances," 95–97.

57. Ibid., 93.

58. Giselbert of Mons, *Chronicon Hanoniense*, ed. G. Pertz, MGH SS rer. Germ., no. 29 (Hanover, 1869), 250–51.

59. Duke Henry was on crusade at the time. Afterward the duke included the Honor of Eye among his titles, "Henricus dei gratia dux Lotharingie marchio Romani imperii et dominus honoris Eye." Cf. Poole, "Alliances," 94–95.

60. Poole, "Alliances," 97.

61. *Pipe Roll 6 Richard I*, PR, NS, 5:76; *Pipe Roll 7 Richard I*, PR, NS, 6:119; *Pipe Roll 8 Richard I*, PR, NS, 7:19, 275; *Pipe Roll 9 Richard I*, PR, NS, 8:77 and 167; *Pipe Roll 10 Richard I*, PR, NS, 9:161; *Pipe Roll I John*, PR, NS, 10:153; *Pipe Roll 2 John*, PR, NS, 12:163; *Pipe Roll 3 John*, PR, NS, 14:120. The payments cease after this last one of Easter 1200, most likely as a result of the treaty of Le Goulet, in which John promised Philip II not to give support to Otto IV. His pension was revived in 1209 when John sought closer relations with Otto IV: see *Pipe Roll 9 John*, PR, NS, 22:105.

very early on. The cathedral prior Adolf,[62] son of Count Everhard of Altena, succeeded his uncle Bruno III of Berg as archbishop in the autumn of 1193. He was already well versed in negotiations, having interceded on behalf of the rebellious Philip of Heinsberg at the Reichstag of Worms in 1187 and having also been sent by his archiepiscopal uncle, Archbishop Bruno III, to negotiate with Henry VI at Speyer concerning the Rhenish rebellion. This latter embassy was sent only a week after Richard was handed over to the German monarch by Duke Leopold V. Adolf then knew well the negotiations that had transpired with Richard during the summer of 1193, and he stood with the other princes as guarantor *(fideiussor)* for the agreement reached then.

On January 6 he received Queen Eleanor and the English justiciar, Archbishop Walter of Rouen, in Cologne, where they remained and celebrated the Feast of the Epiphany together.[63] The queen mother and justiciar had been summoned by Richard in order to receive him upon his planned release on January 17.[64] Then came the offer of additional money from Philip II and John, which necessitated the Mainz conference on February 2–4. Here the German princes prevailed and enforced the agreement allowing Richard's release. In his letter to Ralph de Diceto the archbishop of Rouen writes that the influential figures among the German princes at Mainz were the archbishops of Mainz and Cologne.[65] It was these two archbishops who freed Richard into the hands of his mother as if, according to Roger of Howden, the Lord had freed him from Egyptian captivity.[66]

Upon his release Richard was accompanied by Archbishop-elect Adolf of Altena to Antwerp. En route Adolf prevailed on the king to sojourn in his episcopal city for three days.[67] Richard was sumptuously entertained

---

62. He was elected cathedral deacon in March 1183 and followed his uncle Bruno III as cathedral prior when the latter was elected archbishop in 1191. He had also gone to Rome in 1181 along with the abbot of Siegburg to get permission to raise the bones of Archbishop Anno II: see *REK*, 2:293–94, no. 1459.

63. Ralph de Diceto, *Ymagines historiarum*, 2:112; *REK*, 2:294–95, no. 1466.

64. Eleanor had been active in seeking Richard's release. She had written at least three letters to the pope pleading for him to intercede and obtain her son's freedom: see *Rymer*, 1:72–78.

65. Ralph de Diceto, *Ymagines historiarum*, 2:112; *Böhmer*, 4, 3:135–36, no. 332a.

66. Roger of Howden, *Chronica*, 3:233.

67. Ibid, 3:234–35: "Et est sciendum, quod rex Anglie fuit in captione imperatoris per spatium unius anni, et sex hebdomadarum, et trium dierum. Liberato autem rege, omnes qui aderant prae gaudio lacrymati sunt. Deinde imperator tradidit regi salvum conductum, usque ad portum de Amvers [Antwerp]. Cumque rex Coloniam venisset, archiepiscopus

in Cologne and stayed in the archiepiscopal palace.[68] On the third day Adolf had arranged for Richard to hear Mass in the cathedral, and he added an ingenious twist to the liturgy for the occasion. Rather than using the normal introit for that Sunday, Adolf had the precentor use the introit for August 1—that is, for the Feast of St. Peter in Chains. The introit came from the Book of Acts 12:11.

Now I am sure that the Lord has sent his angel and rescued me from the hand of Herod and from all the Jewish people were expecting.[69]

The archbishop-elect of Cologne had certainly placed himself in a flattering light, appearing now as the angel of the Lord who had rescued Richard from the hand of Herod! This reminder of the archbishop's central role in Richard's release did not go unnoticed. On February 16, while stopping in Louvain along the return journey home, the English king granted a valuable privilege to the merchants of Cologne.[70] They were freed from all tolls, particularly that paid for their guildhall in London, and they were given freedom to come and go throughout England. Here we see the strong commercial current that underlies much of these negotiations.[71] That Richard's ransom was paid *ad pondus Coloniae* says much about the strength of Cologne as an economic center and its trading ties to England.

Coloniae recepit eum cum gaudio; et pro exultatione liberationis illius celebravit Missam in hunc modum: 'Nunc scio vere quia misit Dominus angelum suum, et eripuit me de manu Herodis, et de exspectatione plebis Judaeorum,' etc. Et cum rex inde recederet, praedictus archiepiscopus conduxit eum usque ad portum de Amvers, ubi Renus fluvius cadit in mare." See also Ralph de Diceto, *Ymagines historiarum*, 2:114; *REK*, 2:295, no. 1471.

68. Richard attended to his own personal affairs as well during this stay in Cologne, as a charter dated February 12, 1194, indicates: see *The Cartae Antiquae Rolls 11–20*, ed. J. Conway Davies, PR, NS, 33:141, no. 534 (Feb. 12, 1194). The witness list shows that Richard had a full complement of chancery and other administrative functionaries in his party even at this time.

69. Adolf did not read this text himself or perform the ceremony, as he was not ordained a priest until March 26, 1194. He was consecrated as archbishop the following day, in the presence of Archbishop Conrad of Mainz and Bishop Thietmar of Minden, by Bishop Hermann of Münster: see *REK*, 2:297, nos. 1476–77.

70. *REK*, 2:296, no. 1472; Johann Martin Lappenberg, *Urkundliche Geschichte des Hansischen Stahlhofes zu London* (Hamburg, 1851; reprint, Osnabrück, 1967), 5, no. 5; *Ennen/Eckertz*, 1:605, no. 109; *UGN*, 1:378–79, no. 542; *HUB*, 1:22, no. 40; Bruno Kuske, *Quellen zur Geschichte des Kölner Handels und Verkehrs im Mittelalter*, PGRG, no. 33 (Bonn, 1917–34), 1:3, no. 7.

71. Kienast, "Die Deutschen Fürsten," 10:142.

Before we close the chapter on Richard's crusading exploits and the German nobility we must include the role of Savaric, bishop of Bath, in the negotiations for Richard's release, since he held a unique position in regard to Anglo-German relations. He appears in a curious letter of Henry VI to the prior and chapter of Canterbury in November/December 1191, while Richard was on crusade.[72] The German monarch asks the chapter to elect as the archbishop someone who was satisfactory to him and states that his relative, "our beloved relative and most devoted archdeacon of your church," would convey to the chapter his wishes.

At this time Savaric was the archdeacon of Northampton, and he was related both to the emperor and to Reginald Fitz Jocelin de Bohun, the current bishop of Bath. Savaric had originally been made treasurer of Salisbury by Jocelin de Bohun before 1184 and then acquired the archdeaconry, hence he was clearly in the de Bohun *familia*. In 1186 his income from this prebend was sequestered because of his debts. He had gone to see Richard on some business while the king was wintering in Sicily and in reward received a royal letter that decreed that he enjoyed Richard's consent for election to any bishopric that might be available.[73] Planning ahead, he forwarded the letter to his kinsman Bishop Reginald and went to Rome to gain papal support. When he had heard of the vacancy at Canterbury, the enterprising young cleric devised a plan that would advance both himself and his kinsman: Reginald should be elected archbishop and Savaric would then take Reginald's place at Bath. As a result of his further machinations both the emperor and the king of France wrote letters of support for this idea. We have the reason, then, for Henry VI's letter to the monks of Canterbury. Philip II advised the monks to elect Reginald, whom Savaric had recommended, as he was a wise man and beloved by Philip's father, Louis VII.[74]

In an election disputed by the bishops who had supported Archbishop Walter of Rouen, the monks of Canterbury chose Reginald, and he proceeded to settle affairs in Bath. After Reginald presented the chapter of Bath with the royal letter of consent for Savaric's election

---

72. *Böhmer*, 4, 3:79, no. 192: "dilectus consanguineus noster et ecclesiae vestre devotissimus Savaricus archdiaconus."

73. Appleby, *England without Richard*, 95–98. For the details on Savaric's career see *Chronicles and Memorials of the Reign of Richard I*, ed. William Stubbs, RS, no. 38 (London, 1864–65), 2:lxxxvii–lxxxviii.

74. *Epistolae Cantuarienses*, ed. William Stubbs, RS, no. 38 (London, 1864–65), 2:350–51.

and recommended him, the convent duly elected his cousin as his successor. The archbishop-elect was not to enjoy his new pontificate, as he died on December 27 while on the way to Canterbury. Yet Savaric had succeeded and was now the bishop of Bath and Wells.[75]

No doubt Savaric's kinship ties with Henry VI were the reason for his immediate involvement in the negotiations for Richard's release; he claimed to be a cousin of Henry VI, which was perhaps possible through his mother, Estrangia. He was consecrated bishop in Rome on September 19, 1192, and went directly thereafter to the imperial court. Archbishop Walter of Rouen's letter to Bishop Hugh of Durham informs us that Savaric was busy treating with the emperor for a settlement.[76] Savaric was still present when the meeting at Mainz was held on February 2–4.[77] When Richard was finally released, Savaric remained behind as a hostage for the balance of the ransom, along with Archbishop Walter of Rouen (who had disputed Reginald's election in 1191) and the two sons of Henry the Lion, Otto and William, among others. Archbishop Walter was released after ten thousand marks were paid, and he reached London on May 9, 1194. Savaric may have been released without payment, by virtue of his kinship to the emperor.[78] During his time with Richard in Germany Savaric received two royal letters recommending him for the see of Canterbury; however, his next office was given to him by Henry VI. After his release as a hostage he remained behind in Germany, becoming the chancellor of Burgundy in 1196. He only returned to England after the death of the German monarch, passing his remaining days with the monks of Glastonbury, and he finally died in 1205. Bishop Savaric of Bath, a man well placed, with ties between Germany and England, played an integral role in the negotiations for Richard's release and led an amazing career, with contacts throughout Europe. He is yet another example of the fascinating connections that existed between the two regions during this era. He is surely evidence that Germany was in many ways integrated into the world of western Europe during the Central Middle Ages.

---

75. *MPCM*, 2:395.

76. Roger of Howden, *Chronica*, 3:196–97. In this letter Walter exhorts Bishop Hugh to take part in the upcoming Great Council at Oxford on February 28, 1193. Therefore Savaric had gone to Henry VI sometime between mid-September 1192 and early 1193.

77. Roger of Howden, *Chronica*, 3:231–33; Ralph de Diceto, *Ymagines historiarum*, 2:112–13.

78. *Pipe Roll 7 Richard I*, PR, NS, 6:xvi.

When all was said and done, Richard had benefited more from the intercession of such clergymen as Savaric and Adolf of Cologne than from that of his Welf kinsmen. Indeed traditional ties to the archbishop of Cologne paid more dividends. Once Tancred died on February 20, 1194, Henry VI's attention once again shifted toward Sicily. He quickly concluded another peace with Henry the Lion through the mediation of Count Palatine Conrad of Staufen, whose daughter had married the Welf's son and namesake. By May Henry the Lion was received once again into Henry VI's grace, and his son Henry promised participation in the upcoming Sicilian campaign. Henry the Lion returned to Brunswick and died on August 6, 1195. Welf-Staufen animosity seemed finally at an end, his son Henry being assured of the Count Palatinate of the Rhine. Yet it would reemerge from, of all places, the new count of Poitou. Henry the Lion's son Otto, whose very name expressed Welf aspirations of reviving the Saxon power of the Ottonians,[79] would in time build his German kingship on the foundation of Richard's alliances with the lower Rhenish princes. Now we can finally say that an English king stirred conflict between the Welf and Staufen dynasties, yet it was done to further Richard's regional interests against the Capetian monarch Philip II rather than to achieve an anti-Staufen strike in Germany. We shall soon see just how successful Richard's alliance system of money fiefs proved to be, both in France and Germany.

This chapter in the history of medieval kingship, remarkable because Richard was the most itinerant king of his age, provides us with more than legendary exploits. We see some customary dimensions of medieval political activity and also discover important signs of a changing society. Richard's capture and detention was not a political kidnapping in terms of the seizing of a head of state but rather an act of traditional aristocratic behavior, that is, the taking of hostages to extract pecuniary recompense and ritual retribution. Such ransom demands do not reflect threats to the institutional integrity or development of a state (Richard's realm survived quite nicely during his constant absences) but rather are a part of chivalrous military behavior. Surely Henry VI harbored no intentions of eliminating or torturing Richard; by all accounts Richard was treated very well. Operating here was the traditional chivalric method of settling a feud between parties: use of a social means of conflict resolution rather than political

---

79. For the implications of Otto's royal name see Hucker, *Kaiser Otto IV.*, MGH Schriften, no. 34 (Hanover, 1990), 4–8.

terrorism. Richard was a knight errant, not an anti-Staufen conspirator. He had transgressed both the duke of Austria and the imperial court by his actions while crusading, and he was called to redeem these transgressions when the remarkable occasion to do so presented itself.

Signs of a changing society also appear in Richard's options while incarcerated. He did a remarkable job of negotiating himself out of a difficult situation, but the means with which he negotiated are evidence of the changes. Richard benefited from the rapid growth of trade between England and the Rhineland, with its principal center none other than the city of Cologne. This commerce not only contributed to the enormous wealth extracted from England for his ransom but also gave him negotiating leverage with the Rhenish princes. Drawing from the vast wealth of his kingdom, he not only paid a "king's ransom" but also had enough resources to institute the innovative strategy of money fiefs among the German princes. In some cases land fiefs were given in return for promised vassalage, but the majority of his support was bought with the money income derived from estates. Hence growing economic cooperation between the regions enabled closer diplomatic cooperation.

In this regard Richard was more than an errant knight; he was a remarkably creative diplomat who forged a profoundly new medium for social relationships with German nobles. Traditional forms of social ties, such as marriage unions, operated only within narrow dynastic circles, but the liberal use of money enabled the king to spread his influence far and wide, for now kings had more money than daughters. Since German princes went deeply in debt during the thirteenth century the appeal of money fiefs proved irresistible.[80] Richard had therefore, as a result of the growing money economy of Europe, put Anglo-German diplomatic relations on an entirely new basis for the remainder of the period under study here.[81] Money became the basis for feudal loyalty, and just as it transformed traditional feudal relationships within kingdoms on a local and regional level during this era (the so-called bastard feudalism),[82] so too it transformed interregional personal relationships. From this point onward English kings would employ money to cement social and diplomatic

---

80. Keller, *Zwischen regionaler Begrenzung und universalem Horizont*, 435.

81. Bryce D. Lyon, "The Money Fief under the English Kings, 1066–1485," *EHR* 66 (1951): 161–93.

82. For recent scholarship on bastard feudalism see Michael A. Hicks, *Bastard Feudalism* (London, 1995); John G. Bellamy, *Bastard Feudalism and the Law* (London, 1989).

relations between the Anglo-German political communities. We shall see in the coming chapters the results of this new sort of diplomacy.

The growth of interregional activity and cooperation between the lower Rhineland and England had another dimension beyond the political activities surrounding Richard's imprisonment. Heeding the call to the Third Crusade, a combined flotilla of crusaders from both regions once again followed the pattern of the Second Crusade (1147) and passed through the port of Dartmouth in 1189.[83] These crusaders also paused in Portugal, made pilgrimage to Santiago de Compostella, and entered into temporary service under the Portuguese king (Sancho I). The crusading Cologne burghers, however, who were in the minority this time, seemed to be more interested in commercial activity, and they returned to their city ladened with costly cloth and other items without ever reaching the Holy Land.[84] Here too we see the growing money economy of Europe during the Central Middle Ages, providing in this case as much zeal as had the traditional crusading ideal. The Third Crusade in many ways exhibited the cooperation and interaction that became characteristic between the lower Rhine region and England in this period. Such activity would intensify on the political scene during the civil war between the Welf Otto IV and his Staufen opponents. Once again Cologne was at the center of it all.

The High Point of Anglo-Cologne Relations: The Election of Otto IV as King of Germany

All of the dynamics that led to a close relationship between Cologne and England converged in the years 1198–1216 with a political and diplomatic focus on the person of Otto of Brunswick-Poitou, the second son of Henry the Lion. When the duke had returned from exile to Saxony he left his two youngest sons, Otto and William (who had been born in England), at the English court to be raised. The Pipe Rolls are filled with entries for the expenses of these children, including everything from tutors to the purchase of a horse.[85] The level of Otto's and William's

83. Kurth, "Der Anteil Niederdeutscher Kreuzfahrer," 171–72. See also Runciman, *A History of the Crusades*, 3:9, 26, and Tyerman, *England and the Crusades*, 66.

84. Kurth, "Der Anteil Niederdeutscher Kreuzfahrer," 175.

85. Only two of many such examples are *Pipe Roll 2 Richard I,* PR, NS, 1:26; *Pipe Roll 3–4 Richard I,* PR, NS, 2:112.

integration into Angevin culture and society is revealed by the fact that William is referred to as "Willelmus Anglicus" and by the fact that both spoke French as easily as German.[86]

As noted earlier, Otto and William had also served as hostages for the balance of Richard's ransom. Henry VI remained distrustful of Henry the Lion while in peace negotiations with the duke, yet he wished to be free from the Welf problem in order to pursue a Sicilian campaign. He therefore used the two sons as leverage during the negotiations, refusing the request of other English hostages that he take Otto with him on the Sicilian expedition, and even delaying the return of William from his captivity at the court of Duke Leopold V.[87] Henry VI did, however, ease Otto's confinement by granting him three servants.[88]

By May 1194, the German monarch had made peace with Henry the Lion, whose son Henry of Brunswick had promised to join the Sicilian campaign in return for imperial confirmation of his inheritance, by marriage, of the count palatinate of the Rhine. In fact the Welf patriarch was present along with Archbishop Adolf of Cologne and Count Baldwin of Hainault at Strasbourg, where Henry VI enfeoffed the count of Hainault's son and namesake with the imperial fiefs of Flanders.[89] Otto and William were presumably released around this time.

Otto, however, did not return to Saxony with his brother William, even though his father had died on August 6.[90] He can be found at his

---

86. *Pipe Roll 32 Henry II*, PR, NS, 36:49. Trautz (*Die Könige*, 93) says of Otto's cultural orientation: "No other German lord was so bound to the English kingdom according to his heritage and youth as Otto IV. We must add to this of course that Richard Lionheart in many respects was 'the least English of all the kings of England'; for he spent the greatest part of his life on the continent. And during his years in foreign lands Otto sojourned much longer on French than on English land. Of course he continued here as well as there in the realm of French court and aristocratic culture. As a young man Otto IV certainly spoke just as fluently and with the same preference for French as Henry VII, Charles IV, and Charles V after him." Hucker (*Kaiser Otto IV.*, 19–21) cites evidence that Otto shared his uncle Richard the Lionheart's love for troubadour songs and literature.

87. Ahlers, *Die Welfen*, 169.

88. This letter comes from Ralph de Diceto, *Ymagines historiarum*, 2:118. Cf. *Böhmer*, 4, 3:137, no. 337, and 5, 1:52, no. 185g; *Die Kaiserurkunden*, 2:442–43, no. 4850; Ahlers, *Die Welfen*, 169.

89. *REK*, 2:302, no. 1497.

90. *Chronicon Sancti Michaelis Luneburgensis*, ed. G. Pertz, MGH SS, no. 23 (Hanover, 1874; reprint, 1986), 397. Matilda was known for her piety, in fact she had just given an altar in honor of the Virgin to the church of St. Blasius and endowed the church with land at Deersheim shortly before her death in 1189: see *Die Urkunden Heinrichs des Löwen*, 178–79, no. 121.

uncle's court at Chinon on December 12, where he witnessed a royal charter to the knight Alan Basset.[91] What better evidence is there for showing how integrated Otto had become in the Angevin kingdom? Even before Richard had left for Palestine he granted the county of Yorkshire to his favorite nephew;[92] there was a dispute among the vassals in Yorkshire over this grant, however, and therefore Richard decided to grant Otto the county of Poitou instead in 1196.[93] While Richard and Otto spent Christmas 1194 in Poitou, efforts were underway to arrange a marriage between Otto and Margaret, the only daughter and heir of William the Lion, king of Scotland.[94] William had no son, and when he became seriously ill earlier in the year, he proposed the marriage between Otto and Margaret. His own barons opposed the marriage, however, being unwilling to allow the royal succession to pass through a woman when other male relatives were still living, and William postponed the plans indefinitely. Richard did not wish to lose such an opportunity and in December he sent Hubert Walter (archbishop of Canterbury and justiciar) to the Scottish king to renew the negotiations. This may explain why Otto was present at Richard's court during that month.

William eventually agreed to give the district of Lothian to Otto as a dowry for his daughter, and in return Richard offered Northumberland and Westmoreland. This would have made Otto one of the most powerful princes in northern England and would have assured Richard of a trusted ally along the Scottish border. William, however, learned at this point that his wife Ermengard was pregnant, and he refused to finalize the agreement, hoping that the queen would bear a son. Otto was establishing a track record of near misses that would be the hallmark of his political career. After the marriage plan failed Otto returned with Richard to Normandy, and he was knighted and enfeoffed with the county of Poitou sometime in September 1196.[95] The fact that Richard had been

---

91. *Böhmer*, 5, 1:52, no. 185h.

92. Roger of Howden, *Chronica*, 3:86. Evidence for a trip by Otto to Yorkshire in 1191 appears in the following entry: *Pipe Roll 3–4 Richard I*, PR, NS, 2:61.

93. Roger of Howden, *Chronica*, 4:7; Ralph of Coggeshall, *Chronicon Anglicanum*, 70. Despite Roger of Howden's comment, Ahlers (*Die Welfen*, 170 n. 852) believes that Otto received Poitou in addition to Yorkshire and not in exchange for it. Against this view see Sidney Painter, *The Reign of King John* (Baltimore, 1949), 154.

94. Roger of Howden, *Chronica*, 3:298–99, 308; *Böhmer*, 5, 1:51, no. 185k.

95. Francisque Michel, *Histoire des ducs de Normandie et des rois d'Angleterre* (Paris, 1840), 89. Otto appears again among the witnesses to one of Richard's charters issued on February 4, 1196, at Chinon for Durham priory (Landon, *Intinerary of King Richard I*,

the count of Poitou before becoming king shows the affection that he had for his nephew: he had appointed Otto as his successor in Poitou, a move that positioned the Welf as the future duke of Aquitaine.

Meanwhile, cordial relations were maintained between Henry VI and the English court. The Staufer was consulted in negotiations between Philip II and Richard that resulted in the treaty of Louviers in January 1196.[96] Henry VI had earlier sent a letter to "my dear friend" *[dilecto amico suo]* Archbishop Walter of Rouen (who had been a hostage for Richard), with news of both his conquest of Sicily and Apulia and the birth of his son. It was this son, Frederick II, who would ultimately finish Otto's kingship in Germany.[97]

The remainder of 1196 and the first half of 1197 found Otto in his new county issuing charters and establishing his lordship.[98] By mid-1197 he was back at Richard's court in Normandy, probably to confer with the king about the appointment of new bishops at Poitiers, Limoges, and Périgueux[99] and learning of Richard's plans for renewed warfare with Philip II after obtaining the support of the count of Flanders in late July at Les Andeleys.[100] Otto joined in Richard's subsequent invasion of Auvergne and gained renown for his military prowess. He was again in Normandy by October but returned to Poitou shortly thereafter.[101] Otto was clearly integrated into the Angevin world and appears completely removed from his Saxon ties.[102] Indeed, because of his upbringing at the Angevin court he must have felt more at home in the French-speaking west than in Germany.

---

110), where he is still referred to as the son of the duke of Saxony. Thus Landon (115) places Otto's enfeoffment with Poitou in September 1196. Cf. *Böhmer,* 5, 1:51, no. 1851.

96. The English chancellor and the archbishop of Rheims went to Germany in September of 1195 and returned in November: see Landon, *Itinerary of King Richard I,* 104–5.

97. Ralph de Diceto, *Ymagines historiarum,* 2:125.

98. Ahlers, *Die Welfen,* 174.

99. Ibid., 175.

100. *Diplomatic Documents Preserved in the Public Record Office,* vol. 1, *1107–1272,* ed. Pierre Chaplais (London, 1964), no. 7. Among the witnesses "qui juraverunt in presentia dicti regis Anglie et dicti comitis Flandrie, Bal[de]wini in Normannia," were "Otho comes Pictavie," who appears second on the list behind the royal brother John, and "Hugo de Coloneis." The presence of a Cologne burgher in these negotiations suggests continued contact between the city, its archbishop, and the Angevin king (the archbishop was still receiving his yearly rent from his English fief). This connection would be used again later that year.

101. He appears among the witnesses at Rouen to a royal charter for Archbishop Walter of Rouen dated October 16, 1197: see Landon, *Itinerary of King Richard I,* 123.

102. Ahlers (*Die Welfen,* 187) is right in saying that Otto could even be considered the first foreign king of Germany.

He was a beloved and valued ally of Richard against Philip II and was estranged from his father's homeland.[103] Thoughts of being a German monarch may well have been the furthest thing from Otto's young mind.

The events of the next few months, however, altered Otto's destiny dramatically and had major consequences for the future of the German political community. For Richard attempted to realize a dream of establishing his trusted relative and ally as both the count of Poitou and the monarch of Germany, something every bit as ambitious as the goals of Frederick Barbarossa and Rainald of Dassel in earlier years. Richard's ultimate hope was to apply military pressure to Philip II from territories to the north, west, and east of Capetian crown lands and bottle up his tenacious enemy. Of course, this was not a premeditated geopolitical strategy—little of what Richard did ever was—but rather his response to a remarkable opportunity that came his way as a result of the *Territorialpolitik* of the archbishop of Cologne and the English economic interests of the citizens of Cologne. The attempt to fashion an Anglo-French-German principality for Otto represents the high point of Anglo-Cologne diplomatic relations during the period under study.

In the summer of 1197 Otto's brother Henry, now count palatine of the Rhine, had departed on crusade along with many other German princes, including Archbishop Conrad of Mainz. The Welf prince sailed from Messina on September 1 and headed for Acre. Henry VI's sudden death of typhoid fever in Sicily on September 28 cut short the emperor's plans to join the venture and threw the future of Staufen kingship into serious doubt. The German princes had elected his three-year-old child, Frederick (II), as the German king a year before (in December 1196), but doubts as to the validity of this election persisted.

Adolf of Altena had given his consent to the election of the child Frederick and even taken an oath to this effect before Philip of Swabia, the brother of Henry VI, at Boppard.[104] Yet upon Henry VI's death he initiated new election proceedings that ultimately led to the choice of the Welf Otto of Brunswick-Poitou. Adolf had two momentary advantages: Archbishop Conrad of Mainz was absent on crusade and Philip of Swabia was with the imperial court in Sicily; thus the opportunity presented itself to Adolf, the highest-ranking elector present in Germany, to

---

103. Ibid., 178: "Otto's complete integration in the Angevin lordship domain and his estrangement from his Saxon homeland appeared then definitive."
104. *CRC*, 159; *REK*, 2:308–9, no. 1521.

sanction another election. This move initiated an era in which the archbishops of Cologne became the driving force behind a series of royal elections that involved the English and eventually led to the dissolution of royal power in Germany. We must consider what motivated Adolf to embark on such a venture, in view of its future implications.

The growth of an independent *Territorialpolitik* on the part of the archbishops of Cologne was nothing new by this time. Such a policy reached back at least to Frederick I (1110–31). Frederick had proposed the election of the count of Flanders instead of Lothar of Supplinburg in 1125, so Archbishop Adolf's actions as an electoral prince were not unprecedented. The territorial policies of the archbishops of Cologne were intensified under Philip of Heinsberg, who added tremendous regional power to the see. By 1187 the archbishop held the only double duchy in the empire and the largest feudal contingent next to the emperor. In addition, his cathedral city had developed into the dominant commercial force of the Rhineland region, with strong ties to England. This economic dimension only added to Cologne's independent-minded policy among both the archbishops and the citizenry. By virtue of all this, the archbishop had become the leading political power in lower Germany, and the Cologne burghers had become a force not to be reckoned with lightly. Archbishop Bruno III, the brief successor to Philip of Heinsberg, had also proposed an antiking in the duke of Brabant during the rebellion of 1192–93, which the imprisoned Richard was able to defuse. Adolf, a close confidant of Philip of Heinsberg and nephew of Bruno III, was continuing the policy his predecessors had developed so effectively.[105] There was therefore precedent for the archbishop of Cologne to lead the call for an alternative royal election.

Two other elements are necessary to understand the framework in which Adolf was operating. Firstly, Henry VI's imperium was essentially directed at Sicily, and he gave little attention to the northwestern region of the empire. Thus as Cologne was drawn into the conflicts between the Angevin and Capetian houses by virtue of its regional power, its close economic ties with England, and the growing expansion of Capetian influence in lower Lotharingia, the archbishops could not count on impe-

---

105. Stehkämper ("Adolf von Altena," 16) says of Philip of Heinsberg's legacy: "Yet he left behind for his successors to the ecclesiastical preeminence, territorial superiority, and princely exultation—adorning the prestige claims thoroughly—a real political, military, and economic strength, which was unrivalled among the princes of Germany."

rial support in the region and had to go it alone. In fact they began to consider themselves the responsible territorial authority in the absence of imperial power. The frequent absence of the Staufen kings from Germany only added to the active role exercised by the princes in the administration of the empire.

The second element is tightly wrapped up in the concept of imperial princes *(Reichsfürsten)*. The tradition of elective kingship had been strengthened during the twelfth century through the elections of Lothar (1125), Conrad III (1138), and Frederick Barbarossa (1152), and the electoral princes jealously guarded their prerogative in this area. Indeed the princes considered their imperial prestige best expressed in their electoral rights. The archbishop of Cologne was second in rank behind the archbishop of Mainz in regard to royal elections and possessed the traditional right to crown the king at Aachen. Archbishop Adolf was the leader of princes who perceived a third generation of Staufen kings as an infringement of dynastic kingship at the expense of elective kingship. This was therefore an inheritance struggle—a matter of social order and custom—between the hereditary rights of the princes to elect their kings versus the Staufen dynastic claim to hereditary kingship. We should understand the electoral debate as more of a personal and social conflict than a constitutional one, since both the German princes and the Staufen dynasty considered electoral rights as familial inheritance rather than as an institutional function. These elements then must be taken into consideration when evaluating the motives and actions of Archbishop Adolf in 1197 and beyond.

Henry VI had attempted to obtain the princes' election of his son as early as Christmas 1195, but Adolf had refused.[106] The issue here was over the electoral principle. So much is confirmed by Henry's attempt in the spring of 1196 to circumvent both Adolf's electoral right and also his right to coronation, as Henry turned to Pope Celestine III for the royal anointment of Frederick (II).[107] This was a blatant strike at the customary prerogatives of the archbishop of Cologne and all the German princes as a whole. Henry finally extracted the princes' acceptance of Frederick II at Christmas 1196, with the exception again of Adolf. The archbishop eventually gave his consent at Boppard the following August, doing so only because he had become politically isolated.[108]

---

106. *Annales Marbacenses*, 67.
107. Ibid., 68; Stehkämper, "Adolf von Altena," 25.
108. *CRC*, 159; Stehkämper, "Adolf von Altena," 29.

This then was the background to Adolf's actions upon the death of Henry VI. He only grudgingly gave his consent to Frederick's election and certainly felt that his right to a free election had been undermined. Henry VI's unexpected death, however, changed the situation drastically. There were others who did not want to see the Staufen dynasty's hold on the monarchy continue, and they remembered the precedent for rejecting a minor as king in the election of Frederick Barbarossa. The dangers caused by a minor as king were certainly remembered in the case of Henry IV. In his position Adolf therefore was not particularly anti-Staufen but rather pro-Cologne; he was simply guarding his own territorial interests and electoral prerogatives in repudiating young Frederick.[109]

At Henry VI's death Staufen authority dissolved. Pope Celestine III seized imperial goods and regalian rights in central Italy, the empress Constance drove all Germans out of her Sicilian lands, and the cities and princes of northern Italy took imperial authority for themselves. In addition a movement to replace Frederick as successor to the emperor grew under the leadership of Archbishop Adolf. His earlier troubles with Henry VI and his own independent character, in addition to his territorial power and right to royal election and coronation, made him the natural leader of this rebellion in northern Germany. The absence of the archbishop of Mainz, who traditionally held the right to cast the first vote in royal elections, also left this authority to Adolf by default. He was also motivated by local and regional self-interests as a regional prince.[110] He could not have realized, however, what the consequences of his policy would be for the subsequent political development of Germany, and laying the future fragmentation of royal power in German territories at his feet seems excessive at best and much too modern in outlook at worst. His motives—preserving princely prerogatives and territorial power— are typically medieval and not directed at dismantling the institutional advancement of western monarchy and German national unity.

There soon emerged creative justifications among German princes for the rejection of young Frederick. Some asserted that because he was still unbaptized when they had taken an oath to elect him they were no longer

---

109. Stehkämper, "Adolf von Altena," 34–35.

110. Ibid., 39: "At the same time it would be in no way mistaken [to assert] that territorial interests, English pressures, concern about the commerce of his capital city, excessive desire for power, greed for money, and whatever else could have been the reason, likewise drove the archbishop."

obliged to him. More pragmatic were the claims that he was unable to rule since he was a minor and that many had only elected him because of the pressure of his father.[111] All of these claims countermanded the legal validity of Frederick's election as king. Archbishop Conrad of Mainz had given authority to the archbishops of Cologne and Trier to manage the affairs of the archdiocese of Mainz during his absence on crusade, so Adolf could legally convene an electoral assembly with the cooperation of Archbishop John of Trier.[112] Adolf therefore duly purchased the support of Archbishop John for eight thousand marks; he was so eager to obtain John's backing that he pawned the Cologne cathedral treasury to the archbishop until he could come up with the money![113]

After lining up the support of his vassals among the lower Rhine princes, Adolf called John of Trier, Bishop Conrad of Strasbourg, and other princes to an assembly at Andernach in late 1197.[114] At the same time, a pro-Staufen conference convened at Hagenau under the authority of Philip of Swabia. Duke Bernhard of Saxony, who, like the archbishop of Cologne, had benefited from the dismantling of Henry the Lion's territories in 1190, apparently came to the Andernach meeting fully expecting to be elected.[115] But he took offense at the excessive price asked for his election and turned down the offer, and the meeting came to naught. Adolf was probably not very disappointed at the loss of a Saxon candidate, in view of his territorial holdings in Westphalia. A second election assembly was quickly announced for March 1198 in Cologne, with the lengthy interval intended to allow for further negotiations in search of another candidate.

Adolf's control over events quickly collapsed when Duke Bernhard suddenly joined the Staufen camp, taking with him the valuable east Saxon princes. In fact these Saxon princes eventually managed to get Philip of Swabia to accept the kingship directly (rather than remaining as

---

111. Ibid., 39–40. Concerning the kingship of the unbaptized and the worthiness of a minor for the throne see Fritz Kern, *Kingship and Law in the Middle Ages*, trans. S. B. Chrimes (Oxford, 1939; reprint, Westport, Conn., 1985), 12, 23, 29–30 (originally published in German as *Gottesgnadentum und Widerstandsrecht im frühen Mittelalter* [Leipzig, 1914], 43, 57, 60, 182); Heinrich Mitteis, *Die deutsche Königswahl: Ihre Rechtsgrundlagen bis zur Goldenen Bulle* (Darmstadt, 1977), 36.

112. *REK*, 2:308, no. 1519.

113. *REK*, 2:311, no. 1530.

114. *CRC*, 162–63; *REK*, 2:311, nos. 1531–33.

115. *RNI*, 318, no. 136. This passage comes from a letter of Philip of Swabia, so its details may be questioned for accuracy. But the net result was the same.

the regent for Frederick) and elected him at their own assembly in Thuringia. The tables were quickly turning on the Cologne archbishop. In response Adolf made two new invitations around Christmas 1197, one of which would bring a whole new dynamic to the proceedings and move them in a direction originally unanticipated by the archbishop. He invited Duke Bertold of Zähringen, a bitter enemy of the Staufen, to come to the Cologne assembly as a candidate for election. Adolf also sent an embassy to Rouen and invited King Richard, as a "special member of the empire" *[praecipuum membrum imperii]*, to come and participate in the upcoming election. Adolf admonished the king "in the power of the oath and fealty by which you were bound to the emperor and to the Roman empire" *[in vi sacramenti et fidei, quibus astringebatur imperatori et imperio Romano]* to come and participate; this was a reference to Richard's supposed vassalage status in the empire.[116] The archbishop of Cologne was hoping to gain the support of the Angevin king, who had much influence over the lower Rhenish princes as a result of their oaths of pecuniary vassalage to him after his imprisonment. Their interactions with Richard during the negotiations for his release had formed a bond of cooperation and mutual interests, and the growing economic ties between all parties in the lower Rhineland bound them together as well. Adolf obviously hoped to exploit this network of relationships to recharge his cause, and he hoped that English money might once again bring the Rhenish princes together. His calling of both Berthold of Zähringen and Richard while seeking to placate the pro-Staufen party shows a political dexterity and ingenuity reminiscent of Rainald of Dassel.

Roger of Howden says that Richard declined to participate personally, citing the king's failure to maintain all payments promised to the princes of the lower Rhine. This may well have been true, since the enormous cost of his ransom probably left royal resources thin for some time thereafter (although the archbishop of Cologne was still receiving regular payments). Roger also records that Richard feared to go because he was responsible for the fact that Henry VI remained unburied. This strange statement may be a confusion with the legend of the nasty death of Duke Leopold V of Austria, who was said to have remained unburied following

---

116. Roger of Howden, *Chronica*, 4:37–39; Ralph of Coggeshall, *Chronicon Anglicanum*, 88; Gervase of Canterbury, *Chronicle*, 1:544–45. The *Annales de Burtonensis* (1:195) follow Roger of Howden's account.

his divinely appointed suffering and death after capturing Richard near Vienna. In any case Richard would have shown a lack of discretion if he did not have misgivings about returning to the land of his imprisonment. Instead he sent to Cologne an impressive embassy that included, among others, the bishops of Durham (Richard's current chancellor), Ely, Evreux, and Angers and the count of Aumale. This distinguished party came initially to negotiate for a Welf candidate, namely, Henry of Brunswick, the count palatine of the Rhine.

The inclusion of a Welf candidate had two immediate consequences, both of which were disadvantageous to Archbishop Adolf. First of all the archbishop would never have desired a Welf candidate after his acquisition of the duchy of Westphalia. The specter of reestablishing Welf dominance in Saxony, so near his own territories, was absolutely unacceptable. It was equally unacceptable to the Saxon princes, Bernhard of Saxony foremost among them, who had also been the beneficiary of the fall of Henry the Lion in 1190. Thus Richard's proposal drove the Saxon princes to a quick election of Philip of Swabia and destroyed any opportunity of compromise between the electoral camps.[117] In fact Richard's involvement in the election, which Adolf had invited, was the beginning of the end of the archbishop's control over its dynamics.

When the election assembly convened in early March 1198 in Cologne, Adolf was disappointed on two counts: very few princes came to participate and even his chosen candidate, Berthold of Zähringen, had defected to the Staufen party.[118] Adolf was politically isolated by a small electoral assembly as a result of many defections and by the new impetus of the English party amid the vacuum of other available candidates. Therefore he entered into negotiations with the Staufen camp. He sent Bishop Hermann of Münster to the Thuringian assembly with an offer for a joint election assembly.[119] Perhaps Adolf considered accepting a candidate from the Staufen party after his own plans fell through. But he was most likely unwilling to recognize the candidacy of Philip, who was participating in an unlawful election assembly.

Before Adolf's offer had been received, however, Philip was elected in

---

117. Engels, "Entmachtung," 55. For a fuller presentation of the events surrounding the election in Cologne see Stehkämper, "Adolf von Altena," 42–47; "England und die Stadt Köln."

118. *REK,* 2:313, no. 1538. Berthold had already spent six thousand marks on his election and was apparently offended at further demands: see *Annales Marbacenses,* 72f.

119. *CRC,* 162.

Erfurt through the leadership of the Saxon princes.[120] This further isolated Adolf, since it had occurred without his participation as the highest-
ranking elector present in the empire. Philip had even been crowned,
which was an outright challenge to the archbishop of Cologne's right to
anoint and crown the king-elect. This hereditary right had been the basis
for Adolf's election policy from the beginning, and its oversight left no
room for reconciliation or compromise.[121] Philip's election not only occurred in Thuringia, but also lacked the participation of the archbishops
of Cologne, Mainz, and Trier and of the count palatine of the Rhine.
These were four of the most essential electors. Because Philip's coronation occurred outside Aachen and without the archbishop of Cologne it
was legally invalid. Philip sought to overcome this hurdle by a coronation
on September 8 in Mainz in the presence of Archbishop John of Trier,
who had recently defected from the Cologne party.[122]

Archbishop Adolf had rejected Philip's kingship as illegal, but there
was no other suitable candidate to call on after the loss of the Zähringer.
This series of miscalculations resulted, then, in Adolf accepting the English embassy's suggestion of a Welf candidate—an idea that enjoyed the
support of the burghers of Cologne (we shall consider their role in the
Welf kingship shortly).[123] Just as expediency had forced Rainald of
Dassel to assert English support at the diet of Würzburg, so now his
successor sought a way out of his self-imposed predicament by playing
the English card. It was too dangerous for Adolf to accept Henry of
Brunswick, though, for two reasons. First, because of his lands in both
Saxony and the palatinate of the Rhine, Henry could threaten directly the
lands of the archbishop.[124] Second, Henry was still on crusade and fur-
ther delay in electing an antiking to Philip of Swabia would be disastrous.
The Cologne party had been losing supporters with each passing day, and

---

120. *Böhmer*, 5, 1:6–7, no. 16.
121. Philip sought Adolf's recognition with many promises, but the archbishop refused.
His anger at the affront to his prerogatives is clear in *CRC*, 163: "Hic ergo rumor et
inhonestus eventus primores inferiorum partium graviter afflixit, eo quod indignum sibi et
intolerabile videretur, si contra suam voluntatem Suevus regnasset. Constat tamen, quod
ipse nuncios suos ad archiepiscopum Coloniensem cum precibus transmisit, multa offerens,
sed plura promittens, si ad suam electionem animum vellet inclinare. Sed episcopus hoc sibi
tutum non credens vel honestum, haec facere penitus recusavit . . ."
122. *Böhmer*, 5, 1:9, no. 19a.
123. Stehkämper, "Adolf von Altena," 82.
124. Ibid., 55 n. 176.

the news of Philip's election forced an immediate response from the increasingly dwindling party.

Thus a compromise was struck and Adolf accepted the election of Henry of Brunswick's brother Otto, the count of Poitou. Adolf was reassured by the fact that this Welf did not possess any personal power in Germany and thus would be less of a threat than his brother. The archbishop's hereditary electoral rights and territorial interests were preserved after all. Otto's position of dependence on the lukewarm support of the archbishop of Cologne would prove to be one of the greatest liabilities of his kingship, which seemed doomed from the start. His election was brought about by a small party of princes, and he himself had no direct political or military power in the empire. His power base would always be derivative and thus insecure. Ironically, whereas under Richard England was often a country without a king, his nephew Otto was to be a king without a country.

Count Emicho of Leiningen was dispatched to Otto to offer him the crown at the end of March, and Adolf hurried to Liège to prepare for the Welf's arrival. He also worked in vain to gain the support of the bishop of Liège for Otto's kingship.[125] Adolf then accompanied a compliant Otto to Cologne, where he was solemnly received. Negotiations began with Otto over his election on June 6, for which he was well provided by his English uncle,[126] and the formal election took place three days later among Bishop Conrad of Strasbourg and the princes of the lower Rhine and lower Lotharingia.[127] The assembly then moved to Aachen on June 18 for the royal anointment and coronation, but they met resistance since the city remained loyal to the Staufen. Aachen only capitulated on July 10, and the coronation was held two days later.[128] At this time Otto was also engaged to the daughter of the count of Brabant. Adolf and his cathedral city were quickly rewarded for their support of Otto, who confirmed in Aachen all prior imperial grants of regalian rights and lands to the archbishopric and other privileges to Cologne merchants.[129] Adolf also sent letters of support to the new pope Innocent III after the election, in which he appealed to the merit of Otto's dynastic ties—in particular to the English king—as

---

125. *REK*, 2:314, no. 1540.
126. *Pipe Roll 10 Richard I*, PR, NS, 9:198.
127. *REK*, 2:314, nos. 1541–42; *Böhmer*, 5, 1:56, no. 198c–f.
128. *REK*, 2:315–16, nos. 1544–47.
129. *REK*, 2:316–17, no. 1550.

opposed to the Staufen record on papal relations.[130] Adolf would be receiving papal admonitions to remain loyal to Otto very soon, and this letter would come back to haunt him.

The major English chronicles all record these events with few specifics concerning the role of the English in these negotiations.[131] The Styrian monastic chronicle of Admont, however, makes clear the role played by English money in Otto's election.[132] The pro-Staufen Caesarius of Heisterbach blamed Adolf's greed for English money as the cause of the coming destruction of civil war—indeed it was Adolf who transformed the beast of avarice into human form![133] English funds were liberally distributed among the princes of the lower Rhineland who had already been given money fiefs by Richard, and this had a significant influence on the outcome of the election. Otto himself must have brought considerable wealth from Poitou as well.[134] In addition to monetary support Richard also turned to the papacy for recognition of Otto's kingship. He wrote two separate letters to Innocent III in the summer of 1198 asking him to crown Otto as

---

130. *RNI*, 21–23, no. 9; *REK*, 2:317, no. 1552; MGH Const., 2:25–26, no. 20; *Böhmer*, 5, 1:58, no. 204: Adolf writes to Innocent asking him to confirm Otto's election, to call for his imperial coronation, and to take steps against the supporters of Philip. Adolf even vouches for the reestablishment of the Patrimonium Petri by Otto (July 12, 1198–March 1199). In the letter of the northwestern German princes to Innocent III asking for his confirmation of the election, Adolf appears at the top of the list of signatories ("Ego Adolfus Coloniensis Archiepiscopus elegi et subscripsi")—also listed are Bishop Bernard of Paderborn, Bishop Thietmar of Minden, Abbot Widukind of Corbei, Gerardus "Indensis abbas," Abbot Herbert of Werden, Duke Henricus of Lotharingia, and Count Henry of Cuk (July 12, 1198): see *RNI*, 23–26, no. 10; *REK*, 2:317, no. 1553; MGH Const., 2:24–25, no. 19; *Rymer*, 1:105–6; *Böhmer*, 5, 1:58, no. 203.

131. Roger of Wendover, *Flores historiarum*, 1:272; *MPHA*, 2:65; Ralph de Diceto, *Ymagines historiarum*, 2:163.

132. *Continuatio Admuntensis*, ed. W. Wattenbach, MGH SS, no. 9 (Hanover, 1851; reprint, 1983), 588. After telling of Philip of Swabia's election, the chronicle continues: "Econtra episcopus Coloniensis, ad quem Romani regis unctio spectat, et dux de Lovin, et comes Flandriae, accepta pecunia infinita a rege Anglorum, eiusdem regis sororium Ottonem nobilem de Prunswich, Pictaviensem tunc comitem, Heinrici magni quondam ducis filium, in regem eligunt. Quem etiam Aquisgrani deducentes, ei regalem unctionem conferunt, presentibus duobus cardinalibus et assensum domni Innocenti papae super hoc facto declarantibus" (actually Innocent sent his legate bishop, Guide of Praenestae, only in 1201).

133. Caesarius of Heisterbach, *Dialogus Miraculorum*, ed. Joseph Strange (Cologne, Bonn, and Brussels, 1851), 1:103.

134. *Gesta episcoporum Halberstadensium* (ed. L. Weiland, MGH SS, no. 23 [Hanover, 1874; reprint, 1986], 113) suggests that Otto sold his county back to Richard for means to fund his election: ". . . Ipse autem avunculo . . . suo pro pecunia comicia sua, electoribus suis, quod sitiverant, erogavit."

emperor and vouching for Otto's recognition of papal rights,[135] and he sent his own embassy to Rome to plead for Otto at a cost of over two thousand marks.[136] He also managed to insert his concerns for Otto's kingship in negotiations with the papacy over peace with Philip II of France.[137] Richard's own chaplain was a member of the Anglo-Cologne embassy sent by Otto to the pope to deliver his own announcement of election and coronation.[138]

Papal confirmation of Otto's election became essential even before the Welf was crowned king. On June 29, 1198, while Aachen was besieged by the forces loyal to Otto, Philip of Swabia concluded an alliance with Philip II of France at Worms "against King Richard of England and Count Otto his nephew and Count Baldwin of Flanders and Archbishop Adolf of Cologne and against all of his [Philip II's] other enemies."[139] The leaders of the Welf antikingship are made plain in this statement. Now the Staufen-Welf *Thronstreit* created principally by the archbishop of Cologne was intimately tied to the Angevin-Capetian conflict in France. Richard's hopes of establishing a familial ally in Germany and Adolf's hopes of preventing either Staufen or Capetian incursions against his territorial power had unexpectedly combined to create the first real threat to the political stability of all the territories involved. One can say that, although not as the result of some political master plan by any medieval prince, Germany was now fully integrated into western European politics.

With his uncle's financial and political support Otto was able to endure Philip of Swabia's first attack in October 1198.[140] At this point

---

135. *RNI,* 13–15, no. 4; *Böhmer,* 5, 2:1581, nos. 10627 (July 15–31) and 10628 (August 19).

136. After Richard's death John ordered the payment of 2,125 marks for this embassy: see *Rotuli chartarum in turri Londinensi asservati. Vol. 1, pt. 1, Ab anno MCXCIX ad annum MCCXVI,* ed. Thomas Duffus Hardy (London, 1837), 31; *Rymer,* 1:115.

137. Roger of Wendover, *Flores historiarum,* 1:281; *MPHA,* 2:74.

138. MGH Const., 2:23–24, no. 18; *RNI,* 10–13, no. 3; *Böhmer,* 5, 1:57, no. 202 (July 12, 1198–March 1199). Present also were members from Cologne and Milan. Cologne would prove to be a bulwark of support for Otto, and the inclusion of a Milanese member was surely designed to engender papal sympathy.

139. *Rymer,* 1:107; MGH Const., 2:1, no. 1; MGH Leges (folio), 2:202–3; *Böhmer,* 5, 1:8, no. 18: "contra Richardum Regem Angliae et Comitem Othonem nepotem ipsius et Balduinem Comitem Flandriae et Adolphum Archiepiscopum Coloniae et contra omnes alios inimicos ejus."

140. *CRC,* 165; *REK,* 2:318–19, no. 1558. Roger of Howden (*Chronica,* 4:79) mentions Otto's warfare with Philip in concert with Richard's against Philip II. Roger's account does not, however, agree with the actual events.

Adolf was giving active support to Otto and thus sent an army to meet Philip's on the Moselle River, but this attempt to prevent the Staufen army from crossing over failed. Adolf then retreated first to Andernach and then back to within the safe walls of Cologne. This unfortunately left the countryside unprotected and Philip's army burned Remagen, Bonn, and the surrounding area. After coming within two miles of Cologne, however, the army suddenly returned to upper Germany. Andernach was destroyed during the retreat.

The year 1199 started out positively for Otto, but by midspring his position was drastically altered. Richard had continued to fund him liberally,[141] and both the archbishop of Cologne and burghers of Cologne themselves[142] were actively serving as intermediaries between the two parties. Even Pope Innocent III seemed ready to acknowledge him openly. But his primary patron, Richard I, died suddenly in April at the gates of Chaluz in battle against Philip II.[143] When Richard died so ironically close to Otto's county of Poitou, the young king lost both his financial backing and his political momentum. Otto would then only receive spotty support at best from the English court and have to rely more and more on Cologne and the papacy. A sign of Otto's coming difficulties with the new king of England occurred shortly after the death of Richard. On his deathbed Richard had made John his successor and then willed a sizable portion of his treasury and jewels to Otto.[144] Try as he might during the following years, Otto never got his hands on this legacy, which could have financed him for some time.

Soon after Richard's death the always lukewarm support of the archbishop of Cologne began to waver. The Welf king found himself losing the principal patrons of his kingship and thereby exiled in a foreign land. He could only look to two remaining sources of support: a faraway pope who had not yet declared his full support for Otto, and the remarkable burghers of Cologne.[145] On May 20 Innocent III wrote to Arch-

---

141. *Pipe Roll 1 John*, PR, NS, no. 10, 59–60.

142. Ibid., 129 and 243.

143. John Gillingham, "The Unromantic Death of Richard I," *Speculum* 54 (1979): 18–41.

144. Roger of Howden, *Chronica*, 4:83. Sidney Painter (*The Reign of King John*, 154) believed that this grant probably did not amount to very much. It was, however, large enough that Otto continued to seek it, and the pope would admonish John no less than five times to pay the legacy to his nephew.

145. The death of Richard is noted in the second recension of the Cologne chronicle (*CRC*, 166) with legendary overtones: "Richardus rex Angliae dum quoddam castrum,

bishop Adolf, thanking him for the embassy sent to inform him of Otto's election. It had taken over a year after the election for the embassy to reach Rome and manage a short time of negotiating.[146] Innocent merely replied that he would concern himself, as much as he could, for the honor and advantage of Otto, hoping that the same attitude toward the papal see would be forthcoming from Adolf's party. Perhaps he had been clearer in expressing his intentions during the oral discussions with the envoys, although the fact that he had become the guardian for the young Frederick (II) was presumably cause for concern in the Welf camp. The letter was vague enough that Otto did not reply until the end of the year.

In the summer Otto planned a campaign against Philip in which there was to be a siege of Strasbourg. With the support of troops from Archbishop Adolf and Duke Henry of Brabant (Otto's expected father-in-law) he set out marching up the Rhine. Yet he only reached Boppard and had to give up the effort. Typical of his entire kingship, the help promised by his supporters did not materialize and supplies had run out.[147] Upon receiving the news of Otto's failed campaign Philip of Swabia advanced down the Rhine toward Cologne once again, devastating the region around it. Yet again he made a sudden retreat back to the south after having reached the imposing walls of the city.[148] What role Archbishop Adolf may have played, or neglected to play, in the summer campaigns is unclear, but by the end of the summer suspicion about his loyalty was running rampant in Cologne as a result of the archbishop's negligent attitude toward the Welf king.[149]

Word of Adolf's lack of interest in maintaining the Welf kingship he helped to create even reached the ears of Innocent III, who, although he had not officially recognized Otto, wrote a letter of rebuke to the

---

Limogiae scilicet, obsideret, et circuiens quereret ubi assultus oportunius faceret, telo letaliter percutitur; quod non sine iudicio Dei factum hoc modo probatur. Siquidem episcopus quidam dum sine cause offensam eius incurrisset, in tantum eum persecutus est, ut a propria sede eum exturbaret, precipiens ei, ne deinceps eius se oculis offerret. Ille Romam progressus ad apostolicum se contulit. Qui dum quadam die astaret altari, ipso momento quo Richardus obiit telo videt ipsum telum secus altaris crepidinem lapsum, cui karta fuerat innexa secundum vaticinium Merlini olim predictum: 'Telum Limogiae occidit leonem Angliae.' Sic mortuo rege Richardo, frater eius Iohannes in regem eligitur."

146. *RNI*, 27–29, no. 11; *REK*, 2:320, no. 1563.
147. *CRC*, 167; *REK*, 2:320, no. 1564.
148. *REK*, 2:320, no. 1565.
149. *CRC*, 168; *REK*, 2:320–21, no. 1566.

archbishop sometime in late October or early November.[150] The pope admonished Adolf for not informing him about the events in Germany, saying no one would want to think that Adolf was too busy with worldly affairs that he ceased attending to such clerical violations as perjured oaths. This was a thinly veiled reference to Adolf's oath of loyalty to Otto. Reminding him that punishment for such sin would not be lacking, he ordered Adolf to inform him about the attitudes of the princes and the progress of events. Adolf, however, did not respond to this letter; in fact he would never respond to papal directives throughout this conflict.

Otto was heartened by this show of papal support, and he wrote to Innocent in November/December thanking the pope for returning his embassy. He also apologized for the lack of correspondence and asked for further help.[151] Otto realized that he had to cultivate papal support since King John was stonewalling him in England. Indeed he called Innocent his "only consolation and help" in the letter. Otto had become isolated in northwest Germany and his options were severely limited. The burghers of Cologne—the only consistently loyal supporters Otto would enjoy—were his last line of defense. We have saved the role of the Cologners until this point to have the context of events as a backdrop to their unique involvement in Otto's election.[152] The always independent-minded citizens of Cologne had become sufficiently anti-Staufen by the close of Henry VI's reign that they supported the archbishop's move away from young Frederick, and they were well-enough disposed to English interests, by virtue of their own strong economic relations with the island, to support a Welf candidate when they had little to gain from a revival of Welf power.[153]

Cologne's burghers had been gradually alienated from the Staufen kings beginning as far back as Frederick I.[154] The emperor sided often

---

150. *RNI,* 42–43, no. 16; *REK,* 2:321, no. 1569.

151. *RNI,* 53–54, no. 19.

152. The role of the city in Otto's election has finally entered the general historiography concerning this period: see Bernhard Töpfer, *Deutsche Könige und Kaiser des Mittelalters* (Cologne and Vienna, 1989), 198, Hucker, *Kaiser Otto IV.,* 25–35.

153. For excellent studies of the medieval urban institutions and society of Cologne see Paul Strait, *Cologne in the Twelfth Century* (Gainesville, 1974); Manfred Groten, *Köln im 13. Jahrhundert: Gesellschaftlicher Wandel und Vergassungsentwicklung,* Städteforschung; Veröffentlichungen des Instituts für vergleichende Städtegeschichte in Münster Reihe A: Darstellungen, no. 36 (Cologne, 1995, 2nd ed. Cologne, 1998).

154. For Frederick's economic policies see Johannes Fried, "Die Wirtschaftspolitik Friedrich Barbarossas in Deutschland," *Blätter für deutsche Landesgeschichte* 120 (1984):

with the city's competitors in economic disputes, especially supporting Flanders. He granted a generous privilege to the Flemish merchants in 1173 that allowed free trade down the Rhine under imperial protection and gave them markets at Aachen and Duisburg.[155] He transferred the royal toll from Tiel to Kaiserswerth the following year, making it farther away from Flanders and closer to Cologne.[156] These moves sharply impinged on Cologne's control over trade on the Rhine. They cut particularly deeply since the Flemish wished to transport wine from the upper Rhine regions to England, and this commercial activity was the lifeblood of Cologne's trade with England. That the Cologne merchants were able to counteract Staufen policy by obtaining confirmation of special trading privileges in England from Henry II three years later (1175/76) reminds us how crucial English trade was for Cologne's prosperity.[157] During the wars against Henry the Lion and his subsequent exile, the English economic interests of the Cologne burghers clashed with their archbishop's anti-Welf territorial interests in Westphalia. It was only after the archbishop was reconciled with Henry the Lion that tensions were relieved.[158] The conflict between Archbishop Philip and Barbarossa in 1187–88 moved both archbishop and city firmly against Staufen lordship. Although Philip was reconciled to Henry VI and a final settlement was reached with Henry the Lion, the citizens of Cologne remained cautious. When the Rhenish rebellion of 1193–94 erupted during Richard's imprisonment, the city of Cologne, its archbishop, and the English king were drawn together in opposition to Henry VI's policies. Thus at Henry's death the city was more than willing to support its archbishop's call for an end to the Staufen monarchy.

When Archbishop Adolf sent the embassy to Rouen seeking English participation in the election of a new German king the Cologne

---

195–239; Hugo Stehkämper, "Friedrich Barbarossa und die Stadt Köln: Ein Wirtschaftskrieg am Niederrhein," in *Köln, Stadt und Bistum in Kirche und Reich des Mittelalters: Festschrift für Odilo Engels zum 65. Geburtstag*, ed. Hanna Vollrath and Stefan Weinfurter, Kölner historische Abhandlungen, no. 39 (Cologne, 1993), 367–413; Ulf Dirlmeier, "Friedrich Barbarossa—auch ein Wirtschaftspolitiker?" in *Friedrich Barbarossa: Handlungsweisen und Wirkungsweisen des staufischen Kaisers*, ed. Alfred Haverkamp, Vorträge und Forschungen, no. 40 (Sigmaringen, 1992), 501–18.

155. MGH Const., 1: no. 239; *HUB*, 1:13–15, no. 23.

156. Georg Droege, "Die kurkölnischen Rheinzölle im Mittelalter," *Annalen* 168/169 (1967):30.

157. See Hugo Stehkämper, "Friedrich Barbarossa und die Stadt Köln," 388–413.

158. Kallen, "Philip von Heinsberg," 198.

merchants surely rejoiced. Richard had issued them a major trading privilege in 1194 and they would have been naturally disposed to any suggestions by the English king. They accepted the English recommendation of a Welf kingship in the hope of further commercial benefits. Indeed the burghers opposed the election of the Zähringer in favor of the English proposal and contributed directly to the failure of Adolf's election strategy.[159]

Although a Welf king would have endangered the archbishop's territorial interests, he would not have been a threat to the citizens of Cologne. The Welfs in Saxony had always been indifferent to the city, since little important trade was carried on between Saxony and Cologne. The Cologners also would have been happier with Otto than with Henry of Brunswick for the same reason as their archbishop: fear of the count palatine of the Rhine's blockading the river during a dispute. Evidence for the city's involvement in the election appears from many quarters. The sometimes unreliable Arnold of Lübeck states that the municipal leaders took part in the negotiations.[160] Burchard of Ursperg writes in 1229 that the burghers of Cologne and Strasbourg were among the principle instigators of Otto's kingship (the bishop of Strasbourg was a member of the Cologne electoral assembly).[161] Evidence may suggest that a consortium of Cologne merchants devised the financing scheme needed to obtain Otto's election, since the archbishop was heavily in debt at this time.[162] If this is an accurate scenario, then it appears that Adolf had little choice but to help elect Otto, though he did so out of financial and political need, not out of greed for wealth and power as has been often asserted.[163] Caesarius of Heisterbach, who was born in Cologne in 1180 and grew up

---

159. Stehkämper, "England und die Stadt Köln," 236.

160. Arnold of Lübeck, *Chronica Slavorum*, 217.

161. *Burchardi praepositi Urspergensi Chronicon*, ed. O. Abel and L. Weiland, MGH SS, no. 23 (Hanover, 1874; reprint, 1986), 367.

162. In making this case, Hucker (*Kaiser Otto IV.*, 25–35, 454–56) follows Sonja Zöllner, "Geld und Politik im 12. Jahrhundert: Gerhard Unmaze in Köln," *Geschichte in Köln* 29 (1991): 27; *Der gute Gerhard von Köln—Realität und literarische Bearbeitung* (PhD. diss., Frankfurt am Main, 1990); "Besitzkonzentration in einer mittelalterlichen Großstadt: Grund- und Hausbesitz der Kölner Familie Unmaze in der zweiten Hälfte des 12. Jahrhunderts," in *Hochfinanz—Wirtschaftsräume—Innovation: Festschrift für Wolfgang von Stromer 1* (Trier, 1987), 103–26; *Kaiser, Kaufmann und die Macht des Geldes: Gerhard Unmaze von Köln als Finanzier der Reichspolitik und der 'Gute Gerhard' des Rudolf von Ems* (Munich, 1993).

163. Hucker, *Kaiser Otto IV.*, 32. Groten, *Köln im 13. Jahrhundert*, 10 n. 77 is critical of Hucker's conclusions in this matter.

in the Siebengebirgskloster within the vicinity of the city, lamented such behavior.

> O Cologne, bewail your destruction, which will come to you, because the aforesaid evil [the Welf kingship] arose not only through the fault of the archbishop alone but also by virtue of [your] common sin.[164]

These striking references confirm that the patrician leadership of the city had some measure of participation in and influence over the election of Otto. We shall see more of this in subsequent years, when the city itself would remain the only firm supporter of Otto. A combination of hatred for the Staufen and of the positive economic interests in England moved the burghers of Cologne to support—indeed even invest in—the Welf candidacy proposed by Richard.[165]

The first year of Otto IV's kingship (1199) closed out with an effort by Archbishop Conrad of Mainz (who had recently returned from crusading) to negotiate in Cologne for a settlement of the disputed kingship. In the most definitive reference so far of the Cologne burghers' participation in Otto's kingship, the Cologne chronicle indicates that Conrad came to the city to negotiate with both the archbishop and the citizens of the city.

> Bishop Conrad came to Cologne and held a conference [colloquium] with the bishop of Cologne and the burghers [burgensibus] on this matter; with the negotiations proving impossible, he returned home.[166]

The patrician leaders of the city were consulted by Archbishop Conrad because they played an important role in Otto's kingship from the beginning—that is, from the election.[167] At the very least it is clear that they were a significant element in any equation for a resolution of the

---

164. Caesarius of Heisterbach, *Dialogus Miraculorum*, 1:102: "O Colonia, deplora calamitates tuas, quae venient tibi, quoniam non solum ex culpa solius episcopi, sed etiam ex communi peccato venient mala supradicta." Caesarius's Staufen leaning comes through clearly in this passage, which was to have been a prophecy.

165. This is expressed in Philip of Swabia's rebuke of the Cologne burghers in 1205 (*CRC*, 176): "...civitatem Coloniam, utpote maiestatis ream, quippe de qua tam sibi quam multis ante se regibus opprobria multa illata fuisse conquerebatur, solotenus eversurus."

166. *CRC*, 169: "Cunradus etiam episcopus Coloniam veniens cum episcopo Coloniensi et burgensibus colloquium supra hoc habuit, sed infecto negocio rediit."

167. Stehkämper, "England und die Stadt Köln," 242.

conflict.[168] The negotiations broke down, however, because of the growing distrust between the Cologne patricians and their wavering archbishop. From this point on the city and their new king would basically
have to go it alone, so the burghers would ultimately defend the kingship
Richard I and Archbishop Adolf had wrought with their support.

Once again a political narrative unlike modern scenarios is operative
in the political activities surrounding the ill-fated election of Otto IV.
Traditional political history notwithstanding, there was no carefully coordinated anti-Staufen plot hatched. Rather, a last-minute candidate who
happened to be a Welf was located (because of his kinship ties to the
English king) after several false starts and failed coalitions, and the result
was a flawed coalition like that built around Philip of Swabia's candidacy. Otto, German by birth but an alien in his own homeland, was a
hasty import clearly ill suited to the German political community and an
imperfect candidate for the requirements of Archbishop Adolf of Cologne's *Territorialpolitik*. Behind the scenes we also find the substantial
interregional economic ties between England and Cologne that served as
a conduit for Otto's arrival from the hands of the English court. Archbishop Adolf, the supposed mastermind of anti-Staufen politics, had himself lost control of events, swept along as they were by the initiative and
money of Richard I and the popular support of Otto by the Cologne
burghers.

The personal feudal and familial politics of noble families over hereditary ties and rights, on the one hand, and the economic interests of the
burgher class, on the other, determined the strategies employed here. One
gets the impression that much of the action was improvised rather than
the result of the implementation of carefully constructed strategies and
policies. Certainly there is no evidence here of plots either to build up or
to tear down institutions of western politics: Richard I was not seeking to
extend English hegemony into Germany, Archbishop Adolf was not seeking to destroy the power of kingship in Germany, and Otto had no clear
agenda other than to establish his legitimacy by any means, even by the
recognition of the pope. All parties were merely grasping at straws to
address the immediate personal and regional problems of the moment

---

168. Edith Ennen ("Kölner Wirtschaft im Früh- und Hochmittelalter," in *Zwei Jahrtausende Kölner Wirtschaft*, ed. Hermann Kellenbenz, Rheinisch-Westfälisches Wirtschaftsarchiv zu Köln [Cologne, 1975], 1:152) remarks, "The city participated in imperial affairs
on the same level with the high-placed imperial princes!"

rather than seeking to establish precedents for the long-term constitutional history of their territories.

In many ways the election of Otto IV is the center point of this study, in that it is so representative of the social realities of medieval politics. At no other time will we see the confluence of Anglo-German interregional cooperation between these political communities as integrated as they were here: the king of England and his Saxon Welf relatives, the archbishop of Cologne, the Cologne burghers, and even eventually the papacy all collaborated to fashion Otto's kingship out of whole cloth. Yet the fabric of this cloth was flimsy. It was quickly pulled apart by natural causes (the death of Richard I while pursuing his own vendetta against Philip II), local and regional interests, and the vacillating support of clerical authority. This was because it was cobbled together to satisfy these competing interests rather than to further the constitutional history of Europe.

Hence the kingship of Otto IV may appear as a failure to those who hold modern expectations of state and empire building and the institutionalization of political authority. Yet this troubled kingship succeeds in embodying the quintessential social realities of medieval political life. Just as the "failures" of Barbarossa's and Henry II's kingships should be understood as reminders of the possibilities of medieval politics, so too should Otto IV's kingship teach us something about the realities of political communities as they functioned in 1199 rather than about how they fall short of modernizing political discourse.

5

King John, Otto IV, and Cologne:
A Case Study of Kinship, Kingship,
and Diplomacy between Medieval
Political Communities

The same dynamics that brought about Otto IV's kingship would also be those that frustrated and ultimately destroyed it. In many ways we can consider King John and his royal nephew Otto to have had an affinity of style and result in their respective reigns. Not only did they eventually lose the territories on which their political independence depended, but both would discover how difficult it was to forge a coordinated coalition across different political communities. The history of their so-called alliance is one of repeated false starts and near misses. This was so because both medieval monarchs found themselves so preoccupied with the regional and personal affairs of their own political communities that they were most often in no position to assist each other. When they finally did manage a focused joint military action, their inability to coordinate a collage of feudal levies held together more by money than by personal loyalty proved to be their undoing.

This chapter of Anglo-German relations is the best documented, in both German and English sources, of all those we shall consider, and once again the role of the archbishop of Cologne continues to be pivotal. The archbishop's *Territorialpolitik* is a determinative factor in the development of both Otto's German kingship and John's revived coalition scheme with Rhenish princes. Traditionally historians have evaluated the evidence of both monarchs' inability to realize a reasonably sound strategy as a political failure in state building. When, however, one looks not at the failure of monarchs to build modern-looking political alliances and states but at the nature of social relationships among political leaders in this era, a different picture of the past emerges. John and Otto may be royal failures in modern political terms, but they were normative in medieval social terms.[1]

With the preceding ideas in mind, we shall now consider in detail the troubled kingship of Otto IV. Here the political events of 1200–1214 are understood not as a failure to achieve the modern aspirations of a unified Germany or of effective geopolitical alliances between states but rather as a story that reveals two hitherto neglected themes. First, we shall observe the events distinctly from the point of view of Cologne, whose central role in Otto's kingship still remains generally unknown. Second, we shall study the equally unknown intimate nature of Anglo-German diplomatic relations during this time, complete with the lessons they teach about the nature of relations between medieval political communities.

King John and Otto IV (1200–1205):
Failed or Feudal Kings?

Otto continued in 1200 to seek the assistance promised him at his election by the archbishop of Cologne and the English court. In this endeavor he was aided by the ever more supportive Pope Innocent III, who saw the advantage of ending Staufen reign in the empire. Yet virtually no benefit came to the Welf as a result of papal efforts.

Otto's cause was dealt a heavy blow early on when King John agreed to the Peace of Le Goulet with Philip II of France on May 22. Philip II, already allied with Philip of Swabia, included a clause in the peace agreement that John could help Otto "neither by money nor by soldiers nor by retainers nor by himself nor by anyone unless with our council and assent."[2] This promise would serve as John's excuse for disengagement from his nephew's cause. The Pipe Rolls show no new English money sent to Otto for this year or for 1201, and the money fief of the archbishop of

---

1. Ralph V. Turner's recent book *King John* (London, 1994) is typical of such evaluations of John's reign. In his otherwise outstanding study, Turner only mentions Otto at any length as an anti-French military ally in the context of the Battle of Bouvines, and Otto appears nowhere else as an important kinsman of the Angevin king. John's continental interests are solely political and French, excluding the social and German in the case of Otto. Again modern political and intellectual boundaries neglect actual medieval social ties.

2. *Diplomatic Documents*, 20–23, no. 9: "neque per pecuniam neque per milites nec per gentem nec per se nec per alium nisi per consilium et assensum nostrum." *CRC* (167) makes note of this peace, perhaps aware of its implications for Otto's kingship. Roger of Wendover (*Flores historiarum*, 1:294) specifically points out this clause and its consequences for the Welf-Staufen conflict.

Cologne was also discontinued at this time.[3] In February Otto had already sent his brothers Henry of Brunswick (now returned from crusading) and William of Winchester/Lüneburg (who had also been raised at the Angevin court) to apply some familial pressure on John to release Richard's legacy to Otto. The Winchester annals estimate the total amount of the legacy to have been twenty-five thousand marks of silver in value.[4] John of course refused to grant their request, citing his promise to Philip II at Le Goulet not to aid Otto in any way without the consent of the French king. Innocent also wrote to John in this year and urged him to pay the legacy, but the pope was met with the same response.[5] Innocent then removed this impediment to English support for Otto in November 1201 by freeing John from his oath to Philip, but John did not relent on his decision.[6] His refusal to maintain Richard's money fiefs for the lower Rhenish princes, again because of his oath to Philip, also had a severe effect, since Otto was unable to finance such support on his own. Hence the coalition built on English money that had brought Otto to Germany had dissolved before him as a result of John's exigencies at home. Otto's kingship seemed stillborn.

In fairness to John, his attention was monopolized by affairs in his own realm. Philip II was threatening to recognize the claims of John's nephew Arthur in Anjou, Maine, and Brittany. In addition, the fact that Otto's star was fading before that of Philip of Swabia could hardly encourage John to make further investment in his nephew during such difficult times at home. Through the treaty of Le Goulet John did manage to secure his succession to the entire Angevin realm and received homage from Arthur for Brittany, and thus he achieved his personal and regional goals. Yet he made considerable concessions to Philip II, dismantled Richard's coalition scheme in the lower Rhine, and abandoned his nephew's

---

3. *Pipe Rolls 3 John*, PR, NS, 14:268. This final payment of one thousand marks, issued to cover Otto's debt to the merchant Hugo Oisel of Ypres, came from the profits of the exchange and was probably due to Richard's affairs and not John's, since the calculations reached back two years. Cf. Ahlers, *Die Welfen*, 199; Kienast, "Die Deutschen Fürsten," 10:156 n. 4.

4. Roger of Howden, *Chronica*, 4:116–17; *Annales de Burtonensis*, 1:201–2; *Annales de Wintonia*, ed. Henry Richards Luard, RS, no. 36 (London, 1865; reprint 1971), 2:73; *Böhmer*, 5, 1:562–63, no 215a.

5. *RNI*, 73–74, no. 28. John was admonished to support his nephew as nature demanded, as his own honor was linked to that of his kinsman. This comment would prove prophetic.

6. *RNI*, 161–62, no. 60.

cause. This was a case of feudal obligations overshadowing kinship ties, which was a typical tension in feudal Europe.

As a result of his recent military setbacks and financial woes Otto made efforts to reinforce his position. He carefully nurtured the backing he received from the city of Cologne. On January 6 Otto held court in the city and, in a symbolic move designed to strengthen his own kingship, commissioned the fashioning of three golden crowns for the heads of the Three Kings (Magi). These were to be placed on the very heads of the relics.[7] He then turned to diplomacy and appointed Archbishop Adolf and the bishops Hermann of Münster, Theoderich of Utrecht, and Hugo of Liège to attend a conference sponsored by Archbishop Conrad of Mainz, which was to meet somewhere between Koblenz and Andernach. Conrad was seeking once again to find a resolution to the *Thronstreit* in Germany. Although the conference was scheduled for July 28 it did not convene until December. The participants, who also included Bishop Wolfgang of Passau and Archbishop John of Trier (a recent defector to the Staufen side), came to no concrete conclusions.[8]

Adolf's passive policy toward Otto may have been a decisive factor in the failure of these negotiations. Yet surely the conflict that had arisen between John of Trier and Adolf concerning the Cologne cathedral treasury must have added a measure of rancor to the proceedings. Adolf had originally pawned the cathedral treasury to John until he could gather eight thousand marks as payment for the Trier archbishop's vote in the royal election. Innocent III saw this as an opportunity to pressure both archbishops and assert his authority in the matter of the election.[9] The pope commanded John to return the pledged treasury items and was particularly harsh on Adolf for pawning ecclesiastical property for worldly goals. Adolf was to begin a fast and immediately report to Rome; otherwise he would be suspended by the bishop of Cambrai (an ironic situation given the earlier efforts of Philip of Heinsberg to subject Cambrai to Cologne archdiocesan authority). Adolf did not follow the dictates of the letter, but he soon learned that the new pope was a man to be reckoned with.

The year 1201 saw a barrage of papal letters on behalf of Otto as Innocent III finally came out publicly in support of the Welf. On January

7. *REK*, 2:322, no. 1573.
8. *REK*, 2:322, no. 1576; 326, no. 1592.
9. *REK*, 2:322–23, no. 1578.

5 he wrote to Adolf that since the bestowal of the imperial crown belonged to the pope he had an interest in the disputed election.[10] Innocent explained his own lack of intervention thus far as an effort to show respect for the electoral rights of the German princes. This was a reference calculated to ease Adolf's concerns about his princely privileges. Yet discord still continued, and since Conrad of Mainz's attempt at a reconciliation the prior month had failed, the pope felt he should now intervene. Therefore he sent his legate Bishop Guido of Palestrina, who was to be joined later by Bishop Octavian of Ostia (himself busied in negotiations with Philip II of France). Similar letters were also sent to the other German archbishops and princes.

The legates were to bring news of Innocent's wishes, which were finally made public on March 1.[11] In a letter announcing his support of Otto, Innocent told Adolf that the archbishop should be happy because the Roman church had sanctioned his election of Otto (the irony here is hard to miss); Innocent admonished Adolf to be obedient to the Welf and even seek new supporters. On the very same day, the pope issued another letter to King John, urging him a second time to pay Richard's legacy to Otto.[12] Finally, on June 3, all the princes of the lower Rhine gathered in Cologne and received the legate Guido's document of papal recognition of Otto. Guido excommunicated all those who worked against the Welf kingship, and at the suggestions of Adolf he confirmed a papal dispensation for a marriage between Otto and Maria, daughter of Duke Henry of Brabant, thus assuring the king of his most important ally among the secular princes.

Papal pressure on Adolf continued as the legate Guido remained in the Cologne archdiocese and Innocent continued to write letters of admonishment.[13] In a letter dated September–November of the same year, the pope chided the archbishop in the most severe tone yet.[14] Innocent begins the letter by reminding Adolf that the archbishop himself had elected and crowned Otto and then suggested an imperial coronation. Indeed, it was because of Adolf's strong request that the pope had taken up the Welf's cause. If Adolf wished to remove his hand from the plow now, he would

---

10. *RNI,* 91–94, no. 30; *REK,* 2:326, no. 1594.

11. *RNI,* 118–19, no. 39; *REK,* 2:327–28, no. 1597.

12. *RNI,* 134–35, no. 49.

13. *REK,* 2:239, no. 1605: on September 20 in Xanten Adolf assisted Guido in the consecration of archbishop-elect Siegfried of Mainz.

14. *RNI,* 145–49, no. 55; *REK,* 2:329, no. 1606.

therefore deserve severe punishment for playing a disgraceful game with the apostolic see. Reminding Adolf that the archbishop had spent much already on Otto, even the pawning of the cathedral treasury, Innocent promises him a final reward if he remains loyal. The letter closes, first, with assurances that the pope was acting in support of the princes' electoral rights and against hereditary kingship and, second, with a command to obey all orders from the papal legate. Innocent's reference to Adolf's electoral rights reminds us that the archbishop had entered the conflict in the first place to defend these hereditary rights, and they were the main reason that he opposed papal intervention in the matter. Adolf looked with disfavor on any interjection of either papal or Staufen authority in matters pertaining to the German princes' right to elect their king.

Otto's spirits were greatly buoyed by the papal recognition of his election. English chronicles state that he felt his situation so improved that he promised John military assistance against Capetian France. This was done out of thankfulness to the English court for Richard's support and was also a not-so-veiled reference to Otto's original patron and guarantor of funding.[15] Otto was able to better his own fortunes by a successful military venture in the early months of 1201. Supported by troops from Cologne, Westphalia, and the lower Rhine, and assisted by his brother Henry's supporters in the palatinate of the Rhine, he marched unmolested through Mainz as far as Weissenburg.[16] Otto was even able to install his candidate, Siegfried of Eppstein, in the disputed election of the Mainz archbishopric, but he achieved little else of lasting importance at the time.[17] While at Weissenburg, Otto confirmed with a charter that his brothers Henry of Brunswick and William of Winchester/Lüneburg formally renounced the archbishop's ducal lands in Saxony that were formerly part of their father's duchy.[18] Otto had already made this concession at his coronation in Aachen in 1198, so the confirmation most probably was intended to improve the strained relations between archbishop and king.[19] Perhaps Adolf felt the need for the confirmation after seeing Henry of Brunswick returned to the Rhine palatinate.

---

15. Roger of Howden, *Chronica*, 4:95–96; Roger of Wendover, *Flores historiarum*, 1:290; *MPHA*, 2:83; *Annales de Burtonensis*, 1:200.

16. *REK*, 2:327, no. 1595; Eduard Winkelmann, *Philipp von Schwaben und Otto IV. von Braunschweig* (Leipzig, 1873), 1:206–9.

17. Roger of Howden, *Chronica*, 4:122.

18. *UGN*, 1:396–97, no. 566; *REK*, 2:327, no. 1596 (dated February 3).

19. *UGN*, 1:317, no. 1550; *REK*, 2:317, no. 1550.

Innocent III kept steady diplomatic pressure on both Archbishop Adolf and King John in the following year. In March he warned the English king for a third time to pay Otto the legacy due him, and he now threatened to excommunicate John if he did not do so.[20] In the following month he once again exhorted Adolf to support the Welf, in a letter that was kinder than his previous admonishment.[21] Innocent told the archbishop that he should continue as a supporter of Otto, whom he, next to God, called to the empire. Once again the pope made allusion to Adolf's electoral prerogative. Innocent promised rewards for both Adolf and the Cologne church and instructed him to prepare to bring the king to Rome at a suitable time for the imperial coronation.

John did change his policy toward Otto in 1202, but this was not as much a result of papal diplomatic pressure as it was of renewed personal conflict with Philip II. During the years since the peace of Le Goulet John had no cause to cultivate anti-Capetian allies, but by this year the political landscape had changed. He had become embroiled in conflict with his Poitevin vassal Hugh of Lusignan as a result of marrying the twelve-year-old Isabelle of Angoulême, who had already been betrothed to Hugh. John refused to come to Philip II's court as a vassal himself to have the dispute adjudicated, so on April 30 the French king charged John with contumacy and declared him forfeit of his continental lands. Philip then enfeoffed Arthur with Brittany, Touraine, Anjou, Mainea, and Poitou, as he had threatened to do earlier.[22]

As tensions mounted during this period, John, mindful of Otto's earlier promise to aid him against Philip II, began an attempt to resurrect his brother's coalition structure in the lower Rhineland. This seemed a prudent move, since John had to date lost the allegiance of vassals in Poitou, Anjou, Maine, Touraine, and Normandy, especially after his nephew and rival Arthur of Brittany mysteriously died after John captured him. He therefore initiated payments to Otto and negotiations for an alliance.[23] He also used the economic ties between the regions to his favor. In February he allowed Aachen to import grain from Normandy because of

---

20. *RNI*, 193–94, no. 69 (dated March 28).
21. *RNI*, 189–91, no. 67; *REK*, 2:330, no. 1612 (dated April 5).
22. Ralph Turner, *King John*, 115–27.
23. *Pipe Rolls 3 John*, PR, NS, no. 14, 139, 211, and 289 reveal a heavy traffic of envoys between the regions during this year, including two "trumpeters" of Otto, a gift of a palfrey for the Welf, and the English envoys Ralph of Arden and Gerard of Rodes.

the service they had rendered to him in the past, and on June 4[24] he issued
a letter to the citizens of Cologne in which he thanked them for supporting his nephew and exhorted them to continue in Otto's service—an
ironic rhetorical shift in John's diplomacy.[25] He declared to the Cologne
burghers that he was finally in a position to help the Welf; however, this
endeavor was of course less philanthropic in reality. John also called on
any knights who would be loyal to him in Flanders, Hainault, and
Brabant to come to Rouen for service in return for fiefs of land and
money.[26]

On September 8, 1202, John confirmed a formal alliance with Otto at
La Suze "contra omnes homines."[27] The agreement speaks of the kings
putting past enmities behind them and is signed by all the major magnates
of England. On the same day, John asked the archbishop of Canterbury
and his clerics "most urgently" for a subvention to be used to advance
Otto to the emperorship.[28] John had now returned to the diplomatic and
kinship policy of his brother Richard, but not for the same reasons. This
alliance was only supported as long as it had political value for John's
conflicts with Philip, and it had little in the way of familial loyalty attached to it. It is hard to imagine that Otto could offer any real military
support at this time, but the value of the alliance lay in its usefulness in
negotiations with the French monarch, and it held out the prospect of
papal support.

As positively as Otto's diplomatic relations had improved with England they had deteriorated among the princes of the lower Rhineland
who had initially supported him. In September Otto held a Reichstag at
Maastricht to attend to, among other things, a feud that had broken out
between Duke Henry of Brabant and Count Otto of Guelders. The count
was forced to recognize Duke Henry as his feudal lord. While King Otto

---

24. *Böhmer*, 5, 2:1584, no. 10649.
25. *Rotuli litterarum patentium in turri Londoniensi asservati*, vol. 1, *1 Ab anno MCCI
ad annum MCCXVI*, ed. Thomas Duffus Hardy (London, 1835), 11; *HUB*, 1:31, no. 59;
Lappenberg, *Urkundliche Geschichte*, 6, no. 6; *Böhmer*, 5, 2:1584, no. 10652: "Rex etc.
Civibus Coloniensis etc. Grates vobis referimus multiplices super honore et bonis que
dilecto nepoti nostro Oton. Regi Romanorum domino vestro fecistis. Rogamus vos
attentius ut ita faciatis. Et sciatis quod Dei gratia cooperante in statu tali positi sumus quod
ei bene succurrere possumus. Teste me ipso apud Ponte Arch."
26. *Rotuli litterarum patentium*, 10–12; *Böhmer*, 5, 2:1584, no. 10651.
27. MGH Const., 2:29–30, no. 25; MGH Leges (folio), 2:207–8; *Böhmer*, 5, 2:1584,
no. 10654.
28. *Rymer*, 1:130; *Böhmer*, 5, 2:1584, no. 10653.

was resolving this dispute at the diet, Count Dietrich of Holland invaded Brabant and caused trouble before he was captured after a few days of skirmishing. Duke Henry held Count Otto responsible for this attack and stripped him of all his fiefs.

Archbishop Adolf, who had supported the duke of Brabant, intervened along with King Otto and other princes at the request of Otto of Guelders, and a second agreement was reached through his mediation. The count was given back his fiefs, but he was to appear before the duke and make satisfaction; if he did not his land would then be forfeited for good.[29] Further negotiations were held thereafter in Louvain by the interested parties, who were joined by Archbishop Adolf's kinsman Count Adolf of Berg. After three days of discussions, in which the duke of Brabant must have felt himself abused, he sealed off the exits of the city and ordered the citizens to assemble at a certain location. Fearing evil, Adolf and the count of Berg escaped from the city later that night.[30] It appears that the duke had instigated these measures to keep the count of Guelders from escaping; however, the fact that only Archbishop Adolf and his kinsman left the city while King Otto remained may imply that there was more than just tension between Duke Henry and Count Otto.

As if this aristocratic feuding over status were not enough to distract Otto IV, an open break emerged between Archbishop Adolf and the king upon the former's return to Cologne (suggesting a rupture had occurred in Louvain). Desperate for money, Otto IV had infringed on the minting and toll privileges that he had yielded to Adolf at his election, and it took the intervention of the papal legate Guido to restore peace between them.[31] The details of the settlement are remarkable in that they not only show the allegiance of the Cologne burghers to Otto and the distrust of all about the intentions of the archbishop but also clarify the contingent nature of Otto's kingship. The priors of the Cologne church, the nobility holding fiefs of the archbishopric, the ministerials, and twenty-four burghers (on behalf of the citizens) all swore that they would induce their archbishop to render constant and loyal allegiance to Otto or they would cease their obedience to him. Should a disagreement arise between Adolf and Otto a delegation of three representatives each from the prior, nobles, ministerials, and burghers of the

29. *REK,* 2:331, nos. 1617–19.
30. *REK,* 2:332, no. 1621.
31. *REK,* 2:332, nos. 1622–23; MGH Const., 2:28, no. 24.

city would decide for their respective orders to whom their loyalties would belong. In exchange for this loyalty Otto had to forgo the mint at Aachen and the tolls at Duisburg and Kaiserswerth. The city of Dortmund would serve as security for the debts of the king if he did not settle them with the archbishop by July 24 of the next year. Finally, these provisions were read aloud and the two disputants took public oaths to accept the legate Guido's authority in enforcing the agreement.

Clearly Otto had been seeking creative ways to obtain not only the resolution of aristocratic feuds but also money—both being needed to hold his fragile coalition together. He was heavily in debt to the archbishop of Cologne and had virtually no regalian rights with which to finance his kingship. The presumptive emperor had to forgo any claims to imperial mints and tolls. This indeed is symbolic of the impotence of Otto's kingship in Germany. Since Otto was in this position of dependence on Cologne and its archbishop, there appears to have developed great animosity against Adolf for his failure to provide financial aid. The archbishop had even forced the king to go deeply into debt to him by only loaning Otto funds. We also see again the remarkable role played by the burghers of Cologne, who took the extraordinary oath to enforce their own archbishop's loyalty to the king.

Innocent III had received further reports of Adolf's harsh treatment of Otto and he issued another terse letter of reprimand shortly following the settlement.[32] The pope informed Adolf, to whom he had recently given ecclesiastical jurisdiction over portions of the archdiocese of Trier,[33] that conflicting reports had reached his ears about Adolf's commitment to the Welf cause. He reminded the archbishop again of his electoral rights, which he had exercised freely in support of Otto while Philip of Swabia had been elected in direct contravention thereof. Once again the pope played on Adolf's own interests, even calling him the "creator" of Otto's kingship. Although Otto wrote to Innocent III at this time telling him of the favorable agreements with John and Adolf, the breach with the archbishop would never be healed.[34] Adolf would be ready to defect to the Staufen camp by the end of the following year.

---

32. *RNI*, 216–19, no. 80; *REK*, 2:334, no. 1626.

33. *REK*, 2:334, no. 1625. Innocent had excommunicated Archbishop John of Trier and made this transfer because of John's continued Staufen loyalty. It was, however, a tangible inducement for Adolf to continue supporting Otto's kingship.

34. *RNI*, 220–21, no. 81 (dated September–November, 1202).

Otto's letter to the pope indicates both that Adolf's submission to the king was brought about by the Cologne church and that the Welf alliance with John was contingent on John seeking peace with his Capetian lord. Thus it is clear that no joint hostilities were contemplated at this time against Philip II or Philip of Swabia, and the Anglo-Welf alliance treaty should be understood as defensive rather than offensive.[35] Since Arthur of Brittany's rebellion had been disposed of, the alliance provided John the hope of helpful papal mediation in his conflict with Philip II. Papal legates were in fact sent in May 1203, yet Philip II was unwilling to consider a settlement and continued to press his advantage by taking further territories in Poitou and Normandy. Now John hoped to enforce the defensive nature of the alliance and gain direct assistance from Otto and his princes in the lower Rhineland. He must not have understood the fragmenting power base of his nephew in northwest Germany, nor could he have anticipated the effect that Capetian conquests in northern France would have on the willingness of the lower Lotharingian princes to leave the Welf camp.

In April 1203 Otto wrote John to inform him that he was making some headway in the civil war and was thus prepared to make a one- to two-year truce with the Staufen forces in order to wage war on Philip II along with his brother Henry of Brunswick. In what could only be a familial expression of solidarity to his kinsman rather than a plausible military strategy, he offered to attack at either Cambrai or Reims.[36] Otto's offer was completely unrealistic in the face of the growing dissension among his own supporters, but he seems genuinely committed to providing service in memory of the assistance he received from his uncle Richard. John responded appreciatively in July by sending Otto three hundred marks of silver through merchants of Piacenza.[37]

Hopes for a joint invasion against Philip II in 1204 went for naught, as differences between Otto's allies became more heightened and further undermined his kingship.[38] A feud had broken out between Bishop John of Cambrai and Count Philip of Namur (who ruled Flanders during the

---

35. Ahlers, *Die Welfen*, 210.
36. *Rotuli chartarum*, 1:133; *Rymer*, 1:133–34; *Böhmer*, 5, 1:70, no. 231.
37. *Rotuli de liberate ac de misis et praestitis regnante Johanne*, ed. Thomas Duffus Hardy (London, 1844), 46. John also sent Otto a personal gift of a palfrey: see *Pipe Roll 5 John*, PR, NS, 16:9.
38. King John sent a certain Terricus Teutonicus (Dietrich the German) to Otto to ask for help: see *Pipe Roll 6 John*, PR, NS, 18:212. Cf. *Rotuli de liberate*, 77.

absence of his brother Baldwin), and the duke of Brabant had joined on the side of Namur, along with the count of Los. A peace was arranged with great difficulty in November 1203, but it was soon followed by a violent inheritance struggle after the death of Count Dietrich VII of Holland on February 4, 1204.[39] Meanwhile Archbishop Adolf, the most influential of the regional princes, was now strongly rebuked by the pope for his abandonment of Otto.[40] Innocent declared his amazement at the numerous reports of the archbishop's rejection of the Welf and commanded him to be loyal or face punishment.

With Otto's power base eroding fast he had to cancel his intended invasion of Swabia and wound up instead defending Brunswick against a strong attack by Staufen forces led by Philip of Swabia. He wounded his own cause further by stupidly quarreling with his own brother Henry of Brunswick over inheritance and finances.[41] Henry therefore jumped to the Staufen camp as the first of many defectors in the next few months and was able to recover his palatine lands along the upper Rhine. Without his own brother's support Otto was forced to withdraw and watch Philip of Swabia conquer Thuringia and then receive the homage of Otto's brother and of King Ottokar of Bohemia. By the time the bishop of London arrived in Cologne in late March or early April in hopes of arranging an invasion of France, Otto had lost Archbishop Adolf of Cologne and Duke Henry of Brabant as well as several other lesser Rhineland princes.[42] No German help would be forthcoming against the Capetian under such circumstances. Both John and Otto seemed worthy of the English king's cruel nickname "Lackland." Philip II continued his conquest of Normandy, which was completed on June 24 with the capitulation of Rouen.[43]

The connection between the events in northern France and those in the Rhineland was of course a strong one, and not only because of the Angevin-Welf link. The German princes of northwest Germany were no doubt influenced in their decision to leave the Welf camp by French

39. Winkelmann, *Philipp von Schwaben*, 1:319–23.

40. *RNI*, 256–58, no. 100; *REK*, 2:238, no. 1641. The *REK* shows no evidence of Adolf being with Otto from the time of their falling out in September 1202 to Adolf's open recognition of Philip of Swabia in 1204.

41. Arnold of Lübeck, *Chronica Slavorum*, 226–27.

42. Ralph of Coggeshall, *Chronicon Anglicanum*, 147–48; *Rotuli litterarum patentium*, 39; *Böhmer*, 5, 2:1587, no. 10667.

43. W. L. Warren, *King John* (Berkeley, 1978), 93–99.

advances directly on their western borders. This precarious situation forced Duke Henry of Brabant, for example, into joining the Staufen party, though he demanded that the duke of Swabia work to make peace between Philip II and John as the price for his submission.[44] Count Philip of Namur, who had been administering Flanders for his brother, was forced into a particularly difficult position because of this and eventually joined the Staufen and Capetian parties.[45]

Otto had now lost the three foundations of his military power in Germany—Archbishop Adolf of Cologne, Duke Henry I of Brabant, and his own brother Henry of Brunswick—along with lesser lights like the counts of Berg, Guelders, Mark, Jülich, Arnsberg, Hochstaden, and Kessel. His brother was in an awkward position himself, being torn between kinship loyalty and the lands in Saxony on the one hand, and his palatinate in the Staufen-controlled south on the other, which connected him through his wife to the Staufen dynasty. Otto now looked like his father Henry the Lion, who was himself abandoned by his allies not so long ago.[46]

At this point Adolf finally made his public break with the Welf, whose kingship he had privately opposed from the start.[47] Although the pope's confirmation of Otto's election and subsequent assurances had continually confirmed Adolf's electoral prerogatives, the archbishop was still disturbed about papal involvement in the electoral affairs of Germany. Innocent's claim to decide an election dispute among the German princes would make their electoral rights contingent on papal approval and vulnerable to papal veto. Furthermore, Adolf's territorial interests kept him from supporting the strengthening of Welf power in northern Germany. Finally, the advances of Philip II into northern France and the continued lack of English support for Otto left the archbishop increasingly isolated politically. Thus Adolf's secret negotiations with the Staufen party finally led to a settlement that he could accept.[48]

On January 6, 1205, Philip of Swabia laid down his kingship in Aachen to allow a "free election according to ancient rules," including the

44. Kienast, "Die Deutschen Fürsten," 10:166.

45. Kienast, *Deutschland und Frankreich*, 3:552f.

46. Ahlers, *Die Welfen*, 214.

47. Adolf entered into intense negotiations with Philip's party at Andernach in November, and on the twelfth of the month he met with the Staufen candidate in Koblenz to perform an oath of loyalty: see *REK*, 2:340–41, nos. 1651–52.

48. Stehkämper, "Adolf von Altena," 71.

archbishop of Cologne.[49] In this way Philip submitted to Adolf's view of the princes' hereditary electoral rights as superior to hereditary kingship.[50] The archbishop of Cologne participated in Philip's second election along with the other important electors who had joined the Staufen camp (the archbishop of Trier and the count palatine of the Rhine), and he then crowned the Staufer in Aachen. The participants had managed an election that came the closest of any to the traditional and customary requirements demanded by the archbishop and that preserved his exalted place among the electors. Now that his electoral rights were acknowledged, which had always been the central goal of his imperial politics, there was no stumbling block to Adolf's joining the Staufen side.[51] Adolf was now in a position to help prevent the victory of a Welf candidate and thus a possible threat to archiepiscopal territorial power in the region. And finally, it may well be that Philip of Swabia paid the sizable debt Adolf owed to the archbishop of Trier, in order to regain the cathedral treasury and reconcile the two archbishops; once again, it was debt, not greed, that motivated Adolf.[52] On what was surely a date chosen as a symbolic counterweight to Otto IV's exercise of royal power in Cologne, Archbishop Adolf crowned Philip of Swabia in Aachen on the day of the Feast of the Three Kings (*Dreikönigstag*).

Innocent III moved quickly to counteract the defections from Otto. On October 27, while negotiations between the archbishop and Philip of Swabia's party were underway, he issued a letter to Duke Henry of Brabant ordering him no longer to hold his daughter Maria from her betrothed husband, King Otto. Expecting Adolf to refuse to crown her, the pope told the duke to ask the papal allies Archbishop Siegfried of Mainz and Bishop

---

49. *CRC*, 219–20: "liberam electionem secundum antiquitatis institutum."

50. Stehkämper, "Adolf von Altena," 75: "Royal dynastic claims finally bowed to princely electoral rights."

51. Karl Leyser, "A Recent View of the German College of Electors," *Medium Aevum* 23 (1954):76–87 (reprinted in *Communications and Power in Medieval Europe: The Gregorian Revolution and Beyond*, ed. Timothy Reuter [London and Rio Grande, OH, 1994], 183: "He [Philip of Swabia] had to allow that the archbishop of Cologne had never been wrong, and that without him he could not be properly king. For the formation of the College of Electors this really mattered a great deal more than the writings of the canonists and perhaps even papal propaganda, which, after all, did not remain unanswered in Germany."

52. Stehkämper emphasizes the importance of Adolf's defense of his electoral rights ("Adolf von Altena," 77) and sees Adolf as a "Rechtsfanatiker" (82). He does not, however, give enough emphasis to the possible threat of a Welf kingship to the archbishop's territorial ambitions. For the cathedral treasury issue see Hucker, *Kaiser Otto IV.*, 80–83.

John of Cambrai to do so within a month.[53] Of course the duke ignored this letter, since he had already decided to switch to the Staufen camp. Two days later Innocent issued a letter to the archbishop of Mainz and the bishop of Cambrai, as well as to Prior Bruno of Bonn, telling them to command Adolf one last time to remain loyal to Otto. Innocent held Adolf personally responsible for moving the other princes to join Philip of Swabia—an oversimplification of myriad causations for noble defections from Otto—and threatened therefore to excommunicate him.[54]

It is quite significant that in this letter the pope took care to involve the citizens of Cologne. Their role in the support of Otto was certainly known to Innocent, particularly in contrast to the behavior of their archbishop. The pope had already written letters of encouragement to them on December 12, 1203, and April 23, 1204. In the December 12 letter Innocent assured the burghers that the time was coming when "God willing, you shall receive the reward of your labor, and the [royal] plant that you have planted will bear fruit."[55] In the April letter the pope further elaborated on this imagery.

> For just as a mother cannot forget the son of her womb, thus you are not able to neglect [your] king, whom, as far as concerns the empire, you have begotten. If you maintain your plant and raise profitably what you have planted, you fulfill the care of the planter in a praiseworthy manner. . . . Indeed, although you have borne the burden and heat of the day thus far as if alone, God forbid that others should enter into your labors without you and harvest with rejoicing that which you sowed with great care.[56]

The colorful rhetoric of this letter reminds us of the central role played by the burghers of Cologne in Otto's kingship. In a set of mixed meta-

---

53. *REK,* 2:239, no. 1649.

54. *RNI,* 279–82, no. 113; *REK,* 2:339 no. 1650.

55. *UGN,* 2:6, no. 8; *Ennen/Eckertz,* 1:13, no. 7: "Cum igitur iam tempus immineat, quo dante Domino de labore vestro recipiatis premium et fructus vobis planta proferat, quam plantastis."

56. *UGN,* 2:9, no. 12; *Ennen/Eckertz,* 2:16 no. 10: "Quoniam sicut mater filii uteri sui oblivisci non potest, sic nec vos eidem regi potestis deesse, quem, quoad imperium pertinet, genuistis. Si manutenetis igitur plantam vestram, erigatis utiliter, quod plantastis, impletis laudabiliter sollicitudinem plantoris. . . . Sane cum hucusque [*sic*] pondus diei et estus portaveritis quasi soli, absit, ut alii sine vobis in labores vestros introeant et metant cum exultatione, quod cum anxietate nimia seminastis."

phors, they are described as the mother who gave it birth and the gardener who planted and nurtures it. In point of fact, they were his only support in Germany by this time. King John of England had also written to the citizens of Cologne again on April 11, 1204 (only days before the papal letter arrived), to encourage them to maintain support for Otto.[57] As a reward for their service he also confirmed their trade privileges in England. Later that year, on December 25, John issued an official declaration of these privileges, which were to remain in effect only as long as the city remained loyal to Otto.[58] This was certainly a strong incentive for the citizens to remain with Otto.[59] Yet John provided no further material support for his nephew in his time of greatest need; of course he was in no position to do so.

The most enduring and impressive monument of Cologne support for Otto was fashioned during this crucial year of political isolation. The cathedral chapter, which remained loyal to the Welf despite its archbishop, had commissioned a beautiful reliquary for the Three Kings (Magi), which remains today on the main altar of the Cologne cathedral.[60] During this year, however, a last-minute alteration in the iconographical program was made in an effort to legitimate Otto's waning kingship. On the front side of the reliquary appears the scene of the Adoration of the Magi. Here we find three niches, originally one for each king, to the left of a larger niche for the Virgin and Christ Child, who receive the gifts being offered. Yet in the final production two of the kings were fitted uncomfortably together into the central niche provided for the

57. *Rotuli litterarum patentium*, 40–41; *Rymer*, 1:133; *Ennen/Eckertz*, 2:15, no. 9; Lappenberg, *Urkundliche Geschichte*, 6, no. 7; *HUB*, 1:33, no. 63; Kuske, *Quellen zur Geschichte des Kölner Handels*, 1:4, no. 9; *Böhmer*, 5, 2:1587, no. 10668.

58. *Rotuli litterarum patentium*, 48; *Ennen/Eckertz*, 2:16, no. 11; Lappenberg, *Urkundliche Geschichte*, 6, no. 8; *HUB*, 1:34, no. 69; *Böhmer*, 5, 2:1588, no. 10674. John also forgave the debts of Simon Saphir and Walter Sprok, two citizens of Ghent, "pro amore dilecti nepotis nostri Regi Othonis": see *Rotuli litterarum patentium*, 44; *Rotuli litterarum clausarum*, 1:3. Simon Saphir and Walter Sprok were Flemish merchants who also served as lending agents and middlemen between the two monarchs. This debt may well have been one incurred by Otto himself.

59. Keller, *Zwischen regionaler Begrenzung und universalem Horizont*, 430.

60. Concerning the shrine see Joseph Hoster, "Zur Form der Stirnseite des Dreikönigsschreins," in *Miscellanea Pro Arte: Hermann Schnitzler zur Vollendung des 60. Lebensjahres* (Düsseldorf, 1965), 194–217; Paul Clemen, Heinrich Neuß, and Fritz Witte, "Der Dom zu Köln," in *Die Kunstdenkmäler der Stadt Köln* (Düsseldorf, 1937), 1:337–41; Anton von Euw, "Darstellungen der Hl. Drei Könige im Kölner Dom und ihre ikonographische Herleitung," *Kölner Domblatt, Jahrbuch des Zentral-Dombauvereins* 23/24 (1964): 313ff.

one king, so that a figure of Otto could be placed in the vacant niche. Otto therefore had joined the Three Kings, the city's spiritual patrons, in making an offering to the Christ Child. Otto is represented offering a golden crown, a reminder that he had commissioned three golden crowns for the Three Kings in 1200. Herein is also an echo of the Mass ordo for the Feast of the Epiphany, in which the king offers gold at the *offertorium*. This was a beautifully crafted stroke calculated to raise the prestige of Otto's kingship in a fashion that Barbarossa and Rainald of Dassel would have admired.[61] It also serves as a reminder that Otto's kingship was a Cologner creation.

The patrician leaders of the city did indeed fulfill their oaths and attempted to bring their archbishop back to the Welf party in January 1205.[62] They used the same argument that Innocent III had employed with Adolf, namely, that it was through the archbishop's recommendation in the first place that the pope confirmed the election of Otto. The burghers of Cologne were unsuccessful, however. Thus the provisions of the agreement made in October 1202 finally went into effect: letters that showed joint solidarity against the archbishop were sent to the pope by Otto, the cathedral chapter, and the citizens of Cologne.

Meanwhile, Adolf crowned Philip of Swabia in Aachen on January 6, 1205,[63] and in return the newly anointed king confirmed all of Adolf's regalian rights and privileges—including the duchy of Westphalia, the imperial lands of Andernach and Eckenhagen, and imperial mints, tolls, and markets—and gave him additionally the imperial residence in Brackel and a priory in Kerpen.[64] At this point Adolf had achieved all of his political objectives. He had maintained his hereditary electoral prerogatives and had also obtained confirmation of his regional principality from the Staufer. Adolf seemed now in a strong position. Intervention by Innocent III, however, whose role the archbishop had been extremely wary of, would rob him of his newly won victory.

Once the news of the Aachen coronation reached Rome Innocent wrote again to the new archbishop of Mainz and the bishop of Cambrai, as well as to the *scholasticus* Henry of St. Gereon in Cologne, commanding them to formally excommunicate Adolf. The legates were to remove

61. Stehkämper, "England und die Stadt Köln," 241.
62. Arnold of Lübeck, *Chronica Slavorum*, 255; *REK*, 2:343, no. 1660.
63. *REK*, 2:341, no. 1655.
64. *REK*, 2:341–42, no. 1656; *UGN*, 1:7–8, no. 11.

Adolf from office and hold a new episcopal election if he did not proceed to Rome within a month for discipline.[65] A second letter was given to the burghers of Cologne informing them of the forthcoming sanctions by the papal legates.[66] An additional papal letter was sent sometime thereafter in May, instructing the legates to try once more to regain Adolf's allegiance.[67] Of course the attempt was futile, and on May 19 Adolf was publicly excommunicated and threatened with deposition.[68]

The rift between the archbishop and the city of Cologne had widened significantly now. While attending the Staufen court at Speyer, Adolf complained to his new king about the excommunication and asked for military assistance against his own citizens, who still held to Otto against the archbishop's wishes. Philip and the princes promised a campaign for October.[69] In preparation for the attack, the Rhine was blocked above and below the city in June by Adolf's vassals. The citizens of Cologne, however, took preemptive action themselves, attacking with the support of whatever troops Otto and the duke of Limburg possessed and conquering Hochstaden, whose count was a strong ally of the archbishop. Cologne was fighting not only for Otto but also for its own economic life and independence.[70]

The papal legates responded to the military moves against the city with the formal deposition of Adolf on June 19 in the presence of the Welf king, who was likely very satisfied with the measure.[71] The deposition was followed on July 25 by the election of Bruno IV, the prior of Bonn and a scion of the comital house of Sayn, which was very loyal to Otto.[72] Innocent III wrote to the Cologne church commending them on the election of Bruno IV and also sent separate letters to the people of Cologne and their leaders exhorting them to resist Philip of Swabia. In a December 23 letter, the pope announced his confirmation of Bruno IV's election and told the burghers of Cologne to consider Adolf as excommunicate and deposed.[73]

---

65. *RNI*, 285–90, no. 116; *REK*, 2:343–44, no. 1664.

66. *RNI*, 290–92, no. 117.

67. *RNI*, 292–94, no. 118.

68. *REK*, 2:341, no. 1666.

69. *REK*, 2:344–45, no. 1667.

70. *REK*, 2:345, no. 1669.

71. *REK*, 2:347, no. 1684.

72. *REK*, 3, 1:1, no. 1.

73. *RNI*, 308–9, no. 130; *REK*, 3, 1:2, no. 5 (dated September 23); *REK*, 3, 1:3, no. 11.

Adolf responded to the election of Bruno IV with his own invasion of the territories of the duke of Limburg in August and September. He was then joined by Philip of Swabia's army, which met with the duke of Brabant's contingent during its march to Cologne on September 29. Five days later the city was besieged, but again its strong walls kept the enemy at bay. Philip then turned northward to Neuß and conquered the nearby town, handing it over to Adolf. This provided the deposed archbishop a crucial base of operations from which, with the support of the princes of the lower Rhineland, he could attack Cologne and the lands of the duke of Limburg.[74]

During all these moves, the pope continued to exert moral pressure on those opposing Otto, but he was of little real help. Bruno IV could only remain as the archbishop of Cologne as long as the city held out. Furthermore, Otto received no material support at this time from John, who had become embroiled in his own dispute with the papacy over the election of Stephan Langton as archbishop of Canterbury.[75] Although he had been admonished a fourth and fifth time by Innocent III to pay Otto's legacy, John did little more for Otto than pardon a member of the Welf's court named Hugh de Gurnay from royal "malevolentiam," at the Welf's request.[76] In fact, precisely because of the dispute over the Canterbury election, Otto lost a large sum of money that had been earmarked for him. Three thousand marks had been raised for Otto's cause and were in the hands of the archbishop (this may have been the response to John's request for money from the archdiocese of Canterbury in September 1202 when the formal alliance was promulgated); however, the Pipe Rolls for 1205 and 1206 show no such payment into the royal treasury.[77] Of course John could simply have chosen not to send the money after seeing the collapse of the Welf party. As the winter snows fell in both England and Germany, the respective kings of these realms were isolated

---

74. *REK*, 3, 1:1, nos. 2–3; 3, 1:2, no. 6.

75. The Cologne chronicler was aware of this dispute, perhaps because of its direct implications for the city's needed English support: see *CRC*, 184.

76. *RNI*, 307–8, no. 129 (dated September 22, 1205). Innocent also wrote to the bishops Eustace of Ely, Philip of Durham, and Mangerus of Worcester and to other English magnates on February 17, 1206 (*RNI*, 310–12, nos. 131–32) asking them to pressure the king into paying the legacy. A similar letter was even issued on the same day to Archbishop Geoffrey of York, John's illegitimate brother, commanding him to help his nephew (*RNI*, 313–14, no. 135). For John's pardon of Hugh de Gurnay see *Rotuli litterarum patentium*, 57; *Rymer*, 1:139, *Böhmer*, 5, 2:1589, no. 10680.

77. *Rotuli litterarum patentium*, 48; *Böhmer*, 5, 2:1588, no. 10673.

and mired in their own regional and personal problems. Otto's kingship in particular was clearly being slowly strangled to death.

It should be quite clear by this time that the often described "Welf-English alliance" against the Staufer king had never fully developed and was of no significance for either monarch. This would continue to be so until 1214, where its brief moment of joint action ended swifly in disaster. What are we to make of these bewildering and entangled series of diplomatic conflicts? Do we see here any effective alliances forming anywhere? Who is the "winner" thus far? Again, we find a narrative more typical of medieval social than modern political discourse. There are as many motives for political action as there are political players. Yet all players were fundamentally seeking to defend their own status and prerogatives against any possible diminution. This is true whether we are considering the archbishop of Cologne, the duke of Brabant, Otto IV, Philip of Swabia, the English king, or the archbishop of Canterbury. In origin such disputes were actually self-contained bilateral conflicts. But the social nature of medieval politics assured that they would become intertwined through kinship, lordship, and ecclesiastical ties, even those now extending across regions and political communities in an increasingly integrated Europe.

The result is a web of sociopolitical relationships that put the participants at impossible odds against each other and produced constantly shifting coalitions, with the pope serving as moderator. It is no wonder that interregional relations proved so difficult, given the fact that regional, local, and personal relations were already deeply complex. Surely King John and King Otto IV had failed to fashion a workable coalition, either between themselves or within their own territories. This was partly due to their own lack of ability to lead, but it was also due to the nature of social discourse within and between their political communities. Hence their political failures should teach us about medieval society more than they disappoint us about medieval politics. Both John and his royal nephew Otto are exemplary of the ties that bound medieval society.

From Isolation to Bouvines: Anglo-German Diplomacy and Cologne (1206–14)

The Welf party was so isolated in Cologne that no suffragan bishops who could consecrate Bruno IV of Sayn as archbishop were found in Germany. Therefore, remarkably, two unnamed English bishops were brought in to assist Archbishop Siegfried of Mainz in the ceremony held on June 6, 1206.[78] The Cologne chronicle mentions this event in two passages, each of which account for the presence of English bishops differently. The first says that they had come "by apostolic command" [*iussu apostolici*], the second that they were "sent by the king of England" [*a rege Angliae missis*].[79] A Pipe Roll entry for the eighth year of John's reign suggests that both may have been true.[80] Here a certain William of Leicester, who was an Englishman yet the notary of the archbishop of Mainz, is said to have received the English bishops. Innocent III had not forgotten Adolf of Altena, however, and he wrote to him on June 24 admonishing him to do penance and return to obedience.[81] The change in archbishops may have brought peace within the city of Cologne, but storm clouds had gathered outside and lightning would soon strike.

After Bruno IV's consecration the new archbishop took troops loyal to him and joined Otto on campaign. On July 27 the combined forces of Philip of Swabia and Otto finally met in open battle near Wassenberg (north of Aachen). Otto's forces were put to flight and the newly consecrated bishop fled into Wassenberg Castle, where he was imprisoned. He was later taken to southern Germany and held for over a year under severe conditions in various places, such as Trifels (where Richard I had been detained), Hohenems (near Bregenz), Würzburg, and Rothenburg ob der Tauber. Otto was fortunate enough to escape and retreated back to the city of Cologne.[82] The citizens of the city made up a large part of his fighting force, since Adolf still maintained the loyalties of most of the countryside around Cologne. This looked like the end for Otto's kingship.

Otto and the citizens of Cologne braced for the onslaught that came to the city as Philip's and Adolf's armies approached after the disaster at

---

78. *REK*, 3, 1:4, no. 18.

79. *CRC*, 17: "Bruno electus a Sigefrido Mogontino archiepiscopo Colonie consecratur in archiepiscopum 8. Idus Iunii [June 6], presentibus duobus episcopis, qui ad hoc ipsum iussu apostolici de Anglia illuc advenerant." *CRC*, 223: "Rex autem Otto et Bruno, qui ipso mense in archiepiscopum ordinatus fuerat a Sifrido Mogontino, presentibus duobus episcopis de Brittannia a rege Angliae missus, cum 400 militibus et duobus milibus peditum de Colonia exeuntes, cum eodem confligere statuerunt."

80. *Pipe Roll 8 John*, PR, NS, 20:22: "Et magistro Willelmo de Leicestr' et episcopis qui cum eo ierunt in Alemanniam pro navi in qua transfretaverunt iiii li. et v s. per breve eiusdem. Et item pro alia navi locata ad eundem in servitio R. vi li. et iii s. per idem breve. Et in liberatione ciuisdam probatoris ii s. et x d. de xxxiii diebus." See also Ahlers, *Die Welfen*, 219 n. 1188.

81. *REK*, 3, 1:4, no. 19.

82. *REK*, 3, 1:4, no. 21.

Wassenberg. In September the cathedral deacon Conrad, along with the city's priors and clergy, wrote to Innocent III and described the devastation they had suffered as a result. The church's property had been confiscated outside the city, with much of it burned and the religious abused. Their archbishop had been imprisoned, and the blockade of the city had caused supplies to run out; the burghers of Cologne could not hold out much longer. They therefore pleaded with the pope as the sole support for Otto. A Liège chronicle tells of their bravery in battle at Wassenberg for the Welf cause, but such fidelity only made more misery for them.[83]

Now they were isolated and wearied of the cost of being the only supporter of Otto left in the region.[84] The city capitulated on November 11, 1206, and Adolf sought his restoration as the city's archbishop.[85] A final peace between the city and Philip of Swabia was established in January 1207, in which the citizens agreed to work with Rome toward a reinstatement of Adolf and a recognition of him as archbishop. They also agreed to accept Philip's will should Adolf not succeed in obtaining reinstatement. In return the vassals of Adolf agreed to molest the city and its citizens no longer.[86] The burghers and clergy had been the strongest supporters of Otto all the way until their defeat at the hands of the Staufen siege. They had been more dependable and effective than the other parties that brought about his kingship in the first place: Archbishop Adolf, the Angevin court, and even Pope Innocent III. Indeed they had been the foundation for Otto's kingship from his election until their honorable defeat in 1206, while all others failed him.[87]

Otto escaped from Cologne in the last days of its defense and retreated to his allodial lands in Brunswick. They must have seemed a strange, unfamiliar place of exile since he had never actually lived there for any length of time. His kingship was destroyed and there was little hope of recovery. From here he made a trip to the land of his childhood and visited the court of his hitherto unsupportive uncle John in May 1207.[88]

---

83. *Reineri Annales S. Iacobi Leodiensis,* ed. G. Pertz, MGH SS, no. 16 (Hanover, 1859; reprint, 1994), 660.

84. *CRC,* 224.

85. *REK,* 3, 1:5, no. 24.

86. *REK,* 3, 1:5, no. 25.

87. Stehkämper ("England und die Stadt Köln," 243) concludes, "The city of Cologne held true to Otto to the bitter end because they had initiated his kingship."

88. *CRC,* 224; Roger of Wendover, *Flores historiarum,* 2:35; *MPHA,* 2:108–9; *Annales de Wigornia,* ed. Henry Richards Luard, RS, no. 36 (London, 1869; reprint, 1965)

John realized that the victory of Philip of Swabia would only bode well for his enemy Philip II of France, hence he finally offered monetary assistance to his nephew. John was not thereby proposing a close coordination of activities, however, but rather merely funding Otto further in hopes of prolonging the conflict in Germany and thus delaying a complete Staufen victory.[89]

It is clear that John had expected Otto to come to England, as envoys had already arrived from his nephew and John had then sent Dietrich the German, who was involved in the 1202 alliance negotiations, to accompany Otto to England.[90] Otto met his uncle at Stapleford Abbots in the chambers of the abbot of Bury St. Edmunds[91] and returned shortly thereafter to Saxony with six thousand marks and a fief for his seneschal Conrad of Wijlre.[92] In June John sent Otto a horse as well.[93] The bishop of Norwich also spent 200 pounds on Otto during a visit,[94] and royal gifts were given to Otto's chamberlain John, Hugh de Gurnay, and Lambert of Cologne.[95] Lambert's presence in Otto's entourage indicates a continued support of the Welf by Cologne burghers, as he was the same man who used to collect a yearly feudal rent along with the archbishop of Cologne before its discontinuance. John apparently received a great crown from Otto as a reciprocal gift.[96]

While Otto was making his fund-raising trip to England, Philip of Swabia was consolidating his power in Cologne. On April 22 he celebrated Easter there, and a week later he confirmed the Cologne burghers'

4:395; Nicholaus Trivet, *Annales*, ed. Thomas Hog, English Historical Society Publications (London, 1845; reprint, 1964), 180.

89. Kienast, "Die Deutschen Fürsten," 10:170.

90. *Pipe Roll 9 John*, PR, NS, 22:30; *Rotuli litterarum clausarum*, 1:82 (dated May 6, 1207). Here again we see the financing role of Walter Sprok, who here has loaned Terricus Teutonicus (Dietrich the German) one hundred marks for his trip with Otto. For biographical information on Dietrich the German see Hucker, *Kaiser Otto IV.*, 468–69; Natalie Fryde, *Ein mittelalterlicher deutscher Großunternehmer: Terricus Teotonicus de Colonia in England, 1217–1247*, Vierteljahrschrift für Sozial- und Wirtschaftsgeschichte Beihefte, no. 125 (Stuttgart, 1996).

91. *Annales Sancti Edmundi*, ed. T. Arnold, RS, no. 96 (London, 1890–96), 2:16.

92. *Rotuli litterarum clausarum*, 1:82 (Westminster, May 8, 1207). Otto's seneschal Conrad of Wijrle would continue to receive a money fief from this year onward. The English chronicles assert that Otto received only five thousand marks.

93. Ibid., 1:86 (June 22, 1207).

94. Ibid., 1:82 (Westminster, May 8, 1207).

95. *Pipe Roll 9 John*, PR, NS, 22:105; *Rotuli litterarum clausarum*, 1:87 (July 8, 1207).

96. *Rotuli litterarum clausarum*, 1:77.

freedom from the tolls of Boppard and Kaiserswerth (these were part of the regalian rights given to the archbishop) and generously allowed them to build fortifications within the city's walls.[97] The pope encouraged the city to remain loyal to Otto, but the request was completely unrealistic at this point.[98] By the autumn it was clear that Philip was in full command of the region around Cologne, and the pope entered into negotiations with him. Innocent instructed his legates to work for the release of Bruno and also allowed them, clearly as a quid pro quo concession to the Staufen party, to free Adolf from excommunication if he swore publicly to come to Rome within a month for papal judgment.[99] Obviously a settlement of the Cologne schism had to be reached for Philip of Swabia to have a chance at an agreement with the pope that would lead to imperial coronation. After all, the legitimacy of his kingship rested on the participation of the archbishop as his elector. Meanwhile, Otto remained isolated in Brunswick, and a truce was announced until June 24, 1208.

Philip held a great Reichstag at Augsburg on November 30, where he released Bruno IV and sent him to Rome with the returning legates. In return the legates released Adolf from excommunication on condition that he too went to Rome.[100] Adolf complied and in early 1208 negotiations began. Innocent, however, postponed his decision until the following Advent (November 30); until then Bruno held the spiritual jurisdiction of the archdiocese and Adolf could retain all the fortifications that he had possessed since the imprisonment of Bruno.[101]

Innocent's plan to issue a final judgment in November was affected heavily by the sudden news of Philip of Swabia's murder on June 21, 1208. The Bavarian count palatine, Otto of Wittelsbach, who was betrothed to a daughter of Philip, killed the Staufer in Bamberg when he heard the rumor that the princess was to be married instead to the pope's nephew as a means of reconciling with the papacy.[102] What years of diplomatic and military maneuvering could not accomplish the violent anger of an offended nobleman could, and Otto awoke the next morning more of a king than he had been the night before. He wrote immediately

---

97. *REK,* 3, 1:5, no. 27; *UGN,* 2:11–12, no. 17; Kuske, *Quellen zur Geschichte des Kölner Handels,* 1:5, no. 10.

98. *REK,* 3, 1:5, no. 26 (dated March 13).

99. *RNI,* 339–40, no. 145; *REK,* 3, 1:6, nos. 32–33 (dated November 1).

100. *REK,* 3, 1:6, no. 34.

101. *REK,* 3, 1:6–7, nos. 38, 40.

102. Haverkamp, *Medieval Germany,* 246.

to the pope asking him to send the archbishops of Mainz and Cologne (meaning Bruno IV) to assist him. Bruno then returned to Cologne on September 11 and was received with great rejoicing.[103] The Staufen army quickly disbanded and almost every German prince accepted the weak Otto of Brunswick-Poitou as their king by default. The Capetian suggestion of electing Duke Henry of Brabant as the new king received little serious consideration; in fact, the duke himself declined and joined the Welf camp.[104] At the same time, Innocent wrote to the German clergy as well as to the "judges, jurors, and citizens of Cologne" [*iudicibus, scabinis et civibus Coloniensibus*] and encouraged them to hold fast to Otto.[105] Ironically the death of his rival had raised his kingship from its deathbed: he had been given a second offer to rule in Germany, as unexpected as the first.

Through papal intervention Otto accepted betrothal to Beatrix of Staufen (rather than to Maria of Brabant as originally planned) on November 11 in Frankfurt, in an effort to join the Welf and Staufen dynasties. The wealth of the Staufen family lands in Swabia were now at his disposal. He had finally been given the means to maintain himself. Altogether Otto must have spent around twenty-two thousand marks to secure the princes' approval of his kingship. This money did not come from England, so it was the Staufen lands that made such generosity possible.[106]

Now Otto had been fully acknowledged in Germany and had the power base from which to launch his long-promised invasion of France. Until now Otto had been more of a liability for King John, but as the circumstances changed radically, so did the interest of the uncle in his nephew. Contact had continued between the two in early 1208, and Otto's men Hugh de Gurnay, the seneschal Conrad of Wijlre, Lambekin (or Lambert) of Cologne, and the chamberlain John Lupus all still enjoyed their English fiefs.[107] The timing of these grants indicates that

103. *REK*, 3, 1:7, nos. 41, 44.

104. Innocent III had written letters to Archbishop Bruno IV and other German bishops not to hold another election and thus disturb the new peace. The German princes in turn refused Philip II's suggestion: see *REK*, 3, 1:7, no. 42; 3, 1:8, no. 45.

105. *RNI*, 357, no. 157; *REK*, 3, 1:7, no. 43.

106. Ahlers, *Die Welfen*, 224–25.

107. *Rotuli litterarum clausarum*, 1:114 (May 14, 1208); *Rotuli litterarum patentium*, 1:85 (July 16, 1208). The Westphalian nobleman Bernhard of Horstmar had joined this group as an envoy of Otto in this year: see *Rotuli litterarum patentium*, 1:87 (Westminster, October 25, 1208). John sent Otto yet another horse during this year as well: see *Pipe Roll 10 John*, PR, NS, 23:171.

German embassies had visited England in July and October of 1208. Innocent III had written the English monarch as well, telling him of the great opportunity that lay before Otto to become emperor and exhorting John to support his kinsman.[108] Yet John was himself deeply enmeshed in the dispute with Innocent III over Archbishop Stephan Langton, which eventually led to the king's excommunication and an interdict for England. John was even deposed by the pope in 1213 before he submitted in the face of a French invasion. Thus he was clearly not able to coordinate military activities with Otto and would not be until 1214.[109] Yet another opportunity to coordinate a coalition between political communities was missed because of regional and political problems within each political community.

Talks continued, however, between the two royal relatives. In fact Otto sent his brother Henry of Brunswick (with whom he had been reconciled) to England in 1209, while he was entering negotiations for an imperial coronation. Count Palatine Henry had come officially on behalf of his brother and the German princes to seek John's reconciliation with the pope and Stephen Langton.[110] The Waverly annals record that John, in response to Henry's embassy and a subsequent letter from Otto, sent an embassy of four great men back to Germany to continue these discussions, and he supposedly also softened his treatment of the English church as a result of Henry's visit.[111] Henry had also come for a more practical reason: to obtain further subsidies from his uncle.[112] Otto was obviously in great need of money, both to pay off his princes and to prepare for his imperial coronation. In fact his own seneschal Conrad of Wijlre required an Angevin subvention in order to redeem jewels that he had pawned in Cologne on behalf of the German king.[113] Henry of

---

108. *RNI,* 359, no. 159 (S. Germano-Sora, July 15–early August 1208).

109. His only effort on Otto's behalf, other than the gifts mentioned already and fiefs to Otto's envoys, was the pardon of Harlacus de Marzano at the Welf's request in September 1208: see *Rotuli litterarum patentium,* 1:18.

110. *Annales de Waverleia,* 2:261.

111. This letter is probably the one written by Otto shortly after his imperial coronation in October: see *Acta Imperii Inedita Saeculi XIII et XIV,* ed. Edward Winkelmann (Innsbruck, 1880–85; rpt. Aalen 1964), 1:19, no. 28; *Böhmer,* 5, 1:84–85, no. 266, and 5, 1:98, no. 303. The connection between Otto's imperial coronation in Rome and his intercession with John on behalf of the pope is obvious.

112. Robert of Wendover, *Flores historiarum,* 2:49; *MPHA,* 2:117, 119–20; *MPCM,* 2:524; Ralph of Coggeshall, *Chronicon Anglicanum,* 163; *Annales de Dunstaplia,* 3: 31–32.

113. *Pipe Roll 11 John,* PR, NS, 24:65.

Brunswick left his own son and namesake in England at the tender age of three to be educated, just as his father had done to Otto and William. Thus there are many entries for the maintenance and education of the son in the Liberate Rolls for the year May 1209–May 1210.[114] Payments for envoys of both Henry and Otto appear as well,[115] and both Simon Saphir and Otto's seneschal Conrad of Wijlre received royal privileges that reveal the economic initiatives these men pursued in England along with their diplomatic duties.[116] Henry of Brunswick himself received a sizable financial gift and money fief[117] and even managed a royal grant of trade protection for the citizens of Utrecht.[118]

This busy interregional diplomatic activity was John's way of greasing the wheels for a renewed anti-Capetian coalition now that Otto had a real power base in Germany. His intentions became clear in an encyclical letter sent to the German princes on March 24, 1209.[119] The English king had discussed more than the Langton affair with his nephew Henry, who had brought news from the German princes. John responded by sending back to Germany an embassy of five diplomats to continue the discussions, including a joint military move against Philip II. John had the cheek to assert that since he had supported his nephew for so long it was now time that he was paid back. This makes clear that John's spotty assistance to his nephew was always given in his own self-interest rather than out of kinship obligations. In addition we can suppose that John had asked for a good word on his behalf during the coronation negotiations with the Curia. Philip II at least believed that a joint invasion was in the planning stages, since his excuse for not joining in the Albigensian crusade was the military threat of Otto and John.[120]

---

114. *Rotuli de liberate,* 110–13, 116, 118, 122, 124, 127–29, 132, 134, 138, 141–43, 148–50, 152, 155, 158–59, 163, 164, 166, 169. The son returned to Germany in 1211–12: see *Pipe Roll 14 John,* PR, NS, 30:171.

115. *Rotuli de liberate,* 109, 119, 133.

116. *Rotuli litterarum patentium,* 89; *Rymer,* 1:154 (March 24, 1209). Simon Saphir was also given a letter of free trade in wool between England and Flanders for this year (*Rotuli litterarum patentium,* 90).

117. *Rotuli litterarum patentium,* 89; *Rymer,* 1:154 (March 24, 1209).

118. *Rotuli litterarum patentium,* 90 (March 24, 1209).

119. Ibid., 91–92; *Rymer,* 1:153–54; *REK,* 3, 1:12, no. 59; *Böhmer,* 5, 2:1592, no. 10712 (London, March 24, 1209). This letter was clearly issued in response to the embassy of Henry of Brunswick, Conrad of Wijlre, and Simon Saphir.

120. *Reineri Annales S. Iacobi Leodiensis,* 663. CRC (230) tells of the involvement of crusaders from England, France, and Lotharingia in this crusade, referring to the Albigensians as "Begginos."

Actually, little immediate danger existed. Philip was successful in fomenting rebellion in Wales and Ireland, which would occupy John until 1212. Otto was too busy preparing for his imperial coronation, after which he would alienate the pope and once again be bogged down in a civil war. Although Otto seemed to be in a powerful position, he was highly beholden to the German princes. This feature of his kingship would never change. Early resistance to any real exercise of royal power by Otto in Germany appeared in the rumor floated in 1213 that he planned to create an English taxation system. This was an old charge laid before Henry V and had resurfaced to undermine Otto's resurrected kingship. Indeed his own turncoat chancellor, Bishop Conrad of Speyer, spread the rumor that Otto had planned to draw a regular income for imperial finances from a system of royal brothels.[121] Though likely nothing more than a bad joke, this latter rumor is as unbelievable as the former, and together they confirm the continued weakness of Otto's position in Germany.

The fate of Adolf of Altena was obscured amid all the events since the death of Philip of Swabia. He had returned to Germany from Rome after a decision in his case had been delayed by the pope. After the death of Philip and the subsequent change of the political landscape of Germany, Adolf felt it unsafe to cross the Alps and return to Rome. Innocent rejected his request, brought by a certain cleric named Hermann, to have the case adjudicated by a papal legate in Germany. The pope wrote back on October 23, 1208, addressing Adolf as "quondam archiepiscopus," and ordered him to appear either in person or through representatives so that a decision could be rendered. In a statement that assured Adolf he had lost in the matter, Innocent guaranteed that if he made satisfaction for his error he would be raised to another see in the future.[122] Circumstances looked even bleaker for Adolf when Bruno IV died on November 2 and his successor Dietrich I (1208–12) was elected and invested by Otto on December 22.[123] Otto had hastened to Cologne upon word that the priors were uncertain whom to elect. His first suggestion of Bishop John of Cambrai was rejected and they soon settled on Dietrich, an elderly prior of Holy Apostles Church in Cologne. Dietrich sought to placate Adolf by granting him, with the approval of

---

121. Keller, *Zwischen regionaler Begrenzung und universalem Horizont,* 370.
122. *RNI,* 371–73, no. 166; *REK,* 3, 1:8, no. 47.
123. *REK,* 3, 1:9–10, nos. 51, 53.

the priors, nobility, ministerials, and burghers of Cologne, a rent of 250 marks on the day of his consecration (May 24, 1209).[124] It would seem that the once proud Adolf of Altena was finished, but we shall soon see him again in Cologne.

Although Otto refused as an unacceptable prerequisite for coronation the papal demand for a promise not to recover the papal lands, and although he promised only to make peace with Philip II when the French king returned the Angevin continental lands to King John, Innocent III still crowned Otto emperor on October 4, 1209.[125] These unresolved issues would prove to be the causes for a papal repudiation of the Welf and Angevin monarchs in the long run. After the coronation Otto retired to upper Italy and disbanded his army; there was no planned invasion of Sicily or central Italy at this time. In fact Otto's letter to John asking him to be reconciled to Stephan Langton suggests that Otto maintained good standing with Innocent III through 1209. John anxiously awaited the news of his nephew's coronation, which was brought to him by an archiepiscopal ministerial of Cologne.[126]

The reason for Otto's sudden decision to attack Sicily the next year, a move that ended in his excommunication and deposition by the pope, is therefore a mystery. Since there is little surviving documentation for this moment, it has been the source of much speculation. Some historians have supposed that Otto acted so because he was now under the influence of Staufen advisors who encouraged him to reunite Germany and Italy.[127]

---

124. *REK*, 3, 1:12–13, no. 64. Innocent III confirmed this grant on November 7, 1209 (ibid., 3, 1:13, no. 71).

125. Ahlers, *Die Welfen,* 233.

126. *Rotuli de liberate,* 138. The messenger was a relative of Henry de Zudendorp, a ministerial of the archbishop of Cologne. For a thorough prosopographical study of the Zudendorp family and its remarkable English connections see J. Huffman, "Prosopography and the Anglo-Imperial Connection: A Cologne *Ministerialis* Family and Its English Relations," *Medieval Prosopography* 11, no. 2 (autumn 1990): 53–134; *Family, Commerce, and Religion in London and Cologne,* chapter 6. Concerning the role of the ministerials as archiepiscopal servants see W. Pötter, *Die Ministerialität der Erzbischöfe von Köln vom Ende des 11. bis zum Ausgang des 13. Jahrhunderts,* Studien zur Kölner Kirchengeschichte, no. 11 (Düsseldorf, 1967); Manfred Groten, "Zur Entwicklung des Kölner Lehnshofes und der Kölnischen Ministerialität im 13. Jahrhundert," *Blätter für deutsche Landesgeschichte* 124 (1988): 1–50.

127. Winkelmann, *Philipp von Schwaben,* 2:232; Alexander Cartellieri, *Philip II. August, König von Frankreich* (Leipzig, 1899–1922), 4:288; Karl Hampe, *Deutsche Kaisergeschichte in der Zeit der Salier und Staufer,* 250f.; Mitteis, *Der Staat des hohen Mittelalters,* 269; Thomas Curtis van Cleve, *The Emperor Frederick II of Hohenstaufen* (Oxford, 1972), 72f.

It is questionable, however, whether conquest of Italy was only a Staufen goal and not the goal of every German emperor.

Hans-Eberhard Hilpert's discovery of correspondence from Otto to John written shortly after the imperial coronation sheds considerable light on the subject.[128] According to the newly discovered letters, Otto, as he wintered in northern Italy, asked John to inform him as soon as possible where he should invade France. Otto wished to fulfill his old promise of assistance to his kinsman in the recovery of the old Angevin lands.[129] John had received this offer in late December, but England was still under interdict and the English monarch faced a rebellion in the north country in addition to those in Wales and Ireland. Therefore, John was unable to take advantage of the Welf's offer, and Otto was free to entertain other projects. This was provided by an embassy of rebellious Apulians who approached him in his winter camp and offered their help in conquering the kingdom of Sicily.[130] The offer was appealing in that it would elminate Otto's only remaining enemy and increase his own power, making him independent of the German princes and the pope. Apparently this was enough incentive for Otto to risk his newly revived kingship.

John too could gain advantage from strong Welf control in Sicily, as it would apply pressure on Innocent to settle affairs with him. When he learned of the plan in late January 1210 he sent William Bigod to Otto,[131] and the seneschal Conrad of Wijlre received one thousand marks during a reciprocal embassy to the Angevin court between October 1210 and October 1211.[132] Other imperial envoys were present at the court in this period[133] and John paid more of Otto's debts, thus revealing that Angevin interest in Otto's Italian venture was strong.[134]

128. Hans-Eberhard Hilpert, "Zwei Briefe Kaiser Ottos IV. an Johann Ohneland," *DA* 38 (1982): 125.

129. Ibid., 139–40.

130. Ahlers, *Die Welfen*, 236–37.

131. He appears at the top of a witness list for a charter issued in Parma on June 25 (*Böhmer*, 5, 1:121, no. 423) and also heads the list of witnesses (followed also by "Comes Heinricus de Saxonia") to a charter of Otto IV to the Abbey of San Salvatore on August 21, 1210 (J. F. Böhmer, *Acta Imperii Selecta: Urkunden Deutscher Könige und Kaiser 928–1398* [Innsbruck, 1870; reprint, Aalen, 1967], 226–27, no. 250; *Böhmer*, 5, 1:123, no. 433).

132. *Pipe Roll 13 John*, PR, NS, 28:135.

133. *Rotuli de liberate*, 152, 154, 164.

134. Ibid., 148.

John even paid two hundred marks to obtain regalian jewels for his nephew.[135] Conrad of Wijlre and Lambekin (Lambert) of Cologne continued to hold their English fiefs as well.[136]

Innocent III, who was greatly disappointed after his intensive lobbying on behalf of Otto's kingship, excommunicated the Welf on November 8, 1210, as his army entered Apulia, and the pope released all of Otto's vassals from their oaths of obedience.[137] Immediately several German princes announced their intention to support the kingship of the young Staufer Frederick II, the pope's new candidate, who had been elected once as a child. Innocent, knowing that Archbishop Dietrich I of Cologne was, along with the city, a supporter of the Welf cause, also brought Adolf of Altena out of mothballs.[138] He informed Adolf that the former archbishop was now allowed to perform the Mass and to take any clerical office that was offered to him other than episcopal, to which status he could expect to climb back through papal dispensation. The reasons given for Innocent's change of heart are that the former archbishop had patiently borne the punishment inflicted by the pope and that Otto's recent behavior might suggest that the Welf had behaved unworthily toward Adolf to begin with. Innocent was preparing Adolf for a restoration to the Cologne see if he were willing to support the latest Staufer candidate.

Dietrich I refused to perform the excommunication of Otto in January 1211 that Innocent had commanded him to do and was eventually excommunicated and deposed by the papal legate Siegfried of Mainz (hitherto a Welf partisan) in April of the following year.[139] Siegfried then carefully orchestrated the return of Adolf of Altena to the Cologne see, but Innocent put his confirmation of Adolf in abeyance, allowing Dietrich to seek his own restoration. This way the pope could still keep his options open and even opt for a new election if the conditions warranted it. The city of Cologne, however, remained closed to Adolf, as it was still pro-Welf.[140] Cologne was thus divided between Welf and Staufen loyalties once again.

---

135. Ibid., 156.
136. See *The Red Book of the Exchequer,* ed. Hubert Hall, RS, no. 99 (London, 1896; reprint, 1965), 2:523, for Lincolnshire.
137. The English chroniclers record Otto's excommunication and do not side strongly with the pope in the conflict: see, for example, Roger of Wendover, *Flores historiarum,* 2:55–56; *MPHA,* 2:121.
138. *REK,* 3, 1:16, no. 84.
139. *REK,* 3, 1:18, no. 94; 20–21, no. 107; 21, no. 109.
140. *REK,* 3, 1:21, no. 108.

Now that both Otto and John were under papal excommunication and shared a desire to fulfill a planned attack on Philip II the negotiations for such a move intensified. John had a further incentive to act quickly against his Capetian enemy: now the pope, who had excommunicated him, was allied with Philip II, a consistent supporter of the Staufen house. The threat of a French invasion at the request of the papacy became a real possibility now.[141] In 1211 John's envoy Dietrich the German was sent once again to the emperor, and on May 4, 1212, John wrote to the viscount of Thouars that Otto had sent Count Rainald of Boulogne to England to become a vassal of the English king.[142] In the same month, John had received an impressive embassy of thirty-one men from Otto, including Conrad of Wijlre, Conrad de Dyck, and Roger of Merheim, and he sent to the emperor in return his trusted household advisors Chancellor Walter de Gray, the earl of Winchester Saher de Quincy, his steward William de Cantilupe, and Robert Tresgoz to continue developing their plans.[143] The English ambassadors met Otto at his wedding with Beatrix of Staufen in July 1212.[144] From these intensive negotiations John secured a coalition that included the counts of Boulogne, Flanders, and Bar and the dukes of Limburg and Brabant.[145] The king greased the wheels further with gifts to the imperial envoys and a prebend for one of Otto's clerics.[146] Otto himself received another thousand marks through his seneschal Conrad of Wijlre in October.[147] John did not leave out Otto's brother Henry of Brunswick, to whom he sent Dietrich the German in August with his yearly rent of five hundred marks.[148] By the late summer of 1212 John had, through generous

---

141. Painter, *Reign of King John*, 188.

142. *Rotuli de liberate*, 238; *Rotuli litterarum clausarum*, 1:129; *Rymer*, 1:156–57. Rainald was richly rewarded for his vassalage with nine fiefs throughout England, which he had claimed through his wife's inheritance: see Kienast, "Die Deutschen Fürsten," 10:186–87.

143. *Böhmer*, 5, 2:1596, no. 10737; *Rymer*, 1:156. William de Cantilupe was also responsible to cover the expenses of the German embassy: see *Rotuli litterarum clausarum*, 1:117 (May 24, 1212).

144. *Annales Sancti Edmundi*, 1:21–22.

145. *Rymer*, 1:156–64.

146. *Pipe Roll 14 John*, PR, NS, 30:23. Further mention of regalia for Otto occurs elsewhere (ibid., 44); *Rotuli litterarum clausarum*, 1:117 (Westminster, May 11, 1212), 120 (Westminster, July 14, 1212).

147. *Rotuli litterarum clausarum*, 1:124 (Westminster, October 6, 1212).

148. Ibid., 1:121 (Nottingham, August 6, 1212). The valet Philip mentioned in this entry was the master of Henry's young son and was staying at the English court. Dietrich wound up somehow in prison while in Germany and had to be ransomed on January 2, 1213, for forty-four marks: see *Böhmer*, 5, 2:1597, no. 10748.

spending of English money, virtually re-created the coalition network of his brother Richard among the princes of Lotharingia.

Angevin-Welf plans were suspended once again, however, by events in the autumn of that year. Already in August an outbreak of rebellion was renewed in Wales that forced John to redirect his troops gathered for Poitou to Chester. Then a revolt among the English barons threatened to break out. Otto had also met with setbacks, as the Swabian and Bavarian contingents secretly left his party after the untimely death of his Staufer wife, Beatrix, on August 11, 1212. The marriage had lasted only a month and so kinship ties did not run deep. Unable to stop Frederick II's advance into Germany now, the young Staufer was elected king in Frankfurt on December 5 and crowned in Mainz by Archbishop Siegfried. The coronation was carried out by Siegfried at the behest of Adolf of Altena, who could not be present.[149] Adolf had been reinstated as archbishop of Cologne and was finally allowed to enter the city on May 2 of this year. Consequently he was busy attempting to gain control of its clerics and burghers.[150] In an attempt to maintain the citizens' allegiance Otto had granted them on March 16 the right to raise a penny tax on milling and brewing in order to further fortify their already imposing walls, and as late as November 30 he confirmed again their freedom from tolls at Kaiserswerth and similar privileges at the tolls of Boppard and Duisburg.[151]

Frederick II's success owed much to the support of Philip II of France, who had given him twenty thousand marks of silver. With this money Frederick was able to quickly gain allies and secure his second election in Frankfurt.[152] A formal alliance between the two monarchs was concluded between Toul and Vaucouleurs on November 19, even before Frederick had been elected.[153] Frederick agreed thereby not to make any peace with Otto "once called emperor and with John king of England and their allies" without the consent of Philip II—a clear echo of the Treaty of Le Goulet that reveals the essentially defensive nature of Philip II's intentions.

As Frederick gained momentum in Germany, Otto experienced a defec-

---

149. *REK*, 3, 1:21, nos. 110–11.

150. *REK*, 3, 1:21, no. 109.

151. *UGN*, 2:21, no. 39, and 21–22, no. 40.; *Ennen/Eckertz*, 2:42; Kuske, *Quellen zur Geschichte des Kölner Handels*, 1:5, no. 42; *Böhmer*, 5, 1:142, no. 491. Henry de Zudendorp and Conrad of Wijlre were among the witnesses to the latter grant.

152. Kienast, *Deutschland und Frankreich*, 3:563.

153. *Historia Diplomatica Friderici Secundi*, ed. J. L. A. Huillard-Bréholles (Paris, 1852–61), 1, 1:227–28.

tion from his ranks similar to that of 1204. Furthermore, John faced the very real threat of deposition by Innocent III and a French invasion of England. Once again the Welf-Angevin "alliance" was stillborn because of the different political exigencies of its respective leaders. John finally submitted to Innocent and received England back as a papal fief. He was thus absolved on May 15, 1213, and fortunately nothing had come of the Capetian invasion plans. Indeed papal support proved valuable against his rebellious nobles and the Capetian threat. John's political tenacity and fortitude are quite remarkable here; even as he faced deposition and overthrow by French forces, he was sending huge sums of money to his Welf nephew and to the princes of Lotharingia. On January 28, 1213, he informed Otto that the German envoys Gerard de Rodes and Conrad of Wijlre had been given 8,500 marks. John also acknowledged receiving a certain Master Ywain, who read to him letters from Henry of Brunswick, the count of Boulogne, and Count William of Holland.[154] These letters no doubt concerned the arrangements for a money fief for Count William, who performed homage to John (on March 29) in return for an annual fee of four hundred marks.[155]

The enormous investment in Otto and his coalition at this time (an additional ten thousand marks would be given as well in September)[156] was wasted, since little help could be expected at this juncture. John had hoped for help in the face of a Capetian invasion, which continued to threaten England through the first half of 1213. Yet in April, when the English were nervously awaiting an invasion, Otto had moved his army into eastern Saxony to fight the archbishop of Magdeburg and Hermann of Thuringia in defense of his allodial family lands in Brunswick and Lüneburg.[157] By the time the bishop of Norwich, the count of Salisbury, and William Brewer arrived at Otto's court in early August they realized

---

154. *Rotuli litterarum clausarum,* 1:133; *Rymer,* 1:164–65; *Böhmer,* 5, 2:1598, no. 10753. Ywain received twenty marks for his efforts: see *Documents Illustrative of English History in the Thirteenth and Fourteenth Centuries,* ed. Henry Cole (London, 1844), 242.

155. *Rymer,* 1:168–69. Among those who were witnesses to this deed were Henry of Brunswick, the count of Boulogne, Gerard de Rodes, and Conrad of Wijlre—exactly those men who were participants either in person or by letter in the January embassy to the English court.

156. *Documents Illustrative of English History,* 243. Other royal gifts included more trading privileges for Simon Saphir and Walter Sprok (*Rotuli litterarum patentium,* 98, 100–101) and a marriage arrangement for a certain Peter Jordan at the request of Otto (*Rotuli litterarum clausarum,* 1:132 [York, August 31, 1213]).

157. *Böhmer,* 5, 1:143–44, no. 495; Kienast, "Die Deutschen Fürsten," 10:195.

that the vast sums of money sent to the Welf were being used to arm against the Staufen party rather than in preparation for an invasion of Capetian France.[158] While Otto was fighting in Saxony John made a gesture intended to shore up Welf support at its heart, the city of Cologne. On July 24, 1213, John issued a decree that freed the Cologne guildhall in London from rent and other customs dues, and he confirmed the merchants' right to safe conduct throughout England, though the municipal rights of London were not to be infringed on thereby.[159] This was a reconfirmation of Richard I's grant of 1194, which had released the Cologne merchants from tolls. John had reinstituted these tolls in his confirmations of the Cologne merchants' rights previous to this date.

Otto's fading power in Germany made him once again of little military worth to John, who found a stronger ally in the count of Flanders. The count had turned to John for help after Philip II's forces had invaded his county, and the English king responded with a successful surprise attack on the French fleet at Damme in late May. This victory not only solidified the Anglo-Flemish coalition but also assured England that no French invasion would be coming.[160] Amid the flow of money to Brunswick, John was still able to earmark the amazing amount of twenty-six thousand marks for war in Flanders. On July 13 the first ten thousand were sent, then five thousand were sent between July 28 and August 24, 1213. An additional six thousand would be sent in May–June 1214 and a final five thousand on July 21, 1214.[161] The money sent to Otto, when compared to the expenditures in Flanders for mercenary troops, was comparatively little, and it is clear that John expected Flanders, not Otto's contingent, to play the major role in a joint attack on Philip II. Flanders offered the added advantage of lessening the risk that Philip II would attack England while John invaded Poitou.

In August the embassy of Count William of Salisbury (John's half brother, who would lead the English contingent at Bouvines), the bishop of Norwich, and William Brewer informed the preoccupied Otto of the planned invasion: Count Ferrand of Flanders was expected to engage Capetian forces in northern France until the armies of John and Otto

158. *Rotuli litterarum clausarum*, 1:164; *Rymer*, 1:174.

159. *Ennen/Eckertz*, 2:46–47, no. 41; *HUB*, 1:43, no. 109, and 3:395–96, no. 605; Lappenberg, *Urkundliche Geschichte*, 8–9, no. 15; *Böhmer*, 5, 2:1599, no. 10766.

160. Cartellieri, *Philip II. August*, 4:368–72.

161. *Rotuli litterarum clausarum*, 1:135, 146, 206, 209; *Rotuli litterarum patentium*, 103; *Pipe Roll 16 John*, PR, NS, 35:27; Ralph of Coggeshall, *Chronicon Anglicanum*, 168.

arrived in a pincer movement from Flanders and Poitou. This was calculated to recover all the lands lost by John in recent years as well as those
lands in Flanders and Boulogne that Philip II had confiscated. Otto was
to lead a strike force from Flanders directly to Paris. He welcomed this
initiative, since after his failed campaigns in Saxony and the Rhineland
there was little hope of surviving the steady spread of Staufen power in
Germany. He had hoped rather to undercut Frederick II's French support
and thereby indirectly undermine the Staufer's momentum.[162]

Furthermore, there seems to have been a genuine personal hatred of
Philip II by Otto, perhaps stemming from his days as the count of Poitou.
He had made his uncle John an offer more than once to undertake a joint
invasion of Capetian France and recover the lost Angevin territories. In
fact Otto's hatred became legendary, with a remarkable story appearing
in chronicles from England to Saxony to Italy.[163] The story goes that at a
French tournament, Philip II promised Otto three French cities if Otto
ever became the emperor (according to Matthew Paris and Arnold of
Lübeck they were Paris, Etampes, and Orléans; Thomas de Papia says
they were Paris, Chartres, and Orléans; and the chronicle of Treviso/
Lombardy tells only of the city of Paris). The promise was intended as an
affront to both Richard I and Otto, since Philip considered its fulfillment
beyond the realm of possibility. To add insult to injury, according to
Thomas de Papia, Philip II later offered Otto three dogs named after the
cities as a fulfillment of his promise. Winkelmann believed that Otto had
this legend spread to foment anti-French sentiment in Germany, though
this sounds again more like modern propaganda politics (e.g., Bismarck's
Ems Dispatch) than medieval.[164] Whatever the origin of this legend, it
suggests Otto's hatred of the French king, who after all did try to bring
about the kingship of the duke of Brabant when Philip of Swabia was
murdered. This personal animosity between the monarchs aside, however, Otto determined that the real danger to his throne was not Frederick

---

162. Ahlers, *Die Welfen*, 250.

163. *MPHA*, 2:83; Arnold of Lübeck, *Chronica Slavorum*, 287; *Braunschweigische
Reimchronik*, ed. L. Weiland, MGH Deutsche Chroniken, no. 2 (Hanover, 1877), 591, vv.
4770–816; Thomas de Papia, *Gesta imperatorum et pontificum*, ed. E. Ehrenfeuchter,
MGH SS, no. 22 (Hanover, 1872; reprint, 1976), 509–10; *Chronicon Marchiae Tarvisinae
et Lombardiae*, ed. L. A. Botteghi, Rerum Italicarum Scriptores, 2d ed., no. 8:3 (Città di
Castello, 1916), 4. This Italian chronicle was written ca. 1270 and covers events from 1207
to 1270. I thank Peter Diehl for pointing out this last passage to me.

164. Winkelmann, *Philipp von Schwaben*, 2:154–55.

II but the Capetian Philip II, who funded the Staufen cause in a way he could only wish his Angevin relatives would finance his own.

Otto sent his brother Henry of Brunswick to England once again in October 1213, and final preparations for an attack on Philip II were made in London during January 1214.[165] Count William of Salisbury and Count Ferrand of Flanders were present along with Otto's envoy Ywain.[166] The news that Ferrand had managed to get the duke of Brabant's support through the mediation of the bishop of Liège was well received, and the Brabantine connection was cemented by the traditional social bond of marriage between Otto IV and the duke's daughter Maria.[167] In early February John set sail for La Rochelle while Count Ferrand, William of Salisbury, and Rainald of Boulogne organized in Flanders and Otto assembled his forces from the lower Rhineland princes.[168]

When the armies met in Flanders at Valenciennes in July 1214, five months after the military action had commenced, the element of surprise was long gone and Philip II had had time to strengthen his position in northern France.[169] The Battle of Bouvines (on July 27, 1214, near Lille) was a complete disaster for the anti-Capetian coalition, best exemplified by the loss of sizable troop strength from Otto's contingent through the defection of the dukes of Brabant and Limburg at the last minute. His own father-in-law lost nerve when it counted most. Within a few hours Philip II held the field and had captured Ferrand of Flanders, William of Salisbury, Rainald of Boulogne, William of Holland, and over two hundred knights.[170] Powerfully symbolic of the day's result was the loss of Otto's imperial standard. Having been dropped on the field of battle, the imperial eagle, its wings broken, was recovered by the Capetian forces and eventually sent to Frederick II. The imperial title had indeed passed back into Staufen hands thanks to Capetian military success.

---

165. *Rotuli litterarum clausarum*, 1:152; Böhmer, 5, 1:145–46, no. 497.

166. *Rotuli litterarum clausarum*, 1:159.

167. Kienast, "Die Deutschen Fürsten," 10:270f. To assure the support of the duke of Brabant, Otto was finally married to the duke's daughter. They were originally engaged on the day of Otto's royal coronation some fifteen years earlier: see *Gestorum abbatum Trudonensium continuatio tertia*, ed. R. Koepke, MGH SS, no. 10 (Hanover, 1852; reprint, 1987), 392; *Annales Marbacenses*, 85.

168. Winkelmann, *Philipp von Schwaben*, 2:367–70.

169. Warren, *King John*, 223–24; Hucker, *Kaiser Otto IV.*, 303–19.

170. *Annales Marbacenses*, 85; Roger of Wendover, *Flores historiarum*, 2:106–8; *MPHA*, 2:150–51; Georges Duby, *The Legend of Bouvines* (Berkeley, 1990).

Otto once again escaped capture and fled to his sanctuary, the city of Cologne. There is no reference to the participation of Cologne troops at Bouvines; however, the city was Otto's base of operations in the Rhineland, so his military contingent was composed of a considerable number of men from Cologne and the surrounding region.[171] Otto's stay in Cologne was short. He was driven out by Frederick II's army, and the young Staufer was crowned again at Aachen on July 25, 1215.[172] The city of Cologne had already made its peace with Frederick II in Würzburg two months earlier, when the Staufer confirmed his father's approval of their freedom from the tolls of Boppard and Kaiserswerth.[173] When Otto fled to his allodial lands in Brunswick and Lüneburg, the victory of Frederick II was complete. The schism in the Cologne church was finally resolved as well in early 1216 when both Dietrich and Adolf resigned after a papal order to the priors to elect a new archbishop.[174] Each received a rent of three hundred marks from the archiepiscopal income, and the new archbishop, Engelbert I of Berg (1216–25), was elected on February 29.[175] The era of Cologne-Welf cooperation had thus ended and a new alignment of relations between Cologne, England, and the new German monarch was in the offing.

With the coalition destroyed John remained despondent for several months in La Rochelle.[176] He then accepted a five-year truce at Chinon on September 18.[177] He returned to England and never again ventured off

171. In 1216 Archbishop Engelbert I of Cologne, along with the priors and archdeacons of the Cologne church, confirmed that the lord Gerald of Randerole, who had been lying in prison since the Battle of Bouvines, had pawned through his family and friends the office of bailiff for his "Stiftshöfe" in the Roergau for three hundred marks of Cologne coin in order to obtain his release: see *REK*, 3, 1:28–29, no. 148; *UGN*, 2:32, no. 59. Furthermore, a certain "Ric. de Colonia" was imprisoned in Amiens after the battle (Hucker, *Kaiser Otto IV.*, 314). This confirms that knights from the area surrounding Cologne as well as Cologne burghers participated in the battle.
172. *REK*, 3, 1:24, no. 130; *CRC*, 193. Archbishop Siegfried of Mainz performed the coronation again in the absence of the archbishop of Cologne.
173. *UGN*, 2:25–26, no. 49 (dated May 6, 1215). The Cologne patriciate was eager to obtain confirmation of the city's privileges from each and every royal candidate.
174. *REK*, 3, 1:25, no. 137.
175. *REK*, 3, 1:26–27, no. 138. Archbishop Engelbert I of Berg was the cousin of Archbishop Adolf of Altena, who himself was the nephew of Archbishop Bruno III of Berg. The local power of the counts of Berg was felt most keenly at this time in the cathedral chapter.
176. Warren, *King John*, 224.
177. *Rymer*, 1:192; *Historia Diplomatica*, 1, 1:317; *Böhmer*, 5, 2:1601, no. 10779.

the island. At this point the dynamic of the Welf-Staufen conflict in Germany was effectively severed from Anglo-French politics. John nevertheless hoped that Otto could still be of some service. The Welf's chamberlain John Lupus and notary Ywain visited John at Poitou in August 1214,[178] and on September 1 John sent Otto two thousand marks.[179] In November, after John's return to England, he was visited by Ywain and Otto's seneschal Conrad of Wijlre,[180] and he paid a debt of two hundred marks for Otto to the Flemish merchants Simon Saphir and Walter Sprok.[181] Other messengers from Otto in this month include a certain Colinus, a citizen of Cologne named Henry, a certain Master Jacob, and a priest from Piacenza.[182] John even sent the quite personal gift of eighty barrels of Poitevin wine to Otto in Cologne; apparently Otto's years at the English court and in Poitou had developed in him a taste for French wine and the Rhine variety was not to his liking.[183] In many ways life in Germany had not been to Otto's liking.

King John also sent personal gifts to his nephew's new wife Maria of Brabant: as gifts to the "empress," in January 1215 he gave seven hundred marks each to the two Flemish merchants Simon Saphir and Walter Sprok, and to Gerard de Rodes and one hundred marks to Otto's senschal Conrad of Wijlre.[184] When Conrad of Wijlre returned to Otto in January, Ywain remained behind to manage what had become the only real business left for his Welf lord: he received three French knights who had been captured with Robert of Dreux (a cousin of Philip II) at Nantes.[185] Ywain no doubt

---

178. *Rotuli litterarum clausarum,* 1:169 (August 4): John Lupus was given the "terra de Bernaldesby, que fuit in custodia Theoderici Teutonici." Ywain was awarded an ecclesiastical benefice in England (*Rotuli litterarum patentium,* 120–21 [August 27, 1214]).

179. *Rotuli litterarum patentium,* 121.

180. *Rotuli litterarum clausarum,* 175 (Westminster, November 4, 1214); 176 (Westminster, November 14, 1214); 180 (Westminster, November 28, 1214). The envoys left in January 1215.

181. Ibid., 1:179 (apud Bruli, November 24, 1214); 180 (Westminster, November 28, 1214).

182. Ibid., 1:177, 180.

183. Ibid., 1:179. The wine was delivered by Peter of Poitou in March 1215: see *Rotuli litterarum patentium,* 129 (Tower of London, March 3, 1215). We learn here that the Poitevin barons had also contributed to the gift for Otto.

184. *Rotuli litterarum clausarum,* 1:183 (apud Knapp, January 23, 1215); *Rotuli litterarum patentium,* 126A (apud Knapp, January 23, 1215). Walter Sprok was also given a letter of royal protection for his trading activities on March 5, 1215 (*Rotuli litterarum patentium,* 130).

185. *Rotuli litterarum patentium,* 129 (February 23, 1215).

used these three knights in some kind of prisoner exchange to free German knights who had been captured at Bouvines.[186]

Despite his grave problems with the English barons during the last two years of his life, John continued until his death in 1216 to negotiate with and on behalf of Otto and still referred to him as the emperor. Only months before his death John was negotiating with the count of Los to reestablish allegiance to the Welf.[187] Innocent III died the same year, and Otto died two years later. With them passed the generation that had participated in the era of the Welf-Angevin-Cologne coalition.

We have gone into great detail considering the events 1193–1216 for several reasons. First of all, these years represent the high point of diplomatic interaction and cooperation between Cologne and the Angevin court, whose interests were matched as closely as they would ever be. It was necessary also to present the sizable evidence in order to illustrate just how dependent the Welf king was on both of these parties for his political survival. Of these two, the city of Cologne, at times joined by its archbishop, was the foundation of Otto's kingship in Germany. If he had not had the support of this wealthy, fortified city it is doubtful whether his candidacy would have survived for any length of time. We must remember that he was brought to this position in the first place only through the support of Cologne. Cologne's aid was the result of both the growing interregional economic importance of the lower Rhineland region and the awareness among western European leaders of its strategic and political value in relations between the intertwined political communities of England, France, and Germany. It had become the magnet to which all parties were eventually drawn in their respective relations, and this does much to mute traditional Anglo-French political histories that leave the German realm on the periphery of medieval Western history.

Whereas most historians have considered Otto IV a failure in political terms, we should see him rather as symbolic of the vast changes occurring in Europe that were knitting regions ever more closely together. Otto was

---

186. Hucker (*Kaiser Otto IV.*, 311, 497–98) indicates that Bernard II of Horstmar (the "Westphalian Achilles," crusading knight alongside Richard the Lionheart, and envoy of Otto IV to the English court) participated in the Battle of Bouvines, only to be captured and imprisoned in the Grand Chatelet in Paris. He and Count Conrad of Dortmund tunneled their way out to freedom and escaped, but there were surely many such knights to be ransomed.

187. *Rotuli litterarum patentium*, 189, 100; *Rymer*, 1:212–13; *Böhmer*, 5, 2:1605, nos. 10803–4.

born in Saxony, raised at the Angevin court in France and England, spoke French as effortlessly as German, almost obtained the county of Yorkshire and the kingdom of Scotland early in his career, was the count of Poitou and enjoyed French wine as much as the Rhenish variety, was elected king in Germany and crowned emperor in Rome, married women from Swabia and Brabant, led military campaigns from southern Italy to northeast France, and then retired to his unaccustomed Saxon allods. If this is not a man whose life reflects significant interregional European history (which intimately included Germany), then who was?[188] A visible sign of the interregional and interdynastic fusion in Otto's person and kingship accompanied him on every military campaign: not only did he fight according to English custom under banners, but his own coat of arms was a conflation of the imperial eagle and the three Angevin leopards.[189] Otto's kingship, then, was the product of growing interregional ties between the Rhineland, England, France, and Italy. This historical development both made his kingship possible and ultimately brought it down. We can discern in his experience the new fabric of both power and interdependency in this emerging Europe. Otto stood at the nexus of interregional diplomatic and economic forces well beyond those of Barbarossa's generation, and it is no surprise, then, that he was unable to negotiate these uncharted waters.

------

188. Another excellent example of a life reflecting this comingling of regional political communities is the life of one of Otto IV's secretaries, Gervase of Tilbury. Gervase was born in Essex but raised in Rome, and he both studied and taught law at the University of Bologna. He was present in 1177 at the signing of the Peace of Venice between Frederick Barbarossa, Pope Alexander III, and the Lombard League, an account of which may have been given by him to Roger of Howden and Gervase of Canterbury. He then spent time at the Angevin court in the circle of Henry (the eldest son of Henry II), whose sudden death led Gervase back to the continent. His Angevin connections secured him a series of subsequent posts—with the archbishop of Reims, William II of Sicily, and then Otto IV. Otto made him the marshal of the kingdom of Arles, and after the Welf's fall Gervase seems to have finished his career as the provost of the Benedictine house of Ebstorf in Saxony (1223–24). In 1211 Gervase wrote for the Welf king a compendium of general knowledge known as the *Otia imperialia (Liber de mirabilibus mundi [Otia imperialia]*, ed. G. W. Leibniz, Scriptores rerum Brunsvicensium [Hanover, 1707–10], 1:881–1005, 2:751–84), with a decidedly pro-papal harangue on the superior role of the popes as vicars of God. Thus Gervase's life is exemplary of the social history of relations between the English, French, German, and Italian communities. In the latter respect he is much like Gerard Pucelle during Barbarossa's reign. See *The Dictionary of National Biography,* ed. Sir Leslie Stephen and Sir Sidney Lee (Oxford, 1917–), 7:1120–21; Hucker, *Kaiser Otto IV.,* 407–9.

189. B. Schwineköper, "Eine unbekannte heraldische Quelle zur Geschichte Ottos IV. und seiner Anhänger," in *Festschrift für Hermann Heimpel,* Veroffentlichungen des Max-Planck-Instituts fur Geschichte, no. 36 (Göttingen, 1972), 2:959–1022.

Surely Otto and his uncle John did much by their mercurial and often obstinate leadership style to damage their respective kingships, but Otto no less than John learned the hard way that monarchy in Europe was changing.[190] Although expanding European economic activity enabled kings to harness new means of independent power (e.g., we noted the wealth of England spent to form an anti-Capetian coalition and how both monarchs manipulated privileges to maintain Cologne support), the equally emerging interregional power of the papacy and the regional power of the English and German nobility moved to check the two monarchies from realizing their potential. In this regard Magna Carta meant the same thing as the Golden Bull of Eger and the Battle of Bouvines.

We must point out as well that this result was not carefully crafted by a coalition of princes and the papacy but rather emerged piecemeal out of the complex diplomatic interactions between and within these political communities. Hence interpretations that use modern concepts of strategic alliances and state building (or the failure to do so) miss the social dynamics of these interactions. The political communities did effectively limit royal power in Germany and England, something Frederick II and Henry III would soon discover. As Frederick Barbarossa had reached in vain beyond the political possibilities of his generation to expand royal power within his own realms, so too John and Otto fell short in reaching an effective coordination of royal power between their realms. In the latter case the war fought was not ideological but rather one over allegiances in the social fabric of kinship and lordship.

Modern historians often lose sight of an additional social dimension to this story: that the Welf and Staufen dynasties were closely related during this period of conflict between them and that the claim of blood right was used by all parties to justify their royal legitimacy as much as their disputed elections by the princes. This socially based claim to power is generally overlooked amid the modern historiographical concerns over institutional and constitutional claims to power. Therefore, even the opponents to the Staufen line were chosen by the electoral princes and papacy from a pool of familial candidates close to the Staufen kinship

---

190. John Gillingham's article "The Fall of the Angevin Empire" in *England in Europe, 1066–1453*, ed. Nigel Saul (New York, 1994), 88–96, reflects the historiographical tradition that blames John's personal leadership style (or lack thereof) for the loss of the continental lands: ". . . it was John's special talent to provoke revolt right in the heartland of the Angevin empire. . . . In the final analysis, it was his inability to inspire either affection or loyalty which was fatal" (94–95). Much the same could be said for Otto.

group. It just so happens that as a result of the growing interregional ties of the Central Middle Ages and the marriage policies of European aristocrats, crossovers between regional political communities became a much more common practice.[191] Hence we find so-called foreign candidates for the German throne, of which Otto was the first but certainly not the last. Indeed, where has any historian made more of Otto's kinship ties with John than of their supposedly threatening anti-French military alliance? Here again the modern political categories have gotten more play than have medieval social and dynastic considerations.

In the face of these rival assertions of royal power, the political communities of England, Germany, and the Church ultimately voiced their opposition to the strengthening of royal power, and the result was in fact its limitation in England, Germany, and Italy. Staufen monarchy would now become more and more focused on the Italian portion of the empire, and German princes would further cultivate an independence that resulted in the territorial principalities of the Later Middle Ages. The archbishops of Cologne led the way in this development and thereby dominated their region. Since the era of Philip of Heinsberg the archbishops of Cologne had joined the dukes of Austria as the only German princes with a double duchy, the Austrian dukes holding Austria and Styria after 1191 while the archbishop's duchies straddled both sides of the Rhine. The archiepiscopal rise to regional dominance contrasts markedly with the fall of such powers as Henry the Lion. The archbishops had enfeoffed the various dukes and counts in the region and thereby added further to their political suzerainty.

In fact it was the independent course taken by these powerful archbishops that complicated political affairs in the empire and eventually led to civil war. The practice of king making, which the archbishop of Cologne embarked on in this generation, will continue throughout the remainder of the period under study here and will thereby further involve the English monarchs in German political affairs. The difference between the involvement of Richard I and Richard of Cornwall in German kingship says much about the growing influence exerted by the archbishops of Cologne in the intervening years. Although the archbishops lost their dominant influence at times during the Cologne schism of 1205–16, no

191. Georg Schnath, "Das Welfenhaus als europäische Dynastie," *Streifzüge durch Niedersachsens Vergangenheit: Gesammelte Aufsätze und Vorträge von G. Schnath* (Hildesheim, 1968), 126–45.

political movement in northwest Germany would have been possible without their approval and participation. The very core of the schism itself—a split over which monarch to support—only reinforced the central importance of Cologne's territorial and economic power for any candidate for the throne. When Otto enjoyed its support his kingship was viable, but when he lost it, all was lost.

A final word must be said about the significance of the Welf-Angevin-Cologne coalition. This coalition was never actually effective in bringing about a common goal. The relations between these powers changed repeatedly in both intensity and purpose as a result of the deaths and political exigencies of the various players. Although Otto's election was a moment of success and close cooperation, it contained elements of divergent interests and disunity. Richard and John supported Otto's kingship as part of their efforts at a comprehensive network in northwest Germany against the Capetians.[192] Adolf, however, sought a candidate suitably weak enough to prevent challenges to his territorial power, and Innocent III sought a candidate who would no longer be a threat in Italy. Otto's kingship was therefore a collective creation of princes from different political communities whose ultimate goals had little in common.[193] This problem continued and was exacerbated by regional conflicts that further fragmented their interests and prevented any significant corporate action. His kingship was an interregional creation, with all the potential and limitations inherent therein.

Neither John nor Otto could successfully coordinate their enterprises, because of constant distractions and threats to their own power bases. The archbishopric of Cologne was a constantly changing factor in the equation, as a result of Adolf's independent policy and the subsequent schism. The pope was also pursuing his own program, which often clashed with those of his nominal allies. Hence this coalition, so highly vaunted as an anti-Staufen conspiracy by many modern historians, was in actuality of little real consequence in either the Angevin-Capetian or the Welf-Staufen conflicts. It is time we cease referring to this loose coalition as an effective anti-Staufen alliance.

Just as the story of an Anglo-Welf conspiracy against Staufen kingship during the era of Henry the Lion can be discussed, so can the view that

---

192. Appleby (*England without Richard*, 211) argues that Otto's kingship was the capstone of Richard's anti-Capetian diplomacy.
193. Kienast, "Die Deutschen Fürsten," 10:213.

overemphasizes the role played by the later Welf-Angevin-Cologne coalition during Otto's kingship. If anything, the city of Cologne itself was the bulwark of Welf kingship. The citizens of Cologne and the Cologne church remained fiercely loyal to Otto despite the vacillations of King John, Archbishop Adolf,[194] and Pope Innocent III. They were indeed, to borrow Innocent's imagery, the gardener who tended the plant of Welf kingship, while all others left the cause when it no longer advanced their own interests. It would be more appropriate to speak of a Welf-Cologne alliance than a Welf-Angevin coalition for most of this period.[195] We now leave this central period in Anglo-German and Anglo-Cologne diplomacy and enter the last phase of this study. By 1216 the political landscape of Europe had been altered dramatically, and Anglo-German relations would take on a new cast accordingly.

194. Some historians, such as Leonard Ennen (*Geschichte der Stadt Köln,* 1:33), have blamed Adolf of Altena and his greed for money and power for the destruction of both the countryside and the German kingship in the civil war. But Stehkämper ("Adolf von Altena," 83) argues that the Staufen party was also responsible, citing Henry VI's overbearing assertion of imperial rights as causing the conflict with the German princes to ignite in the first place. We must remember also that the Staufen party was the first to officially override Frederick II's election and raise Philip of Swabia instead.

195. Georg Scheibelreiter ("Der deutsche Thronstreit 1198–1209 im Spiegel der Datierung von Privaturkunden," *MIÖG* 85 [1977]: 36–76) presents an interesting piece of evidence for how much Adolf loathed Otto's kingship: none of his charters were dated according to the Welf's regnal years. Moreover the pope does not appear for dating purposes in any of Adolf's charters. Yet the Cologne church did date its documents according to Otto's regnal years. Indeed, one charter of St. Maria ad Gradus in 1207 was dated "... regnante rege Ottone, sub Brunone Coloniensi archiepiscopo," although the city had officially been reconciled by this time with Philip of Swabia (Philip even celebrated Easter in Cologne) and Adolf of Altena was reasserting his control over the archiepiscopate.

6

Cologne Archbishops: *Territorialpolitik,* Marriage Negotiations, and Imperial Relations with England

The diplomatic landscape of Europe had changed profoundly as a result of the Battle of Bouvines and the passing of the generation that had struggled there. Philip II's victory laid the foundation for the extension of Capetian royal power at the expense of the Angevin dynasty, while the English monarchy was repeatedly required thereafter to submit to baronial demands at home as embodied in the Magna Carta. In Germany the confusing *Thronstreit* had finally been decided in favor of another Staufen candidate, Frederick II, whose attentions rested much more on his Sicilian kingdom than on the German realm. We have, then, a point in time when the political communities of Italy, Germany, France, and England were all undergoing fundamental changes in form and function. Nowhere better do we see the dynamics of this transformation reflected than in the diplomacy of the archbishops of Cologne, wherein all these European communities were intertwined and manipulated to serve the local and regional *Territorialpolitik* of the Cologne episcopal principality. The principality itself increasingly became the property of local aristocratic dynasties through membership in the cathedral chapter.

The Archbishop and the Unlikely Marriage I: A Failed Union of Regional Politics and Interregional Diplomacy

By 1218 all the leaders of western and central Europe, with the exception of Philip II of France, had died and been succeeded by a new generation—a situation identical to that after the Third Crusade. Even the city of Cologne had a new archbishop, Engelbert I of Berg (1216–25). Two other elements would influence the political alignment of Europe in the thirteenth century and help define the roles played by the English kings and the archbishops of Cologne. The first was the Sicilian focus of Frederick II's monarchy, which meant the definitive end of imperial influence and power in northern Germany. This development resulted in the archbishop of Cologne's complete independence from imperial authority and the final consolidation of his regional power. In essence, the *Territorialpolitik* begun by Philip of Heinsberg was perfected during Frederick II's reign.

The second element was the continued expansion of the Capetian monarch's power eastward. The former Angevin territories surrounding and including Normandy had already been absorbed into the Capetian domain, and subsequently Champagne, Flanders, the Arelate, the county of Burgundy, and Lotharingia were all objects of Capetian expansion during the remainder of the period under study here. Although this was not part of a grand, systematic plan by the Capetian monarchs, the era of French royal consolidation of power had begun.[1]

Such a growing force on the border of the Cologne archbishop's principality was a direct threat to his own territorial power, especially since imperial power was fading in Germany. Thus traditional ties with England were of utmost political value. In fact after the end of the Anglo-Welf era the archbishops of Cologne continued to be the primary point of contact for Anglo-German diplomatic relations. Therefore the traditional England-Cologne tie endured in the face of a common threat: namely, the king of France. It must be emphasized of course that the archbishops maintained this relationship for the defense of their own regional power and had little real interest in joining in an English offensive against Capetian France. This reluctance would continually frustrate Plantagenet expectations.

The continuity of other forms of interregional cooperation was maintained in the wake of the great political defeat at Bouvines. This is best exemplified by yet a third crusading endeavor that brought the citizens of Cologne and Englishmen into contact. Spurred on by exhortations from Pope Innocent III in 1213 and in 1216 and by Pope Honorius in January 1217, crusaders from Cologne and its province, along with many Frisians, left on May 29, 1217, with 112 ships and followed the previous crusading route to Dartmouth, where they arrived on June 1.[2] The leader

---

1. Fawtier, *Capetian Kings of France*, 156–68.
2. *Ennen/Eckertz*, 2:47, no. 42; 2:58, no. 50 (incorrectly dated 1215); 2:65, no. 55. Cf. Kurth, "Der Anteil Niederdeutscher Kreuzfahrer," 215–45.

of the German contingent was a certain Oliver, the master of the schools of Cologne cathedral.[3] Disembarking ten days later, under the joint leadership of Count William of Holland and Count George of Wied they made the traditional pilgrimage to Santiago de Compostella and landed at Lisbon on July 14. Once again the king of Portugal convinced them to assist him against the Moors. Although many Frisians refused to delay their passage to Palestine, the others besieged Alcacer on behalf of the king, and the city capitulated on October 21. After wintering in Lisbon the crusaders then continued on to the East.[4] This pattern had now been followed three times in seventy years, with the Cologne and Flemish burghers thereby establishing valuable trading ties with Lisbon.[5] The practice of crusaders from northwest Germany stopping at Lisbon and the growing trading ties between the regions were no mere coincidence.[6]

Although Anglo-German relations continued to develop, one traditional tie faded after the defeat at Bouvines. As has already been shown, King John tried until his death to maintain the viability of Welf influence. During the minority of his young son Henry III relations with the Welf house would be continued briefly, but to no result.[7] After Otto IV's death on May 18, 1218, his brother Henry of Brunswick made peace with Frederick II and thereafter limited himself to administering the Welf allodial lands. During negotiations in early 1219 concerning handing over the imperial insignia, the Welf Henry wrote to Henry III that he would coordinate his future plans with the English king;[8] however, the Plantagenet court saw now that there was little value in continued close ties with the Welfs. They would turn rather to the archbishop of Cologne, who, as we shall see, held a great deal of influence at the imperial court and thus was

3. Haverkamp, *Medieval Germany,* 249.

4. *CRC* (339–48) has an extensive account of this crusading venture, and both Roger of Wendover (*Flores historiarum,* 2:226) and Matthew Paris (*MPCM,* 3:32–33) tell of the participation of those from the province of Cologne.

5. Kurth, "Der Anteil Niederdeutscher Kreuzfahrer," 245–51; A. H. de Oliveira Marques, *Hanse e Portugal na Idade Media* (Lisbon, 1959).

6. For studies of the English in Portugal see D. W. Lomax, "The First English Pilgrims to Santiago de Compostela," in *Studies in Medieval History Presented to R. H. C. Davis,* ed. H. Mayr-Harting and R. I. Moore (London and Ronceverte, 1985), 165–79; Anthony Goodman, "England and Iberia in the Middle Ages," in *England and Her Neighbours, 1066–1453: Essays in Honour of Pierre Chaplais,* ed. Michael Jones and Malcolm Vale (London, 1989), 73–96; idem, "Before the Armada: Iberia and England in the Middle Ages," in *England in Europe, 1066–1453,* ed. Nigel Saul (New York, 1994), 108–20.

7. Ahlers, *Die Welfen,* 262–66.

8. *Diplomatic Documents,* no. 28.

better placed to further English interests. Although Anglo-Welf diplomatic contact continued between the years 1221–23 out of kinship, the Plantagenet court realized that the Welfs could no longer provide effective help against the Capetian king.[9] The relationship essentially dwindled away, except for one brief attempt in 1229 to revive the Welf kingship.

Frederick II had broken with his papal patron and thus been excommunicated in this year by Pope Gregory IX for failing to undertake a promised crusade. The emperor then proceeded to go on crusade in 1228–29 even under this sentence, and the vexed pope sent his legate Otto of St. Nicholas into Germany to make the call for the election of yet another antiking. The legate was blocked from entering Germany and accomplished little; however, Henry III took up the papal plan in the hope of gaining papal support against the new French monarch. Otto "the Child," son of the Welf William of Winchester/Lüneburg, wrote to the English king detailing his release from captivity by his enemies amid a local skirmish, and in return Henry III sent a letter of congratulations on March 6.[10] In it Henry alluded to the planned antikingship and asked Otto to send envoys to him by Pentecost. An embassy under the leadership of a cleric named Galfried was present at the English court on April 4, although Henry III had not requested a response until Pentecost.[11] Henry immediately sent Galfried on to Rome[12] and wrote a letter to Otto telling him of Galfried's trip to confer with Pope Gregory IX.[13] He issued a second letter to Pope Gregory, wherein he thanked the pope for his role in obtaining Otto's release from imprisonment and asked Gregory to increase Otto's honor and to recommend him to the imperial princes for election when the time was right.[14]

These plans were defeated by the unexpected return of Frederick II in June 1229 and the refusal of the German princes to consider Pope Gregory's call to elect an antiking. Otto "the Child" of Lüneburg for his part remained aloof from any direct move against the emperor. His own position was quite insecure even in his own lands after recent imprison-

---

9. *Rotuli litterarum clausarum,* 1:471, 508, 514, 541, 546.

10. *CCLR Henry III,* 1:233; *Rymer,* 1:308; *Böhmer,* 5, 2:1635, no. 11039.

11. *CCLR Henry III,* 1:121. Galfried received a yearly rent of five marks on April 4, 1229: see *CPR Henry III,* 2:243; *CCLR Henry III,* 1:233 and 234.

12. On April 5 Galfried received one hundred shillings as a gift for the trip: see *CLR Henry III,* 1:123.

13. *CCLR Henry III,* 1:234, *Rymer,* 1:308–9; *Böhmer,* 5, 2:1636, no. 11040.

14. *CCLR Henry III,* 1:234; *Rymer,* 1:309; *Böhmer,* 5, 2:1636, no. 11041.

ment, and any influence he had in the empire was virtually nonexistent. Otto sent his nephew Hermann to the English court in July[15] and a second embassy in September of the same year,[16] at which his decision to refuse to stand as an antiking was made known. He then visited England the following summer, but no revival of the English-Welf coalition resulted.[17] Indeed after Otto returned to Saxony his visit was quickly forgotten in the face of the surprise announcement of a marriage between the emperor, Frederick II, and Isabella, the sister of Henry III, on November 15, 1235. The Plantagenet house had thereby abandoned its kinship ties with the Welf to reestablish such ties with the Staufen dynasty.

Perhaps Otto benefited indirectly from this marriage, since English efforts may have been behind Frederick's recognition of Otto as duke of Brunswick-Lüneburg in the same year.[18] In any case this year marked the definitive close to the traditionally close Welf-Angevin relationship. Now that the Welf restitution question was finally resolved and the simultaneous rapprochement with the Staufen emperor had been successfully concluded with a marriage union, the Welfs thereby became superfluous to the Plantagenets and faded from the political landscape in both England and Germany. The archbishops of Cologne served thereafter as the conduit for English diplomatic relations with Germany. To understand how the emperor so unexpectedly married an English princess, and the role of the archbishop of Cologne in the matter, let us return to the early years of Henry III's reign.

Anglo-German diplomatic relations reached a low ebb after the debacle of Bouvines and the death of King John. The long minority of Henry III and Frederick II's attention to Italian affairs prevented any close alignment of mutual political interests between the two dynasties. France enjoyed a series of truces between the Capetians and Plantagenets that lasted almost a decade after Bouvines. This peace was broken in 1224, however, when the new French monarch, Louis VIII, invaded Poitou and hostilities between the two traditional enemies were renewed. Louis had strengthened his position in preparation for an attack on the

15. *CLR Henry III*, 1:224 (July 18).

16. Ibid., 1:143; *Böhmer*, 5, 2:1636, no. 11049 (September 26).

17. A royal writ to the constable of Windsor commands him to allow Otto to hunt freely in the forest: see *CCLR Henry III*, 1:365–66; *Böhmer*, 5, 2:1640, no. 11080.

18. Ahlers, *Die Welfen*, 266. See also K. Brandi, "Die Urkunde Friedrichs II. vom August 1235 für Otto von Lüneberg," in *Festschrift für Paul Zimmerman* (Wolfenbüttel, 1914), 33–46.

228 The Social Politics of Medieval Diplomacy

remaining Angevin continental lands through a renewal of the Capetian-Staufen alliance initiated by Philip II.[19] Frederick II had no intention, however, of entering directly into western European political conflicts. The agreement served only to shield him from western interference as he concentrated on Italian affairs.[20] His promise to prevent any German princes from making alliances with the Plantagenet house must have concerned the regents of Henry III, however.

The English were clearly isolated by both moves of the French monarch, who then sought the additional step of a marriage union with the Staufen house. Frederick II seemed agreeable, and a meeting to discuss this possibility was set for November 19, 1224, at a location between Toul and Vaucouleurs. The English court was in no position to derail these increasingly dangerous ties between the French and imperial monarchs and could only hope that their traditional German ally, the archbishop of Cologne, would intervene on their behalf.

English hopes for Archbishop Engelbert I's intervention were based on three factors. Firstly, he was in a position to affect imperial policy. Frederick II had appointed Engelbert as the regent for his nine-year-old son, King Henry (VII), who was the likely candidate for any French marriage.[21] The emperor, moreover, had made Engelbert the imperial regent north of the Alps, since Frederick was most often in his Italian lands.[22] Therefore Engelbert would naturally play a leading role during these negotiations. Secondly, the archbishop had traditional economic ties to England, which were the foundation of the episcopal city's wealth. Finally, Engelbert had cause to prevent any expansion of Capetian power, particularly in the Low Countries. Such a development threatened his own territorial principality and therefore drew him to maintain an anti-Capetian policy.[23]

19. *Historia Diplomatica*, 2, 1:461–63; MGH Leges, 2:253; MGH Const., 2:125, no. 99; *Böhmer*, 5, 1:311, no. 1509. The agreement was signed at Catania in November 1223, and in it the emperor promised, "de rege Anglie sic erit, quod nullam cum eo faciemus confederacionem nec cum heredibus suis, nec a nostris fieri permittemus, ubicumque impendiendi habeamus potestatem." Concerning the dating of this agreement see Kienast, "Die Deutschen Fürsten," 16:18 n. 1.

20. Kienast, "Die Deutschen Fürsten," 16:18.

21. Engelbert had crowned Henry (VII) as king at Aachen on May 8, 1222; see *REK*, 3, 1:62, no. 352.

22. *REK*, 3, 1:55, no. 303 (dated November 1220).

23. Kienast, "Die Deutschen Fürsten," 16:21; idem, *Deutschland und Frankreich*, 3:587; Wand, "Die Englandpolitik der Stadt Köln," 85; Trautz, *Die Könige*, 102–3; Julius

Engelbert had maintained active diplomatic contact with the English court from the beginning of his pontificate. Sometime after his consecration he wrote a letter to the young English king asking that the king restore the Honor of Eye to the duke of Brabant,[24] and his envoys to the English court are evidenced often in subsequent years.[25] In fact Engelbert sent ambassadors to England as tensions were growing between the English and French monarchs in the spring and summer of 1224.[26] Because of his powerful position as imperial regent north of the Alps the archbishop received many foreign dignitaries who sought to do business with the empire, yet his own territorial needs necessitated a policy sympathetic to English interests.[27]

Engelbert seems to have had no involvement in the renewal of the Capetian-Staufen alliance at Catania; indeed he was preoccupied at the time with negotiations between the king of Denmark and King Henry (VII).[28]

Ficker, *Engelbert der Heilige, Erzbischof von Köln und Reichsverweser* (Cologne, 1853), 133.

24. *Diplomatic Documents*, 108, no. 157 (dated 1216–24). The duke of Brabant had written a similar letter to the justiciar Hubert de Burgh (ibid., 108, no. 158). The Honor of Eye was restored to the duke before January 2, 1225: see *Rotuli litterarum clausarum*, 2:10.

25. *Rotuli litterarum clausarum*, 1:432 (Winchester, October 6, 1220); 461 (Northampton, June 11, 1221 [the envoy mentioned here—John Lupus—remained in the service of the archbishop of Cologne after Otto IV's kingship ended; cf. *Historia Diplomatica*, 2:783; *Rymer*, 1:461; *Böhmer*, 5, 2:1614, no. 10878]); 471 (Westminster, October 1, 1221 [cf. *Böhmer*, 5, 2:1616, no. 10887]); 506 and 508 (July 19, 1222); 522 (Westminster, November 19 and 21, 1222 [the envoy mentioned here—Conrad of Wijlre—also remained in the service of the archbishop after Otto IV's kingship came to an end]); 576–77 (Tower of London, December 5, 1223 [cf. *Historia Diplomatica*, 2:783–84; *Böhmer*, 5, 2:1619, no. 10911]). This last entry involved Archbishop Engelbert as imperial administrator, since Bernard of Horstmar, another former servant of Otto IV who remained in the archbishop's service along with John Lupus and Conrad of Wijlre, is mentioned here. Bishop Radulf of Speyer, a knight named Anselm, and a cleric named Bertram—all called messengers of the Roman king (i.e., Henry)—also appear at the English court at the same time as Bernard of Horstmar's embassy, and they are given money to defray their travel costs (*Rotuli litterarum clausarum*, 1:578; *Böhmer*, 5, 2:1619, no. 10912). This last entry further confirms Engelbert's involvement in the December embassy, as he was the guardian of young King Henry.

26. *Rotuli litterarum clausarum*, 1:599 and 600 (Westminster, May 21 and 22, 1224), 601 (Westminster, May 26, 1224), and 610 and 634; *REK*, 3, 1:75, no. 442; *HUB*, 1:54, no. 165; *Böhmer*, 5, 2:1621, no. 10923 (Bedford, July 9, 1224).

27. *REK*, 3, 1:84, no. 527. Caesarius of Heisterbach declares in his *Vita Engelberti* that the archbishop had made pontifical robes and also a golden altar chalice that cost more than five hundred marks and that was bejeweled with precious stones given to him by the kings of England, France, Denmark, Bohemia, and Hungary.

28. *REK*, 3, 1:71, no. 409.

He would later inform English envoys that he had been unaware of the treaty's conclusion.[29] In any case Engelbert's political machinations on November 19, 1224, at a meeting between himself, King Henry (VII), and King Louis VIII along the German-French border would more than satisfy English expectations.[30] Cardinal Legate Conrad von Urach, the archbishops of Mainz, Trier, and Besançon, and many other bishops, dukes, and imperial princes were also present at this conference. The stage was set for an important display of unity among the participants. Yet despite Frederick II's instructions to reach a settlement with the French king and the pope's willingness to accept it, Archbishop Engelbert refused to allow the marriage agreement to go through. Upon his return home Louis VIII complained loudly to both emperor and pope about the interference of the imperial regent and even offered large sums of money to assure a marriage agreement. The Cologne archbishop outmaneuvered the French king, however, sending embassies directly from Toul to both England and the emperor as well as a letter to the pope.

The mission of the envoys to England was to expedite an alternative to the Capetian marriage offer. Engelbert furthered this cause in his letter to the pope. Here he declared two reasons for his refusal to allow the French marriage alliance: because it was directed against England, to which the pope owed special protection; and because it would be detrimental to the Roman Church. Engelbert urged the pope to use his influence on the emperor to bring about a union with the Plantagenets instead. The envoys to Frederick II asked the emperor not to accept the Capetian offer until Engelbert had received word about the success of his envoys in England.[31] This embassy to England did not come as a complete surprise to the English court, since a series of important German envoys had been there during the previous months.[32]

---

29. *Diplomatic Documents*, 109, nos. 160–61; *Shirley*, 1:251, no. 213. The English were evidently satisfied with Engelbert's record of a pro-English policy.

30. *REK*, 3, 1:77, no. 463.

31. *Chronica Albrici monachi Trium-fontium*, ed. P. Scheffer-Boichorst, MGH SS, no. 23 (Hanover, 1874; reprint, 1986), 914. *Diplomatic Documents*, 109, no. 161 and *Shirley*, 1:251, no. 213 continue Engelbert's conversation with Bishop Walter of Carlisle, where the aforementioned actions of the archbishop are recounted. Cf. Ficker, *Engelbert der Heilige*, 126–27; Wand, "Die Englandpolitik der Stadt Köln," 85; Kienast, "Die Deutschen Fürsten," 16:21–23.

32. Kienast ("Die Deutschen Fürsten," 16:24) believed that Frederick II knew of the alternative marriage negotiations with England and was perhaps playing a double game with France and England at this time. There is, however, no other evidence that Frederick

This was a remarkable effort by the archbishop of Cologne to redirect imperial policy away from the deepening rapprochement with France and toward England instead. Engelbert had in effect stalled the momentum for a Capetian-Staufen marriage union, a most disadvantageous development for the English, and sent embassies to Sicily, Rome, and England exhorting emperor, pope, and king to work instead toward the isolation of France. This was, in effect, a complete reversal of imperial policy. These actions say much about the political power wielded by Engelbert at this time, since even attempting such an audacious strategy would have been unimaginable to most other imperial princes. Although Engelbert's policy was no doubt in his own best territorial interest, England would never be served better by an archbishop of Cologne than at this moment.[33] Evidence survives showing that the English court was aware of the archbishop of Cologne's plans even before the November 17 conference. Bishop Walter Mauclerc of Carlisle was provided with forty marks on October 22 in preparation for an overseas embassy, and a certain Lambekin, nuncio of Archbishop Engelbert, was present at the English court on the same day.[34] Therefore it appears that counterplans were afoot a month before the Toul-Vaucouleurs meeting transpired.

Details of the Cologne-Plantagenet counterproposal to the Capetian offer became clear on January 3, 1225.[35] The English regents issued letters of credence on behalf of the young king to both Archbishop Engelbert and Duke Leopold VI of Austria. Bishop Walter of Carlisle, Master Alanus Martel of the English Templars, Prior Robert of the English Hospitallers, Chancellor Henry de Cornhill of London, and a knight named Nicholas de Molis are listed as members of the English embassy to

---

II's interests reached beyond his own affairs in Italy. Furthermore the envoys, even those specifically designated as representing the Roman emperor, had come from central or northern Germany and most likely were under the authority of Archbishop Engelbert (as imperial regent) and King Henry (VII). Any marriage arrangement would have also required the assent of Henry (VII) himself, who was still under the tutelage of Engelbert. Therefore the Cologne archbishop's active role in these matters was based on his own initiative rather than on the instruction of the emperor, who had in fact ordered that a marriage union be arranged with the Capetian house.

33. Haverkamp, *Medieval Germany*, 252–53.

34. *Rotuli litterarum clausarum*, 1:627, 652 (Westminster, October 22, 1224).

35. *CPR Henry III*, 1:558; *Rymer*, 1:275–76; *Historia Diplomatica*, 2, 2:824–25; *REK*, 3, 1:78, no. 473; *Böhmer*, 5, 2:1622, nos. 10931–33. The envoy Nicholas de Molis was a household banneret at the court of Henry III and became sheriff of Yorkshire in 1239; see Robert C. Stacey, *Politics, Policy, and Finance under Henry III (1216–1245)* (Oxford, 1987), 63 n. 68.

Germany. The second letter of credence to Duke Leopold VI indicates that Henry de Cornhill and the knight Nicholas de Molis were being sent to Austria to discover the duke's position regarding a marriage union; they would then return to Cologne to inform Bishop Walter, Master Alanus, and Prior Robert of the duke's wishes. As the letter of credence states, the English embassy was sent in response to a prior embassy of Duke Leopold VI to the English court "for a marriage between us and your daughter," that is, for a marriage between Henry III and a daughter of the duke. This earlier Austrian initiative took place in late 1221, at which time the English regents had responded in a less than enthusiastic way.[36] In a brief letter in the name of Henry III, thanks had been given to the duke for sending a certain "magistrum B. archidiaconum Marchie"[37] concerning the marriage offer, and a desire to bring the matter to a conclusion was expressed; however, the Plantagenet regents could not accept the conditions suggested by the duke. Since additional details were not clear to the regents, an English canon was sent with the Austrian envoy back to the duke for further discussions. The English did not wish to break off these negotiations, yet they clearly seemed reticent about the offer.

No mention is made of subsequent negotiations during the years 1222–23, which suggests that this first effort came to naught. Yet it was an important channel that Archbishop Engelbert took up in his efforts at arranging an Anglo-imperial marriage union. In hopes of avoiding an increased Capetian threat to his own territorial interests, the Cologne archbishop was attempting to fashion a double-marriage agreement hearkening back to that arranged by his predecessor Rainald of Dassel.[38] The English, for their part, were anxious to find continental allies and were

---

36. *Rymer*, 1:252; *Böhmer*, 5, 2:1617, no. 10890. The letter is dated December 15, 1221. *Pipe Rolls 5 Henry III*, PR, NS, 48:201 contains an expense for a certain "Roberto de Alemannia nuncio R. eunti in nuncium R. . . . ." at Michaelmas 1221.

37. Erich Zöllner ("Das Projekt einer babenbergischen Heirat König Heinrichs III. von England," *Archiv für Österreichische Geschichte* 125 [1966]: 58–62) has identified this envoy as Bernhard, a prior from Friesach and chaplain of Duke Leopold. The *Rotuli litterarum clausarum* mentions (1:483) a royal command to the chamberlain to pay out 110s. 2d. to Andreas Bukerel for a silver cup, a golden brooch (*firmaculum*), and a golden ring "ad opus prepositi Frisacensis, nuncii ducis Austrie," and also mentions (501) a royal payment on June 24, 1222, of five marks for a horse and an additional five marks to defray the costs of a return trip home for Bernhard. Therefore the trip back to Austria must not have occurred until late June or early July 1222. Cf. Ficker, *Engelbert der Heilige*, 127–34.

38. Wand, "Die Englandpolitik der Stadt Köln," 85.

hopeful that a double marriage (a marriage between Henry III and Duke Leopold VI's daughter Margaret and another between Henry III's sister Isabella and the emperor's son King Henry [VII]) would begin to reverse the political gains of the Capetians, which had come at their expense.[39]

The first sign of new movement in these marriage negotiations comes from a writ of *liberate* attested by Bishop Peter des Roches of Winchester and dated July 21, 1224.[40] Here the abbot of Stratford received twenty marks for his expenses for "going on a mission to Germany." In October and December of the same year, German envoys were in England.[41] Letters exchanged between the English court and the various intermediaries in Cologne provide us with detailed accounts of the complicated negotiations that ensued in January 1225. On February 10, shortly after his arrival in Cologne, Bishop Walter of Carlisle sent a lengthy progress report to Henry III.[42] After the bishop set sail from Dover on January 22, a dangerous winter trip across Channel waters almost resulted in shipwreck. Bishop Walter, however, landed safely at Gravelingen and then proceeded onward to Cologne, where his party arrived on February 1. Here they were met by an archiepiscopal ministerial who was previously at the English court, Henricus de Zudendorp, and an English cleric named John. These two men had just returned from the imperial diet at Ulm, where they had requested that the archbishop return to Cologne to meet the English embassy.[43]

A meeting between Engelbert and the English party was delayed a few more days because of the late arrival of the Templar and Hospitaller representatives. Upon their coming the two joined Bishop Walter in the initial conference with the Cologne archbishop on February 7 at the Abbey of Altenberg.[44] After thanking the archbishop for his efforts against the Capetian-Staufen union, the English party learned of several

39. Kate Norgate, *The Minority of Henry III* (London, 1912), 253–54; Charles Petit-Dutaillis, *Étude sur la vie et le Règne de Louis VIII* (Paris, 1894), 263–70; Stacey, *Politics, Policy, and Finance under Henry III (1216–1245)*, 166. D. A. Carpenter's *The Minority of Henry III* (Berkeley, 1990) has no discussion of these marriage negotiations.

40. *Rotuli litterarum clausarum*, 1:465, 495.

41. Ibid. 1:471, 483.

42. *Diplomatic Documents*, 109–11; *Shirley*, 1:249–54; *Historia Diplomatica*, 2, 2:833–39; *REK*, 3, 1:78–79, nos. 481–82; *Böhmer*, 5, 2:1622, no. 10934.

43. At the Ulm diet Engelbert witnessed the confirmation by King Henry (VII) of the toll privileges given to the burghers of Cologne by Henry VI and Frederick II: see *UGN*, 2:61, no. 111.

44. *REK*, 3, 1:78–79, no. 482.

new developments, some of which were not encouraging. Engelbert's envoys to the Austrian court had not yet returned and the archbishop himself had to depart to Saxony, where urgent imperial business required him.[45] Engelbert, however, declared his loyalty to the English cause and told the envoys of his actions after the meeting at Vaucouleurs-Toul. After the Ulm diet Engelbert had also sent Bernard of Horstmar to the emperor at San Germano to persuade Frederick II to reject the French offer.[46]

News concerning the Austrian marriage proposal was therefore still uncertain, and recent developments had made the English initiative for a Staufen marriage union doubtful as well. At the Ulm diet both the kings of Bohemia and Hungary had put forth their daughters as marriage candidates for King Henry (VII) along with large sums of money, and of course the French offer was still standing.[47] Now the English court was competing with no less than three other royal offers of marriage. Declaring that there was danger in delay, the archbishop counseled the English embassy to make a suitably large offer of dowry money to the emperor immediately.

When Engelbert was asked in return what an appropriate amount might be, his response was quite striking. He said that, although he loved the English king very much, it would be inappropriate for an imperial officer and a *consanguineus* of the German king to make such suggestions. Yet he swore before an altar to advance the English cause and even intimated that the English king could gain back all lost continental lands through the marriage union. The closing remark was a clear reference to imperial military aid against Capetian France. Engelbert's behavior here is curiously reserved, relying more on the English eagerness to advance their cause than on his own imperial influence. He then departed to attend to affairs in Saxony and indicated that he would be back in Cologne on February 20.

---

45. A sign of how important Engelbert thought the negotiations with the English were can be seen in the fact that the archbishop returned to meet with the English envoys after all members of the embassy had arrived, even though he had already set out on a day's journey toward Saxony to resolve imperial affairs there.

46. We have met this Westphalian nobleman before in connection with the kingship of Otto IV and the Battle of Bouvines. Concerning the career of Bernard and his service to the Welf cause and to the archbishops of Cologne see Ficker, *Engelbert der Heilige*, 137–39.

47. For the marriage King Ottokar I of Bohemia offered thirty thousand marks, and Duke Ludwig of Bavaria offered fifteen thousand additional marks since the king's daughter was his niece. The fifteen-year-old King Henry is said to have refused Ottokar's daughter, however. In addition the king of Hungary had sent an offer of his daughter to the emperor, along with *pecuniam maximam*.

Chancellor Henry de Cornhill of London and the knight Nicholas de Molis, the envoys to the Austrian court, arrived in Cologne on the Saturday after Engelbert departed for Saxony. Since the archbishop had not yet heard from his own envoys to the Austrian court (one of whom was the son of Duke Leopold VI) and desired to send still other messengers along with the English envoys, Henry and Nicholas remained in Cologne until Engelbert returned. Bishop Walter closed his February 10 letter to Henry III with a conviction that the embassy would require a lengthy stay in Germany, although the Templar and Hospitaller representatives could not stay longer than Easter.[48] Therefore he exhorted the king to send replacements for Master Alanus and Prior Robert and reiterated that great sums of money were needed both to secure the success of the embassy and to pay for their expenses. Walter seems decidedly discouraged at the outset, an attitude that was quite in keeping with the mounting obstacles confronting the English envoys. Continual delays and lack of money would come to define this diplomatic effort.

The same attitude, albeit more forcefully expressed, was held by Chancellor Henry de Cornhill. In a letter filled with frustration and striking rhetoric, he wrote to the bishops of Bath, Salisbury, and Chichester shortly after his arrival in Cologne about mid-February concerning the obstacles facing the envoys.[49] Henry, sounding unhappy about being commissioned with this task, complained principally about the lack of financial support for the endeavor. He even sarcastically compared the envoys to the apostles, "who were ordered to take nothing on the way," and pointed out that such poor preachers should never be sent to negotiate a marriage. Saying that the envoys had not yet met the angel of Tobias (Raphael, who led Tobit's son safely to his father's money),[50] the chancellor declared that he would rather have been sent to Acre at a suitable time than "to this people, raving and lacking in reason and moderation."[51]

Henry de Cornhill informed the bishops also that Henricus de Zuden-

---

48. Easter Sunday fell on March 30 in the year 1225.

49. *Diplomatic Documents*, 112–13, no. 163; *Shirley*, 1:254–56, no. 214; *Böhmer, 5*, 2:1624, no. 10950.

50. This allusion is to the apocryphal Book of Tobit, especially chapters 5–12.

51. "... ad populum illum furiosum et ratione modestiaque carentem." The phrase *furor Teutonicus* became a commonplace in the twelfth century: see E. Dümmler, "Über den furor Teutonicus," in *Sitzungsberichte der königlich-Preussischen Akademie der Wissenschaften zu Berlin, Philosophische Klasse* (Berlin, 1897), 112–27. John of Salisbury made use of this term in an 1165 letter to Thomas Becket: see *Letters of John of Salisbury*, 2:54.

dorp, an archiepiscopal ministerial, was to join him on the trip to Austria. There had been some doubt about whether Henricus felt himself able to undertake such a venture safely, and he would not go "without his comrade the knight" [*sine socio suo milite*]. This concern was apparently also aired by the Cologne ministerial in his own letter to the English king. His participation was arranged with the understanding that the English embassy would pay for his expenses, a step that was unnecessary considering the wealth of the archbishop of Cologne but most probably done in an effort to maintain the archbishop's goodwill. Henry de Cornhill did not expect to return from Austria before Easter week, both because of the distance involved and also because of the delays in arranging Henricus de Zudendorp's travel necessities.

The English court responded directly to the letters sent by Bishop Walter, Henry de Cornhill, and Henricus de Zudendorp by sending money. On February 27 a royal writ issued funds for their travels, including means for the participation of Henricus de Zudendorp.[52] On March 2 Henry III sent identical letters to Bishop Walter, Henry de Cornhill, and Nicholas de Molis informing them of the funds being sent for the trip to Austria.[53] Yet no mention appears anywhere about the sizable amount of money that would be required to attract either the emperor or the duke to accept an English marriage offer.

While Bishop Walter sojourned in Cologne, Henry de Cornhill and Nicholas de Molis were joined by Henricus de Zudendorp and made their venture to Austria in early March. No progress was made for the English cause, however; in fact Duke Leopold VI responded in a confusing letter to Henry III that he had already placed the entire matter in the hands of Archbishop Engelbert of Cologne.[54] To complicate the matter more the Welf Henry of Brunswick wrote to the bishop of Chichester at this time complaining that he had been frozen out of the negotiations and asking the bishop to intercede on his behalf so that he might become involved in

---

52. *Rotuli litterarum clausarum*, 2:20–21. Note that the bishop of Bath, one of the recipients of the letter written by Henry de Cornhill, witnessed the writ for these funds.

53. *Rotuli litterarum clausarum*, 2:70. After stating his regret that the Hospitaller and Templar representatives had to leave at Easter, the king mentions the sending of Walter de Kirkeham to replace them. He also informs the English embassy that he had issued funds to cover the expenses of Henry de Zudendorp. Also sent at this time were royal letters to Master Alanus and Prior Robert acknowledging their need to depart at Easter to attend to the affairs of their respective orders (ibid., 2:71).

54. *Diplomatic Documents*, 113, no. 164 (March 1225).

the matter.[55] It was beginning to appear that both the duke of Austria and the emperor were using delaying tactics, and Archbishop Engelbert showed no sign of direct intervention during the subsequent months.

On March 22 the English king wrote to Archbishop Engelbert as well as to the bishop of Carlisle and his companions, who had by now returned from Austria.[56] He informed them of the imminent arrival in Cologne of the abbot of Beaulieu ("de Bello Loco") and the abbot of Robertsbridge ("de Ponte Roberti"), who would explain to them his wishes *viva voce*. In particular Bishop Walter was instructed to send his cleric John to inform the pope about the status of the negotiations. There was obviously little news that John could bring to the Curia. Indeed the English party would languish in Cologne as the months dragged on into the summer.[57]

Sometime in late May or early June Bishop Walter wrote again to Henry III, acknowledging the arrival of the abbot of Beaulieu and Henry de Cornhill.[58] As the bishop indicated in the letter, these two had been sent back to England to advise the court and had returned to Cologne a second time with further instructions.[59] Bishop Walter sounds wearied in this letter; he declares his constant loyalty to the royal family yet requests that the king defend not only the royal honor but the bishop's own reputation as well. The negotiations were obviously stalled at this point.

Frederick II was ultimately the reason behind all the temporizing. As his primary interest was in Italian affairs, he wished to reach a comprehensive settlement with Pope Honorius III. Therefore any marriage agreement had to be made in concert with this goal.[60] Bernard of Horstmar,

---

55. Ibid., 113–14, no. 165 (dated February–March 1225). This echo of the past involvement of the Welfs in Anglo-imperial affairs went unheeded at the English court, which preferred to continue to rely on the intercession of the archbishop of Cologne.

56. *Rotuli litterarum clausarum*, 2:71. Henry de Cornhill and Nicholas de Molis are addressed along with Bishop Walter in the letter to the English envoys. The new envoy Walter de Kirkeham is also mentioned.

57. The *Rotuli litterarum clausarum* (2:38) records a payment to a certain Bruno of Cologne of thirty pounds as reimbursement for money that the Cologne merchant lent to Bishop Walter for expenses incurred in the city. This payment was issued on May 12, 1225.

58. *Diplomatic Documents*, 117, no. 172; *Shirley*, 1:260–61, no. 218; *Böhmer*, 5, 2:1624, no. 10950 (May–June).

59. The *Rotuli litterarum clausarum* (2:26, 71, 72) indicates that the abbot of Beaulieu left for Cologne around April 8 and left England on his second mission about May 29. Henry de Cornhill apparently had permanently returned to England sometime before June 25 (ibid., 2:46, 47).

60. Kienast, "Die Deutschen Fürsten," 16:26–27.

who had been in attendance at the imperial court at San Germano on behalf of the Archbishop of Cologne since the January diet at Ulm, informed the English court of this complication.[61] The duke of Austria, for his part, was awaiting the result of the negotiations between pope and emperor so that he could coordinate his marriage policy accordingly. Eventually the mutual interests of both emperor and duke would finally lead to the exclusion of the English in the final marriage settlement.

The lengthy stay of the English embassy in Cologne necessitated additional funding, which was once again obtained by a third party in Cologne and then reimbursed by royal command on June 24.[62] This was an extremely frustrating and lonely sojourn for the envoys in Cologne, especially since Archbishop Engelbert was absent from the February meeting at Altenberg Abbey until August.[63] During this time he was in the itinerant court of young Henry (VII), constantly attending to affairs of the kingdom as the imperial regent, at such locations as Soest, Schwäbisch-Hall, Würzburg, Nuremburg, and Nordhausen. Other than the presence of Bernard of Horstmar at the imperial court in San Germano, there is no evidence of any direct diplomatic activity by the archbishop on behalf of the English cause during these months. Once again we must note how local and regional affairs overshadowed any interregional diplomacy, even when the archbishop of Cologne was involved.

Henry III encouraged Bishop Walter and Nicholas de Molis to wait patiently for the replies of the emperor and duke of Austria as the months passed from June to July, and ninety marks were advanced to them for their continued stay in Cologne.[64] The duke, however, had been busy advancing his own cause before the imperial court as the English waited. In June Leopold VI made his way to San Germano via Venice and Rome; the latter stop was no doubt to obtain papal support for his plans.[65] During the crucial months of June and July the duke was able to overcome Bernard of Horstmar and other German princes and gain Frederick

---

61. *Diplomatic Documents,* 120, no. 179; *Shirley,* 1:258, no. 216; *REK,* 3, 1:80, no. 488; *Böhmer,* 5, 2:1623, no. 10939 (March–July 1225).

62. *Rotuli litterarum clausarum,* 2:46; *Böhmer,* 5, 2:1624, no. 10947. The moneylender mentioned here—Henry Lupus—may well have been a relative of John Lupus, the chamberlain of Otto IV.

63. *REK,* 3, 1:79–82.

64. *Rymer,* 1:280; *Böhmer,* 5, 2:1624, no. 10948 (Westminster, July 7, 1225).

65. Duke Leopold VI had just benefited from the intervention of a papal legate, Bishop Conrad of Porto, in negotiations concerning border disputes with Hungary during the months preceding the duke's trip into Italy: see Zöllner, "Das Projekt," 68–70.

II's support for a marriage between his daughter Margaret and the young King Henry (VII). Frederick, for his part, accepted the Austrian marriage union because of its value for his Italian activities.[66]

In the end, therefore, the English plans for a double marriage were destroyed, since Henry (VII) and Margaret, who were now engaged, had been the two spouses sought for Henry III and his sister Isabella. The duke's success was the result of the emperor's unwillingness to accept either the English marriage offer supported by Archbishop Engelbert or the Bohemian marriage offer supported by other powerful princes.[67] Young Henry (VII) had himself refused to marry the Bohemian princess. Although Archbishop Engelbert had successfully fended off French, Bohemian, and Hungarian offers for a marriage with his ward, he could not gain the support of Henry (VII)'s father for the English proposal.[68]

Engelbert received an imperial letter informing him of Frederick II's decision in favor of the duke's proposal and forwarded a copy to Bishop Walter, who then sent Nicholas de Molis to England with the news. The Cologne archbishop moved quickly to assuage an angry and disappointed English court, sending a letter to ask that Bishop Walter not return home until Engelbert received Bernard of Horstmar from the imperial court.[69] The archbishop desired to make one more effort at changing the emperor's mind. He was also aware that Bishop Walter wished very much to return home after receiving the bad news. Engelbert's envoy, Henricus de Zudendorp, also wrote to Henry III to exhort him not to abandon the apparently failed negotiations just yet.[70] Presenting himself as a liege vassal (a very strong statement of loyalty to the English), Henricus informed the English court that the matter of the marriage, with which the duke of Austria had interfered, was still open

---

66. Kienast, *Deutschland und Frankreich,* 3:589. Frederick II was also thereby able to remain on good terms with France without becoming involved in Anglo-French affairs: see Kienast, "Die Deutschen Fürsten," 16:29.

67. Bishop Conrad of Regensburg appears to have played a key role in the success of Leopold VI's marriage offer to the emperor: see *Notae S. Emmerammi Ratisbonensis,* ed. Ph. Jaffé, MGH SS, no. 17 (Hanover, 1861; reprint, 1990), 574.

68. In an effort to placate Engelbert, Frederick II granted him and his successors with the "predium" at Richterich because of the "fidem puram et devotionem laudabilem necnon et grata valde et accepta servitia, que Engelbertus venerabilis Coloniensis archiepiscopus, dilectus princeps noster, nobis et imperio exhibuit iugiter et exhibet excessanter" (*REK*, 3, 1:82, no. 1225).

69. *Diplomatic Documents,* 126–27, no. 188 (late July or early August).

70. Ibid., 127, no. 189.

and had only been prorogued for a time. Therefore he urged that Bishop Walter's stay in Cologne not be cut short.

Thus the possibility of an imperial marriage was still held out to the English by the Cologne party, although any hope of an Austrian union was obviously not a desirable, or even an available, option at this juncture. Time, however, was needed to achieve such a difficult task, and Bishop Walter was anxious to return home. Therefore Engelbert wrote to Abbot Henry of St. Pantaleon in Cologne, ordering him to arrange the translation of the heads of St. Felix and St. Audactus from the church's altar to a newly prepared shrine at Holy Apostles' Church.[71] Engelbert then asked Walter, as a favor to the canons of Holy Apostles' Church, to consecrate these relics as well as many others that were held at the church. Walter consented, and the consecration service took place on July 15.[72] The bishop granted a thirty days' indulgence in honor of this event.

The arrangement and carrying out of the translation and consecration must have busied Walter until mid-July and given him a measure of purpose and prestige, but by the time of his letter to the justiciar Hubert de Burgh in early August he was again seeking permission to return to England.[73] Walter informed Hubert that the archbishop had recently been more attentive to his affairs and had assured him that the letter announcing the decision of the emperor ought not to worry the English, as the archbishop was busy in negotiations with the imperial court to amend it. Word from San Germano came in the form of a letter from the master of the German Hospitallers and Bernard of Horstmar, which led Engelbert to believe that the matter was progressing nicely. In fact the delay, which had become a hallmark of the entire affair by this point, was caused by the intense negotiations that Frederick II was holding with Pope Honorius III. Walter expected therefore that this delay would be a lengthy one and asked Hubert to allow him to return home, even though this would greatly displease Archbishop Engelbert. Response from England to his request did not arrive until August 27, when a royal letter

71. *REK*, 3, 1:81, no. 501. The distance between St. Pantaleon and Holy Apostles' Church was sufficient to have allowed a sizable procession for the occasion.

72. Walter's charter of confirmation survives in Cologne: see *Ennen/Eckertz*, 2:95, no. 87; *REK*, 3, 1:81, no. 501; *Böhmer*, 5, 2:1624, no. 10949.

73. *Diplomatic Documents*, 126, no. 187; *Shirley*, 1:259–60, no. 217; *Böhmer*, 5, 2:1624, no. 10947. Archbishop Engelbert was not in Cologne until the month of August: see *REK*, 3, 1:82, no. 507.

was sent that exhorted Walter to continue his valuable service in Cologne and to wait until Michaelmas (September 29) before determining whether he could return to England with the blessing of the archbishop of Cologne.[74] The English court still held out hope that Engelbert could salvage a marriage union from the ashes of the recent diplomatic failure.

According to the Cologne Chronicle, Bishop Walter finally received an opportunity to present the English case at the royal diet of Frankfurt sometime between late August and October;[75] however, the German princes looked with disfavor on the offer, and Walter returned empty-handed to England. Engelbert had only managed a formal hearing of the English proposal but could not get the princes to support it. Walter of Carlisle's ten-month embassy in Germany went therefore entirely for naught.[76] As if to punctuate the failed initiative, Archbishop Engelbert was suddenly murdered by his own nephew, Count Frederick of Isenburg, on November 7 as a result of a dispute between them.[77] This squabble, based on local, dynastic, and kinship politics, had significant consequences for interregional politics as well. Henricus de Zudendorp, in a letter to the English king informing him of Engelbert's murder, declared that the marriage negotiations would have reached a positive end had the archbishop not been killed.[78] Henricus de Zudendorp maintained contact with the English court during the remainder of the year, but the cause was clearly at an end.[79] On November 29, 1225, a double marriage was in fact celebrated at Nuremburg: King Henry (VII) wedded Margaret of

---

74. *Rymer*, 1:282; *Historia Diplomatica*, 2, 2:850–51; *REK*, 3, 1:83, no. 512; *Böhmer*, 5, 2:1624, no. 10954.

75. Concerning the dating of this diet see Eduard Winkelmann, *Kaiser Friederich II.* (Leipzig, 1889–97), 1:458, 539ff.; Kienast, "Die Deutschen Fürsten," 16:29 n. 3. Engelbert was present in Frankfurt on October 21: see *REK*, 3, 1:83, no. 519.

76. *CRC*, 255: "Heinricus rex curiam habuit Frankinvort; ubi quidam episcopus missus a rege Anglie cum ceteris ipsius legatis affuit, laborans, ut ipse rex matrimonium contraheret cum sorore regis Anglie. Sed cum talis contractus displicuisset principibus nec potuisset habere processum, nuncii inacte reveruntur."

77. *REK*, 3, 1:87–88, no. 569. A few months earlier Engelbert, at the command of both the pope and the emperor, had forced his nephew to cease interfering in the rights of the religious foundation in Essen, where Frederick held the office of advocate. This dispute was the source of conflict between the archbishop and his nephew (*REK*, 3, 1:82–83, no. 511). Engelbert's murder was noted in detail in the *Annales de Dunstaplia* (3:96). Count Frederick's family held powerful positions in the church. His two brothers were the bishops of Osnabrück and Münster.

78. *Diplomatic Documents*, 129, no. 193; *Shirley*, 1:274, no. 227; *REK*, 3, 1:87–88, no. 569; *Böhmer*, 5, 2:1625, no. 10957.

79. *Rotuli litterarum clausarum*, 2:88 (Westminster, December 11, 1225).

Austria, and her brother Henry married Agnes of Thuringia.[80] English concerns were further stirred when King Henry (VII) joined his father's pro-Capetian policy and agreed with Louis VIII of France on June 11, 1226, never to make a *confederatio* with the English king or his heirs without Louis's approval.[81]

The English had lost both their most valuable German ally and the opportunity to link themselves by marriage to either the imperial family or a German ducal family. This failure had significant reverberations at the English court, since Henry III would soon thereafter (1232) level a charge against the justiciar Hubert de Burgh that he had secretly hindered Duke Leopold VI of Austria from a dynastic union with England. This topped the list of accusations of treason made by the young king against Hubert and so it had been a festering point of contention for him.[82] That the emperor and his son had in the end affirmed the defensive alliance agreement with Louis VIII only added to the frustration and embarrassment of this failed diplomatic initiative.

Although this chapter in Anglo-German diplomacy was a frustrating one, there was little real fear concerning any Capetian-Staufen power bloc. The Capetians saw this *confederatio* as essentially defensive diplomacy, and Frederick II's participation derived its purpose more from his gratitude for Capetian help during the *Thronstreit* than from determined plans for a dynastic union or joint military action. Once again, the "alliance" was based more on personal ties of commitment than on institutional or geopolitical dictates. Furthermore, the minority of Louis IX, filled as it was with feudal rebellions and Plantagenet successes in regaining much of the territory lost between the Loire and Garonne, proved that the "alliance" afforded no real value to the Capetians.

In fact even the prospect of an English marriage union with a German dynasty was renewed when King Ottokar I of Bohemia, whose marriage proposal had also been rebuffed by the imperial court, suggested in mid-

---

80. Zöllner, "Das Projekt," 72.

81. MGH Const., 2:405, no. 290; *Historia Diplomatica,* 2, 2:875–76; *Böhmer, 5,* 1:727, no. 4008. This treaty has language identical to the agreement of November 1223 by Frederick II at Catania. The "confederatio" was renewed by Frederick with Louis IX in August 1227 (MGH Const., 2:147, no. 115) and in May 1232 (MGH Const., 2:215–16, no. 174) and by Henry (VII) on June 29, 1232 (MGH Const., 2:424–25, no. 313).

82. Roger of Wendover, *Flores historiarum,* 3:32. Cf. Kienast, "Die Deutschen Fürsten," 16:29; Zöllner, "Das Projekt," 72–73.

1226 that the English king marry his daughter. This was a welcome offer, since Hubert de Burgh had failed again in 1226 to arrange a marriage for Henry III with the daughter of Peter of Dreux, duke of Brittany.[83] On July 3, 1226, Henry III wrote a letter to Ottokar acknowledging the reception of his envoy and asking credence for his own ambassadors, who were sent to the Bohemian king to give Henry's response *viva voce*.[84] Ottokar sought the good offices of the new archbishop of Cologne, Henry I of Molenark (1225–38), who was quite willing to continue the traditional intermediary role that Cologne's archbishops played with the English court. Envoys representing the archbishop of Cologne were present at Westminster during the early months of 1227, where intensive negotiations were underway.[85]

The support of the German king, Henry (VII), and his new guardian, Duke Ludwig of Bavaria (who had replaced the murdered Archbishop Engelbert), was essential for such an important marriage union, as it was hoped that they could persuade Frederick II to be amenable. The careful negotiations of the early months of 1227 were successful in this regard, and a certain Prior Conrad of Speyer arrived at the English court in early April bringing news of Henry's and Ludwig's approval.[86] Why these two German princes, who had followed the emperor's pro-Capetian policy since 1226, should choose to support an Anglo-Bohemian marriage is unclear; however, the influence of the archbishop of Cologne may be behind this shift.[87] Henry of Molenark's involvement in these

---

83. Sidney Painter, *The Scourge of the Clergy: Peter of Dreux, Duke of Brittany* (Baltimore, 1937), 34–48.

84. *Rymer*, 1:286; *Böhmer*, 5, 2:1626, no. 10970. On July 4 Henry III ordered the payment of one hundred shillings to Ottokar's envoy named Lambert: see *Rotuli litterarum clausarum*, 2:126.

85. *CLR Henry III*, 1:15 (Westminster, January 7); 17 (Westminster, February 10); 27 (Westminster, April 11, 1227). Note in these entries the continued service of the Zudendorp family as ambassadors of the archbishops of Cologne to the English court.

86. On April 13 Henry III wrote to the German king and his guardian of the arrival of Prior Conrad, who had informed him of their desire to establish a "confederatio." The English king then sent a Master Henry and a cleric named Bernard to Duke Ludwig to advance the matter further: see *Rotuli litterarum clausarum*, 2:210; *Rymer*, 1:292; *Historia Diplomatica*, 3:322; *Böhmer*, 5, 2:1628, no. 10984. On 30 March Prior Conrad received a gift from the English king: see *CLR Henry III*, 1:25.

87. Kienast ("Die Deutschen Fürsten," 16:47–48) suggests that Duke Ludwig of Bavaria sought personal advantage thereby in the matter of the inheritance of Welf lands in Germany. But it is difficult to imagine how the English king could have possibly intervened in this matter.

negotiations was most welcomed by Henry III, who carefully nurtured a trusting relationship with him throughout the affair.[88]

Diplomatic exchanges continued through the summer months[89] and appeared to be reaching a positive culmination when a joint council of several English and German princes was planned for September at Antwerp.[90] Yet once again the possibility of an Anglo-German marriage union was shattered by the opposition of the emperor.[91] Indeed Frederick II had just renewed his alliance with the Capetians at Melfi in August.[92] Frederick owed a great deal to Capetian support during his struggle with Otto IV for the German kingship, and he therefore remained inclined to maintain his traditional diplomatic ties with France and avoid any entanglements in Anglo-French disputes, by agreeing to a German marriage union with England akin to the old Welf ties. No subsequent mention is made of the planned Antwerp negotiations, either in English or German sources. Although contacts concerning the marriage continued into 1228, yet another English attempt to procure a dynastic union with a German aristocratic house resulted in frustration.[93]

Throughout the decade of the 1220s the archbishops of Cologne made their highest interregional diplomatic priority the arrangement of a marriage union between the Plantagenet royal house and a German prince, if not the son of the emperor himself. Although Engelbert I of Berg and Henry of Molenark failed at each turn, their unwavering allegiance to aspirations in the face of opposition from the emperor and several German

---

88. *Rotuli litterarum clausarum*, 2:210; *Rymer*, 1:293; *REK*, 3, 1:96, no. 624; *Böhmer*, 5, 2:1628, no. 10986. These sources contain a carefully worded letter from the king to the archbishop (from Westminster, dated April 13, 1227), which is full of encouragement and blandishments.

89. Lambekin, the representative of Henricus de Zudendorp, was present at Westminster on June 1, and Prior Conrad was there on June 5 along with a Bohemian envoy, Count Arnold of Hückeswagen: see *CLR Henry III*, 1:36.

90. On September 4 at Windsor King Henry III issued letters of credence for the intended English envoys: the archbishop of York; the bishops of Coventry and Norwich; the counts of Pembroke, Gloucester, Hertford, and Albemarle; the constable of Chester; and Ralph, son of the royal seneschal: see *CPR Henry III*, 1:161; *Rymer*, 1:295–96; *Böhmer*, 5, 2:1630, no. 10997.

91. Wand, "Die Englandpolitik der Stadt Köln," 87.

92. MGH Const., 2:147, no. 115.

93. Henry III gave gifts to Bohemian envoys on February 12, 1228 (*CLR Henry III*, 1:68, 76, 88), and a letter of Henry III to King Ottokar of June 24, 1228, expressed the wish that the negotiations be continued (*CCLR Henry III*, 1:107). The count of Hückeswagen was present for the last time at the English court, along with an envoy of the bishop of Olmütz, on November 24, 1228 (*CLR Henry III*, 1:110).

princes and the machinations of the French king is remarkable. Henry III, for his part, found only frustration and failure in his endeavors with the German princes during this decade. No doubt part of this was caused by his own lack of a focused diplomatic policy,[94] yet his plans were also dashed by the growing particularism among the German princes and the distancing of the last Staufen emperor from direct involvement in political affairs north of the Alps. This same dynamic of the growing independence of German territorial principalities in the absence of imperial authority was responsible at the same time for the Cologne archbishops' turning to the English as a strategic counterbalance to Capetian France, as well as for an increasing inability to form a consensus among the German princes that could be considered a unified imperial policy.[95] This was a lesson that Henry III would learn again most thoroughly during the German kingship of his brother, Richard of Cornwall; and his son Edward I would also learn how impossible it had become to build an anti-Capetian coalition under such conditions in Germany. The English failure to successfully manage the regionalism and particularism among the German princes in the 1220s was a precursor of things to come.

By now it is not a new notion that local, regional, and dynastic concerns drove medieval politics much more than did institutional, constitutional, or state-building requirements. This social reality always made interregional diplomacy between political communities fragile and unstable, whether in the age of Saxon, Salian, or Staufen monarchs or in the time of territorial princes in Germany. It must also be pointed out that the focus of all the aforementioned intensive interregional diplomacy involving England, France, all regions of Germany, Italy, and the papacy was not about ideologies, states, or geopolitical power blocs but rather about the traditional social institution of marriage. The competition for dynastic unions, while not the stuff of modern diplomacy, still formed the social reality within which medieval politics were pursued, on either a local, regional, or interregional basis.

---

94. Stacey, *Politics, Policy, and Finance under Henry III (1216–1245)*, 166. Concerning Henry III's political needs vis-à-vis France Stacey concluded (167), "Hubert de Burgh's proposed German alliances were a supreme irrelevance." While the German marriage negotiations were not irrelevant to Anglo-French affairs, the English effort was marked by a lack of initiative and creativity, in contrast, for example, to the effort of the duke of Austria.

95. In addition to the emperor's pro-Capetian policy, the lack of unity among those princes participating in the guardianship of Henry (VII) hindered the fulfillment of English hopes for a marriage union. See Trautz, *Die Könige*, 102–3.

The Archbishop and the Unlikely Marriage II: A Short-Lived
Union of Regional Politics and Interregional Diplomacy

Frederick II's lack of interest in any dynastic ties between the princes of Germany and England—ties that would only have complicated his traditionally good relations with France—had done much to frustrate English initiatives in the 1220s. Yet the appearance of a fiery new pope, Gregory IX, resulted in increasing hostility between the Curia and the emperor, and thus Frederick found it politically expedient to nurture a favorable relationship with Henry III in subsequent decades. The religious force of the papacy therefore obtained what the money and dynastic prestige of the Plantagenets could not: a marriage union.

After being excommunicated by the pope on Michaelmas 1227, ostensibly for neglecting to fulfill his crusading vow, Frederick II began immediately to seek English support for his cause. An imperial envoy, the falconer Lambert, was present at Westminster in February 1228.[96] Lambert brought with him a letter of lament by the emperor about the great difficulties that prevented him from embarking on the promised crusade. No doubt it also contained a request for Henry's intercession, to which the king responded favorably. On February 20 Henry wrote to Frederick, informing him that he had shown the emperor's letter to a papal cleric named Master Stephan and that the king was sending a plea to the pope to receive the emperor back in peace.[97] This letter to Gregory IX was issued on the same day.[98] In July Henry responded to another letter from the emperor[99] by exhorting him to undertake the promised crusade in defense of the Holy Land.[100]

Although Frederick gained Henry's intercession with the pope, it availed him little in the short term. In fact the English king's advice to the emperor was essentially to fulfill his crusading obligations, the neglect of which had occasioned his excommunication in the first place. There was

96. *CLR Henry III*, 1:69 (February 19, 1228).
97. *CCLR Henry III*, 1:94; *Rymer*, 1:299–300; *Böhmer*, 5, 2:1631, no. 11011.
98. *CCLR Henry III*, 1:93; *Rymer*, 1:299; *Böhmer*, 5, 2:1631, no. 11010.
99. *Historia Diplomatica*, 3:48–50; *Böhmer*, 5, 1:345, no. 1716, from *MPCM*, 3:151–53. This letter is addressed to both the king and the English nobility. In it Frederick complains about his excommunication and uses Henry III's father John and Count Raymond of Toulouse as examples of the pope's desire to make princes his vassals. Furthermore, Frederick apologizes for his delay in crusading, blaming it on rebellion in Sicily and poor health.
100. *Shirley*, 1:331, no. 272; *Böhmer*, 5, 2:1633, no. 11024 (dated July 15, 1228).

therefore little to encourage the emperor to intensify his contacts with the English court, although he did send word to Henry III and Richard of Cornwall in 1228 and 1229 of his successes in the Holy Land.[101] Indeed, it was only in the period during which Frederick II fulfilled his crusading vow (albeit against papal wishes, since an excommunicate crusader seemed a contradiction) that the emperor established key ties to the English kingdom.

Peter des Roches, bishop of Winchester, and William Brewer, bishop of Exeter, led the English contingent that departed on crusade in June 1227.[102] They were joined by several English nobles, among them Philip Daubeny, William Paynel in 1228, and Gilbert Marshal (soon earl of Pembroke) in 1229. As preparations for Peter des Roches' departure were underway in 1226, Henry III wrote to Frederick II on Peter's behalf requesting that the bishop accompany the emperor to fulfill a crusading vow taken by Peter in 1221.[103] This began a significant cooperation between the English bishops and the German emperor during the crusade. The two bishops were key leaders on this campaign and became close advisors to Frederick II, despite his excommunicate status. Peter des Roches was appointed by the pope to organize preaching, and both bishops coordinated the refortification of crusader sites like Sidon and Jaffa.[104] Peter in particular worked closely with Frederick II's advisors, such as Hermann von Salza, the master of the Teutonic Knights, whose rule he borrowed for the English Order of St. Thomas. These English ecclesiastical ties would prove valuable for Frederick II in the coming years.[105]

---

101. *Historia Diplomatica*, 3:93; *Böhmer*, 5, 1:351, no. 1738, from *MPCM*, 3:173–76, and from Roger of Wendover, *Flores historiarum*, 2:365–69. This letter was no doubt sent in response to Henry III's letter of July 15, 1228, which encouraged Frederick to undertake the crusade in defense of the Holy Land. See also *CCLR Henry III*, 93; *Rymer*, 1:187; Roger of Wendover, *Flores historiarum*, 4:187–93; *MPCM*, 3:300–305.

102. Simon Lloyd, *English Society and the Crusades, 1216–1307* (Oxford, 1988), 75, 83; Christopher Tyerman, *England and the Crusades*, 98–101.

103. *Rotuli litterarum clausarum*, 2:204. It is highly likely that Frederick offered money, provisions, and transportation to the English crusaders: see Thomas Curtis van Cleve, *Emperor Frederick II*, 194.

104. Tyerman, *England the Crusades*, 101: "The activities of the two bishops were widely and proudly reported by English chroniclers, and Bishop Brewer was received 'with honour' on his return to his diocese in 1229, as was his colleague in 1231."

105. Another sign of Anglo-German interregional cooperation appears in 1228. The Franciscans in Germany had no theology teacher until this year, when the minister general sent an Englishman named Simon to the convent in Magdeburg. Shortly thereafter another Englishman and encyclopedist, Bartholomaeus Anglicus, taught there as well after lecturing in Paris.

Back home Henry III, who had taken a crusading vow himself but failed to fulfill it, continued as a loyal supporter of the papacy.[106] He even went so far as to explore Gregory IX's aborted plans for an antikingship in Germany using the Welf Otto "the Child" of Lüneburg in 1229 (as mentioned earlier in this chapter). When Frederick II returned from his crusade and learned of Henry III's complicity in the proposed Welf antikingship, he sent the Plantagenet court a clear response in 1232 by notifying them of his decision to renew the *confederatio* with the Capetian house.[107]

By this time almost twenty years had passed since any close, lasting diplomatic contact existed between England and the empire, with continuing ties to the archbishop of Cologne being the exception.[108] At this point diplomatic matters looked as if they would continue along Capetian-Staufen/papal-Plantagenet axes. But a rapid shift in Staufen relations with both the papacy and the Capetians during the 1230s resulted in the last significant dynastic union between a powerful German emperor and the English royal house during the remainder of the Middle Ages. The archbishop of Cologne would of course play a prominent role in this final confluence of interests.

A warming in relations between Frederick II and Henry III began only in the years following the emperor's reconciliation with Pope Gregory IX in 1230 (the Peace of Ceprano). Signs of a thaw can be discerned in Henry's favorable reply to the emperor's request that he support the cleric Lando, nephew of the archbishop of Messina, in his studies at Paris in 1233.[109] In the same year, Bishop Peter des Roches of Winchester, who had replaced Hubert de Burgh as justiciar, sought to capitalize on his positive crusading relations with Frederick II by seeking the recently reconciled emperor's influence with the pope concerning the confirmation of John Blund as archbishop of Canterbury.[110] The bishop of Win-

---

106. Tyerman, *England and the Crusades*, 53.

107. *Historia Diplomatica*, 4:354; MGH Leges, 2:293; *Böhmer*, 5, 1:394–95, no. 1986 (dated May 1232).

108. We have already seen the archbishop's role in the marriage negotiations of the 1220s, and diplomatic contacts continued into the 1230s: see *CLR Henry III*, 1:169.

109. *Shirley*, 1:412–13, no. 340; *Böhmer*, 5, 2:1648, no. 11133. Henry indicated to Frederick that he had sent thirty pounds Parisian to Lando, and he promised to seek in time a suitable "beneficium" for Lando through one of the prelates of his kingdom.

110. *MPCM*, 3:243. John Blund's candidacy proved unsuccessful and Edmund of Salisbury was consecrated instead. In any case imperial intercession did not influence the pope's decision in this matter.

chester's initiative failed to free John Blund from the odor of simony; however, the fact that the emperor was now considered a diplomatic channel for English interests suggests a rapprochement between the two parties.[111] This development eventually reached its fullest expression in marriage negotiations during 1234–35.

Matthew Paris tells us that the emperor sent two German Hospitallers to England in February 1234 to initiate negotiations concerning a marriage between himself and the English king's sister Isabella.[112] She was the same princess whom Henry III had proposed for Frederick's son Henry (VII) a decade earlier. Henry responded positively to the overture in March after consulting his nobles, and on November 15 the emperor issued a declaration of the terms agreed on.[113] The decree also empowered Petrus de Vinea, the influential imperial procurator, to finalize the details of this settlement (particularly concerning the dowry) at the English court.[114] The Cologne archbishop, Henry of Molenark, was also commissioned to give an oath in support of the agreement, since the

---

111. In his eulogy of Peter de Roches, Matthew Paris (*MPCM,* 3:490) indicates that the bishop played a central role in the reconciliation between the pope and emperor. Therefore diplomatic contact between bishop and emperor was already apparent before the Blund affair.

112. Both *MPCM* (3:318–27) and *MPHA* (2:378–81) have extensive accounts of the marriage between Isabella and Frederick II.

113. *Treaty Rolls Preserved in the Public Record Office,* Vol. 1, *1234–1325,* ed. Pierre Chaplais (London, 1955), 6, no. 9; *Historia Diplomatica,* 4, 1:503–6; MGH Const., 2:230–31, no. 188; MGH Leges, 2:307; *REK,* 3, 1:123, no. 816; *Böhmer,* 5, 1:407–8, no. 2063; *Rymer,* 1:346–48 (dated November 15, 1234, at Foggia). Throughout these entries Rymer has incorrectly indicated the dates of the documents a year late (i.e., 1235–36).

114. Petrus de Vinea became well known at the English court. As a reward for his service he received a yearly pension, with installments evidenced in nine of the next twelve years. He also obtained royal support for his nephew Johannes de Vinea, who was studying at Paris. Petrus even wrote a remarkable letter to Henry III in his later years requesting English citizenship: "Apulus vester a vobis in fidelem regis per regie munificentie gratiam adoptatus adoptari in municipem Anglie supplicat per eandem, ut non solum devotus fidelis regis et domini, sed regni filius habeatur et civis." He was very influential in the *ars dictaminis* of the English chancery, which used a letter collection of his as models for letters: see Ernst Kantorowicz, "Petrus de Vinea in England," *MIÖG* 51 (1937): 43–48. For Petrus de Vinea's influence on the imperial chancery see Gerhart B. Ladner, "Formularbehelfe in der Kanzlei Kaiser Friedrichs II. und die 'Briefe des Petrus de Vinea,' " *MIÖG Ergänzungsband* 12 (1933): 92–198, 415. Concerning this last matter, Hagen Keller (*Zwischen regionaler Begrenzung und universalem Horizont,* 480) has concluded, "And the works of Petrus de Vinea, until his downfall in 1249 the most important advisor of the emperor, became well known throughout all of Europe: letters and writings in which the emperor was raised far above all people into a divine sphere, even considered a saint."

archbishop of Cologne was still the natural and trusted diplomatic intermediary between the empire and England.[115]

Frederick notified the pope of these negotiations,[116] and the pope then wrote to Henry III and strongly encouraged him to agree to the marriage.[117] Petrus de Vinea arrived in England and a settlement was quickly reached by the end of February 1235.[118] Henry III declared his pleasure over the marriage in a letter to his sister Joan, the queen of Scotland,[119] and informed both the pope and the cardinals of his approval.[120] The dowry was set at a sizable thirty thousand marks sterling (20,000 pounds), which was to be paid in six installments until Easter 1237. No doubt installments were required since the raising of such money was difficult on short notice.[121] Provision was also made for Isabella to be handed over to the archbishop of Cologne on April 17 for transport to the emperor, but the trip would actually take place a month later.

---

115. Kienast ("Die Deutschen Fürsten," 16:76–77) refers to the archbishop of Cologne in this matter as "der natürliche Vermittler eines deutsch-englisches Bundes."

116. *Historia Diplomatica,* 4, 1:515–16; MGH Const., 2:231–32, no. 189; *Böhmer,* 5, 1:408, no. 2067 (dated November 9, 1234).

117. *Rymer,* 1:348.

118. Henry III informed the emperor of the reception of Petrus de Vinea (*Rymer,* 1:349; *Böhmer,* 5, 2:1651, no. 11151), who declared imperial acceptance of the final agreement on February 22, 1235: see *Treaty Rolls,* 3–4, no. 5; *Historia Diplomatica,* 4, 1:522–24; *REK,* 3, 1:124, no. 824; MGH Const., 2:234–35, no. 191; MGH Leges, 2:310; *Rymer,* 1:355; *Böhmer,* 5, 2:1651, no. 11153. This is essentially the same text as that of Frederick II's November 1234 declaration, including the clause concerning the archbishop of Cologne. Here are demands that the archbishop swear to escort Isabella to the emperor and, should unexpected problems arise, return her to England.

119. *CCLR Henry III,* 3:167; *Shirley,* 1:459–60, no. 383; *REK,* 3, 1:124, no. 825; *Böhmer,* 5, 2:1651, no. 11154; *Rymer,* 1:356–57 (Westminster, February 23, 1235). This letter informs us that the dukes of Brabant and Limburg were to join the archbishop of Cologne as escorts for Isabella. Subsequent references only mention the duke of Brabant, however.

120. *Treaty Rolls,* 6, no. 8, and 7, no. 12; *Böhmer,* 5, 2:1652, no. 11156; *Rymer,* 1:359–60 (dated February 25, 1235). In these letters the king, declaring his consent to the marriage according to the pope's advice, implores the pope and cardinals to secure the emperor's aid in the recovery of his rights, which he expected in exchange for his readiness to comply with the emperor's wishes. This is certainly a reference to the lost Angevin lands.

121. *Treaty Rolls,* 1–3, no. 1; MGH Const., 2:231–32, no. 189; MGH Leges, 2:308; *Böhmer,* 5, 2:1651, no. 11152; *Rymer,* 1:353 (dated February 22, 1235). Henry III issued a formal notice to the emperor of the entire agreement on the day it was settled: see *Treaty Rolls,* 3, no. 2; *Böhmer,* 5, 2:1652, no. 11157; *Rymer,* 1:349. Installments were scheduled as follows: three thousand marks due ten days after Easter 1235; two thousand marks due at the Feast of St. John the Baptist (June 1235); five thousand marks due at Michaelmas 1235; five thousand marks due at Easter 1236; five thousand marks due at Michaelmas 1236; ten thousand marks due at Easter 1237.

Special arrangements were made for the arrival of Archbishop Henry of Molenark. A letter informing him of the conclusion of the marriage agreement was issued on the same day as that sent to the emperor.[122] On March 2 a royal order was given to the chamberlain John de Colmere to choose four casks of the best royal wine in his custody, perhaps the Rhine wine that Cologne merchants brought in abundance to England, and have it stored at New Temple in London in preparation for the archbishop's arrival.[123] The balance of March and April were needed to complete preparations for Isabella's trip to Germany, during which time Bishop William Brewer of Exeter was assigned, among others, to accompany Isabella into Germany.[124] Hence Frederick II had clearly benefited from the good offices of the two bishops he had worked with during their crusade.[125] On the day after the initial payment of three thousand marks was made to Petrus de Vinea[126] both the archbishop of Cologne and the

---

122. *Treaty Rolls,* 3, no. 3; *Ennen/Eckertz,* 2:165, no. 162 (dated incorrectly as 1236); *REK,* 3, 1:124, no. 826; *Böhmer,* 5, 2:1651, no. 11155; *Rymer,* 1:357 (February 27, 1235).

123. *CCLR Henry III,* 3:55 (March 2, 1235).

124. Royal orders went forth to gather several ships at Orwell (*Rymer,* 1:358–59, dated March 24), and chaplains were sent to care for Isabella at Dover (*CCLR Henry III,* 3:73, dated April 11). Isabella's sizable entourage was assembled in late April (*CLR Henry III,* 6:246, no. 2196: "To the king's sister Isabel 200 m. of his own gift, and to divers persons going with her to Almain as follows for their expenses: W. bishop of Exeter 100 li.; John Mar' 10 m.; Hobert Hues' going with two other knights (se tertio milite) 100 m.; Walram le Tyeis (Teutonico) 50 li.; Bartholomew Pecche 40 m.; Robert de Muscegros 60 m.; Robert de Bruera 50 m.; William de Houeton, chaplain, 20 m.; William Pepin, clerk, 5 m.; Roger de Essewell 10 m.; Master Gilbert le Leche (Phisico) 15 m.; Roger Pilet, usher of her chamber, 5 m.; John de Sauden, cook, 5 m.; William le Sauser 5 m.; William son of Henry Dispens' 100 s.; William de Derneford, butler, 100 s.; Richard le Taillur (Scissori) 5 m.; William de Tayden, her yeoman (vadletto), 5 m.; William Malet, her palfrey-keeper, 5 m.; Hamon, marshal of her household and horses, 100 s.; Thomas de Erlham, falconer, going with gerfalcons, 5 m.; brother of Henry de Hauville, going with gerfalcons, 5 m." [Westminster, April 23]), and the ships were provisioned and moved to Sandwich (*CCLR Henry III,* 3:84 [Westminster, April 30]). Meanwhile messages concerning these preparations were sent to the emperor (*CLR Henry III,* 6:246, no. 2198 [Westminster, April 24]), pope, and cardinals (*Rymer,* 1:359–60, dated April 25).

125. In 1235 Henry III gave the Teutonic Knights an annual fee of forty marks to maintain one knight in the Holy Land. This must have had some connection to the marriage and perhaps reflects the influence of Bishop Peter de Roches of Winchester.

126. *CLR Henry III,* 6:247, no. 2206 (Westminster, May 2, 1235). On the same day Petrus de Vinea was granted his yearly fee of forty marks: see *CLR Henry III,* 6:247, no. 2208. On May 3 Henry III promised the full payment of the dowry's remainder and submitted himself and his successors to ecclesiastical censure as security for it: see *Treaty Rolls,* 9, no. 17; *Böhmer,* 5, 2:1652, no. 11158–59; *Rymer,* 1:361–62.

duke of Brabant, having now arrived in London, swore oaths concerning their guardianship of the young princess.[127]

Both Matthew Paris and Roger of Wendover have lengthy accounts of Isabella's departure from London on May 6 and her passing through Sandwich, Antwerp, and Cologne on the way to Worms.[128] Her arrival in Cologne on May 24 and subsequent monthlong stay are described with great detail in both these chronicles, as well as in the Cologne Chronicle.[129] Honored by an extremely festive procession from Antwerp to Cologne, Isabella was led through the main streets of the ancient imperial city with pomp and celebration that would rival any parade in present-day Cologne during Karneval. As evidence of both her beauty and charm, she is said to have meekly removed her headdress so that the curious onlookers, especially the noble matrons of Cologne, could behold her loveliness. She sojourned about a month at the Priory of St. Gereon (which lay outside the 1106 city walls but within the extended walls of 1180), amid continual celebrations in the city. No doubt these carefully planned festivities were designed to curry favor both with the English king, who maintained the city's trading privileges in his kingdom, and with the emperor. The *adventus* of Isabella in Cologne continued long in the folklore of the city and eventually was immortalized on the huge wall that still stands in the Isabellensaal of the municipal building known as the Gürzenich and by the Isabellenstraße.

The delay in Isabella's passing on to Worms was occasioned by the rebellion of Frederick II's son, King Henry (VII), who was duly captured and imprisoned at Heidelberg. Henry had joined the Lombard cities in 1232 when his father had confirmed the *Statutum in favorem principum,* which granted regalian rights to the secular princes and greatly weakened

---

127. *Treaty Rolls,* 10–11, nos. 19–20; *Historia Diplomatica,* 4, 1:541–42; *Ennen/ Eckertz,* 2:159–60, no. 158 (dated incorrectly as 1236); *REK,* 3, 1:125, no. 828; MGH Const., 2:235–36, no. 192; *Böhmer,* 5, 2:1652, no. 11160; *Rymer,* 1:360–61 (dated May 3). As reward for his service Henry III returned to the duke of Brabant the Honor of Eye on May 7 (*Rymer,* 1:340; the grant was confirmed on October 10, 1235 [*Treaty Rolls,* 30, no. 83] and again on February 6 and 10, 1236 [*Rymer,* 1:352]).

128. See *MPCM,* 3:319, where the German ambassadors are impressed by Isabella's beauty, and the arrivals of the archbishop of Cologne and the duke of Brabant are recorded. For Isabella's travels from London to Sandwich to Antwerp see *MPCM,* 3:320–21 and *REK,* 3, 1:125, no. 829; *Böhmer,* 5, 1:988, no. 5286I. See also Roger of Wendover, *Flores historiarum,* 3:108–11.

129. *MPCM,* 3:321–23; Roger of Wendover, *Flores historiarum,* 3:111; *CRC,* 266. Cf. *REK,* 3, 1:125, no. 831.

Henry's royal power in Germany. Once he put down the revolt of his own son and heir, Frederick instructed the archbishop of Cologne and the bishop of Exeter to bring Isabella to Worms, where the marriage took place with suitable ceremony on July 15.[130] Shortly thereafter Isabella's English attendants returned home and she began her new life as the twenty-one-year-old wife of the emperor.[131]

Various reasons for Frederick's marriage initiative with England have been put forth. Kienast has argued that the emperor agreed to the marriage to achieve a counterbalance against Louis IX's increasing dominance in the Arelate,[132] and we know that the marriage disturbed the French king, who feared this was a shift away from the often renewed understanding between the Staufen and Capetian rulers.[133] We cannot forget, moreover, that the sizable dowry was a valuable resource, particularly in Frederick's preparations for war with the Lombard cities. In this regard one could compare the marriage to that between Emperor Henry V and Matilda in 1114. Perhaps the emperor was also concerned about his succession, now that his son Henry (VII) was proving increasingly rebellious.[134] Another incentive may have been the establishment of a final peace with the Welfs (relatives of the English royal house), which occurred in the same year as the Staufen-Plantagenet marriage, although these events were probably only loosely connected.[135]

In his choice of bride, Frederick followed closely the advice of Pope Gregory IX, with whom he was recently reconciled. The emperor needed a young princess who was capable of bearing children and came from a high social rank, preferably a daughter of royal blood. Gregory IX, for his part, desired a marriage for Frederick that would link him to a dynasty that was

---

130. *MPCM*, 3:323–24; *Annales Marbacenses*, 97; *Continuatio Eberbacensis*, ed. G. Waitz, MGH SS, no. 22 (Hanover, 1872; reprint, 1976), 348; *Historia Diplomatica*, 4, 2:728; *REK*, 3, 1:125, no. 833; *Böhmer*, 5, 1:414, no. 2099a.

131. *MPCM*, 3:324.

132. Kienast, "Die Deutschen Fürsten," 16:75; *Deutschland und Frankreich*, 3:603–4.

133. Early on, both Frederick II and Pope Gregory IX assured Louis IX that this marriage in no way damaged the special "amicitia" between emperor and king. The pope's letter was issued on April 16, 1235: see *Historia Diplomatica*, 4, 1:536–37. Frederick II's letter was also issued on this date (ibid., 4, 1:539–40).

134. Trautz, *Die Könige*, 104.

135. Ernst Kantorowicz (*Kaiser Friedrich II.* [Berlin, 1927], 372) considered the marriage "so to speak as the beginning of that celebrated settlement of the Staufen-Welf dispute, which resulted thereafter." Kienast ("Die Deutschen Fürsten," 16:75 n. 2) agrees, but Trautz (*Die Könige*, 104) concludes, "Of course, the two events are only very loosely tied together" (translations mine).

favorably disposed toward the Curia. There was no more loyal monarch to be found than Henry III; indeed this very loyalty would eventually frustrate the emperor during his second excommunication and papal deposition.[136] On both counts the English king and his sister Isabella fitted the bill exactly. No doubt Frederick and Gregory remembered Princess Isabella from the marriage negotiations for Henry (VII) in 1224–25.

We have already noted papal encouragement for Henry III to accept the marriage proposal, as well as papal assurance to Louis IX that the marriage would not impede Capetian-Staufen friendship. Hence the Curia was closely involved in these proceedings, which reminds us of the Italian aspects of the marriage plan. In any case the huge dowry, rather than any interest in entangling himself in a broader European coalition, was a major incentive for Frederick's personal activities in Italy. Adhering to such a view avoids casting a medieval dynastic union in terms of a modern European conception of geopolitical alliances and the balance of power.[137] Here the driving forces of interregional diplomacy were dynastic and regional political exigencies rather than the search for military alliances. This will become quite clear in the coming years. Once again the basis for such interregional diplomacy was the traditional social institution of marriage between dynastic houses. Modernist "alliance" interpretations of these events have relied heavily on the English chroniclers, who declare that the English court expected imperial military assistance in regaining the lost Angevin lands from Louis IX. We have already seen Henry's request that the pope work toward this end with the emperor, and both Matthew Paris and the Dunstaple chronicler leave no doubt about English expectations from the marriage.[138] In fact Matthew Paris

---

136. Trautz, *Die Könige*, 104. Kienast ("Die Deutsche Fürsten," 16:75 n. 1) believed that at their meeting in the summer of 1234 the pope suggested to the emperor the idea of marriage with an English princess. But Matthew Paris credited the emperor himself with the initiative already in February 1234.

137. Trautz (*Die Könige*, 105) wisely points out, "One should consider the dynastic marriage alliances of the Middle Ages less militarily and geographically, but rather think of the corresponding documentary evidence in comparison to marriages in large peasant families, in which attention is given to the dowry, to the multifaceted value of in-law relations, and to the possible succession of heirs."

138. *MPCM*, 3:325. Stacey (*Politics, Policy, and Finance under Henry III (1216–1245)*, 180) has followed the view of these accounts "Henry scored perhaps the greatest diplomatic success of his reign when he married his sister Isabella to Emperor Frederick II of Germany. The match cost Henry a dowry of £20,000, but it provided him with the most powerful ally he could have against the Capetians. . . . in the emperor, Henry had an ally whose connections and claims to overlordship stretched from Jerusalem to Denmark, and from the Alps

even states that Frederick offered such assistance in January 1236, when he asked that Richard of Cornwall be sent to attack France with imperial military support.[139] The English nobility supposedly rejected this offer, since it would have been dangerous to send the only male heir to the throne, who was considered too young (although he was twenty-seven years old) for what the nobles felt was a dubious venture. According to Paris the nobles were still willing to send members of their own circle should the emperor agree, but nothing more came of the affair.

The actual correspondence on this matter, which has survived, reveals a different picture of the events. Shortly after the marriage of Frederick II and Isabella, the English king issued a response to the emperor's request that Richard come and visit the imperial court.[140] Henry gladly agreed to the request but expressed a serious concern about whether safe conduct could be assured for the trip. In addition he sent the cleric William de Kilkenny to convey further information and promised to send envoys to a planned meeting between the emperor and French king. There is no mention of any planned military activity in this letter or in the subsequent letter sent in late January 1236.[141] In the latter the king declared that Richard could not at present leave the kingdom because of pressing business in Wales, Scotland, and Ireland; but this was only a postponement of Richard's eventual visit.

If the emperor's proposal were truly military in nature it was badly timed, since the English were at this very moment ratifying a five-year truce with the Capetian court.[142] Therefore it seems more likely that

to Aquitaine. The marriage opened up to Henry the prospect of forging a truly continental alliance by which to recover his own ancestral lands. This dream of such a European-wide alliance continued to animate Henry's diplomacy right up until the eve of his 1242 Poitevin expedition." We must note, however, that there is no such explicit promise made by the emperor in the marriage contract to this end. Matthew Paris (*MPHA*, 2:479) declares, "Insuper, cum sororem ipsius regis Ysabellam sibi matrimonio copulaverat, promisit Frethericus memoratus, quod juvaret potenter et efficaciter ipsum regem, ut revocaret a dominio regis Francorum terras suas ultramarinas, sed, optenta nobili puella cum xl milibus marcarum, nihil fecit de praemissis." Paris then uses this broken promise as justification for Henry III's allowing papal legates to collect money in England that was used to fund the war against the emperor. For the Dunstaple annals see n. 145.

139. *MPCM*, 3:340. Cf. the final paragraph in *MPHA*, 2:386–87; *Böhmer*, 5, 1:421, no. 2136.

140. *Shirley*, 1:474–75, no. 393; *Böhmer*, 5, 2:1653, no. 11169 (both dated ca. June 1235); *Rymer*, 1:366 (dated incorrectly as June 29, 1236).

141. *Treaty Rolls*, 14, no. 29; *Shirley*, 2:9–10, no. 419 (late January, 1236).

142. *Treaty Rolls*, 14, no. 27 (dated February 3, 1236). The treaty had been negotiated at Melun on July 31, 1235. Therefore mention of a meeting between emperor and French

Frederick actually intended Richard simply to visit and perhaps to intercede for him diplomatically before the Curia or contemplate plans for a crusade.[143] Matthew Paris made more out of the recent marriage union and the emperor's request for Richard of Cornwall than was justified. Frederick II was in no position to enter into such a military campaign and was more intent on collecting his wife's vast dowry as he prepared to deal with the Lombard cities.[144]

Perhaps the Dunstaple chronicler's expectation of some sort of imperial support against Capetian France is understandable given the significant thirty-thousand-mark dowry.[145] The payment of such a large amount of sterling proved extremely draining on the royal resources, and a general scutage of two marks on all fiefs (royal or not) was demanded as a feudal aid.[146] All religious houses, irrespective of whether they were royal foundations or not, were also expected to contribute. Such an excessive request for feudal aid, especially as it was for the king's sister and not for his eldest daughter, naturally resulted in complaints and therefore in delays in the collection of these funds.[147]

Royal instructions for the assembling of the second installment, due in June 1235, were issued in June; however, the disbursement did not occur until August 20.[148] The third installment of five thousand marks, due at Michaelmas, appears to have been sent to the emperor in late October

---

king in the first letter (ca. June 1235) may have been part of the negotiations surrounding this peace treaty.

143. As we shall see, Frederick II would again make a request for Richard of Cornwall to visit him in 1238 and intercede diplomatically on his behalf.

144. Kienast, "Die Deutschen Fürsten," 16:78.

145. *Annales Dunstaplia,* 142: "Eodem anno Fredericus, imperator Alemanniae, duxit in uxorem Ysabellem, filiam Johannis regis Angliae, accipiens pro dote triginta milia marcarum. Pro quibus petitum et concessum fuit generale scutagium duarum marcarum per totam Angliam, non solum de feodis habitis in capite de rege, sed etiam de aliis cultis. Domus etiam religiosae tam de fundatione regis, quam aliae, ad hoc suum auxilium praestiterunt. Dictus item imperator consilium et auxilium in adquisitione et defensione juris sui regi Henrico promisit." Of course the issue of the exact meaning of "consilium et auxilium" remains unclear.

146. Stacey, *Politics, Policy, and Finance under Henry III (1216–1245),* 43.

147. *Annales de Burtonensis,* 1:364.

148. The second installment of two thousand marks, due in June, was not paid until August 20, 1235 (*CLR Henry III,* 6:263, no. 2261), although a royal command for its collection was issued in June: see *CCLR Henry III,* 3:110 (Woodstock, June 18, 1235). These imperial envoys were also given a small gift for their patience: *CLR Henry III,* 6:263, no. 2260 (Westminster, August 20, 1235).

1235.[149] The fourth installment, due at Easter 1236, did not arrive on time either; only on June 30 did Henry III inform the emperor that the five thousand marks were finally being sent.[150] Henry also asked to delay the payment of the fifth installment, due at Michaelmas 1236, until Easter 1237 and to delay the final installment of ten thousand marks, due at Easter 1237, until the following Michaelmas. The emperor, however, was not so accommodating, and the final payment was made by July 1237.[151]

There can be no doubt that Frederick II was anxious to obtain the balance of the dowry, since he moved against the Lombard cities in this year.[152] Henry III had to seek an aid from Ireland for the dowry,[153] and dispensations from scutages owed were still being issued years after the dowry was paid off[154]—facts indicating that collecting the money proved to be quite difficult.[155] There is no evidence that either Frederick II himself

---

149. *CCLR Henry III*, 3:154 (Westminster, October 24, 1235).

150. *Historia Diplomatica*, 4:884; *Rymer*, 1:364–65; *Böhmer, 5*, 2:1656, no. 11189 (Bristol, June 30, 1236).

151. Brother Giles Bertaud (most likely the "frater Egidius de Hospitali Sancte Marie Teutonicorum in Hibernia" mentioned in n. 155) and Master Walter (de Ocra) were present at the English court from May until the reception of the final ten thousand marks in July. Their presence in May indicates imperial expectations that the final installment would be paid at Easter according to the marriage agreement: see *CLR Henry III*, 1:269 (Windsor, May 11, 1237). In late June the king ordered Hugh de Stocton and Hugo Pateshull (*thesaurii*) to pay "dilectis nobis fratri Egidio Bertrando et nunciis domini Imperatoris decem milia marcarum" as the final payment: see *Rymer*, 1:373; *Böhmer, 5*, 2:1659, no. 11209 (Woodstock, June 26 or 28, 1237). The payment was not actually made until the next month: see *CLR Henry III*, 1:275 (Westminster, July 17, 1237). While the imperial envoys awaited the final installment, the king had each given a cup as a gift: see *CCLR Henry III*, 3:466 (Woodstock, July 5, 1237).

152. Matthew Paris (*MPCM*, 3:364) made note of the conspicuous presence of imperial envoys at court who sought to collect the dowry.

153. *CCLR Henry III*, 3, 509–11 (Westminster, November 2, 1236), 571–75 (Nottingham, October 5, 1237). Hence the king was still trying to collect an aid in Ireland at least three months after the final installment was paid to the emperor.

154. *CCLR Henry III*, 1:290 (King's Cliffe [Clyve], August 21, 1237), 4:39 (Tewkesbury, April 7, 1238), 4:181 (Westminster, March 25, 1240), 5:344–45 (Chester, October 29, 1245), 5:509 (Woodstock, April 30, 1247). These Close Roll entries indicate that collections were continuing well after the final installment was paid to the emperor.

155. *Rymer*, 1:362–63; *Böhmer, 5*, 2:1655, no. 11182: In a curious entry Henry III grants safe conduct to Magister Walter de Ocra, "clericum et nuncium karissimi fratris nostri [i.e., Frederici imperatoris] et dilectae sororis nostrae Isabellae, Romanorum Imperatricis," during his stay in England, Wales, and Ireland (Winchester, May 19, 1236). It seems, according to the following entry, that even the king was unsure of Walter's activities in Ireland and Wales: see *CCLR Henry III*, 3:368 (July 23, 1236). Perhaps Walter had joined

or the English court considered this massive dowry an investment in some joint military campaign against Capetian France, despite what English chroniclers and some modern historians have said. For the Plantagenet house it represented a prestigious dynastic tie to the imperial family, for the pope it was evidence that the wayward Frederick had finally mended his ways as a Christian ruler, and for Frederick it meant valuable resources for a redoubled effort to control Italy. Once again divergent dynastic, local, and regional political goals were united for a time in the social symbol of unity, marriage. Because each party to this union between dynasties differed in their goals the union was as fragile as the marriage on which it was built. The following years would bear this out.

Although the marriage did not in fact result in imperial military support against the French, it seems to have forged a genuinely cordial kinship bond between the rulers. Frederick sent Henry exotic gifts, such as leopards and a camel,[156] and the English king reciprocated with falcons—creatures beloved by the emperor and hand-picked by his personal falconer.[157] These gifts were punctuated by Henry III's intercession once again before the Curia on behalf of his imperial brother-in-law. The imperial marshal, Henry de Aeys, and Walter de Ocra were present at the English court in February,[158] and in late June 1236 the advocate of Aachen came as imperial envoy to the English court, informing the king of the Lombard uprising.[159] In response Henry sent messengers to Rome with letters on behalf of Frederick to gain papal support for the suppression of the rebellion.[160] Diplomatic contact over these matters contin-

---

Giles Bertaud (*frater Egidius de Hospitali Sancte Marie Teutonicorum in Hibernia*) in collecting the dowry aid.

156. *MPCM,* 3:324–25 (1235); 334 (1235); 369 (1236). Henry III gave some of the horses received here to his vassals: see *CCLR Henry III,* 3:309 (Nottingham, September 1, 1236), 417 (Rochester, February 14, 1237).

157. *CCLR Henry III,* 3:296 (Woodstock, August 2, 1236).

158. *Treaty Rolls,* 14, no. 28 (dated February 24, 1236); *Historia Diplomatica,* 4, 2:809–10; *Shirley,* 2:89, no. 418 (dated February 2, 1236). In this letter Henry III thanks the emperor for sending word concerning a "causam inauditam" (most likely news of a massacre of Jews at Fulda) and promises the return of Walter de Ocra soon with the king's response to the embassy.

159. For Henry III's letter of response, in which he expresses his indignation over the arrogance of the Lombards, see *Historia Diplomatica,* 4:883–85; *Böhmer,* 5, 2:1656, nos. 11189–90; *Rymer,* 1:364–67. Matthew Paris (*MPCM,* 3:376–77) indicates that a certain Baldewin de Vere was also sent on a secret mission to the imperial court at this time. His mission probably concerned Henry's request for a delay in the payment of the dowry.

160. Henry also took this opportunity to send a letter to his sister, the new empress, in which he asked after her welfare: see *Rymer,* 1:366–67; *Böhmer,* 5, 2:1654, no. 11170.

ued,[161] with a ministerial envoy of the archbishop of Cologne present at Westminster on April 20, 1237.[162] In June Frederick even called for a general meeting of western princes at Vaucouleurs, to which the English king offered to send Richard of Cornwall, but the meeting was eventually postponed.[163] In the meantime the emperor took matters into his own hands, and in December of that year he issued a joyful letter to Richard of Cornwall informing him of the great imperial victory at Cortenuova.[164]

The year 1238 saw developments that looked as though they would draw Anglo-imperial relations closer together than they had been since the kingship of Otto IV a quarter of a century earlier. In early February the emperor once again invited Richard of Cornwall to visit him in Sicily while the earl was en route to the Holy Land on crusade, and the emperor offered Richard advice concerning the endeavor.[165] This was likely another effort to obtain Richard's good offices before an increasingly hostile Curia, although the earl had been invited once before to visit and this second request was an offer in support of Richard's crusade. It was also timely because the empress was to bear a son on the eighteenth of the same month, knowledge of which the English court must have possessed. In fact the emperor wrote to Richard of Cornwall again on March 3, informing him of the birth of the child, who was named Henry in honor of his royal uncle.[166] The emperor also expressed the hope that this child would further strengthen the bonds between the respective royal families.[167] Frederick II had reason to rejoice, as the marriage had given him the male heir he had hoped for.

Frederick II also must have rejoiced in the additional support Henry III

---

161. Imperial envoys were at the English court at least in August and December 1236: see *CCLR Henry III*, 3:301, 401.

162. *CLR Henry III*, 1:263. The coordination of imperial and papal diplomacy at this time can be seen in the envoy who received an advance on Petrus de Vinea's yearly rent on March 19: see ibid., 1:270.

163. *MPCM*, 3:393–94. The meeting was called "de negotiis arduis, tam imperium quam alia regna contingentibus tractaturi." Distrust of Frederick, especially by the French, prevented this meeting. Cf. *Böhmer, 5*, 1:451, no. 2258a.

164. *Historia Diplomatica*, 5:132; *Böhmer, 5*, 1:462, no. 2291, from *MPCM*, 3:441–44 (Cremona, December 4, 1237).

165. *Historia Diplomatica*, 5:164; *Böhmer, 5*, 1:465, no. 2312, from *MPCM*, 3:471–72 (Vercelli, February 11, 1238). See also Tyerman, *England and the Crusades*, 106–8; Lloyd, *English Society and the Crusades*, 91.

166. *MPCM*, 3:474–75 (Turin, March 3, 1238) and *MPHA*, 2:204. Cf. *Historia Diplomatica*, 5:166; *Böhmer, 5*, 1:466, no. 2316; *Rymer*, 1:374.

167. *MPCM*, 3:474.

provided against the Lombard cities shortly after Easter of the same year. Moving beyond diplomatic intercession at the Curia, the English king sent one hundred knights under the leadership of Henry de Trubleville to serve in the emperor's army in the siege of Brescia.[168] Henry did so in response to an evocative letter of appeal by Petrus de Vinea to all European kings to come to the aid of the emperor.[169] Henry de Trubleville and his troops gained renown for their martial abilities during this campaign, according to Matthew Paris.[170] The *Annales Placentini* record that the English knights fought with many other contingents, among which was the army of the archbishop of Cologne; we have further evidence of Anglo-Cologne cooperation, this time in far off Italy.[171] This would prove to be the only instance in which Henry III would aid the emperor in the face of papal opposition.[172] The venture cost the English king at least eight thousand marks, which was rather expensive during the period when he had been gathering thousands of marks for his brother's crusade.[173]

Henry's motivation for offering military suport may have been the hope that aiding Frederick's success in Italy might be rewarded in the future by reciprocal support against Capetian France. Yet it is more likely that he did this to further his brother's crusading expedition. If the emperor could be freed from Italian affairs, he would then be able to focus his attention on the Holy Land and therefore assist Richard, an offer that had already been generally made by the emperor in any case.[174] Given Henry III's religious convictions and predilection to support both his brother and the crusading ideal, aid for Frederick in this instance should

---

168. *MPCM*, 3:485–86; *MPHA*, 2:408. The siege of Brescia began on August 3, 1238 (*Böhmer*, 5, 1:476, no. 2375a). Henry de Trubleville had served the king as seneschal of Gascony in the late 1220s (*Shirley*, 1:317–21, nos. 261–63) and had been in the service of the empress earlier in the same year, for which he was duly rewarded: see *CCLR Henry III*, 4:30 (Tower of London, February 25, 1236).

169. Haverkamp, *Medieval Germany*, 258–59.

170. *MPCM*, 3:491.

171. *Annales Placentini Gibellini*, ed. G. Pertz, MGH SS, no. 18 (Hanover, 1863; reprint, 1963), 479. Although this collection of armies may contain exaggerations, contingents from Cologne and England certainly did fight alongside each other at Brescia.

172. This military assistance, along with that of other princes, gave the emperor great confidence that he would be victorious over the rebel cities. Such an attitude frames a letter sent from Frederick to Henry III: see *Historia Diplomatica*, 5:207; *Böhmer*, 5, 1:469, no. 2336.

173. *CPR Henry III*, 3:221. An additional thousand marks was put toward this venture: see *CLR Henry III*, 1:365 (Rochester, February 9, 1239).

174. Stacey, *Politics, Policy, and Finance under Henry III (1216–1245)*, 126.

not be seen as inconsistent with his unwavering propapal conduct.[175] It is ironic that historians have made more of the supposed plan for Staufen military aid against Capetian France (which never came) than of this direct military assistance in Italy provided by Henry III. Yet even so, it was done primarily to support dynastic and crusading goals rather than to build a military alliance system.

Relations between the emperor and the English court were so intimate at this point that even Simon de Montfort could turn to the emperor for letters of support as he sought papal dispensation for his secret marriage with Eleanore, the king's sister. The marriage was displeasing to Richard of Cornwall, but since Simon was in the good graces of Henry III at this time (Henry had secretly approved the marriage), it is likely that the king had something to do with the favorable reception Simon received at the imperial court.[176] At this point Anglo-imperial relations had become extremely close, even close enough for the mediatory role of the archbishop of Cologne to recede for a time. Yet the increasingly strained relations between emperor and pope would prove to be the undoing of this Anglo-imperial harmony, as it had been so often before.

The Archbishop and the Unlikely Marriage III: The Divorce of Regional Politics and Interregional Diplomacy

Two ongoing developments, begun in the political community of Germany in the second half of the twelfth century, received new vigor from 1238 on and ultimately resulted in a permanent alteration of traditional Anglo-German diplomacy with Cologne at its center. These were the renewal of Staufen-papal animosity and the regional *Territorialpolitik* of the archbishops of Cologne. Frederick II's falling out with Gregory IX, which resulted in a second excommunication and, more importantly, a papal declaration of deposition, forced the English king to choose between his kinship ties to the emperor and his religious scruples.

---

175. For the importance of crusading in Henry III's personal and diplomatic policies see Simon Lloyd, "King Henry III, the Crusade, and the Mediterranean," in *England and Her Neighbours, 1066–1453: Essays in Honour of Pierre Chaplais*, ed. Michael Jones and Malcolm Vale (London, 1989), 97–119.

176. *MPHA*, 2:404–7; *MPCM*, 3:479–80, 487. Henry III had approved this secret marriage, but Richard of Cornwall led a party at court that opposed the secret nature of the negotiations. See Christopher Brooke, *From Alfred to Henry III (871–1272)* (New York, 1969), 228.

Unfortunately for Frederick, Henry III's submission to the papacy would dominate his diplomacy in this matter.

Equally as significant for English ties to Germany was the pontificate of the new archbishop of Cologne, Conrad of Hochstaden (1238–61).[177] His interest was that of Philip of Heinsberg and Adolf of Berg writ large: the consolidation of his territorial principality at all costs. The regional interests of his double duchy and vast archbishopric ultimately overshadowed any concern in advancing either imperial or English policies. Although he remained intimately involved in these interregional relations, his diplomacy and that of his successors was fundamentally different from the traditional Anglo-Cologne diplomatic discourse of the past. His participation in Anglo-imperial diplomatic affairs served only the advancement of his territorial goals. Indeed, he would become the kingbroker of Germany before his pontificate was over, and he would draw the English into his political machinations.[178] Anglo-imperial diplomacy was thus subordinated to the territorial interests of the Cologne archbishop.

Archbishop Conrad of Hochstaden was typical of the ecclesiastical princes of Germany at this time. With the absence of direct imperial control in northern Germany the archiepiscopal office had passed into the hands of local aristocratic families, which placed their sons in the cathedral chapter and thereafter competed for the ultimate prize of the archiepiscopacy. The local noble houses of Berg, Altena, Hochstaden, Falkenburg, and others provided the archbishops, who therefore functioned within their aristocratic milieu both as regional territorial princes as well as ecclesiastical prelates. Benjamin Arnold has recently shown exceptionally well that this regionalization of political power in Germany was not a cause for the failure of German kingship but the creative response by princes to the lack of imperial authority in their territories.[179] The German princes did not usurp royal prerogatives and power in the Central Middle Ages but rather maintained their local power based on inherited rights and institutions that operated outside of imperial jurisdiction. Because the imperial court lacked sufficient personnel for a central

---

177. See Hermann Cardauns, *Konrad von Hochstaden, Erzbischof von Köln (1238–1261)* (Cologne, 1880); Stehkämper, "Konrad von Hochstaden."

178. Wand, "Die Englandpolitik der Stadt Köln," 88: "His policy toward England was determined by its utility for his territorial power. He subordinated everything to this: city, empire, church, and his English policy."

179. Arnold, *Princes and Territories in Medieval Germany*, 5; *Count and Bishop in Medieval Germany*, 28.

government, the emperors actually encouraged such regionalism as a form of shared rule. Since they were bearers of the mantle of universal leadership as the secular head of Christendom and as rulers of no less than three (and sometimes four or five) kingdoms each, the German emperors had functions well beyond their personal capacity, and therefore all members of the German political community accepted the shared responsibilities. Bemoaning the decline of centralized state government in the territories of the empire during this era is misplaced since there was really none to begin with (outside of Sicily); emperors willingly transferred jurisdictional powers to the princes.[180] Hence if we set aside modernist evaluations of centralized state building as the business of politics, we can see this period as one of creative adaptation rather than decay and fragmentation.

Such creative regionalism in Germany proved to be a nightmare for Anglo-German diplomatic relations, however. Although English monarchs would still attempt to forge anti-Capetian coalitions with the numerous independent German princes, the lack of a centralized royal or imperial power in Germany would result in vast amounts of English money spent in vain. Thus the absence of strong imperial power in Germany (assured with the politics and passing of Frederick II) and the loss of a consistently pro-English ally in the archbishop of Cologne would bring to an end the era of traditionally close Anglo-Cologne diplomatic relations as an avenue for achieving positive Anglo-German relations.

The second excommunication of Frederick in 1239 and the papal declaration of deposition at the Council of Lyon (1245) did much to dissolve the growing ties between the Plantagenet and Staufen courts. During the years 1239–41 Henry III continued to hope for a resolution between pope and emperor, but he remained submissive to papal demands. He allowed the sentence of excommunication against Frederick to be read throughout England and the collection of papal taxes that were then used to support the enemies of the emperor.[181] Frederick was naturally incensed by this policy of his brother-in-law, which he saw as unnatural: nobody should support, even passively, aggression against one's kin. These years saw a

---

180. Frederick II's *Confederatio cum principibus ecclesiasticis* (1220) and *Statutum in favorem principum* (1231), which gave both ecclesiastical and secular princes in Germany extensive regalian rights in their territories, are the two major examples, though German kings and emperors gave such concessions to individual princes often.

181. *MPCM*, 3:545. Matthew Paris was apparently sympathetic to Frederick's reminder of the kinship ties between the Plantagenets and Staufen.

flurry of imperial letters sent to the Plantagenet court and to the English baronage at large, railing against papal injustices and against the willingness of Henry III to accept Gregory IX's injunctions.[182] Imperial letters and envoys were sent to Westminster to implore Henry to expel the papal legates from England,[183] but Henry responded consistently that he had to obey papal and ecclesiastical commands above all the princes of the world, and he even rebuked the emperor for the petty matter of not allowing Isabella to wear the imperial crown in public.[184]

This did not necessarily mean that Henry opposed Frederick. Kinship ties still meant something to him,[185] but he felt compelled to acknowledge the papal decree of excommunication.[186] He did, however, continue to seek a peace between pope and emperor, which created animosity at the Curia.[187] Richard of Cornwall, returning from his crusade, was also en-

---

182. *MPCM*, 3:574–75 (April 1239), 3:631–38 [*Historia Diplomatica*, 5:840–46; *Böhmer*, 5, 1:534, no. 2910 (March 1239)], 4:26–29 [*Historia Diplomatica*, 5:920–23; *Böhmer*, 5, 1:541, no. 3019 (April 1240)]. See also *MPHA*, 2:429–30; *Rymer*, 1:382 (these letters are incorrectly dated 1238 in *Rymer*), 383–87. In the letter of October 29, 1239 to the English magnates (*Rymer*, 1:385–86) Frederick complains: "quale, quantum, et quam grande sit matrimonii et affinitatis vinculum, quod inter regem Angliae et Romanum principem est contractum, et qualiter illud voluntas Dei excelsi firmavit per sequentia pignora filiorum, et quos fructus ex eo, per consequens, credatur inter regem et imperium proventuros . . . Ha Deus! sustineret haec hodie, si viveret, Henricus senior rex Angliae? Non utique, quia nec minora hiis aequanimiter tolerabant." Once again Frederick calls on kinship ties.

183. *Annales de Theokesberia*, ed. Henry Richards Luard, RS, no. 36 (London, 1864; reprint, 1965), 1:115–16. Imperial envoys appear often at the English court during 1240 and 1241: see *CCLR Henry III*, 4:172 (February 8, 1240); *CLR Henry III*, 2:93 (Reading, October 7, but must be December 7, 1241). Walter de Ocra was present twice during the year 1241: see *Rymer*, 1:393–94 (May); *CLR Henry III*, 2:80 (October 20), 81 (October 21). Petrus de Vinea received his pension during this time as well: see *CLR Henry III*, 1:400 (July 4, 1239), 1:477 (July 4, 1240), 2:78 (October 11, 1241). And envoys of Isabella arrived in England then: see ibid., 1:501 (October 16, 1240).

184. *MPCM*, 4:4–5 (Placentiae, October 29, 1240). Cf. *Rymer*, 1:237; *Historia Diplomatica*, 5:464–67.

185. Ironically Henry III appealed to ties of affinity in his intercessory letter to Frederick on behalf of the count of Provence, who had failed to carry out the emperor's command to attack the count of Flanders: see *MPCM*, 4:23 (1240). Similar letters were sent by Richard of Cornwall and the French king, Louis IX, when the emperor then commanded the count of Toulouse to attack the count of Provence: see ibid., 4:105–6 (1241).

186. Henry's policy of neglect toward Frederick proved unpopular in England for two reasons: because of the financial cost of papal taxes imposed on the clergy to support the war against Frederick, and because this war was waged against Henry's brother-in-law with disregard for the military situation in the Holy Land. See William E. Lunt, *Financial Relations of the Papacy with England to 1327* (Cambridge, MA, 1939), 197–205.

187. *MPCM*, 4:5 (1240). Henry even sent three hundred marks for use by royal envoys at the papal court: see *CLR Henry III*, 2:81 (Westminster, October 25, 1241).

listed to intervene at the papal court on behalf of the emperor. Yet even the prestigious crusading knight was unable to soften Gregory IX's heart regarding Frederick II.[188] Richard's efforts were, however, still rewarded with a splendid visit in Frederick's Sicilian kingdom.

The emperor, for his part, proved to be just as resistant to Henry's requests for a truce,[189] and English hopes for a profitable relationship with the emperor faded with the close of the year 1241.[190] Not only had Gregory IX died, and not only had Frederick inflamed the conflict further by the capture of a number of cardinals, but the primary link between the German and English monarchs—the empress Isabella, whom Matthew Paris called the "glory and hope of England" [gloria et spes Angliae]—also died.[191] Isabella, the fourth wife of the emperor, died in childbirth after having given life to four other children.[192] Frederick's sad letter announcing her December 1, 1241, death carried the hope that Henry, his son by Isabella, might continue the special relationship established between the two royal families.[193] Yet a growing estrangement in Anglo-imperial diplomatic relations actually resulted.[194] Henry III

---

188. MPCM, 4:145–48 (cf. MPHA, 2:452–53; Historia Diplomatica, 5:1158–59). According to Matthew Paris (MPCM, 4:46–47) the papacy had even interfered with Richard's original plans to sojourn with the emperor while heading to the Holy Land. Richard set out on crusade, stopping first at St. Giles, where papal legates and the archbishop of Arles forbade his proceeding further. He refused to embark at Aiguesmortes at their insistence and went on to Marseilles, then la Roque, where he sent a messenger to the emperor.

189. Frederick had refused to admit the Lombard cities to a truce between himself and the pope or give safe conduct to any prelates going to a council called to resolve the conflict. He complained once again to Henry upon this occasion about the papal legate Otto and the declaration of his excommunication in England (MPCM, 4:65–71).

190. Stacey, Politics, Policy, and Finance under Henry III (1216–1245), 182; Fawtier, Capetian Kings of France, 151. Lloyd (English Society and the Crusades, 221, 225–26) mistakenly reads Henry III's policy toward the excommunicant Frederick II as a strategy to dismantle the Staufen inheritance for the Plantagenets. This is as flawed a conclusion as the similar view of relations between their predecessors and namesakes Frederick I and Henry II.

191. MPCM, 4:175–76; Historia Diplomatica, 6:25–27; Böhmer, 5, 1:575, no. 3264 (Coronata, January 30, 1242). Frederick had only in August of this year written to Henry about the death of Gregory IX: Historia Diplomatica, 5:1165–67; Böhmer, 5, 1:569–70, no. 3225.

192. H. Decker-Hauff, "Das staufische Haus," in Die Zeit der Staufer: Katalog der Ausstellung im württembergischen Landesmuseum (Stuttgart, 1977), 3:358–59, 366.

193. Matthew Paris (MPCM, 4:83) noted the cordial affection that Frederick II held for the English as a result of his wife Isabella.

194. Henry III himself grieved greatly at the death of his sister and commissioned over one hundred thousand meals for the poor as alms in memory of Isabella over several years: see CLR Henry III, 2:124 (Winchester, April 30, 1242; cf. Issues of the Exchequer; being a

became involved in a war with the Capetian king and could no longer hope for assistance from Frederick, who was bound up in his confrontation with the papacy.

An attempt was made by Henry III in 1242 to recruit German military support in his war against the French king. Embassies were exchanged during the months of May and June as he made his way to Saintes in preparation for an invasion of Poitou.[195] The support of the princes of the Rhineland and the Low Countries was especially sought, with the counts of March, Flanders, and Hainault agreeing; however, for the first time this coalition of German princes lacked the archbishop of Cologne.[196] Of course no direct assistance came from Frederick either,[197] and the German princes proved to be of no help in the end; in fact the count of March even switched to the Capetian side by September.[198] That Frederick did not provide assistance to Henry may seem just recompense for the English king's propapal policy in the face of continued requests for support from the emperor in the preceding years. Frederick did not alter his

---

collection of payments made out of His Majesty's revenue, from Henry III to Henry VI inclusive, ed. Frederick Devon [London, 1837], 19; cf. Devon, 27). Petrus de Vinea still was receiving his pension at this time: see *CLR Henry III,* 2:128 (May 4, 1242), 204 (Westminster, December 9, 1243), 281 (Woodstock, December 12, 1244), 306 (Westminster, June 4, 1245); *CCLR Henry III,* 5:491 (Clarendon, December 10, 1246); *CLR Henry III,* 3:156 (Clarendon, December 14, 1247).

195. *CLR Henry III,* 2:134 (Portsmouth, May 7, 1242); Henry then sent Petrus de Burdegala (Bordeaux) and Bartholomew de Peche with letters of credence to Frederick "ad tractandum vobiscum super quibusdam articulis, de quibus aliquando per nuncios vestros tractatus habitus fuit nobiscum" (Saintes, June 17, 1242): see *Rymer,* 1:406–7; *Böhmer,* 5, 2:1684, nos. 11391–92. Henry borrowed money from Florentine merchants to pay for Bartholomew's expenses on this or a subsequent embassy, which was reimbursed the following year: see *CCLR Henry III,* 5:38 (August 6, 1243).

196. *Rymer,* 1:407; *Historia Diplomatica,* 6:904–5: Richard of Cornwall, now returned from crusading, also signed this agreement with the German princes (Saintes, July 5, 1242).

197. Henry had proposed an alliance to Frederick against all men except for the pope: see *CPR,* 3:309 (June 19, 1242). This limitation on Henry's involvement in an alliance was precisely the element that made the offer of no value to the emperor.

198. *CCLR Henry III,* 4:530–32; *Shirley,* 2:25–27, no. 434; *Böhmer,* 5, 2:1685, no. 11396; *Rymer,* 1:325–26. Henry wrote to Frederick, complaining of the treason of the count of March (September 19, 1242). He also sent a letter of woe on January 8, 1243, about his continued failure to capture Poitou (*Historia Diplomatica,* 6:905–7; *Rymer,* 1:414; *Böhmer,* 5, 2:11402); although Henry appealed to the kinship tie between the two rulers, it did not move the emperor to send aid, nor did Henry's efforts at gaining the good offices of Petrus de Vinea (*Rymer,* 1:414–15; *Böhmer,* 5, 2:11403). An imperial envoy was present in England in February 1243, but he brought no promises of imperial military aid with him: see *CLR Henry III,* 2:169 (Westminster, February 9, 1242).

position, either, in the years to come. Walter de Ocra was often at the English court trying to stop the collection of money by the papal legates.[199] Henry, however, continued his acquiescence to the legates' demands, and the collection of money continued.[200]

Once again conflict between emperor and pope proved a major hindrance to the maintenance of close Anglo-imperial relations. Diplomatic contact continued throughout the remainder of Frederick II's reign,[201] and numerous letters were exchanged,[202] especially after Frederick's deposition at the Council of Lyon in 1245.[203] But the promising relations of the 1230s faded in the 1240s as neither monarch could or would advance

---

199. *MPCM*, 4:161–62; *MPHA*, 2:492. Walter de Ocra reported to the emperor that he could not find the papal legates. Frederick then had all the cities of Italy under his control searched, especially for use of English money, and the collectors were eventually captured. Walter de Ocra's appearances at the English court are recorded in the following sources: *CCLR Henry III*, 5:146 (Windsor, December 18, 1243); *CLR Henry III*, 2:209 (Westminster, January 9–10, 1244), 2:275 (Westminster, November 15, 1244). On November 17 Walter collected Petrus de Vinea's yearly rent, along with his own and that of John, dean of Capua: see *CLR Henry III*, 2:277, 3:94–95 (Marlborough, November 21, 1246), 3:95 (Clarendon, November 25, 1246).

200. Matthew Paris (*MPCM*, 4:313) records Walter de Ocra's plea made before the English court in 1244 that these collections be stopped.

201. *CLR Henry III*, 2:232 (Westminster, May 4, 1244), 2:278 (Westminster, November 19, 1244), 2:297 (Windsor, April 23, 1245), 2:302 (Reading, May 5, 1245), 3:1 (Chester, October 29, 1245), 3:7 (Woodstock, November 18, 1245), 3:21 (Westminster, January 23, 1246), 3:53 (Dover, May 15, 1246), 3:68 (Oxford, July 23, 1246), 3:68 (Faringdon, July 24, 1246), 3:126 (Windsor, June 1, 1247), 3:127 (Windsor, June 6, 1247). Henry sent new falcons to the emperor in 1248: see *CCLR Henry III*, 6:88 (September 20, 1248).

202. For a letter of May 18, 1241, from Frederick to Henry declaring Frederick's conquest of Faenza see *MPCM*, 4:126–29; *Historia Diplomatica*, 5:1123–25; *Böhmer, 5*, 1:564, no. 3205. Elsewhere (*MPCM* 4:173–74) Frederick complained to a 1241 embassy of English clerics, which sought to achieve a peace between pope and emperor. In 1244 Frederick asked Henry for an English embassy to be present at his negotiations with the pope (*MPCM*, 4:332), and Frederick offered to submit himself to the counsel of the kings of England and France and their barons, once again asking Henry to stop papal exactions in England (*MPCM*, 4:371–72).

203. In 1245 Frederick complained to Henry III (*MPCM*, 4:475–78) and to the English barons (*MPCM*, 4:538–44; *Historia Diplomatica*, 6:331–32; *Böhmer, 5*, 1: nos. 3495–99) about the papal declaration of his deposition, and in the following year both he and Walter de Ocra wrote to Henry III of an alleged papal plot on his life (*MPCM*, 4:570–77, dated Salerno, April 15, 1246). Such worries were not without foundation, as even Petrus de Vinea attempted to have the emperor poisoned in 1249 and thereby forfeited his career. He was arrested, blinded, and died a suicide (*MPCM*, 5:68–69). On February 27, 1245, the emperor also wrote to Richard of Cornwall of his readiness to go on crusade (*MPCM*, 4:300).

the interests of the other. Indeed, their respective political concerns actually shared little common ground. Although Henry promised Frederick that his envoys were going to the Council of Lyon to work for a reconciliation, the fact that they were even attending the council was a nod to papal authority and so would have given the emperor little reassurance.[204] Perhaps the best symbol of Henry III's loyalty to his religious scruples at the expense of Frederick II was the king's gift in 1244, along with sixty bezants, of a golden seal of the emperor to help pay for decorating the reliquary of Edward the Confessor; here imperial substance was submitted by Henry to a higher religious cause.[205]

Henry, the son of Frederick II and Isabella, did not long outlive his mother and thus was unable to serve as a unifying factor between the Staufen and Plantagenet families in the years after 1250. He informed his royal uncle in 1247 that he had been given authority to rule the kingdom of Sicily.[206] Frederick II made the Calabrians and Apulians swear allegiance to Henry in that year,[207] and the young ruler even had occasion to intercede for his uncle with Louis IX.[208] The *spes Anglorum et gloria* (a name given by Matthew Paris to both Henry and his mother, Isabella) died in 1254, and with him died the last vestiges of kinship ties between a powerful German emperor and an English king throughout the remainder of the Middle Ages.[209]

The final component in this weakening of Anglo-imperial diplomatic ties was fashioned by the policies of the new archbishop of Cologne.

---

204. *CCLR Henry III*, 5:356; *Rymer*, 1:434; *Historia Diplomatica*, 6:290–91; *Böhmer*, 5, 2: nos. 1692–93. In March 1245 Frederick had written Henry, congratulating him on the birth of a son (probably Edmund) and asking for reports more often: see *Historia Diplomatica*, 6:267–68; *Böhmer*, 5, 1:612, no. 3462.

205. *CCLR Henry III*, 5:156 (Reading, February 7, 1244).

206. *Rymer*, 1:893; *Historia Diplomatica*, 6:504; *Böhmer*, 5, 1:645, no. 3611. Frederick also wrote to Henry informing him of his hope that the pope would eventually baptize his son Henry: see *Historia Diplomatica*, 6:502–3; *Böhmer*, 5, 1:645, no. 3610. Frederick's final will stipulated that Henry was to inherit his father's kingdoms of Germany, Sicily, and Italy if his half brother, Conrad (IV), should die without heir and that Henry was also to receive either the kingdom of Arles or Jerusalem (whichever Conrad wished), and one hundred thousand ounces of gold was made available to recover the Holy Land: cf. Van Cleve, *The Emperor Frederick II*, 529–30; David Abulafia, *Frederick II: A Medieval Emperor* (London, 1988), 406.

207. *MPCM*, 4:613.

208. *MPCM*, 3:49–50.

209. *MPCM*, 3:336; *MPHA*, 3:100. Henry's half brother, Conrad (IV), announced the death of his brother to the English court and blamed the delay in notification on his own overwhelming grief: see *Böhmer*, 5, 1:846.

Conrad, a scion of the comital houe of Hochstaden, concentrated on strengthening a grip on his territorial principality[210] and therefore wanted little to do with the schemes of either the emperor or the English king.[211] We have already seen that he was not among those Rhenish princes who were willing to support Henry III's invasion of Poitou in 1242. The main reason for this was his conflict with Count William of Jülich, who eventually captured him and held him prisoner for most of the year.[212] This conflict was occasioned by the fact that Conrad refused to declare his allegiance to the emperor in 1241 along with the duke of Limburg, the counts of Berg, Jülich, and Los, the lord of Heinsberg, and the city of Cologne, and therefore warfare was waged against the archbishop in an effort to force him to submit.[213] In the autumn of 1241 Archbishop Conrad had formed a pact with the imperial regent Archbishop Siegfried of Mainz to reject the emperor. Both ecclesiastical princes had done so primarily out of regional territorial interests rather than out of specific plans to destroy Staufen power in the empire.

Frederick's second papal excommunication, coming two years before this conflict in the environs of Cologne, had released Archbishop Conrad from any allegiance to the emperor,[214] and thereafter he remained a constant foe of Staufen rule. Conrad supported the papacy, but only because it served his own territorial interests. In December 1244, on the eve of the Council of Lyon, Conrad and Archbishop Siegfried of Mainz

---

210. Conrad was extremely successful at extending the regional power of the archbishopric, which ironically only lacked control over the city of Cologne itself: see Stekhämper, "Konrad of Hochstaden," 108.

211. Wand, "Die Englandpolitik der Stadt Köln," 89: "He did not want to serve in any foreign politics, even if it were English, but his own politics." In 1241 Conrad did write to Henry III, requesting his aid against the invading Tartars: see *MPCM,* 4:111; *REK, 3,* 1:151, no. 1010 (dated March). Conrad was not alone in this, however, as Duke Henry of Brabant issued a request for assistance to Henry III and to the bishop of Paris. Frederick II informed the English king about the Tartar threat: see *Historia Diplomatica,* 5:1148–54; *Böhmer,* 5, 1:567, no. 3216 (dated July 3, 1241). The initiative, however, appears to have originated among the Franciscans via Cologne, since a certain Franciscan in the city had already forwarded to the duke of Brabant a letter of Jordan, warden of Pinsk (Franciscans in Bohemia and Poland), about the Tartars: see *Böhmer,* 6:83–84. Therefore the call was a general one to Christian princes to come and defend central Europe against the Tartars, not an isolated request from Conrad to the English (cf. *Historia Diplomatica,* 5:1216–18). Conrad certainly could not call on the emperor at this time.

212. *REK, 3,* 1:156–57, nos. 1046–55. Matthew Paris (*MPCM,* 4:188) records Conrad's imprisonment but is incorrect about the details.

213. *REK, 3,* 1:155–56, no. 1044.

214. *MPHA,* 2:474.

made a hurried trip to Lyon and met with the exiled Pope Innocent IV.[215] There they promised the pope that they would elect a new king if he should depose the emperor, and they prevailed on him to at least renew Frederick's excommunication. Although Conrad did not remain in Lyon to participate in the council the following year, his work had already been done: Frederick was deposed, a new election was called, and the pope even declared a crusade against the Staufer.

The archbishop moved quickly against Frederick after the declaration of deposition. In August 1245 Conrad either accompanied or gave safe conduct to the papal legate Philip of Ferrara on his way to negotiate with Landgrave Henry Raspe of Thuringia (who was ironically Frederick II's appointed imperial regent since 1242),[216] and on May 22, 1246, the Thuringian prince was elected antiking near Würzburg.[217] Matthew Paris noted the central role played by Conrad of Hochstaden in Raspe's election. Indeed, this effort was not to be Archbishop Conrad's last venture in kingship diplomacy.[218] The pope moved quickly to support the antikingship established under the leadership of Conrad, who was in the vanguard of the forces that battled the Staufen partisans.[219] Matthew Paris was not the only English chronicler who heard details of Conrad's role in this rebellion; the chronicle of Bury St. Edmunds contains a detailed passage for the year 1246.[220]

Conrad had in Henry Raspe the regionally isolated monarch he needed in order to restrain royal or imperial encroachment on his territorial prerogatives. He served the same function in Germany as Frederick II had in Italy before the papal excommunication and deposition decrees. Raspe's kingship, however, did not last long, and a new antiking was needed upon his death in 1247. Once again Archbishop Conrad took the lead in the second election, which took place outside Cologne (since the city was still pro-Staufen), in nearby Worringen, on October 3, 1247.[221] The candidate

215. *CRC*, 286; *REK*, 3, 1:171, no. 1167.
216. *CRC*, 288.
217. *REK*, 3, 1:181, no. 1257. The archbishops of Cologne and Mainz elected him, with the consent of the archbishop of Trier.
218. *MPCM*, 4:495.
219. *MPCM*, 4:545, 548.
220. *The Chronicle of Bury St. Edmunds,* ed. Antonia Gransden, Nelson Medieval Texts (London, 1964), 13–14.
221. *REK*, 3, 1:190, no. 1335. The archbishops of Mainz, Trier, and Bremen, along with other suffragan bishops, participated in this election. William was only received in Cologne after granting the city extensive privileges.

selected was Count William of Holland, whom the electors found suitable both because of his connections in the region[222] and because of his isolated political standing in Germany. He was even more acceptable to Conrad, since William owed his very election to the archbishop.[223]

At this point Archbishop Conrad enjoyed considerable political success. After reducing the pro-Staufen imperial city of Aachen, which endured a six-month siege before surrendering, William was duly made king on November 1, 1248, "by the hand of Archbishop Conrad of Cologne."[224] The anti-Staufen forces had begun to drive Frederick II's son Conrad (IV) back to Italy[225] and even had the boldness to admonish him to cease the ways of his father.[226] In 1249 Archbishop Conrad also gained control of the wealthy imperial monastery of Fulda.[227] Matthew Paris rebukes Conrad, whom he describes as "a militaristic and warlike archbishop" [*armipotens et belliger archiepiscopus*], for draining the wealth of Fulda to serve his military purposes. To be sure, this must have added a tidy sum to his already vast resources. In addition, Innocent IV made him a papal legate for Germany on April 30, 1249, with full powers "that he might tear out and destroy, disperse and ruin, that he might establish and smooth out."[228] The new king, however, saw only limited success in achieving the submission of the imperial cities of Cologne, Kaiserswerth,

---

222. *MPCM*, 4:624: "Ipse [William of Holland] enim comes et episcopus Leodiensis [Henry of Guelders, bishop of Liège] fuerant consobrini; dux insuper Braibantiae [*sic*] avunculus ejus fuit; archiepiscopus quoque Coloniensis ipsius amicus extitit indissolubilis et quadam affinitate conjunctus."

223. The dependent nature of William of Holland's kingship is clearly reflected in the numerous concessions granted and large amounts of money borrowed from various sources to maintain himself. See, for example, *Die Urkunden Heinrich Raspes und Wilhelms von Holland 1246–1252*, ed. Dieter Hägermann and Jaap G. Kruisheer, MGH DD, no. 18 (Hanover, 1989), 1: nos. 2, 3, 28, 29, 30, 41, 45, 67, 71–75, 84, 93, 135, 166, 167. These charters alone are either issued from Cologne or signed by Archbishop Conrad, and all of them confirm concessions to or pawning of property to raise money from the citizens of Cologne, Duisburg, and Aachen, various local churches and monasteries, seafaring merchants, the counts of Berg and Henneberg, the duke of Limburg, the burgrave of Kaiserswerth, even the archbishops of Salzburg and Embrun (Arelat).

224. *REK*, 3, 1:201, nos. 1427, 1429; *MPCM*, 5:17, 25–26. William as king was so dependent on Conrad's support that he even had to mortgage the city of Dortmund to the archbishop to obtain twelve hundred marks: see *REK*, 3, 1:202–3, no. 1437; *Die Urkunden Heinrich Raspes und Wilhelms von Holland 1246–1252*, no. 67 (December 23, 1248).

225. *MPCM*, 4:634.

226. *MPCM*, 4:653.

227. *MPCM*, 5:74. See *REK*, 3, 1:204, no. 1453.

228. *REK*, 3, 1:206–7, nos. 1470–71: "ut evellat et destruat, dissipet et disperdat, edificet et planet."

Dortmund, and Aachen. He never made it even as far as the middle Rhine, because of the successful resistance of the cities of Boppard, Frankfurt, and Gelnhausen.

Initially relations between William of Holland and Archbishop Conrad were positive, and they even boded well for renewed ties between the archbishop and England. By this time Isabella had died and Henry III had already given up on Frederick II in favor of the papacy. The final stroke would come when Frederick II died the following year. The Plantagenet court had particularly good relations with the count of Holland, whose wife was a Welf princess. By this time even the city of Cologne had joined the antiking after receiving a significant privilege from William.[229] Therefore conditions appeared similar to those of Otto IV's era: an antiking had been elected under the aegis of the archbishop of Cologne and was supported by a league of Rhenish cities and princes. Yet the political interests of the antiking and archbishop were once again quite different, and a local dynastic conflict led to a clash between these two that altered the political landscape of northern Germany and had lasting implications for Anglo-German diplomacy.

The old dynastic conflict between Flanders and Holland over the county of Zeeland erupted once again in early 1254,[230] and Archbishop Conrad sided with the Flemish faction that opposed the king.[231] Before his election as king of the Romans (*rex Romanorum*) William had been in conflict with Countess Marguerite of Hainault/Flanders over the feudal sovereignty of western Zeeland (land in imperial Flanders), and he now used the discord between Marguerite's sons (the half brothers John of Avesnes, count of Hainault, and William Dampierre, heir to Flanders) to weaken her position.[232] At the July 1252 diet of Frankfurt William

229. *Die Urkunden Heinrich Raspes und Wilhelms von Holland 1246–1252*, 28–31, nos. 2–3; *UGN*, 2:166–68, nos. 318–19; *Ennen/Eckertz*, 2:266f., nos. 265–66 (dated October 9, 1247). William reconfirmed the privileges and customs of Cologne at Speyer on February 24, 1255: see *UGN*, 2:223, no. 411.

230. Werner Reese, *Die Niederlande und das Deutsche Reich* (Berlin, 1941), 288; Kienast, "Die Deutschen Fürsten," 16:124–39.

231. *REK*, 3, 1:243–44, no. 1795.

232. In 1246 a settlement was brokered by Louis IX that John of Avesnes, although older than his stepbrother William, was to be given the county of Hainault and feudal lordship over Namur, while William received the county of Flanders. Needless to say, John was very displeased with this decision. In 1248 another settlement was made between Countess Marguerite and William of Holland concerning the control of western Zeeland by William's brother Florence. Marguerite retained control of the islands but was to do homage for them to William. This, however, did not allow William to exercise direct control

decreed Marguerite forfeit of the imperial Flemish fiefs because she had not come to do homage for them within the prescribed time, and he gave them to her despised son John of Avesnes, who was also the brother-in-law of William (John, who married William's sister Adelaide, had strong ties with England as well: we shall see him again as the imperial seneschal for Richard of Cornwall).[233]

William hoped that his good relations with England might result in support for this dangerous venture against Flanders, a possibility that must have worried Archbishop Conrad since this complex web of feudal ties and disputes threatened to bring both Plantagenet and Capetian forces into his backyard.[234] He therefore allied himself with Countess Marguerite of Flanders, her son William, and Charles of Anjou, promising as long as he lived to provide military assistance against the brothers John and Baldwin of Avesnes.[235] Charles of Anjou, the brother of King Louis IX, entered the fray for two reasons. Firstly, he was administering the French kingdom while Louis IX was on crusade, and he wished, no less than did Archbishop Conrad, to be a strong influence in the Netherlands. Secondly, his support was rewarded by Marguerite, who offered him the county of Hainault. Although this was an illegal act and Hainault was still in the control of John of Avesnes, Charles accepted the offer in October 1253, and as count of Anjou, Provence, and now Hainault he was drawn further into the increasingly chaotic dispute.

Because of his territorial exigencies, Conrad fell away from the anti-king of his own making in much the same way as Adolf of Altena had fallen away from Otto IV. In neither case did the archbishops want to see the establishment of a strong monarchy within their sphere of influence. That Conrad had allied himself with Charles of Anjou out of concern for possible English intervention on behalf of either William of Holland or John of Avesnes represents a major shift in archiepiscopal policy. Since he

over these strategic islands. In addition John of Avesnes had to acknowledge the loss of his claims over Flanders.

233. MGH Const., 2:465–67, no. 359 (July 11, 1252).

234. William of Holland sought to strengthen his English ties, and John of Avesnes wished to obtain direct English support at this time, but Henry III responded that he was too involved in negotiations concerning the kingdom of Sicily and Apulia for his son Edmund to be deflected by other business: see *MPCM*, 5:493; *CCLR Henry III*, 8:261 (August 3, 1254). Cf. *MPCM*, 5:434–37, 6:253–54. Marguerite also counted on Capetian assistance since she held Flanders as a fief of the French king, and she hoped for English support since she also held an English fief: see *CPR Henry III*, 4:387, 553.

235. *REK*, 3, 1:243–44, no. 1795.

now had a French ally and had spurned William, there was little chance of close diplomatic ties with England.[236] Tensions between William and Conrad were further increased when the archbishop became embroiled in a feud with Bishop Simon of Paderborn during the same year, over the archbishop's ducal rights in Westphalia. William and the papal legate Peter Capoccio intervened personally for the release of Simon from Conrad's prison, but the effort resulted in an attempt on their lives at the archbishop's instigation: a fire was set in the city of Neuß, where the negotiations were taking place, and both king and legate barely escaped.[237] Because of this act, Conrad received a sentence of excommunication by the papal legate and was obliged to send several envoys to Rome to work for his release. Thus by 1254 Conrad had alienated himself not only from the Staufen claimants to the throne but also from the pope, his own antiking, and the English court. He had impoverished all of his traditional diplomatic contacts in the furtherance of his own territorial policies and was now quite isolated for the next two years.

New political life was restored to him in surprising fashion upon the sudden death of William of Holland in January 1256. The antiking, who had done precious little to deal with the political order in Germany, died in battle near Hoogwoud in West Friesland while attempting to assert his comital authority there against the Frisians.[238] During the nine years of William of Holland's antikingship the German princes had continued to operate their affairs without the presence or need of royal intervention. This political pattern was not new; it emerged during the reign of Henry VI and became quite pronounced during Frederick II's reign, which was almost entirely spent by him in Italy.

---

236. A final peace to the Flanders-Holland-Hainault conflict could only be reached after the death of William of Holland at the hands of the Frisians in January 1256. Louis IX, now returned from his ill-fated crusade, once again intervened and declared the *Dit de Péronne* on September 24, 1256: Marguerite was to pay Charles of Anjou the enormous amount of 160,000 pounds Tournais for his military assistance, and John of Avesnes and his brother Baldwin were forced to do homage to Charles of Anjou for the county of Hainault, which was to revert to him only after the death of Countess Marguerite of Flanders. John and Baldwin were also forced to surrender their lordship over the county of Namur, given to them by William of Holland, and to secure the consent for it from the next German king within a year of his election.

237. *REK*, 3, 1:247–48, no. 1818 (January 1255).

238. *Chronicon Hanoniense quod dicitur Balduini Avennensis,* ed. Georg Waitz, MGH SS, no. 25 (Hanover, 1880; reprint, 1974), 461–62; *Menkonis Chronicon,* ed. G. Pertz, MGH SS, no. 23 (Hanover 1874; reprint, 1986), 546; *Annales Stadenses,* ed. G. Pertz, MGH SS, no. 16 (Hanover, 1859; reprint, 1994), 374.

Once again, the archbishop of Cologne and the other elector princes were called on to choose a new king. Although at geographical antipodes in the empire, both dynasties came to represent the same sort of limited power inherent in the German kingship. William of Holland was dead and Frederick II's heirs were struggling to survive in southern Italy. Hence the same requirements applied to this election as had existed in all royal elections since that of Otto IV. No prince felt the need to choose a candidate who would unify the German territories, as they had been governed successfully for decades without this type of monarch. Furthermore, no available candidates had personal power that extended beyond a territorial principality, power needed to forge such a unity if it had been desired. Hence the German political community understood the job description of the *rex Romanorum* differently than did the political communities of France and England. The German king was to confirm and maintain the existing territorial principalities rather than consolidate them. But where, then, could the electors turn for such a candidate? Conrad of Hochstaden would turn to the traditional source of diplomatic support for the archbishops of Cologne: England. This time the results would be quite different, not so much for Conrad, but for the Plantagenets.

The reign of Frederick II saw what seemed like a rapprochement between the Plantagenet and Staufen houses. Continued efforts by the English court at obtaining a German princess for Henry III with the help of the archbishop of Cologne met with frustration until Frederick himself initiated a marriage union. On the surface the conditions seemed to be much like those of the period under Frederick I: the emperor was engaged in a vicious struggle with the papacy over the Italian kingdoms, and the English king was plying the Cologne connection to draw the German princes into a continental coalition scheme against Capetian France. Yet some very important changes had occurred since Frederick I's reign. The English monarch was now firmly committed to the papacy, and this proved to be the major hindrance to any close involvement between the Staufen and Plantagenet houses. Only during the brief periods of peace between emperor and pope did Henry III feel free to develop relations with Frederick II. Again we are reminded that religious scruples played as crucial a role in medieval politics as did kinship ties or the bonds of lordship. In Henry III's case it proved to be the predominant factor.

In addition, the last Staufen emperor had left Germany to the imperial princes, and the era of particularism and the building up of territorial principalities was well underway. The archbishops of Cologne—Conrad of Hochstaden especially—were exemplars of this development, and thus their political interests became increasingly territorial and independent in nature. Little of the service rendered to either the emperor or the English king did not have their *Territorialpolitik* at heart. This overriding concern had removed Conrad from cooperation with any royal authority and had at times even put him at odds with papal authority. No longer could the English court count on the archbishop of Cologne as a certain ally whose interests were naturally coordinated with their own. Therefore the nature of Anglo-German diplomacy was radically altered by the middle of the thirteenth century, since these relations were traditionally managed by the Cologne archbishops. When the decline of strong monarchical power in Germany in the closing years of Staufen rule was added to the mixture, maintenance of English diplomatic ties with Germany became even more difficult.[239] The political regionalism of Germany would frustrate the English court just as it would subsequent German monarchs: the stillborn kingship of Richard of Cornwall and Edward I's failed attempt to revitalize the old anti-Capetian coalition scheme with German princes serve as the closing acts to the course of Anglo-German diplomacy.

This transformation of diplomatic relations between Germany and England, and particularly between Cologne and England, was mirrored by economic relations between the two regions. Increasingly the merchants of Cologne were losing their monopolistic control over English trade with Germany, and their London guildhall was soon to be transformed into the Stalhof of the German Hansa under the growing leadership of Lübeck. Thus the unique combination of characteristics that formed the intimate relations between Cologne and England since the eleventh century began to unravel during the changing world of Frederick II's reign. There was still one last moment of significance in Anglo-Cologne and Anglo-German diplomacy, in the candidature of Richard of Cornwall as *rex Romanorum*, but even this cooperation was short-lived and its results only furthered the estrangement of the archbishops of Cologne from England.

---

239. Kienast, "Die Deutschen Fürsten," 16:217.

7

Epilogue: The Quixotic Kingship
of Richard of Cornwall and
Anglo-Cologne Diplomacy during
Edward I's Reign

This chapter closes our study of the diplomatic life of the Central Middle Ages. It is a fitting place to leave off, since the unique combination of factors that made Cologne a nexus for Anglo-German relations was then dismantled. The promise of interregional political cooperation between the English and German political communities, which had yielded precious little to date, could no longer be sustained in its traditional modes by the close of the thirteenth century. Major changes in the makeup and functions of the political communities in these two realms made the old channels of diplomacy ineffective. Despite the changes, however, a great deal of continuity can be discerned in the ways these political communities related both among and between themselves. These continuities serve to remind us of the fragility of institutional achievements in contrast to the longevity of social constructs.

Richard of Cornwall and Anglo-Cologne
Diplomatic Relations

In considering the German kingship of Richard of Cornwall we shall not go into great detail concerning all aspects of his candidature and attempts to enforce his royal authority in Germany, since such studies can be found in several other places.[1] We shall concentrate rather on the role played by

---

1. Cardauns, *Konrad von Hochstaden, Erzbischof von Köln*, 42–50; J. F. Bappert, *Richard von Cornwall seit seiner Wahl zum deutschen König* (Bonn, 1905); C. C. Bayley, "The Diplomatic Preliminaries of the Double Election of 1257 in Germany," *EHR* 62 (1947): 457–83; N. Denholm-Young, *Richard of Cornwall* (Oxford, 1947); C. C. Bayley,

the archbishop of Cologne in this affair and then on the consequences of Richard's reign for Anglo-German diplomatic relations in general and for Anglo-Cologne relations in particular.

The German kingship, long an object of contention between the Staufen house and the papacy, had now ceased to function within this framework after the end of Staufen rule. In fact it had become the object of contention between German magnates, as in the cases of Henry Raspe and William of Holland. Every effort was made to find a candidate whose power and resources matched the limited job description of the *rex Romanorum*. Such nominees naturally enjoyed only regional power within the German political community, which was appropriate.

With the era of the so-called Interregnum,[2] however, this dynamic moved beyond the borders of the German kingdom. The royal dignity became an object of contention among European dynasties, which sought it not for its own sake but as a means to other, non-German dynastic ends. Hence the German kingship can be understood at this point as a signal of the emergence by the late thirteenth century of medieval political activity that was interregional in nature. The European political communities had become interrelated to an extent unknown before, and this created new interregional dynastic possibilities as well. Hence traditional social behavior involving hereditary claims and estate building would be extended beyond previous boundaries. The synthesizing of ancestral regional political interests with the growing interregional ties between European political communities transformed the German kingship from its original role as the leader of the German tribes and the emperor-elect of Christendom into both a protector of the regional German principalities and also a sign of cross-regional ties between Germany and other parts of Europe. When seen in this way, The German kingship is an indicator of

---

The Formation of the German College of Electors in the Mid-Thirteenth Century (Toronto, 1949), 63–77; Stehkämper, "Konrad von Hochstaden," 106–16; T. W. E. Roche, *The King of Almayne* (London, 1966); Roswintha Reisinger, *Die römisch-deutschen Könige und ihr Wähler 1189–1273*, Untersuchungen zur deutschen Staats -und Rechtsgeschichte, NF no. 21 (Aalen, 1977), 71–88.

2. Alexander of Roes notwithstanding, *Interregnum* is a term I shall not use here, since it contains modern nationalist assumptions, namely, that it is illegitimate for a "foreign" monarch to rule over a given people, and hence that any monarch between the Staufen and Habsburg dynasties was in fact no king at all. This flies in the face of medieval social realities, wherein dynastic ties served to identify one's "national" origin for succession. Consider in this regard both the papacy and the generations of Capetian-Plantagenet conflicts, not to mention the candidacy of Otto IV.

European integration rather than of German disintegration. The kingships of Otto IV and Frederick II were, in this sense, the first of such *reges Romanorum*. The election of the next German king therefore engendered not only interest outside of Germany but now also an active participation in the process. This fusion of interregional dynastic claims and the particular need of the German princes for a monarch who would ratify rather than reconsolidate their territorial principalities created the possibility of an English nobleman as the German "king of the Romans." One can hardly say that Germany was not integrated into the life of western Europe during the Central Middle Ages.

The archbishop of Cologne in particular has been credited—or blamed—in great measure for auctioning the royal office to European ruling houses, which it is said proved to be the final blow to the prestige and authority of the German kingship and a major impetus to the political fragmentation of Germany.[3] Yet if we recall the political requirements for the successor of William of Holland and the interregional candidates now available to all German electors, we can conclude that the archbishop of Cologne acted in consonance with his fellow princes in choosing Richard of Cornwall. Hence he was not a destroyer of German political or constitutional unity but a preserver of an effectively administrated and fully functioning regionalist Germany. We shall see that, although more powerfully and effectively than most, he behaved in a normative way within the context and particular needs of his own political community.

Richard's candidacy for the office of *rex Romanorum* can only be understood in the context of his brother's dynastic politics, which had the dual goals of increasing the Plantagenet prestige among European ruling houses and recovering the lands lost by his father.[4] Having emerged from a lengthy minority, he was anxious, though perhaps ill equipped, to achieve a restoration of Plantagenet power akin to what his grandfather had enjoyed. We have already seen that benefits repeatedly failed to accrue from the Plantagenet-Staufen marriage union, because of Henry III's willingness to follow papal dictates. Matthew Paris states that the pope himself had already offered the German crown to Richard of

---

3. For a study on the role of the archbishops of Cologne as an elector of the German kings see Franz-Reiner Erkens, *Der Erzbischof von Köln und die deutsche Königswahl: Studien zur Kölner Kirchengeschichte zum Krönungsrecht und zur Verfassung des Reiches*, Studien zur Kölner Kirchengeschichte, no. 21 (Siegburg, 1987).

4. Bayley, "Diplomatic Preliminaries," 457–58; F. M. Powicke, *King Henry III and the Lord Edward* (Oxford, 1947), 1:245.

Cornwall in 1247 (along with such other candidates as Otto of Guelders, Henry of Brabant, and King Hakon of Norway) before William of Holland eventually was selected.[5] Richard is said, however, to have declined the offer. Whether or not this report is accurate,[6] the pope approached the earl three years later with an offer of the Sicilian crown.[7] Richard was unwilling to supplant his nephew Henry (son of Isabella and Frederick II) or to bear the huge cost of a military campaign of conquest, so the papal offer eventually devolved on Charles of Anjou.[8] After Charles proved impossible to negotiate with, the offer rebounded back to the English court, and Henry III accepted the offer in the name of his son Edmund.[9] Thus we must note the formative role papal influence played on Henry III's diplomacy. His diplomatic ideal was a folding together of dynastic and papal aggrandizement.

Nowhere was this confluence clearer than in the hapless Sicilian venture. The candidacy of Edmund for the crown of Sicily proved to be a financial and political disaster for Henry III from the start. His own brother Richard even joined the baronial opposition in October 1255 that refused to grant the king's request for a loan of forty thousand marks to finance the venture.[10] Yet Edmund's candidacy served as the springboard for Richard's own German venture in 1257. When approached with the idea, Henry III was most willing to support his brother's candidacy for the German throne, since it would eliminate two of his problems at once. Firstly, it would separate Richard from the baronial opposition to Edmund's Sicilian kingship; and secondly, it would assure that no German king would be elected who was hostile to Plantagenet dynastic ambitions in Sicily.[11] Henry certainly also hoped for a candidate who was favorable to the Church and not subservient to the Capetian king. Richard, for his part, eventually chose to pursue the title out of a desire to raise his own dynastic honor; he was an ambitious prince who was not unfamiliar with

---

5. *MPCM*, 4:201.

6. It seems unlikely that Richard would have opposed Frederick II through an anti-kingship, and his presence was too essential in England as a mediator between king and baronage at this time.

7. Bayley, "Diplomatic Preliminaries," 460–61.

8. Conrad IV wrote a letter of gratitude to Richard for refusing to join the papal plot against him: See *MPCM*, 5:458.

9. *MPCM*, 4:457 (dated February 12, 1254).

10. Ibid., 5:520–21. See A. Wachtel, "Die sizilische Thronkandidatur des Prinzen Edmund von England," *DA* 4 (1941): 98–178.

11. Bayley, "Diplomatic Preliminaries," 465.

the empire.[12] As we shall see, Richard was responsible for initiating negotiations for his own candidacy and in so doing behaved well within the social expectations of his political community in seeking to advance his family's prestige by having two reigning kings in Europe. Royalty outside England was something to be grasped now, thanks to the growing interregional dynastic ties established in the Central Middle Ages.

For the second half of the equation we must return to the lower Rhineland, in particular to the regional dynastic disputes of John of Avesnes, count of Hainault, and the involvement of Archbishop Adolf of Cologne. John of Avesnes was wise enough to see the dangerous consequences for himself of a pro-Capetian candidate on the German throne after the death of William of Holland.[13] John's mother, Marguerite of Hainault/Flanders, had favored the sons by her second marriage to William of Dampierre over John and Baldwin by her first husband Bouchard of Avesnes. This meant that the Dampierre branch would inherit Flanders and Namur while John was left with Hainault. In an effort to counteract this John had married the daughter of William of Holland and had thereby drawn the German king into the conflict. We have already seen (see chapter 6) that William of Holland sought to confiscate from Marguerite the territories of imperial Flanders found in Zeeland. As a result of this dispute Archbishop Conrad of Cologne had abandoned William of Holland and sided with the countess in hopes of avoiding the arrival of Capetian and Plantagenet troops so near his territories.

With the sudden death of King William, however, John of Avesnes had lost his strongest ally and was isolated by the Francophile branch of his family in Flanders, Zeeland, and Namur. To make matters worse Louis IX had returned from his crusade and as feudal suzerain was seeking to adjudicate the final settlement in the Avesnes-Dampierre dispute. John's vulnerable position must have been the motivation for a trip to England in early February 1256, at which time he and his brother Baldwin were awarded a sizable yearly pension by none other than the earl of Cornwall.[14] William of Holland had been dead only a few days upon the

<hr/>

12. Trautz, *Die Könige*, 115–16.
13. For a detailed study of John of Avesnes's role see Henry S. Lucas, "John of Avesnes and Richard of Cornwall," *Speculum* 23 (1948): 81–101.
14. Upon Richard's advice John was awarded a yearly pension of two hundred pounds on February 5, 1256 (*CPR Henry III*, 4:461), and his brother Baldwin received a pension of one hundred pounds on April 17 (*CPR Henry III*, 4:468). Denholm-Young (*Richard of Cornwall*, 86) argues: "Richard was a man of great deliberation and it is safe to assume that

arrival of John, who may have suggested Richard as the next king. This piece of advice might well have engendered the pension. John had often been at the Plantagenet court in previous years seeking English support in his inheritance dispute,[15] and William of Holland may have even suggested him as the next king of the Romans in 1251.[16] Since the failed coalition at Bouvines the English court had followed with interest the tangled affairs of the lower Rhineland and obviously was well acquainted with John of Avesnes. Their diplomatic cooperation deepened as the candidacy of Richard of Cornwall was jointly explored. John would prove useful as a Plantagenet ally in the lower Rhineland to counteract his kinsmen in pro-Capetian Flanders and Namur. The impetus for this diplomacy was dynastic advantage for both John of Avesnes and Richard of Cornwall, rather than any sort of geopolitical stratagem to create a coherent Anglo-Gascon-Sicilian-German "empire" or hopes of either strengthening or weakening the institution of German kingship.

The English initiative moved tentatively forward. On March 27 Henry III wrote to William Bonquer, his ambassador currently in Rome negotiating a rescheduling of debt payment to the papacy, to agitate for a German king who would be favorable to English interests (so as not to damage the Sicilian project). He also requested that an Anglophile cardinal be sent to Germany to move the electors in this direction, since the French held aspirations for a Francophile German king.[17] No specific mention of Richard appears in the letter, yet he might have been one of the few suitable candidates on the short list. The Curia proved rather cool to the idea and dragged its feet; in particular the prospect of Plantagenet monarchs on the thrones of Germany and Sicily looked too much like the dreaded Staufen threat of the recent past. On June 12 Henry III had letters of credence issued to Richard de Clare, earl of Gloucester and Hereford (and Richard of Cornwall's stepson), and to the royal seneschal Robert Walerand, "for certain services and negotiations of ours" with the German princes; doubtless this concerned Richard's proposed candidacy.[18]

---

this [grant to John of Avesnes] was no sudden whim. There seems no reason to reject the obvious implication that this was the first step towards acquiring the crown, and that the initiative came from Richard himself."

15. Matthew Paris records that John had asked for military help from Henry III, who declined citing English involvement in the Sicilian project (*MPCM*, 5:493).

16. Lucas, "John of Avesnes," 93.

17. *Shirley*, 2:114–16, no. 507; *Böhmer*, 5, 1:990, no. 5287.

18. MGH Const., 2:479, no. 376; *Böhmer*, 5, 1:990–91, no. 5288.

We know nothing about the particulars of this mission, yet almost certainly these envoys came to Cologne to sound out Archbishop Conrad, who could potentially benefit from Richard's candidacy. He had become politically isolated through his conflicts with William of Holland and the papal legate Peter Capoccio (see chapter 6) and needed not only a candidate who could make his support financially worthwhile but one who was also on good terms with the papacy and whose political power was suitably distant from his territorial principality. Richard satisfied every condition and therefore might hope for his support.[19] In addition, Richard tolerably satisfied the dynastic dimension of legitimacy, since he was the first cousin of Emperor Otto IV (who had married Beatrix of Staufen) and was Emperor Frederick II's brother-in-law. Thus he was among those select few who were related to the kings of Europe. In a great irony so typical of the social webs of feudal and dynastic ties, John of Avesnes and Archbishop Conrad, enemies with regard to William of Holland's kingship, were now potential allies with regard to Richard of Cornwall's kingship.

Conrad found himself in a peculiar position. The remarkable opportunity for an election free of dynastic pressures had presented itself to the electors, but there was no candidate possessing general recognition as the successor to the Staufen dynasty. Furthermore, Archbishop Gerhard of Mainz, who possessed the traditional right of leading the election and casting the first vote, was in the duke of Brunswick's prison. Thus Conrad was in a position similar to that of Archbishop Adolf in 1197/98. We do not know whom Conrad had initially desired as a royal candidate; but we can say that he had to act quickly to counteract the early initiative of the Saxon princes (one of which was in possession of the archbishop of Mainz), who nominated one of their own, Otto of Brandenburg, as a candidate. Given his current political isolation, a new king from Saxony would have been a serious threat to his territorial authority in Westphalia.[20] Furthermore, the southern German princes were consulting one another about whether to support the four-year-old Staufen Conradin

19. Ennen, *Geschichte der Stadt Köln,* 1:122.

20. Strong kinship ties bound Duke Albrecht of Brunswick, his brothers John and Otto (margraves of Brandenburg), and Duke Albrecht of Saxony; they would eventually nominate Otto as their royal candidate. See Manfred Groten, "Konrad von Hochstaden und die Wahl Richards von Cornwall," in *Köln, Stadt und Bistum in Kirche und Reich des Mittelalters: Festschrift für Odilo Engels zum 65. Geburtstag,* ed. Hanna Vollrath and Stefan Weinfurter, Kölner historische Abhandlungen, no. 39 (Cologne, 1993), 483–509.

(whom the pope had expressly forbidden as a candidate) or perhaps King Alfonso of Castile (the grandson of Philip of Swabia) as heir to the Staufen dynasty.

Given these exigencies, the English envoys had to await the outcome of the archbishop's trip to Prague in mid-July to discuss the royal election with King Ottokar II of Bohemia. Conrad remained with the king in Prague until August 10, so they clearly pursued extensive negotiations. That this trip was the private initiative of the archbishop of Cologne is clear by the small, personal entourage that accompanied him.[21] His return trip took Conrad via Saxony and included a stop to visit the captive Archbishop Gerhard of Mainz at the court of Albert of Brunswick, either to inform him of the prospect of release through English money in exchange for his vote[22] or to gain Gerhard's support for King Ottokar II's candidacy.[23] Yet another factor, the need for ransom money on behalf of the archbishop of Mainz, contributed to the complex collage of political and economic needs resulting in the selection of the wealthy earl of Cornwall. Whatever were the internal dynamics of these murky negotiations between the electors, it was clear by August of 1256 that neither the northern electors as the anti-Staufen faction nor the southern electors as the pro-Staufen could agree on an internal, German candidate. This opened the door to external candidates with dynastic ties to the German throne: enter Richard of Cornwall and King Alfonso of Castile.

---

21. *REK*, 3, 1:257, nos. 1903–7. Conrad had earlier sought Ottokar II as yet another antiking against William of Holland in 1254–55, with the support of Countess Marguerite of Flanders: see A. Busson, "Über einen Plan an Stelle Williams von Holland Ottokar von Böhmen zum römischen König zu erwählen," *Archiv für Österreichische Geschichte* 40 (1869): 131–55; Bayley, "Diplomatic Preliminaries," 469 n. 1. Conrad was accompanied on this trip by two of Ludwig II of Bavaria's vassals, Philip of Falkenstein and Werner of Boland, among others. Ludwig (the count palatine of the Rhine and duke of Bavaria) had supported the candidacy of the Staufen Conradin, whose guardian he was, but the reception of the German princes to this idea was negative. The pope had also forbidden Conradin as a candidate (*REK*, 3, 1:257, no. 1905, dated July 28, 1256). The presence of these men of Ludwig suggests that Archbishop Conrad had assurances that Conradin's candidacy would be withdrawn. Ottokar, for his part, was interested in obtaining a candidate who would confirm his claims in Austria, which he had annexed in 1251. He made no assurances of his support for Richard, however, until it was clear that the earl enjoyed certain support among the electors.

22. *Annales Moguntini*, ed. G. Pertz, MGH SS, no. 17 (Hanover, 1861; reprint, 1987), 2. Gerhard of Mainz was eventually ransomed by Richard with eight thousand marks in exchange for his vote, according to the Hamburg annals.

23. Groten, "Konrad von Hochstaden," 496. Ottokar II was on good terms with the Saxon princes, and Otto of Brandenburg was his brother-in-law. Perhaps Conrad sought to resurrect his earlier plan to raise Ottokar to the German throne (see note 21).

Richard of Cornwall's candidacy must have been a topic of discussion in Prague and Brunswick, and perhaps Conrad managed the tacit approval of Ottokar II and Gerhard to explore such an option; in any case Conrad delivered Gerhard's vote by December. John of Avesnes and his kinsman Nicholas of Fontaine, the bishop of Cambrai, took advantage of such a diplomatic opening and were in Bavaria during October concluding negotiations with another elector, Ludwig II. John and Nicholas were spurred on by Louis IX's *Dit de Péronne* on September 24, which subjected them even more to French domination in Hainault by favoring the pro-Capetian Dampierre branch of the family. Not only would Richard of Cornwall protect their territorial interests in Cambrai and Hainault (which were imperial fiefs and therefore not under the jurisdiction of the French king), but the new German king held the power of approving John's lordship over the county of Namur. Bishop Nicholas shared John's fears of Capetian encroachment into his own principality and felt keenly the same pressure from Louis IX's decision against John of Avesnes. So he joined the mission to gain Count Ludwig's vote for Richard.

On November 26 in Fürstenberg near Bacharach the terms were concluded for Ludwig's electoral vote: he was to marry a Plantagenet princess with a dowry of twelve thousand marks sterling, and Richard was to renounce any claim to the kingdom of Sicily—an apparent safeguard for Conradin's claims there, although Henry III's son Edmund had also made a claim. Finally, the treaty was voided if Richard did not appear in Germany by the Feast of St. John (June 24, 1257). John of Avesnes even placed one of his sons as a hostage until the promised dowry payment was made good. Bishop Nicholas, Dean Otto of Aachen, and other lesser lights served as pledges.[24] The proposed marriage would never materialize in the future (in fact no princess appears eligible at this time), but such was the social glue used to cement Ludwig's vote for Richard.

John of Avesnes and Bishop Nicholas of Cambrai went directly thereafter to Cologne and worked out with Archbishop Conrad the final details of the agreement, which was signed at Zündorf (Zudendorp) on December 15.[25] The archbishop extended the negotiations almost three weeks

24. MGH Const., 2:479–82, nos. 377–80; *Acta Imperii Inedita*, 1:583–84, nos. 738–39; *Böhmer*, 5, 2:11765–68. Ludwig agreed to a marriage "cum filia fratris regis Anglie sive sororis eiusdem, si filia fratris non fuerit."

25. *REK*, 3 1:260, no. 1925; *UGN*, 2:232, no. 429; MGH Constr., 2:482, no. 383; *Böhmer*, 5, 2:1733, no. 11771. John of Avesnes and Bishop Nicholas of Cambrai signed this document as authorized agents of Richard. Zudendorp was a suburb of Cologne, now known as Zündorf.

before he obtained the major concessions needed for his vote: if elected with Conrad's help, Richard would protect the Cologne church and all its possessions and soften the harsh attitude that the cardinal legate Peter Capoccio and the Roman church held against the archbishop. Capoccio had excommunicated Conrad after the incendiary incident at Neuß (see chapter 6), so the archbishop made use of Richard as a valuable mediator to reconcile himself with the papacy. If Richard could not manage this by next Easter, he was to pay Conrad an indemnity of two thousand marks sterling. Furthermore, Richard agreed never to establish agents or judges between the Moselle, Aachen, and Dortmund without the advice and consent of the archbishop, and he agreed to recruit no noble, knight, or burgher without the advice and consent of both Conrad and John of Avesnes. This was essentially a confirmation of episcopal regalian rights in the region.[26]

Conrad was to receive eight thousand marks for his services, while the *scholasticus* of St. Severin in Cologne was to receive one thousand marks and the citizens of the city were to receive two thousand marks. This latter three thousand marks would fall to Conrad if Richard did not accept the kingship by January 13 or if he was not satisfied with the electoral votes of the archbishops of Cologne, Mainz, and Count Palatine Ludwig. Otherwise the three thousand marks would be deducted from the eight thousand marks promised to Conrad. Cologne burghers were established to handle the accounting of this money, and the archbishop's advisors were to receive an additional four hundred marks for their services. Conrad had reached a settlement with Richard's representatives before the full complement of German electors had met to elect Richard and before the English baronage had been consulted for their approval to this venture. Hence Richard knew the political concessions required and the financially based nature of his kingship well before he was elected. He also knew that Conrad's support for his election was lukewarm at best and obtained by promises and funding designed to secure the archbishop's territorial independence. When all was said and done Conrad had accepted a king not of his own initiative, but he was able to extract the same securities needed from any candidate to protect his territorial principality. Thus, Conrad was not so much a kingmaker in this instance (though many have asserted so) but rather more of a kingbroker.

---

26. Wand, "Die Englandpolitik der Stadt Köln," 93.

An embassy of the archbishop of Cologne's men Walram (brother of the count of Jülich), Frederick of Schleiden, and Magister Theoderich of Bonn was quickly dispatched to the Plantagenet court to overcome any reservations by the English magnates. Matthew Paris recounts at length the arrival of German princes at Westminster during Christmas 1256, bringing news of Richard's candidacy.[27] They were granted an audience before the body of English magnates and declared that Richard had been elected unanimously to the kingship of Germany. Nothing could be farther from the truth, but the English magnates could not have known otherwise at this point. If they had, they would have been more resistant, since the Crown was already excessively indebted because of the Sicilian project. The German envoys brought letters—from the archbishop of Cologne and other unnamed princes—declaring that Richard had been elected with a unanimity unknown before in the empire.[28]

This exaggerated claim took the assembly by surprise as it was designed to do, and when they hesitated, King Henry seized the initiative and called for acceptance of this heaven-sent offer.[29] Baronial concerns about the viability of Richard's kingship were blandished with rather rhetorical responses: Richard was advised not to consider the sad fate of Henry Raspe and William of Holland, as he was not being foisted on the German people by the pope as they were (yet another misleading statement). The envoys even promised him that, like Octavian of old, he could draw his private revenues from the vast income of the German kingdom and that he had faithful supporters both in England and Germany on whose aid he could rely. Here the rhetoric passes into the realm of pure fantasy and deception. Finally, Richard was admonished to remember the

---

27. *MPCM*, 5:601–5.

28. Groten ("Konrad von Hochstaden," 506–7) argues that the German princes did not intentionally deceive the English magnates about the unanimity of Richard's election, ascribing the lack of clarity merely to English confusion about the electoral process. This argument is difficult to sustain, however, given the importance of the venture for Plantagenet dynastic politics and the clear cooperation on the part of the archbishop's party. Conrad is referred to here with the high-sounding title of "sacri imperii prothocancellarius."

29. Hans-Eberhard Hilpert ("Richard of Cornwall's Candidature for the German Throne and the Christmas 1256 Parliament at Westminster," *Journal of Medieval History* 6 [1980]:185–98) asserts correctly that the the Christmas parliament was carefully planned by the Plantagenet court to avoid noble dissension over Richard's kingship given their current discontent about the Sicilian project. The issue here was taxation for these questionable foreign endeavors as far as the magnates were concerned, and thus nothing was disclosed about the cost of Richard's kingship. Hilpert also emphasizes the complicity of the German envoys in deceiving the English magnates about the status of the election in Germany.

example of his ancestor Robert Curthose, who had rejected the kingdom of Jerusalem and thereby incurred the wrath of God. The charade was then completed by Richard's tearful and humble acceptance of the offer and by his swearing that he would rather burn in hell than be guided by selfish interests. We can find no better example of the priority of dynastic goals over the "interests of the state" in modern political terms. Here the medieval social practice of dynastic advancement superseded any notion of what was in the best interest of the English state.

On the following day, Richard and the Christmas parliament formally accepted the election agreement drawn up on December 15, and his brother placed the royal seal of England on the document. The only alteration made was moving the deadline for a reconciliation between Archbishop Conrad and Cardinal Legate Capoccio to August 15, 1257.[30] This remarkable confluence of dynastic, local, and regional social, economic, and political interests had resulted in a new creation: an interregional kingship. Its most important artisans were a German archbishop (Conrad of Cologne), an embattled count of Hainault (John of Avesnes), and two royal brothers in England (Henry III and Richard of Cornwall), a combination of members from different political communities who found a common way to advance their private interests. Archbishop Conrad in particular had succeeded in securing the third candidate in the last seven years who was suitable for assuring Conrad's territorial principality.

Richard of Gloucester and John Mansel returned with Conrad's envoys to tie up any loose ends, and Conrad hurried to meet Count Palatine Ludwig to carry out the formality of an election.[31] On January, 13, 1257, the two electors, with Conrad voting on behalf of the imprisoned Archbishop Gerhard of Mainz, solemnly chose Richard outside the city walls of Frankfurt, a location unused heretofore for royal elections. They were unable to enter the city because it was under the control of the supporters of an alternative candidate: Alfonso X of Castile. Furthermore, the other electors (the archbishop of Trier, the margrave of Brandenburg, and the duke of Saxony) refused to participate in the election.[32] It was not until January 30 that Ottokar II of Bohemia gave his consent to Richard's

---

30. *REK*, 3, 1:260–61, no. 1926; MGH Const., 2:484, nos. 384–85; *UGN*, 2:233–34, no. 430: *Böhmer*, 5, 1:991, nos. 5288a, 5289 (dated December 26, 1256).

31. *MPCM*, 5:604.

32. *MPCM*, 6:341–42 contains a letter of Archbishop Conrad of Cologne and Count Palatine Ludwig declaring Richard's election under less than ideal circumstances.

election.³³ This was certainly not the situation that was portrayed at Christmas.

The Cologne archbishop's greatest performance was still to come. Between March 20 and April 8 he sojourned at the English court at the head of a tightly knit group of German princes from the lower Rhineland to do homage to Richard.³⁴ The timing of this embassy was very important, as it arrived just after the mid-Lent parliament at which archbishops from southern Italy were present. They were there to treat concerning the Sicilian project. Hence the sequence of the two embassies, between which Richard of Gloucester and John Mansel returned from Germany with news of Richard of Cornwall's election, reflects the intertwined nature of these two endeavors. Richard's coronation would assure no interference by a hostile German monarch in the establishment of Edmund on the throne of Sicily. Matthew Paris says that Conrad's embassy concealed the fact that Richard's election was less than unanimous and that its members proceeded to do liege homage to the earl of Cornwall.³⁵ In a scene most remarkable for its bluntness concerning the nature of Richard's kingship, an exchange occurred that reveals Conrad's perspective on the relationship between the German episcopate and the German king. After doing homage and receiving in exchange five hundred marks and a jeweled mitre, the archbishop of Cologne placed the mitre on his head and remarked:

---

33. *Annales de Burtonensis*, 391–92.

34. *REK*, 3, 1:262, no. 1942; *MPCM*, 5:624–26. Of the aristocracy present, the bishop of Liège, Henry of Guelders, was a former archdeacon of Cologne and was adversely affected by the *Dit de Péronne* because John of Avesnes had held Hainault from him in fee beforehand. The bishop of Utrecht, Henry of Vianden, was related to Archbishop Conrad on the matrilineal side. Count Florence V of Holland was the brother of William of Holland and thus was brother-in-law to John of Avesnes, who had married Adelaide in 1246. Therefore all of these princes had common kinship and feudal ties and thus similar interests in seeing Richard as king of Germany.

35. Matthew Paris (*MPCM*, 5:657) states that they also hid from Richard himself that Alfonso X was elected by another party of electoral princes (the archbishop of Trier, the margrave of Brandenburg, and the duke of Saxony). Since this second election took place on April 1, 1257, while Conrad was at the English court, it seems unlikely that any news of it would have reached the German embassy in time. They may, however, have known before their departure from Germany that this electoral congress had been planned. This may help to account for the exaggerated claims that they employed to woo the English barons, since time was of the essence in the face of a disputed election. Certainly the margrave of Brandenburg and duke of Saxony had voted against Conrad's candidate to check the Cologne archbishop's territorial expansion into Saxony after the humiliation of Bishop Simon of Paderborn during 1254–56.

Count Richard has enriched me and my church with this noble treasure; and indeed I, just as I have placed my mitre on my head, shall place on his head the crown of the kingdom of Germany or rather of the Romans. He mitred me, and I shall crown him.

The last line of Conrad's striking statement shows the complete reversal of the traditional relationship between regnum and sacerdotium in Germany. Unlike earlier times, when German kings struggled to mitre the bishops by whom they themselves were crowned, now an imported king was elected and crowned by a bishop who mitred himself with a royal gift after nineteen years of independent episcopal rule as a territorial prince! This king was elected to *maintain* the bishop's independent territorial principality rather than to rule as a centralizing force in Germany. Truly the European scene had changed dramatically from the beginning to the end of the Central Middle Ages.

Conrad departed shortly thereafter to make preparations for Richard's coronation in Aachen, but not before obtaining further gifts.[36] He was given the right to send servants throughout England to collect an offering for the rebuilding of the Cologne cathedral, which had burned down in 1248.[37] Perhaps Conrad had convinced Henry III that a gift for the restoration of the shrine of the Three Kings would reap divine support for the Plantagenet dynastic dream of enthroning three kings in England, Germany, and Sicily. In any case, much English money went into the building of that beautiful gothic cathedral, which still stands today in Cologne with a current capacity to hold twenty thousand people. Conrad also obtained a pardon for a certain Master Adam de Lynton for the murder of a merchant in the city.[38] Shortly thereafter, he obtained the knighting of a vassal to the bishop of Utrecht,[39] and a cleric of his was given a robe as a gift.[40]

---

36. *MPCM*, 5:627–28.

37. *CPR Henry III*, 4:591; *Rymer*, 1:640; *Ennen/Eckertz*, 2:373, no. 373; *REK*, 3, 1:263, no. 11943; *Böhmer*, 5, 2:1736, no. 11796. Matthew Paris (*MPCM*, 5:35) records the destruction of the first Cologne cathedral, which he calls the mother and matron of all the churches in Germany.

38. *CPR Henry III*, 4:548 (Westminster, April 8, 1257).

39. *Diplomatic Documents*, 202, no. 297. Henry's fulfillment of this request occurred a month later: see *CCLR Henry III*, 10:53 (Merton, May 12, 1257). Note that the Feast of the Ascension—the day on which the king "ad instanciam archiepiscopi Coloniensis [the knight] cingulo milicie decorabit"—was the same day that Richard of Cornwall was crowned in Aachen by Archbishop Conrad of Cologne.

40. *CCLR Henry III*, 10:56 (Westminster, May 24, 1257).

Richard was duly crowned in Aachen by Conrad on May 17—appropriately on the Feast of the Ascension.[41] His wife Sanchia was also crowned, and Richard's son Henry (by his first wife, Isabella) was knighted on this occasion. Henceforth he was styled Henry of Almain, a title that expressed the Plantagenet hope that Henry would succeed his father as king of the Germans. Richard rewarded John of Avesnes for his valuable diplomatic services by making him royal seneschal in Germany, and Bishop Nicholas of Cambrai was appointed royal chancellor.[42] The new king was quite taken by the entire event, especially by the large military contingents that the archbishops of Cologne and Mainz brought to Aachen. In a letter to his nephew Edward, he advised the future king of England that he would do well to have such militant ecclesiastics in England.

Behold! What spirited and warlike bishops we have in Germany; I do not think that it would be harmful to you at all if such were created in England, whose service you would be able to use against the troublesome assaults of rebellions.[43]

Either this was written in the excitement of the moment, or Richard had not fully comprehended the nature of his kingship and its relationship to the ecclesiastical princes at this time in Germany.

The flood of royal privileges and grants of regalian rights began rightly

---

41. *MPCM*, 5:640–41; *REK*, 3, 1:263, no. 1949. Cf. Gervase of Canterbury, *Gesta regum continuata*, ed. William Stubbs, RS, no. 73 (London, 1879–80), 2:206; *Annales de Dunstaplia*, 202–3; *Chronicon vulgo dictum Thomae Wykes*, ed. Henry Richards Luard, RS, no. 36 (London, 1869; reprint, 1965), 4:111–17. Thomas Wykes indicates that the money paid by Richard to the German princes for his election was to be paid in Cologne coinage.

42. John of Avesnes would not long enjoy the hopeful opportunities before him as a result of his long labor to achieve Richard's kinship. He died the day before Christmas 1257, barely a year after he had secured his new patron's position.

43. *Rymer*, 1:622–23; *Böhmer*, 5, 1:995, no. 5294 (dated May 18, 1257). Concerning the military retinues of German bishops see Timothy Reuter, " '*Episcopi cum sua militia*': The Prelate as Warrior in the Early Staufer Era," in *Warriors and Churchmen in the High Middle Ages: Essays Presented to Karl Leyser*, ed. Timothy Reuter (London, 1992), 79–94; Benjamin Arnold, "German Bishops and Their Military Retinues in the Medieval Empire," *German History* 7, no. 2 (1989): 161–83; Wilhelm Janssen, " '*Episcopus et dux, animarum pastor et dominus temporalis*': Bemerkungen zur Problematik des geistlichen Fürstentums am Kölner Beispiel," in *Geschichtliche Landeskunde der Rheinlande: Regionale Befunde und raumübergreifende Perspektiven. Georg zum Gedenken*, ed. Marlene Nickolay-Panter, Wilhelm Janssen, and Wolfgang Herborn, Veröffentlichungen des Instituts für Geschichtliche Landeskunde der Rheinlande, Bonn (Cologne, 1994), 216–35.

after Richard's coronation and are too many to cover here in detail.[44] He dispensed with what little royal authority was left in Germany, in an effort to gain the support of the princes and cities. After confirming the privileges of the city of Aachen on May 22,[45] Richard then went to Cologne, where he confirmed for the burghers the generous privileges that William of Holland had previously granted them.[46] He also affirmed the December 15, 1256, election agreement on June 3 so as to assure the territorial rights of the archbishop.[47] Shortly thereafter, Henry of Almain returned to England with the other English magnates who had accompanied Richard to Aachen, and the new king proceeded up the Rhine distributing privileges and vast sums of money in an effort to secure a foundation for his kingship.[48]

Detailed consideration of Richard's subsequent kingship in Germany is not needed here, as it can be found elsewhere. A summary of his actions and relations with the archbishops of Cologne will suffice. His first trip up the Rhine reached as far as Mainz, where he stayed until mid-September. After gaining the submission of the archbishop of Trier through monetary inducement and being entertained by the recently ransomed archbishop of Mainz, he returned to Cologne for the winter. Hopeful plans concerning a trip to Rome for imperial coronation were deferred until the next spring. Richard probably participated therefore in the settlement of a dispute between Archbishop Conrad and the citizens of Cologne on March 20, 1258,[49] and in a trade settlement that favored foreign merchants on the following day.[50] He then returned to Mainz, where he celebrated Pentecost and the subjection of Worms and Speyer.

Before his kingship had taken full root, news of the baronial revolt in England and papal temporizing concerning his imperial coronation forced a return to England, where he arrived on January 28, 1259. His return was

---

44. See *Regesten der Reichsstadt Aachen I, 1250–1300*, ed. Wilhelm Mummenhoff, PGRG, no. 47 (Bonn, 1961).

45. *REK*, 3, 1:263, no. 1953.

46. *UGN*, 2:239–40, no. 441; *Ennen/Eckertz*, 2:369–71; *REK*, 3, 1:264, no. 1955 (May 27).

47. MGH Const., 2:486, no. 387; *REK*, 3, 1:264, no. 1960.

48. *MPCM*, 5:653. It appears that Richard was left to his own devices amid the German princes, since no Englishmen appear as witnesses in the charters that Richard issued in Germany.

49. *REK*, 3, 1:267–68, nos. 1990–92; *Ennen/Eckertz*, 2:378, no. 382; *UGN*, 2:235, no. 434.

50. *REK*, 3, 1:268, no. 1994; *UGN*, 2:237, no. 436.

also essential because his English wealth was the basis for his power in Germany and he had to protect his own English interests, even at the expense of accepting the Provisions of Oxford. Upon his departure Richard appointed Archbishop Conrad his vicar and defender of the king's peace in northern Germany up to the Weser River, and a promising beginning was cut short.[51]

Richard's second trip to Germany proved much less successful. After settling affairs in England he departed from Dover on June 20, 1259, but his time away had been costly. The archbishop of Mainz and duke of Brabant had switched their loyalty to Alfonso X of Castile, and Archbishop Conrad was embroiled once again in a conflict with the citizens of his episcopal city. Having secured regional power Conrad began to focus on the submission of the traditionally independent Cologne burghers. He had already shown signs of falling away from his chosen king, just as he had done with William of Holland and as the archbishop's predecessor had done with Otto IV. Having managed to install a distant, wealthy, yet politically limited king who could not interfere with his territorial affairs—the job description that had come to be for the *rex Romanorum*—even papal admonition to remain loyal to Richard went unheeded.[52] During this brief stay in Germany Richard finally came to realize the emptiness of his kingship; he now knew that all the German princes wanted were regalian rights and generous installments from his vast financial resources in exchange for the honor of the royal title. Furthermore, papal temporizing on the matter of his imperial coronation and even an open recognition of his election made the situation even more hopeless.

Richard would return to Germany twice more after this venture, and then only to prevent the loss of his title. Never again did he take the *regnum Romanorum* as seriously as he did the affairs of his native land, and papal recognition was no longer a goal sought after in earnest. He held court at Worms in late September and there gave Conrad the authority to invest bishops on his behalf.[53] Richard had abdicated almost all royal prerogatives and returned to England in late October. He now was a king in absentia. The Cologne archbishop and other German princes had gained the kind of king they needed, and in this sense Richard was a success. Indeed, he functioned very much as the later Staufen kings, whose power base lay outside of Germany and whose Italian affairs kept

---

51. *REK*, 3, 1:272–73, no. 2029 (December 1258).
52. *REK*, 3, 1:276, no. 2051 (April 30, 1259).
53. *REK*, 3, 1:286, no. 2125 (September 1259).

them outside of the German realm just like Richard's English affairs kept him more active along the Thames than along the Rhine. In this sense there was continuity between Frederick II's reign and that of his brother-in-law. Only those hoping for centralized state building and the exercise of real royal power in Germany at this time, be they members of the Plantagenet court or modern historians employing modern political categories, should be disappointed.

Archbishop Conrad of Cologne died in 1261 and was succeeded by Count Engelbert of Falkenburg, who continued his predecessor's *Territorialpolitik* and concentration on the submission of the last stronghold against archiepiscopal authority—the city of Cologne itself. This former cathedral prior, who now combined the positions of count and ducal archbishop, was the archetype of Cologne archbishops, at once ecclesiastical and secular lords on a grand scale. Richard's investiture of Engelbert occurred a month after his election by the cathedral chapter. In what is the best example of the nature of Richard's German kingship as well as of the diplomatic relationship between the Cologne archbishop (and the German princes in general) and the English court at this time, the investiture of the archbishop-elect with regalian rights was done through a letter.[54]

Engelbert presumably performed the appropriate oaths upon Richard's return for a third trip through Germany, on which he embarked in late June 1262. Richard traveled up the Rhine as far as Strasbourg, returning to Frankfurt in late autumn. Englebert accompanied Richard in his travels, as evidenced by his witnessing one of Richard's charters issued at Boppard.[55] At the outset of his third *iter* Richard sojourned in Aachen, where he gave the imperial coronation insignia (a golden crown, royal vestments with his heraldic arms, a scepter, and an imperial orb) to the Marienkapelle for use in future coronations. This proved to be one of the few lasting consequences of his kingship in Germany.[56] By mid-October

---

54. *REK*, 3, 2:2, nos. 2188–89; *Acta Imperii Inedita*, 1:457–58, no. 570; *UGN*, 2:286, no. 509 (London, November 8–9, 1261). Engelbert was expected to give an oath of loyalty to Richard the next time the distant king returned to Cologne.

55. *REK*, 3, 2:9, no. 2219 (September 3, 1262).

56. Armin di Miranda, "Richard von Cornwallis und sein Verhältnis zur Krönungsstadt Aachen," *Annalen* 35 (1880): 65–92. This article began the speculation that the head on the famous Aachen bust of Charlemagne might actually be that of Richard. Furthermore there is discussion on the Rathaus used by Richard as his curia. The following articles continue the debate on Richard's role in the Aachen Schatzkammer: Albert Huyskens, "Der Plan des Königs Richard von Cornwallis zur Niederlegung eines deutschen Krönungs-

reports of Henry III's failing health and rumors of Simon de Montfort's return to England spurred Richard back home, and after a short stay in Mainz (until December 3) he returned down the Rhine.

During the years 1263–67 Richard was absorbed in defeating the Montfort regime and thus left his German kingdom in perfect neglect.[57] Only in August 1268 did he make one more attempt to travel up the Rhine in hopes of being invited to continue to Rome. Of all Richard's trips up the Rhine this was the most empty of shows; the past four years of neglect had caused his slight influence in Germany to fade completely.[58] After stopping in Cambrai he sojourned at the castle of the lord of Falkenburg, twelve miles northwest of Aachen. The lord of the castle was Dieter of Falkenburg, whose brothers were Archbishop Engelbert II of Cologne and the count of Cleve. Dieter had been a supporter of Richard since his coronation in Aachen, and in the past he had sided with the burghers of Cologne in their battles with Conrad of Hochstaden, but the raising of his brother to the archiepiscopate changed his position dramatically and he became a partisan of Engelbert's efforts to subject the burghers to episcopal authority. In fact he had been captured and imprisoned by the citizens of Cologne during a feud in 1263, and despite a settlement reached on August 25 of that year, Dieter remained hostile to the city.[59]

As Richard arrived at Falkenburg Castle Archbishop Engelbert II sat in

---

schatzes in Aachen," *Annalen* 115 (1929): 180–204, which contains the text of Richard's 1262 grant; idem, "Noch einmal der Krönungsschatz des König Richard von Cornwallis," *Annalen* 118 (1931): 136–43; Paul Kirn, "Mit welcher Krone wurde König Sigmund in Aachen gekrönt?" *Annalen* 118 (1931): 132–36. Both Richard and his second wife, Sanchia, are listed in the necrology of the Marienkirche in Aachen: see *Necrologium ecclesiae beatae Mariae virginis Aquensis*, ed. Christian Quix (Aachen, 1830), 12.

57. In a curious letter, Pope Urban IV issued a command to Archbishop Engelbert II of Cologne to obey the papal legate, Cardinal Guy of Sabina, whose task it was to prevent the German princes from supporting the rebellious English magnates against Henry III: see *REK*, 3, 2:16, no. 2272; *Calendar of the Entries in the Papal Register relating to Great Britain and Ireland*, vol. 1, *1198–1304*, ed. W. H. Bliss (London, 1893), 397–98 (Orvieto, November 27, 1263). This may have been a general effort on the pope's behalf to support Henry III, yet what role any German prince (the archbishop of Cologne in particular) would or could have played in the English rebellion remains unclear. Richard's political impotence in Germany is reflected in his reply to Philip (his treasurer) and Werner of Falkenstein in 1266 that because of the long war in England he did not have the means to grant their request (*Acta Imperii Selecta*, 311–12, no. 384). No doubt the matter concerned finances in Germany.

58. Denholm-Young, *Richard of Cornwall*, 139.

59. *REK*, 3, 2:14–15, no. 2261.

the prison of Count William of Jülich, a supporter of the Cologne burghers. Engelbert had been there since October 1267 as a result of yet
another struggle between city and archbishop and was to languish there
until May 1271.[60] Here again we see the predominance of local, dynastic,
and jurisdictional disputes in the archbishop's politics. Engelbert II had
finally met his match in the combined forces of the wealthy and powerful
patricians of Cologne and factions of the local aristocracy. His imprisonment at the hands of the count of Jülich lasted a remarkable three and a
half years. When finally released he used good judgment and left the city
to dwell in Bonn and Brühl thereafter.

The archbishop himself had shown no loyalty to or interest in Richard
and it appears that the king had also given up on Engelbert by this time.
In fact upon the archbishop's release in 1271 Richard promised his assistance to the city of Cologne if Engelbert did not uphold the agreement
reached,[61] and later that year he commanded Engelbert to pay the count
of Jülich the two thousand marks promised at his release.[62] These would
be two of the last royal commands that Richard would promulgate from
England before his death on April 2, 1272.

Richard of Cornwall's arrival in 1268 had interrupted Dieter's plan
to carry out a surprise attack on Cologne with the assistance of Duke
Adolf of Limburg and the lord of Heinsberg (Dieter's brothers-in-law).
The ultimate goals of the attack were the submission of the burghers
and the release of Engelbert from imprisonment. The plan was to undermine the city wall and enter the city on the night of October 14, but
somehow news of this reached the patrician leaders of the city and they
soundly defeated the invaders. Dieter was killed and his brother the
archbishop remained in prison at Nideggen Castle.[63] Amid all of this
chaos Richard of all things became enamored with the beautiful fifteen-
year-old daughter of Dieter named Beatrix.[64] Richard had Beatrix taken

---

60. *REK*, 3, 2:35, no. 2388.

61. *REK*, 3, 2:44, no. 2442; *Ennen/Eckertz*, 3:34, no. 45; *UGN*, 2:361–62, no. 611
(Wallingford, May 20, 1271).

62. *REK*, 3, 2:46, no. 2456; *UGN*, 2:365, no. 618 (September 13, 1271).

63. *REK*, 3, 2:38, no. 2401, known in Cologne's history as the "Schlacht an der
Ulrepforte."

64. Frank R. Lewis, "Beatrix von Falkenburg, the Third Wife of Richard of Cornwall,"
EHR 52 (1937): 279–82. Richard was fifty-nine years old at the time but was drawn to
Beatrix by her legendary beauty. The Oseney chronicler described her as the "gemma
mulierum" (*Annales de Oseneia*, ed. Henry Richards Luard, RS, no. 36 (London, 1869),
4:223–24.

for protection to her uncle, Philip of Bolanden-Hohenfels, whose lands were in the palatinate between Bingen and Kaiserslautern. He also began negotiations for marriage with her.

After stopping in Aachen he went next to Cologne on December 15, where he spent Christmas. Moved more by Beatrix's beauty than by the plight of her archiepiscopal uncle, he set out in early 1269 on his well-worn route up the Rhine, meeting the archbishop of Trier in Koblenz and the archbishop of Mainz in his cathedral city. On March 7 Richard was in Worms, only a day's travel from Philip of Bolanden's castle, and he held an Easter diet there (April 14). At the diet, he achieved the only notable deed of this final visitation: the abolition of all tolls on the Rhine except for the traditional imperial tolls at Boppard and Kaiserswerth. Pentecost was spent in Frankfurt, and then Richard married Beatrix at Kaiserslautern on June 16. Then, having run out of money by this time and with the pope still delaying an invitation to Rome for imperial coronation, Richard returned to England with the announced intention of showing his new wife the vast lands he possessed there. By July 9 they had reached Mainz, and they arrived at Dover on August 3, 1268. Richard was never seen again in Germany.

Since Engelbert II was in such bad straits, the marriage to his niece availed Richard nothing politically speaking. According to Thomas Wykes, Richard had married her simply out of infatuation over her beauty, which he was unable to be away from for even one night.[65] Sadly, Beatrix outlived Richard by only five years, perhaps near Oxford at Beckley or Wallingford, and died in October 1277. She was buried at the Oxford Franciscan church where she is remembered in a stained-glass window.[66] There were no children from this Anglo-German marriage.

It is unfair to evaluate Richard of Cornwall as a failure with regard to his German kingship. The lack of papal support, Alfonso X's rival claim to the throne, and Richard's constant need to be in England as a result of the baronial revolt from 1258–65 were all forces that limited his effectiveness in Germany. Indeed, one could even say that he sacrificed his German kingdom for the needs of his homeland.[67] During the fifteen years of

---

65. See *Chronicon vulgo dictum Thomae Wykes*, 223, where Wykes speaks of Beatrix's "incomparabilis forma."

66. She is depicted wearing a velvet cap, a crown, a tight wimple, and an ermine-trimmed cloak.

67. Roche, *The King of Almayne*, 217.

his kingship, he spent barely four in his German kingdom, yet this is not a worse track record than those held by the Staufen rulers. It is more appropriate to see Richard of Cornwall's kingship in a social context rather than in a constitutional or institutional manner. This was more a struggle over dynastic and territorial claims than a struggle to preserve royal power in Germany. Both Richard of Cornwall and Alfonso X of Castile were closely related to the Staufen dynasty: Alfonso was the grandson of Philip of Swabia, and Richard was the nephew of Emperor Otto IV as well as the brother-in-law of Emperor Frederick II. Both candidates could trace their bloodlines to several *stirpes regiae* reaching across Europe. Hence these medieval princes' behavior was normative, rather than an anomaly, in medieval political history. They sought the advancement of hereditary familial claims rather than the advancement of a modern nation-state in Germany and should be judged therefore on their success or failure as dynastic estate builders rather than on their record as state builders.

The forces that defeated Richard and Alfonso before either kingship could take root were the territorial interests of the German princes and their consequent need to secure regalian rights. The long absences of Frederick I, Henry VI, and Frederick II had prepared the way for this circumstance long before Richard was called to the throne. From the machinations surrounding his election onward Richard's kingship was, as far as the German magnates were concerned, a means of gaining wealth and jurisdictional rights for the maintenance of their territorial principalities in exchange for the royal title. We cannot paint Richard as a naive idealist who was disillusioned by the greedy German princes, because he was aware of the financial and juridical nature of his candidacy from the very beginning and willingly entered the fray.[68]

Medieval chroniclers decried the mercenary nature of the sale of the German kingship and the lack of real interest in Richard as king on the part of the German princes.[69] Matthew Paris asserted that the German

68. Lucas, "John of Avesnes," 101: "As happened so frequently in other elections to the Roman imperial dignity, so in the candidacy of Richard of Cornwall and Alfonso of Castile, local political, economic, and dynastic considerations guided the issue."

69. Modern historians like Hugo Stehkämper ("Konrad von Hochstaden," 106) have commented on this. Kienast (*Deutschland und Frankreich*, 3:639; "Die Deutschen Fürsten," 16:147) has summarized the affair as follows: "Henry III's brother . . . must have been a quite suitable candidate for the electoral princes. A party under the leadership of the traditionally England-friendly Cologne archbishop gave him their votes in exchange for a lucrative greas-

magnates' homage was an expensive reward for Richard's money. The chronicler then concluded metaphorically that it would be better to lose a sword or arrow in the depths of the sea than to have one's enemy extort it from you.[70] Paris's criticism reached further when he cited Richard's treasury as a central reason for his election and quoted the contemporary satirical statement that money had wedded Cornwall to Rome.[71] This was obviously a not-so-veiled reference to the German electoral princes and the prospect of Richard's imperial coronation.

The annals of St. Rudbert in Salzburg openly declare the quid pro quo monetary nature of Richard's election.[72] The Hamburg annals follow suit by declaring that Richard threw money at the feet of the German princes like water and concluding, "O foolish England, which is willingly stripped of so much money. O foolish princes of Germany, who sell their noble prerogative for money."[73] Perhaps the most striking of such accounts concerning Richard's kingship is found in the Strasbourg *Ellenhardi Chronicon*, which, although not reflecting Richard's activities exactly, does characterize the nature of his relationship with the German princes in remarkably blunt fashion.

> Now the bishop of Cologne passed over to England after this and led Duke Richard of Cornwall, whom he and the bishop of Mainz had elected king, from there [to Germany]. Richard gave much money to them and to other bishops of Germany and nobles of the land. And since he was thus far sumptuous in riches, he was conveyed by the princes of Germany to each city and town of the empire on the Rhine River and was received honorably by all the citizens because of reverence for the princes who traveled with him. When, however, King

ing of the palms." C. C. Bayley ("Diplomatic Preliminaries," 481–82) criticizes the "clique of mercenary princes absorbed in Territorialpolitik" and "the paramount influence of money in forwarding the pretension of those who struggled for the rags and tatters of the Hohenstaufen inheritance."

70. *MPCM*, 5:626–27.

71. *MPCM*, 5:603: "Elegerunt, inquam, ipsum comitem Ricardum, tum propter ejus fidelitatem, constantiam, et sapientiam, tum propter sui thesauri abundantiam. Unde quidam, sed satiricus, satis inquit satirice, 'Nummus ait pro me, nubit Cornubia Romae.' "

72. *Annales Sancti Rudberti Salisburgensis*, ed. W. Wattenbach, MGH SS, no. 9 (Hanover, 1851; reprint, 1983), 794. Here the avarice of Richard's electors is contrasted with the supposed virtue of Alfonso's electors.

73. *Annales Hamburgenses*, ed. J. M. Lappenberg, MGH SS, no. 16 (Hanover, 1859), 383–84: "Stulta Anglia, quae tot denariis sponte est privata. Stulti principes Alimanniae, qui nobile ius suum pro pecunia vendiderunt!"

Richard had come all the way to the city of Basel his wealth ran out; thereupon the princes of Germany abandoned him, saying that they did not choose him because of his character but because of his wealth, and they gave him a petition of repudiation, and he returned by another way into his own country. The memory of this king faded like a sound.[74]

These continental accounts, however, come from regions that supported Alfonso X, and Matthew Paris is known for negative comments about foreigners in the context of the Poitevin problems at the English court under Henry III. What else should Paris have expected? Had not the English kings been buying the homage of German princes with money fiefs since the reign of Richard I? In fact, Richard of Cornwall's kingship should also be understood as a traditional Plantagenet money fief to German nobles writ large. This time the coalition of German princes was bought not to offset Capetian forces but to accept a Plantagenet scion as their king. We shall see the continued use of these money fiefs during Edward I's reign, with the same results. Since Richard had no feudal lands in Germany to grant to his princes in return for their homage and fealty, money was the only tie that bound them to him.

First and foremost among the German princes who both accepted a Plantagenet money fief for loyalty and yet expected an extremely limited Plantagenet kingship in Germany was the archbishop of Cologne. He played the role of kingbroker in Richard's election and was also the one who benefited most from his kingship.[75] A Cologne chronicler went so far as to say that Conrad "substituted" Richard of Cornwall as the third king in line after Henry Raspe and William of Holland.[76] The fact that Richard, like Otto IV and William of Holland before him, was in essence only a Rhineland king reflects the predominance of the ecclesiastical princes of Cologne, Mainz, and Trier in his party, with Cologne exercis-

---

74. *Ellenhardi Chronicon*, ed. Ph. Jaffé, MGH SS, no. 17 (Hanover, 1861; reprint, 1987), 122.

75. Matthew Paris (*MPCM*, 5:604) leaves no doubt about who was preeminent among the German princes: "Inter omnes hos magnates supereminens est archiepiscopus Coloniensis, qui coronare tenetur regem Alemanniae apud Aquisgranum, ab antiqua et approbata consuetudine."

76. *Chronica presulum et archiepiscopum ecclesie Coloniensium*, ed. Gottfried Eckertz, *Annalen* 4 (1857): 208: "Sed eodem Wilhelmo [of Holland] ad regnum electo in brevi postea per Frisonum gentem in bello interfecto dictus Conradus archiepiscopus tercium ad regnum substituit, Richardum videlicet ducem Cornubie fratrem regis Anglorum."

ing the leadership among these three. The stamp of Cologne was so affixed to Richard's kingship that even his royal seal was similar to the municipal seal of the city.[77]

The period of Richard's German kingship was a transitional era in Anglo-German diplomacy in general and in Anglo-Cologne relations in particular. The growing territorial principalities in Germany and the subdivision of imperial power had been long in coming, and now its fruits, while showing vitality and creativity in Germany, proved frustrating for English diplomacy. The Plantagenet court could no longer expect a unified political policy in Germany, and this made diplomacy quite cumbersome and confusing at times. Long unfulfilled expectations of a unified imperial alliance against Capetian France were more impossible now than ever, and thus the empire's strategic importance for England began to diminish.

Diplomatic relations with the archbishop of Cologne in particular exemplify this development most clearly. After gaining legal confirmation of his independent territorial power through the kings of his own making, the archbishop no longer needed the English as an ally against the old threat of imperial authority as had archbishops in the days of the Staufen rulers. The archbishop himself was now the preeminent power in northern Germany, whose political focus was regionally defined by his *Territorialpolitik*. Ironically, the only force left to reckon with, the independent-minded citizens of Cologne, would be the only community to successfully resist subjection to archiepiscopal power. Furthermore, little direct English support or money could be expected after the baronial opposition to the overseas schemes of Henry III enforced the Provisions of Oxford. Since there was no longer an imperial power to negotiate with, the Cologne archbishop's important mediatory role became increasingly anachronistic. The traditional English policy of diplomacy with the empire via Cologne had become anachronistic by the late thirteenth century.

The failure of English continental schemes regarding the thrones of Germany and Sicily and the recovery of the Angevin lands made the archbishop of Cologne a less important ally as well. The Treaty of Paris (1259), in which Henry III renounced claims to Normandy, Anjou, and Poitou, formally ended the "Angevin Empire." Since Gascony was the only continental fief held thereafter by the English king, Cologne was

---

77. Toni Diederich, *Die alten Siegel der Stadt Köln* (Cologne, 1980), 54.

now of little strategic importance. Thus by the end of Henry III's reign the dynamics that had defined close diplomatic relations between Cologne and England for the past two hundred years were replaced by a new political landscape in which England and Germany would increasingly diverge in interests. We now have only to consider briefly the final episode to this history of Anglo-Cologne-German diplomatic relations: the era of diplomacy between Edward I and the new Hapsburg kings.

Anglo-Cologne Diplomatic Relations during Edward I's Reign

By 1274 a new generation of leadership had risen to power in western Europe. The history of their diplomatic activities reflects a changed political environment from the traditional order we have observed during the Central Middle Ages. This new environment lacked the traditional characteristics inherent in prior Anglo-German diplomatic relations, and correspondingly the Anglo-Cologne connection lost its importance as a conduit between England and Germany.

By this date new kings appeared on the thrones of England, Germany, and France, and a new archbishop of Cologne had succeeded Engelbert II. Rudolf I of Hapsburg was indifferent to the Roman tradition of the German kingship and strove more to expand his family's territorial holdings than to wrestle with the papacy over an imperial coronation. Philip III of France and his son Philip IV concentrated on territorial expansion in southern France and the Mediterranean and thereby increasingly became the successors of the Staufen monarchs as the antagonists of the papacy. Edward I of England succeeded his father after a period of turmoil in England, and his preoccupation was understandably the strengthening of the English crown. Ruling after the "Angevin Empire" had dissolved, his attempts at foreign ventures were constantly frustrated by conflicts closer to home, in Wales and Scotland. Finally, Siegfried of Westerburg, the new archbishop of Cologne, would continue the tradition of local interests in his *Territorialpolitik,* which would result in an ill-fated final showdown with the city of Cologne. The old nexus of interests that had drawn the German and English political communities together through the mediation of the archbishop of Cologne was a thing of the past. Edward's failed attempts to revive it—through a marriage union with the Hapsburg dynasty and later by a reprise in 1294–98 of Richard I's old anti-Capetian coalition with German princes—only underscored the anachronistic nature of traditional diplomacy between the English and German political communities.

We shall briefly consider these events as an appropriate epilogue to Anglo-German/Anglo-Cologne diplomatic relations during the Central Middle Ages. The complete details of these two events have been dealt with at length elsewhere, therefore the focus here will again be on the role the Anglo-Cologne connection played and on their significance for the history of Anglo-German political relations.[78]

In the autumn of 1277, at about the time that Beatrix of Falkenburg died, the heir to her husband as *rex Romanorum*, Rudolf of Hapsburg, commissioned envoys to negotiate a marriage between his second son, Hartmann, and Edward's daughter Joan.[79] The project was the idea of Edward's aunt Margaret, the dowager queen of France. She hoped that Rudolf would endow Hartmann with the kingdom of Arles. This included Provence, the inheritance of which had been given to her sister Beatrice, wife of Charles of Anjou. We discover at the outset, then, that the impetus for this marriage was yet another dynastic reach for inheritance claims and not an anti-French alliance. Edward offered a ten-thousand-mark dowry in exchange for Rudolf's obtaining the kingdom of Arles for his son. In addition, Edward promised to mediate a peace between Rudolf and the count of Savoy, who were embroiled in a conflict that could have proven a hindrance to the marriage proposal. An agreement was reached after two years of leisurely negotiations, and preparations were made for Hartmann to visit England;[80] but the scheme ended abruptly on December 21, 1281, when Hartmann drowned in a shipwreck on the Rhine before ever reaching England to receive his bride.

Remarkably, Rudolf waited until August 1282 to inform Edward of

---

78. Trautz, *Die Könige*, 115–91; Johann Franzl, *Rudolf I.* (Graz, Vienna, and Cologne, 1986), 183–90; Michael Prestwich, *Edward I* (Berkeley, 1988), 317, 386–93; Ruth Köhler, *Die Heiratsverhandlungen zwischen Eduard I. von England und Rudolf von Habsburg: Ein Beitrag zur englisch-deutschen Bündnispolitk am Ausgang des 13. Jahrhunderts* (Meisenheim am Glan, 1969); Carl Henze, *England, Frankreich und König Adolf von Nassau 1294–1298* (Ph.D. diss., Kiel, 1914); Friedrich Bock, "Englands Beziehungen zum Reich unter Adolf von Nassau," *MIÖG Ergänzungsband* 12 (1933): 198–257; Vincenz Samanek, "Der angebliche Verrat Adolfs von Nassau," *Historische Vierteljahrschrift* 29 (1935): 302–41; Geoffrey Barraclough, "Edward I and Adolf of Nassau: A Chapter of Mediaeval Diplomatic History," *Cambridge Historical Journal* 6 (1940): 225–62.

79. *Rymer*, 2:88. The documents pertaining to these marriage negotiations can be found in the following locations: MGH Const., 3:153–60, nos. 161–72; *Rymer*, 2:96, 110, 112–15.

80. *Rymer*, 2:132 (Westminster, April 28, 1279).

his son's death.[81] We can only conclude from this laxity in diplomatic activity that by now the proposed union did not play a significant role in bringing about closer ties between the parties.[82] In fact Edward's interest in his aunt's project was slight, to say the least. The negotiations were handled almost exclusively by the Grandison family, and the entire endeavor looks more like a Savoyard initiative than an English one.[83] Hence this failed effort should not be seen as an effort between the English and German monarchs to forge an anti-Capetian alliance in the fashion of years gone by.[84] Rudolf was interested in this union for the prestige it would bring to his new kingship and for the sizable dowry involved; operative here were altogether typical dynastic interests rather than a desire to form a strategic alliance.

The other matter worth noting here is the conspicuous absence of the archbishop of Cologne in his traditional role of mediator in such negotiations. Siegfried of Westerburg (1274–97) had spent most of his career in the service of the church of Mainz, where his kinsman Werner of Eppstein was the archbishop. It was probably Werner's intercession that gained Rudolf's support for Siegfried in the disputed archiepiscopal election of 1274.[85] As archbishop he became deeply embroiled in conflicts with the citizens of Cologne and the local comital families as a result of his attempts to force their submission to his authority. Siegfried was preoccupied with constant local struggles until he lost the great Battle of Worringen on June 5, 1288, and was driven from Cologne for good. The city still celebrates this date as its independence day.[86] This final showdown

81. Rudolf informed Edward of his son's death in a letter, declaring that Hartmann's death broke only the bands of kinship and not those of friendship: see *Rymer*, 2:215 (August 17, 1282).

82. The papacy had been negotiating for a marriage union between the Habsburgs and the Angevins at this time as well.

83. Otto de Grandison was also involved in the negotiations between Count Philip of Savoy and King Rudolf: see *Acta Imperii Angliae et Franciae ab anno 1267 ad annum 1313: Dokumente Vornehmlich zur Geschichte der Auswärtigen Beziehungen Deutschlands*, ed. Fritz Kern (Tübingen, 1911), 19–20, nos. 32–34 (February 12, 1282).

84. Prestwich, *Edward I*, 317–18.

85. Rudolf wrote to the pope to secure approval of Siegfried's election (*REK*, 3, 2:65, no. 2591).

86. *REK*, 3, 2:168–71, no. 3193; *UGN*, 2:517, no. 870. Two English chronicles mention this battle and Siegfried's subsequent imprisonment, although the matter is there represented as a conflict between nobles: see *Annales de Waverleia*, 407; *Chronicle of Bury St. Edmund*, ed. Antonia Gransden (London, 1964) 92. See also Edith Ennen, "Erzbischof und Stadtgemeinde in Köln bis zur Schlacht von Worringen (1288)," *Gesammelte Abhandlungen zum europäischen Städtewesen und zur rheinischen Geschichte* (Bonn, 1977), 388–404.

between archiepiscopal authority and the rights of the burghers of Cologne and the surrounding comital families was a decisive break in the regional power of the archbishops. The goal of their *Territorialpolitik* since Philip of Heinsberg had become the consolidation of a regional principality extending from Lotharingia into Saxony. They had achieved this rather effectively by the course of the thirteenth century through successfully fending off imperial and papal incursions into their secular and ecclesiastical sovereignty. But local politics ultimately determined the role of the archbishops in the region, and after this major defeat any real archiepiscopal authority in the city came to a sudden end. The archbishops' rule over the counts and margraves of the Rhineland, Saxony, and the Lotharingia faded as they ceased to even rule their own episcopal city. Siegfried was therefore in no position to serve Rudolf as his ambassador to the English, nor was he particularly interested in doing so. In the history of Anglo-German diplomacy this is a noticeable changing of the guard.

Siegfried sought good relations with the English court for the economic benefits it brought to him and the city. On April 26, 1276, he sent an envoy, the knight Wenemar of Gymenich (whom he refers to as his "consanguineus"), with a letter of introduction.[87] The archbishop indicated that he wished very much to follow in the footsteps of his predecessors, who were always "familiares" of the English kings, to assure himself and the Cologne church of Edward's favor. Hence he offered his services to the king and asked him to receive Wenemar in good faith. The knight established such strong diplomatic ties at the English court in the following years that in 1281 King Edward issued a letter asking King Rudolf to attend to the requests of Wenemar and his brother, the prior of Wetzlar.

Wenemar's business was the acquisition of the imperial castles of Kerpen and Werden, while his brother's concern remains unspecified.[88] Wenemar eventually purchased the castle of Kerpen from his sister Beatrix, as is indicated by the charter of August 2, 1276, which Siegfried confirmed.[89] Here we also learn that Wenemar had trading contacts in England, because he intended to make certain payments to her for the purchase "of our goods, which we are allowed to sell in England." That

---

87. *REK*, 3, 2:80, no. 2669; *Rymer*, 2:1067 (Aachen, April 26, 1276).
88. *Acta Imperii Angliae et Franciae*, 10–11, no. 18 (May 1281).
89. *REK*, 3, 2:83, no. 2686.

Wenemar mortgaged this castle to Siegfried on the same day shows that the archbishop was interested in acquiring control of the imperial castle to strengthen his local power and that he thereby benefited directly from Wenemar's English connections.[90] This business is exemplary of the fact that Siegfried's interests were local in scope and had little to do with any diplomatic initiatives involving the English. Edward, for his part, did not respond to the archbishop's general offer of service until eighteen years later.

Siegfried played only a minor role in Edward I's 1294–98 campaign against France, the last in the series of failed English military ventures on the continent during the thirteenth century. In 1293 a break in peaceful relations between England and France occurred as a result of a feud between Norman and English merchants along the coast of Gascony.[91] Philip IV called Edward, as his vassal for Gascony, to appear before the French Parliament and answer for the English merchants' behavior. Edward naturally refused, and Philip promptly declared him forfeit of his Gascon lands. In response Edward devised a two-pronged military venture against France to enforce his Gascon rights. A defensive operation was planned for Gascony, while Edward himself would fight alongside a sizable coalition of continental magnates arrayed against Philip from the north. Anthony Bek, bishop of Durham, advised the king to buy these continental allies, in particular the new German king, Adolf of Nassau, and the archbishop of Cologne, along with the king of Aragon and the counts of Savoy and Burgundy.[92] The strategy seemed promising, since Edward had recently married his daughters to important lower Rhenish princes and therefore a kinship network existed on which to build an anti-Capetian coalition.[93]

Bishop Bek played a central role in forming the strategy of this ill-fated scheme, which hearkened back to that of Richard I but was fashioned

---

90. *REK*, 3, 2:83, no. 2687. Wenemar eventually redeemed the castle and sold it in 1282 to an enemy of the archbishop. Siegfried later besieged the castle for two months before capturing and destroying it in March 1284 (*REK*, 3, 2:138–39, no. 3013).

91. Prestwich, *Edward I*, 377–400.

92. *The Chronicle of Pierre de Langtoft*, ed. T. Wright, RS, no. 47 (London, 1866–88), 2:200–204.

93. Margaret had married John of Brabant on July 8, 1290, and Eleanor married Count Henry III of Bar in September 1293. Elisabeth would also marry Count John I of Holland on January 1, 1297. Although these marriages were not originally directed against the French king (since the engagements were contracted during a period when Edward and Philip were on good terms), they were kinship ties that now could be called on.

under considerably different political circumstances. He was sent during the early summer of 1294, along with Archbishop John of Dublin, Hugh Despenser, Nicholas Segrave, and Count Florence of Holland, to negotiate with King Adolf and Archbishop Siegfried.[94] Adolf proved at first quite willing to join Edward's adventure, since he was concerned about the eastward expansion of Capetian influence. Archbishop Siegfried of Cologne and Count Florence of Holland represented the German king at negotiations in Dordrecht, and a settlement was quickly reached by August 10.[95] Adolf was promised a subsidy of forty thousand pounds by Christmas of the same year and a further payment of twenty thousand pounds when Edward began the planned campaign. Both monarchs promised to join their armies at a date and location still to be determined and to remain allies until a positive conclusion was reached in the campaign.

Archbishop Siegfried's interest in joining the coalition was, however, purely monetary in nature. The Anglo-Cologne diplomatic connection had by now become a mercenary relationship in which the cash-strapped archbishop was only one of several German princes offering military contingents for sale. He was motivated by the prospect of English money for the advancement of his territorial interests rather than by any sense of personal ties to the English court and its cause: *Geldpolitik* and *Territorialpolitik* were the foundations of Siegfried's *Englandpolitik*.[96] Siegfried's own envoys, the brothers Eustace and Gerlach de Pomerio (the former a knight, the latter a canon of the Marienkapelle in Aachen), were commissioned by Edward to receive the archbishop's oath and were provided six thousand marks to give Siegfried in exchange. The archbishop committed

---

94. *Treaty Rolls*, 89–90, nos. 212–14; MGH Const., 3:489–90, nos. 509–10; *REK*, 3, 2:212–13, no. 3420. A general letter of credence was issued for these envoys, and two particular letters were directed to King Adolf of Nassau and Archbishop Siegfried of Cologne (Westminster, June 20, 1294). For the details of this coalition see Bock, "Englands Beziehungen"; Samanek, "Der angebliche Verrat Adolfs von Nassau"; Barraclough, "Edward I and Adolf of Nassau."

95. MGH Const., 3:490–92, no. 511; *REK*, 3, 2:213, no. 3422. Siegfried's copy of this agreement resides now at the Historisches Archiv der Stadt Köln (no. 3/599). Adolf confirmed this treaty on August 21, 1294, in Nuremburg (MGH Const., 3:492–94, nos. 512–13), and Edward did so on October 22 at Westminster (*Rymer*, 2:659–61). Siegfried was a natural choice to represent King Adolf at the negotiations, both because of Cologne's traditional ties to England and because Adolf owed his election to Siegfried: see Trautz, *Die Könige*, 133.

96. Franz-Reiner Erkens, *Siegfried von Westerburg (1274–1297): Die Rechts -und Territorialpolitik eines Kölner Erzbischofs im ausgehenden 13. Jahrhundert*, Rheinisches Archiv, no. 114 (Bonn, 1982) 368–69.

himself to send an army for six months in support of Edward—the army was to be composed of one thousand mounted men, of which three hundred were to be knights—in exchange for ten thousand marks to be paid in full by Christmas 1294 and the promise of an additional two thousand pounds at a later date.[97]

Similar costly purchases of six-month military commitments secured the services of such magnates as the duke of Brabant, the counts of Bar, Guelders, and Katzenellenbogen, and the lords of Cuyk and Montjoye/Falkenburg.[98] Capetian pressure prevented the valuable count of Flanders from also joining, and Count Florence of Holland, although promised eighty thousand livres, fell away from the coalition as a result of the favor Edward showed the duke of Brabant (the king's son-in-law). Support from the counties of Flanders and Holland (acquired by the pressure of an economic embargo on wool exports to Flanders and by a marriage

---

97. *Treaty Rolls,* 105, no. 247; *REK,* 3, 2:215, no. 3433; 3, 2:334–35, no. 3433a; *Acta Imperii Angliae et Franciae,* 64, no. 89 (Westminster, November 12, 1294); *CCLR Edward I,* 3:376 (dated the same). For more details on this treaty see the PRO King's Remembrancer Memoranda Roll 70, m. 24a (= Lord Treasurer's Remembrancer Memoranda Roll 68, m. 38b), King's Remembrancer Memoranda Roll 70, m. 101b: "De obligacione archiepiscopi Coloni mittenda ad Scaccarium" (May 15, 1297). For further payments made to Siegfried and other allies of Edward I see Pipe Rolls 144, m. 31; 146, m. 54. The exchequer account of Robert de Segre for the period November 1294–November 1295 (text published in Bock, "Englands Beziehungen," 252) indicates payments of the original ten thousand marks and two additional payments totaling 3700 pounds. In addition Siegfried's brother received 100 pounds and his nephew 60 pounds during this year.

Edward had written Siegfried on November 6, informing him of the plans for a future meeting of Adolf's forces with his own. This letter must then have been brought to the archbishop by his own vassals, the brothers Eustace de Pomerio and the canon Master Gerlach of Aachen, who were sent to receive the archbishop's oath. These two brothers served as the messengers between Cologne and Westminster during the entire period of this alliance, and it may very well be that they had served Richard of Cornwall during his kingship, since they seem so well known at the English court: see *Treaty Rolls,* 103, no. 241; *REK,* 3, 2:214, no. 3430 (London, November 6, 1294). In the following year, Edward informed Siegfried of the delay in these secret plans to join armies: see *Treaty Rolls,* 109, no. 255; *REK,* 3, 2:217–18, no. 3448 (Llanfaes, April 28, 1295). The letter issued to King Adolf (*Treaty Rolls,* 109, no. 254) was also sent from Llanfaes, where Edward was busied with the Welsh revolt. Hence he asked the king to delay their appointed meeting date from the Feast of St. John the Baptist (June 24) to the middle or end of August.

98. *Treaty Rolls,* 106, no. 249; *REK,* 3, 2:217, no. 3445 (Conway, April 6, 1295). Archbishop Siegfried must have gained Count Rainald of Guelders' participation, since he and his vassal Eustace de Pomerio (or de Gardinia) were present at Rainald's taking of the oath, and since Rainald promised as well not to wage war against either King Adolf or the archbishop of Cologne.

union with the new count of Holland) came only in 1297, when the venture was virtually stalled out.

The campaign, although supported by vast amounts of English money, never came to full fruition. A dangerous rebellion broke out in Wales that was not suppressed until 1295, and then Edward was forced to deal with John Balliol in Scotland the following year. Valuable time had been lost since the initial purchase of German allies, and by the time Edward finally began his futile Flemish gambit in 1297 the opportunity had passed for the coalition to function.[99] Edward's crises in Wales and Scotland, combined with the short-term allegiance of the German mercenary princes, assured that his grand plan was doomed to failure. In fact the majority of the fighting actually occurred only in Gascony. Because King Adolf (who faced his own increasing domestic political threats) failed to join Edward's contingent, and after the devastating news of the earl of Warenne's defeat at the hands of the Scots at Stirling Bridge, Edward was forced to seek a diplomatic way out. First an uneasy truce was arranged, and then the mediation of Pope Boniface VIII led to a final agreement at Montreuil in June 1299 that essentially restored the status quo ante.

Archbishop Siegfried never carried out his military obligation in exchange for the large amount of English sterling advanced to him. He died in Bonn on April 7, 1297, still awaiting the time when Edward would finally appear in Flanders (Edward did not arrive until August of that year).[100] His successor, Wickbold of Holte (1297–1304), was no stranger to English diplomacy. During Siegfried's pontificate Wickbold was both cathedral archdeacon in Cologne and provost in Aachen. He was consulted along with the archbishop during these years and was given the titles of *familiaris* and *secretarius* by Edward I[101]—the latter title was

---

99. By this time, for instance, a dispute had broken out between Archbishop Siegfried and the duke of Brabant over the money that was intended for the archbishop. In an attempt to hold the fragile coalition together Edward sent Bishop Walter of Coventry/Lichfield, Otto of Grandison, and Wymburne canon John de Berwick to Siegfried to settle this dispute, assure the archbishop of his money, and meet with the other coalition partners in preparation for the arrival of the English army (*Treaty Rolls*, 178, no. 433, and 179–80, nos. 435–45; *REK*, 3, 2:225–26, nos. 3503–6; *Rymer*, 2:751–55). They also were empowered to negotiate a peace treaty with France with the aid of the cardinals in Rome (*Treaty Rolls*, 181, no. 446). Edward's Flemish campaign took place between the months of August 1297 and March 1298, but Archbishop Siegfried had died in April 1297.

100. *REK*, 3, 2:230, no. 3535.

101. *Treaty Rolls*, 102, no. 237; *REK*, 3, 2:215, no. 3432; *Rymer*, 2:662 (Tower of London, November 7, 1294).

given only to the most trusted and faithful counselors of the king and was one that Archbishop Siegfried received as well.[102] Wickbold was even promised a prebend in the church of Dublin (set at the value of between eighty and one hundred marks),[103] yet it appears that he never received it despite a subsequent reminder of the offer to Edward.[104] Since Wickbold was elected archbishop later that year, the matter became moot. Yet despite such intimate diplomatic relations, once Wickbold entered into his pontificate there is no further evidence of close contact between him and the English court. As soon as he had local and regional archiepiscopal matters to be concerned with he too lost interest in further joint ventures with the English royal house.

Although Edward had been drawn into this conflict by Philip IV, the entire military venture proved to be the most unsuccessful of his reign. In the fashion of Richard of Cornwall, Edward had only a record of massive payments to continental princes to show for his efforts. The debt incurred as a result of the 1294–98 war with France was as follows: the defense of Gascony cost approximately 256,000 pounds and the continental coalition about 165,000 pounds (although some 250,000 pounds had originally been promised). When the cost of the Flanders campaign (another 50,000 pounds) is figured in, a total of 480,000 pounds were spent, with roughly 34 percent going to the German princes.[105] Edward learned the hard way that by this point in time the political interests of the northwestern German magnates and the English monarchy were too divergent to revive the age-old monetary diplomacy of Richard I. Gone were the days when the political needs and concerns of the two regions could be naturally intertwined. Although money fiefs could still get the attention of continental princes, they were not enough of a force to bind them to an effective coalition with England or to maintain any lasting diplomatic relationship. The political communities of Germany and England had moved, therefore, in different directions. The English magnates increasingly resisted "foreign" ventures on the continent, while German barons likewise concentrated on their local and regional affairs within the German kingdom. France and Italy ceased to be common grounds for Anglo-

---

102. L. B. Dibben, "Secretaries in the Thirteenth and Fourteenth Centuries," *EHR* 25 (1910): 430–44.

103. *CPR Edward I*, 3:103 (Tower of London, November 6, 1294).

104. *Treaty Rolls*, 179, no. 434; *Rymer*, 2:755–56; *REK*, 3, 2:225–26, no. 3505 (February 7, 1297).

105. Prestwich, *Edward I*, 399–400.

German diplomatic cooperation, since the German kings' desire to be emperors under the papal crown faded with each passing year and since the English kings found the old Angevin lands beyond their reach.

One could say that in the long run the traditional social rights of inheritance had won out. The hereditary rights of the noble houses outlasted royal claims to hereditary sovereignty in Germany, and the hereditary rights of the English nobility survived Plantagenet dynastic claims to sovereignty in France. In the years 1337–41 Edward III would once again try to ply the German princes with a liberal distribution of money fiefs to gain their aid against the French king, but the results were the same as in the ventures of Richard of Cornwall and Edward I. His only reward was the empty title of imperial vicar given to him by Emperor Ludwig. Diplomatic relations between England and Germany in the fourteenth century could certainly be considered a vicarious relationship.[106] By that century it had become clear that the real tie that bound the regions together was no longer the old political communities but the new economic forces: the era of the Hanse was dawning.[107] Now the burghers of Cologne, rather than their archbishop, would dominate their city and region; the archbishop's customary rights had been curtailed significantly by these very representatives of an ever expanding world of interregional urban commerce. The interests and power of the newer commercial communities had begun their gradual ascendancy over the interests and power of the traditional medieval political communities of England and Germany as the cohesive force for interregional cooperation.

---

106. In 1348 some of the German elector-princes offered Edward III the German crown so that he might serve as an antiking to Charles (IV) of Bohemia, but Edward's brother-in-law, Margrave William of Jülich, convinced him there was no future in his candidacy and so he rejected the offer. In the 1390s Richard II was considered as a possible replacement for Charles's incompetent son Wenceslas. Richard II's marriage to Anne of Bohemia (the sister of Wenceslas) made this an obviously inappropriate option, however. When their eventual candidate, Rupert, died in 1410 the name of the Lancastrian Henry IV was floated for a time among the electors. Thus the English royal house remained a popular option for wealthy but distant candidates after Richard of Cornwall, but the English princes had clearly learned something from their predecessor.

107. See Horst Buszello, "Köln und England (1468–1509)," *Köln, Das Reich und Europa, MSAK* 60 (1971): 431–67. For the commercial aspects of royal elections during the thirteenth century see Stehkämper, "Geld bei deutschen Köningswahlen."

Conclusion: Reflections on the Nature of Political Life and Interregional Diplomatic Activity during the Central Middle Ages

Now that we have considered the roughly 250 years of interregional diplomatic relations between England and Germany during the Central Middle Ages, some general conclusions are in order. Firstly, taken as a whole, the history of these relations is one of false starts and near misses. In essence, neither party shared similar political goals, and they were not often in position to aid each other in their respective affairs. This stands in remarkable contrast, though, to the extent of diplomatic and dynastic ties that were established between the regions during this period. Although the results of these contacts cannot be considered fruitful, they cannot be said to have been insignificant or marginal either.

Secondly, the modern notion of geopolitical and international alliances, which has characterized most studies on Anglo-German diplomatic relations to date, is an anachronistic means of interpreting medieval politics.[1] Concepts such as balance of power, and state and empire building may have a place in the era of Bismarck, Victoria, and pre–World War II Europe, but they do not reflect the conditions under which political communities interacted during the Middle Ages. Rather, medieval political affairs revolved around domestic concerns of a given political community, and any foreign diplomatic or dynastic relationship served to enhance the noble family's prestige and to gain means (such as large dowries) for achieving local and territorial goals. Indeed this very dynamic prevented Anglo-German diplomatic relations from achieving a long-lasting result, since both parties had such different internal interests.

---

1. Important exceptions are Trautz's *Die Könige* and Ahlers's *Die Welfen.*

Anglo-Norman/Salian diplomatic relations never developed beyond a general contact, as the respective monarchs were busied with internal affairs. Henry IV and Henry V were embroiled in the Investiture Controversy and its resulting civil war and thus were politically isolated from the western kingdoms, while William the Conqueror and his heirs concentrated on consolidating power in their new kingdom. So different were their concerns that each kingdom eventually reached separate settlements with the papacy concerning investiture; not even the shared dispute with the papacy provided a common cause to rally around.

The first half of the twelfth century saw a continuation of this distant diplomatic relationship. Henry V focused on reaching a settlement with the papacy and consolidating his lordship in Germany. His marriage to the English princess Matilda provided him with a large dowry with which to accomplish these goals but did not result in lasting ties of affinity between the two ruling houses. Nor did it provide any military support for Henry I against France. The period from 1125 to 1152 was one of virtual silence as far as diplomatic ties are concerned. In Germany Lothar III and Conrad III spent their energies trying to overcome civil war and consolidate some measure of lordship in their realm. Likewise in England the chaos of Stephen's reign left little room for diplomatic initiatives toward the empire.

Angevin-Staufen relations represented an era of renewed contact, although the fruits of this interaction were few. Frederick I remained politically isolated because of the papal schism, and his attention was fixed on regaining imperial prerogatives in Italy. Henry II embarked as well on a restoration of royal rights after the confusing years of Stephen's reign, and he too became embroiled in conflict with ecclesiastical authority. Yet neither of these commonalities drew the monarchs together, despite the aggressive efforts of Rainald of Dassel to arrange a double-marriage union and use the Becket controversy to move Henry II against Pope Alexander III. Instead Henry II skillfully employed the threat of joining the imperial side and wrung domestic concessions from the pope. Once again the emperor's breach with the papacy and the attention of both rulers to important internal affairs prevented two of the greatest monarchs of the Middle Ages from ever establishing a mutually advantageous diplomatic relationship.

In 1177, after the Peace of Venice, Frederick I extricated himself from political isolation and began an initiative toward the West. Yet here he was to take a new direction that in the long run created another hindrance to close Anglo-imperial relations: he began a rapprochement with the Capetian house that would be continued by his Staufen successors. Furthermore, the fall of the Welf Henry the Lion became another hurdle to Angevin-Staufen relations; but there was never a threat of an Anglo-Welf alliance directed against the emperor, and the hurdle was eventually overcome. Matters were further complicated, though, after Henry the Lion's fall from power, when many German princes in northwest Germany began to align themselves increasingly with English interests. This was done not only because of anti-Staufen sentiment and the new fear of Capetian intervention against them but also because of the growing importance of trade relations between this area and England. Cologne and its archbishop led the way in the region, following a pro-English policy for both of these reasons. As Frederick focused his attention on Italy the new dynamic of increasingly independent German territorial princes would continue to alter the nature of Anglo-German diplomatic relations during the remainder of the period under study here.

Frederick's son, Henry VI, was left to deal with his father's unfinished business upon Barbarossa's sudden death while on crusade. Henry centered his reign on two endeavors: consolidating his kingship in Germany and enforcing his claim to the kingdom of Sicily. The combination naturally aroused the opposition of both the German princes and the papacy. Meanwhile Richard I patched up his dispute with Philip II of France only long enough to go on crusade and become embroiled in other controversies that ultimately led to his capture and imprisonment at the hands of Henry VI. This timely event provided Henry with the means to address his two main goals: a massive ransom to pay for a campaign against Tancred in Sicily, and alliance with a monarch whose friendly ties with the princes of the Welf-Rhineland opposition could help to settle Henry's conflict in Germany. These were both internal matters for Henry and not part of a strategy to involve himself in some sort of international alliance structure. The Staufer monarch skillfully used the threat of Philip II's offers to gain Richard's intercession with the troublesome princes of the Rhine (the archbishop of Cologne among them) and gained the financial means to wage war against Tancred as well.

Richard did not return empty-handed to England, however. He strengthened his personal ties with the princes of the lower Rhineland, many of whom worked for his release from captivity, and through money fiefs he established a series of mercenary vassals who would later be called on to assist against the French king. He was unable to make use of this strategy during the brief remainder of his reign, which was spent attempting to reestablish his lordship in the Angevin territories after a long period of Capetian meddling during his absence. Germany had now been decisively drawn into the world of diplomatic affairs in western Europe. Henry VI, for his part, concentrated on Mediterranean matters, shifting the attention of Staufen emperors away from Germany even more thoroughly than had his father. Henry's early death left Germany in a state of political confusion from which it would take twenty years to recover. During these two decades diplomatic cooperation between the English court and a number of German princes (the archbishop of Cologne, the other magnates of the lower Rhineland, and the Welf dynasty specifically) intensified to a level unknown before or after.

The result of this close cooperation was the kingship of Otto IV. During the civil war between partisans of the Welf and the Staufen candidates (Philip of Swabia and Frederick II) two important developments emerged. Firstly, the process of regionalization was hastened, a process in which the imperial magnates became territorial princes and German kingship was limited. This would complicate future diplomacy between England and Germany, since each German prince increasingly pursued his own independent diplomacy. Therefore, achieving some measure of consensus among the princes was a most vexing proposition. Secondly, other western European political communities were now drawn into the conflict over the German throne. Not only the papacy, a traditional participant in such disputes, but also the English and French courts were involved, each supporting their own candidate. The Staufen house remained linked to the Capetians, and the Welf house was dependent on its Plantagenet kinsmen. This was the closest thing to what one could call some sort of international alliance system in the modern sense, yet it bore quite medieval characteristics: dynastic and personal ties rather than geopolitical or ideological reasons as the foundation of the coalition, poor coordination of execution, constant vacillating of magnates from side to side depending on incentives, and a series of brief, intermittent campaigns without decisive results.

After the ultimate collapse of the Anglo-Welf coalition, which was actually never well coordinated or strongly and consistently supported by King John, a long period of distant diplomatic ties between England and Germany ensued. Frederick II, mindful of the support he had received from the Capetians during the civil war, remained sympathetic toward the French monarch. Yet he restricted his energies to the reunification of the Sicilian and German kingdoms: Frederick never assisted the Capetians in an invasion of Plantagenet-held territories, nor did he become involved in the Albigensian crusade. Any direct involvement by Frederick II in the affairs of western Europe remained distant. When the possibility of a marriage union with the Capetian house was actually considered by Frederick, Archbishop Engelbert of Cologne, among others, created enough interference that the emperor eventually chose an Austrian princess instead for his son. This began a period in which the archbishops of Cologne, driven by their own territorial exigencies, would try unsuccessfully to fashion a marriage union between the Plantagenet house and a German prince.

Only Frederick II himself brought such a union about, when he took the English princess Isabella as his wife. Once again we cannot consider this marriage as some sort of geopolitical move on Frederick's part. He simply needed a young princess of royal stature capable of bearing children, and Pope Gregory IX required that she come from a ruling house that was loyal to the papacy. Furthermore, Frederick needed a large dowry to finance his planned campaign against the Italian cities. These needs were all typically medieval, being dynastic and territorial in nature. Isabella was chosen because she met all these requirements, not because she was a means of forging an anti-Capetian policy with the English ruling house. Once again we see the familiar pattern: a hopeful beginning to close Anglo-imperial diplomatic relations was cut short, not primarily by the death of Isabella, but, as before, by renewed discord between pope and emperor. Frederick's second papal excommunication and deposition were recognized by the papal vassal Henry III, who realized that Frederick was therefore in no position to provide him with support against Louis IX. Although the English court seems initially to have expected such assistance, Frederick himself never made such a formal commitment as part of the marriage agreement. Frederick, for his part, gained little political benefit through the Plantagenet marriage union. Henry did intercede diplomatically before the Curia on the emperor's behalf, but the English king's loyalty to Frederick was always subordinated to the interests of the papacy. Precisely this made the Plantagenets diplomatically useless to Frederick. Here again the lack of shared political interests and needs dashed a promising opportunity for closer relations. Both monarchs were not seeking involvement in a foreign alliance scheme in the modern sense; rather, they were concentrating on pressing internal affairs. Frederick's energies were focused on maintaining his claims in Sicily, while Henry's were focused on maintaining his claims in Gascony; and each hoped in vain that the other would lend assistance.

Since Frederick II based his power in Sicily, the development of independent territorial principalities continued unabated in Germany. At his death these princes, the archbishop of Cologne foremost among them, ushered in the last phase of medieval politics relevant to this study. Here they assured their independence and territorial power by electing candidates whose political authority in Germany ranked far below their personal wealth. Richard of Cornwall's kingship was a prime example of this policy, which completed the transformation of Anglo-German diplomatic relations into a mercenary activity. Henry III's grand dynastic plan to place his son and brother on royal thrones only resulted in the expenditure of vast sums of English money to German princes and in the imposition of the Provisions of Oxford by the English barons.

Such a change in the nature of Anglo-German diplomatic relations, compounded as it was by the independent foreign policy of each German prince, made the management of interregional diplomacy exponentially complex. The large sums of English money distributed by Edward I (and again later by Edward III) were finally unable to meld the divergent political agendas of the German and English political communities into one shared objective. In fact Edward's attempt at reconstructing the coalition scheme originally envisioned by Richard I was as poorly coordinated and implemented as had been King John's earlier undertaking with Otto IV. In both cases the planned joint military venture against Capetian France was continually delayed by domestic political exigencies, which ultimately derailed the coalition's intended effectiveness. Thus numerous attempts at a coordinated political coalition between England and Germany were constantly frustrated because the two communities shared few common interests and because neither had the timely opportunity to assist the other in internal affairs. By the early fourteenth century the radically different worlds of the two political communities made any combined diplomatic coalition between them impractical and anachronistic—indeed one could even say irrelevant.

The failure of any lasting political coalitions between England and Germany should not, however, be seen as merely a series of failed attempts at establishing an international alliance scheme solely directed against France and/or the papacy. As has been said before, such notions result from forcing modern geopolitical concepts onto a medieval culture. A study of Anglo-imperial diplomatic relations instead presents an exemplary history of the nature of medieval politics. Any geographically extended kingdom or coalition of kingdoms was exceedingly difficult to maintain and coordinate. Staufen efforts at maintaining a multiregnal entity met with continual frustration, as did Angevin efforts at enforcing their lordship on the continent, in Wales, and in Scotland, and as did Angevin domestic struggles with the English nobility.[2] This was not a history of failures in "empire building" in the modern sense but rather evidence of how impossible it was in the Middle Ages to enforce one's personal lordship over vast territories. The lesson of Charlemagne's empire was to be relearned time and again. The momentum of particularism and local/regional rebellion constantly worked against the process of centralization. Particularism was victorious in Germany and was gradually overcome in England only after the distant continental lands were finally lost.

Furthermore, these monarchs were not engaged in international intrigue but rather sought to enforce their lordship and dynastic claims in territories that were *within* their realms. In fact it was necessary attention to the needs of internal or domestic affairs that constantly hindered coordinated efforts and policies between the English and the German monarchs. They sought ties with each other for dynastic, economic, and diplomatic reasons that served their domestic needs rather than the needs of imperialistic foreign adventures. It is important to remember that English and imperial armies never fought against a common enemy (in particular France) on foreign soil except on crusade. Finally it should be said that Anglo-imperial diplomatic relations, for all their unfulfilled expectations, often functioned as a crucial dynamic in Anglo-French and papal-imperial struggles. Although they did not accomplish much in and of themselves, they did contribute significantly to the outcomes of these other two, more traditionally studied interregional political relationships. Seeing medieval Anglo-French and papal-imperial politics from the perspective of the Anglo-imperial connection gives us a new

---

2. John Gillingham, "The Fall of the Angevin Empire," in *England and Europe, 1066–1453*, ed. Nigel Saul (New York, 1994), 91: "In trying to rule the whole Angevin empire, John was trying to hold together lands which did not yet automatically belong together. The empire was a recent creation. It had been cobbled together in a series of succession disputes, and it was quite on the cards that another succession dispute would pull it apart again." Timothy Reuter, "The Medieval German *Sonderweg?*" in *Kings and Kingship in Medieval Europe,* ed. Anne J. Duggan, King's College London Medieval Studies, no. 10 (London, 1993), 199: "The *regnum Teutonicum* under Barbarossa was easily twice the size of the kingdom effectively ruled by Louis VII, while Henry II's England or Normandy were hardly larger than a single German duchy. Given the techniques of government available in the high middle ages it is difficult to suppose that the *Reich* could have been ruled in a more intensive fashion for any length of time."

angle on the European diplomatic scene and on the nature of political life during the Central Middle Ages.

By now it should be clear why this study of Anglo-imperial diplomatic relations places special emphasis on Cologne and its archbishops— namely, because the Anglo-Cologne connection was exemplary of the history of Anglo-German diplomatic relations as a whole. Archbishop Frederick I of Cologne was involved in the early diplomatic contacts established between the two regions as a result of Henry V's marriage to Matilda in 1114. After a long lull caused by the civil wars of the early twelfth century, Rainald of Dassel was the mastermind behind the reestablishment of diplomatic ties between the emperor and the English court. Indeed he was more responsible for reviving and sustaining these ties than were either Frederick Barbarossa or Henry II. Yet much to his chagrin Rainald discovered that neither monarch had any real common ground on which to build an alliance. Philip of Heinsberg played an important role in the fall and restoration of the Welf Henry the Lion, whose restoration created yet another opportunity for renewing diplomatic ties between the Plantagenet and Staufen rulers. Adolf of Altena played the Anglo-Welf dynastic relationship to his advantage, as the broker of Otto IV's kingship.

After the failure of the Anglo-Welf venture, Archbishop Engelbert I of Berg revived the long-dormant Anglo-imperial connection in an effort to counterbalance a growing Capetian influence in his region. This effort failed too, as had all the previous attempts; nonetheless it was yet another archbishop of Cologne who authored the initiative. After the death of Engelbert I, Anglo-Cologne diplomatic relations took on a new, more mercenary look under the pontificates of his successors: Conrad of Hochstaden, Engelbert II of Falkenburg, and Siegfried of Westerburg. These three archbishops no longer considered the traditional Anglo-Cologne connection a decisive element in their territorial politics. Rather, their attention was turned toward the strengthening of their own principality, and commitments to either England or the empire became secondary. After a history of false starts in the forging of a lasting diplomatic bond between England and the empire, the need for the Cologne archbishops to continue pursuing this goal had finally ended. Both the Staufen and Angevin empires had ceased to exist as unified forces by the end of the thirteenth century, and therefore the mutual needs of the archbishops and the English kings became negligible. Only offers of English money continued to induce the archbishops to side with the Plantagenets. After Richard of Cornwall's purchased kingship and Edward I's purchased coalition scheme the transformation of Anglo-Cologne diplomatic relations was complete. The archbishops of Cologne, who were the closest of the continental allies of the English and who were the traditional mediators of English interests in Germany for over two centuries, had become merely one of several mercenary princes whose services could be bought at the right price. Of course English diplomacy had created and nurtured this mercenary relationship through the use of money fiefs since the reign of Richard I.

Close diplomatic ties with England had become unnecessary for the archbishop of Cologne by the early fourteenth century. He was securely established as a powerful territorial prince in Germany and no longer needed the English as a means of gaining or preserving such power.[3] Furthermore, the end of English control over regions in northern France limited its strategic value to the archbishop. Finally, Cologne's dominance in German trade with England also came to an end at this time. Therefore the archbishop had less incentive to nurture this valuable economic connection than he had had before. Hence by the end of the thirteenth century the archbishop of Cologne had as little in common with England as had the emperors of the previous centuries. His territorial needs prevented him any longer from service to the English crown for the advancement of English interests on the continent. Just as Henry III and Frederick II found themselves increasingly estranged after the passing of Isabella, who was so triumphantly received in Cologne, so too the archbishops of that city saw the diminution of their ties to England after the era of mutual interests had come to an end.

So much for the leitmotiv of Anglo-German diplomacy during the Central Middle Ages. What new perspective does this story open up for our understanding of the nature of medieval political life? In essence it is one that considers political deeds as fundamentally social activities *within* a given political community rather than as institutional or constitutional acts. Accordingly diplomacy is the social discourse *between* political communities. Historians have long been comfortable with the social dimensions of dynastic politics in feudal Europe when studying *Familienpolitik* in the context of local or regional communities. But this perspective is

---

3. It should be remembered that the archbishop's territorial powers were not only gained through the use of English money but also confirmed through the royal charters of Richard of Cornwall. Cf. Wand, "Die Englandpolitik der Stadt Köln," 95: "With the help of England the Cologne archbishops had raised their territory to the strongest principality [Partikularmacht] in the empire."

generally not applied to *Familienpolitik* when it occurs on an inter-regional basis between houses of different political communities. Then it becomes political history in the traditional sense, complete with "foreign" relations and military "alliances." This is because modern political and intellectual boundaries have been superimposed on medieval social categories when it comes to "national histories." The concept of inter-regional *Familienpolitik* is appropriate, however, in an age of increasing interregional activity and integration between political communities as occurred during the Central Middle Ages. The so-called Interregnum of Richard of Cornwall's kingship has a much different ambience when considered in the light of its interregional social (e.g., dynastic) aspects rather than in an institutional or constitutional manner. From a social point of reference we are constantly reminded of the contingent nature of medieval politics, based as it was on the social fabric of political communities vulnerable to the vagaries of death, disease, inheritance, and religious scruples. This is not the stuff of impersonal institutions that develop inexorably toward modernity.

Perhaps most importantly, when we look at medieval politics as a social rather than an institutional phenomenon, the German and English kingdoms do not look so markedly different. We ought to reevaluate the often cited notion of Germany's *Sonderweg*, given that both kingdoms shared the characteristics of itinerant kingship, limited monarchy, powerful archbishops, multiregnal territories, intervention by the papacy, and by the thirteenth century a growing reticence on the part of their respective noblemen to participate in "foreign" campaigns beyond their own community for the sake of their monarch's prestige. Indeed, we can see parallels in the success of the nobility and clergy to enforce their hereditary rights over those of the kings' claims to sovereignty. Although the English monarchy succeeded in maintaining hereditary rule over elective kingship, it was nonetheless a limited kingship that recognized legal restrictions to power in favor of ancestral aristocratic rights. In this respect Frederick II's *Statutum in favorem principum* (1231) and John's *Magna Carta* (1215) share much in common.[4]

4. Keller, *Zwischen regionaler Begrenzung und universalem Horizont*, 490. David A. Carpenter ("England in the Twelfth and Thirteenth Centuries, in *England and Germany in the High Middle Ages*, ed. Alfred Haverkamp and Hanna Vollrath [Oxford and New York, 1996], 125) concludes: "England had not divided into semi-independent principalities on the German model. But the great magnates had achieved the same results by different means."

The histories of the German and English political communities exemplify the fragility of institutional achievements based on the shifting
realities of dynastic marriages; interregional ties disturbed by competing regional interests; personal ties cut short by death, rebellion, religious scruples, and schism; and so forth. Such domestic political
exigencies were exponentially more complex in the sphere of interregional diplomacy between these political communities. Hopefully,
then, this study has helped to show that medieval Germany was not so
different from the other kingdoms of western Europe and thus needs to
be more integrated into the fabric of medieval studies in Anglophone
scholarship.[5]

A social history approach to German political history in particular
reminds us that the lack of a centralized government in medieval Germany should be mourned only by those whose modern institutional expectations have been frustrated and not by those seeking to grasp actual
medieval realities.[6] It is hard to fault medieval Germany for a decline in
the centralized, institutionalized state, since one never existed in the first
place. Karl Leyser has rightly pointed out that even as powerful a monarch as Frederick Barbarossa, whose imperial government was as developed as that of the Capetians, ruled essentially through social rather than
institutional means.[7] Hence German political history in general and
Anglo German diplomatic history in particular are not stories of failure
in the modern sense of institutional political history but rather reminders
of the contingent and personal nature of medieval society and politics.
Study of medieval Germany broadens a medievalist's understanding of
the medieval political community and its social dimensions. Medieval

5. For example, see Haverkamp's chapter "Germany in the Context of Europe" in
Medieval Germany, 352–63.

6. Susan Reynolds, *Kingdoms and Communities in Western Europe, 900–1300,* 2d ed.
(Oxford, 1997), 289: "Nationalist teleology is a poor guide to the values of the past." D. J. A.
Matthew, "Reflections on the Medieval Roman Empire," *History* 77, no. 251 (October
1992): 363–90: "Studying the unification of the western nations has become a modern
historical obsession, but in the Middle Ages rulers and subjects had other preoccupations."

7. K. Leyser, "Frederick Barbarossa: Court and Country," in *Communications and
Power in Medieval Europe: The Gregorian Revolution and Beyond,* 148: "The governmen-
tal actions of Frederick Barbarossa were for the most part a chain of sporadic dispute-
settlements and displays of favour. They acquired their coherence not through governmen-
tal technique but through the social centre from which they proceeded [e.g., the imperial
assemblies]." Leyser has shown also that Barbarossa's curia was comparable to that of the
Capetians: see his "Frederick Barbarossa and the Hohenstaufen Polity," *Viator* 19 (1988):
156, 159.

Germany was not so much of a political aberration in Europe as is often suggested.[8]

In this social context the archbishops of Cologne appear not as destroyers of German constitutional unity but as typical medieval noblemen. The office of archbishop fell under the control of local aristocratic dynasties through the cathedral chapter, and the holders of the archiepiscopate accordingly behaved in usual dynastic fashion when building a territorial principality to fill the increasing void of imperial influence north of the Alps. It was in turn the resistance of the Cologne burghers and local comital families that eventually limited the archbishop's regional power. Hence the opportunities for interregional diplomatic activity between Germany and England were constantly conditioned by the political struggles of the archbishop of Cologne's local and regional political communities.

Ultimately this study is a call to reevaluate the intentions and motivations we ascribe to medieval political figures and to reconsider whether we ought to privilege those who look more modern than their contemporaries. This has major significance for how Anglophone historiography chooses either to include medieval Germany as a normative community in European history or to exclude it as an anomaly. The story of medieval Anglo-German diplomacy reveals that diplomatic intentions and motivations were based much more on medieval social categories than on modern political goals.[9] It looks more like a social history of familial and personal coalitions held together by personal ties of kinship and lordship

---

8. Timothy Reuter, "The Medieval German *Sonderweg?*" 210–11: "The German rulers were not alone in ruling over a polycentric realm, or in having to cooperate with their leading men; it is only because rulers elsewhere with hindsight seem to have been the drops around which the rain-clouds of the modern state could form that they have in anticipation been so readily invested with its qualities. . . . it is not just German historians who need a greater willingness to consider medieval rulership and politics as style rather than institution." John Gillingham insightfully explores this thesis in his article "Elective Kingship and the Unity of Medieval Germany," *German History: The Journal of the German History Society* 9 (1991): 124–35.

9. W. L. Warren put it superbly in *The Governance of Norman and Angevin England, 1086–1272* (Stanford, 1987), 1, when he wrote: "Nowadays we tend to think that the kind of society any state has is determined by the type of government it has. In the Middle Ages the type of government it was possible to have was largely determined by the kind of society over which it was trying to rule. Government was more about controlling and managing society than about changing it. It is true that government developed at the will of the enterprising rulers; but a successful ruler was like a gardener training an apple tree: he might prune and cut back, select and encourage, but he would work only with what was already there. It is proper to begin not with the structure of government but with the structure of society."

than a history of impersonal institutions, geopolitical alliances, and state building. But since we moderns find our identities in a state rather than in an estate, we tend to be disappointed that estate building defined medieval German political and diplomatic life more than did state building. Such a mentality has historically privileged Anglo-French forms of political development over the political development of central Europe, since those forms emerged from the Middle Ages with a centralized, rather than a polycentric, political structure. Yet a comparative sociohistorical (rather than a national and constitutional) approach to medieval Germany reveals that the *regnum Teutonicum* was not all that different from western European political communities in the ways that it maintained diplomatic relationships with western Europe and ultimately restricted royal power. When we peer over modern political and intellectual boundaries, we sometimes see that the "other" is more comprehensible than we thought.

Appendix: The Archbishops of Cologne

Bruno I of Saxony	953–65
Anno II	1056–75
Hildulf	1076–78
Sigewin	1079–89
Hermann III	1089–99
Frederick I	1100–1131
Bruno II of Berg	1132–37
Hugo of Sponheim	1137
Arnold I	1138–51
Arnold II of Wied	1151–56
Frederick II of Berg	1156–58
Rainald of Dassel	1159–67
Philip I of Heinsberg	1167–91
Bruno III of Berg	1191–93
Adolf I of Atena	1193–1205, suspended
Bruno IV of Sayn	1205–8
Dietrich I	1208–12, suspended
Adolf I of Altena	1212–16, reinstated
Engelbert I of Berg	1216–25
Henry I of Molenark	1225–38
Conrad of Hochstaden	1238–61
Engelbert II of Falkenburg	1261–74
Siegfried of Westerburg	1274–97
Wickbold of Holte	1297–1304
Henry II of Virneburg	1304–32

Select Bibliography

Primary Sources

Acta Imperii Angliae et Franciae ab anno 1267 ad annum 1313: Dokumente Vornehmlich zur Geschichte der Auswärtigen Beziehungen Deutschlands. Ed. Fritz Kern. Tübingen, 1911.

Acta Imperii Inedita Saeculi XIII et XIV. Ed. Edward Winkelmann. 2 vols. Innsbruck, 1880–85. Reprint, Aalen, 1964.

Acta Imperii Selecta: Urkunden Deutscher Könige und Kaiser 928–1398. Ed. J. F. Böhmer. Innsbruck, 1870. Reprint, Aalen, 1967.

Annales Cameracenses. Ed. G. Pertz. MGH SS, no. 16, 509–54. Hanover, 1859.

Annales de Burtonensis. Ed. Henry Richards Luard. RS, no. 36, 1:421–87. London, 1866. Reprint, 1965.

Annales de Dunstaplia. Ed. Henry Richards Luard. RS, no. 36, 3:3–420. London, 1866. Reprint, 1972.

Annales de Theokesberia. Ed. Henry Richards Luard. RS, no. 36, 1:43–182. London, 1864. Reprint, 1965.

Annales de Waverleia. Ed. Henry Richards Luard. RS, no. 36, 2:129–412. London, 1865. Reprint, 1971.

Annales de Wintonia. Ed. Henry Richards Luard. RS, no. 36, 2:3–128. London, 1865. Reprint, 1971.

Annales Hamburgenses. Ed. J. M. Lappenberg. MGH SS, no. 16, 380–85. Hanover, 1859.

Annales Herbipolenses. Ed. G. Pertz. MGH SS, no. 16, 1–12. Hanover, 1859.

Annales Hildesheimenses. Ed. G. Pertz. MGH SS, no. 3, 90–116. Hanover, 1839. Reprint, 1986.

Annales Magdeburgenses. Ed. G. Pertz. MGH SS, no. 16, 105–96. Hanover, 1859.

Annales Marbacenses. Ed. Herman Bloch. MGH SS rer. Germ., no. 9. Hanover, 1907. Reprint, 1979.

Annales Moguntini. Ed. G. Pertz. MGH SS, no. 17, 1–3. Hanover, 1861. Reprint, 1987.

Annales Palidenses. Ed. G. Pertz. MGH SS, no. 16, 48–98. Hanover, 1859.

Annales Pegavienses. Ed. G. Pertz. MGH SS, no. 16, 232–70. Hanover, 1859.

Annales Placentini Gibellini. Ed. G. Pertz. MGH SS, no. 18, 457–581. Hanover, 1863. Reprint, 1963.

Annales Sancti Disbodi. Ed. G. Waitz. MGH SS, no. 17, 4–30. Hanover, 1861. Reprint, 1987.

Annales Sancti Rudberti Salisburgensis. Ed. W. Wattenbach. MGH SS, no. 9, 758–810. Hanover, 1851. Reprint, 1983.

Anonymi Chronica Imperatorum Heinrico V dedicata. Ed. F. J. Schmale and I. Schmale-Ortt. Ausgewählte Quellen zur Deutschen Geschichte des Mittelalters, no. 15, Darmstadt, 1972.

Archiv für die Geschichte des Niederrheins. Ed. Theodor Josef Lacomblet. 7 vols. Düsseldorf and Cologne, 1832–69.

Arnold of Lübeck. *Chronica Slavorum.* Ed. J. M. Lappenberg. MGH SS rer. Germ., no. 14. Hanover, 1868. Reprint, 1978.

Barlow, Frank, ed. *The Letters of Arnulf of Lisieux.* Camden Society, 3d ser., no. 61. London, 1939.

Braunschweigische Reimchronik. Ed. L. Weiland. MGH Deutsche Chroniken, no. 2, 591, vv. 4770–816. Hanover, 1877.

Bresslau, H., ed. *Die Werke Wipos.* MGH SS rer. Germ., no. 61. Hanover and Leipzig, 1915. Reprint, Hanover, 1977.

Briefsammlung der Zeit Heinrichs IV. Ed. Carl Erdmann and Norbert Fickermann. MGH Epistolae: Die Briefe der deutschen Kaiserzeit, no. 5. Weimar, 1950.

Brunos Buch vom Sachsenkrieg. Ed. Hans-Eberhard Lohmann. MGH Deutsches Mittelalter, no. 2. Leipzig, 1937.

Caesarius of Heisterbach. *Dialogus Miraculorum.* Ed. Joseph Strange. 2 vols. Bonn and Brussels, 1851.

———. *Die Wundergeschichten des Caesarius von Heisterbach.* Ed. Alfons Hilka. 3 vols. PGRG, no. 43. Bonn, 1937.

Calendar of Inquisitions Miscellaneous (Chancery) Preserved in the Public Record Office. Vol. 1, *Henry III and Edward I.* London, 1916.

Calendar of Inquisitions Post Mortem and Other Analogous Documents Preserved in the Public Record Office. Vols. 1–4, *Henry III and Edward I.* London, 1904–13.

Calendar of Liberate Rolls Preserved in the Public Record Office: Henry III. 6 vols. London, 1916–64.

Calendar of Patent Rolls Preserved in the Public Record Office: Edward I. 4 vols. London, 1894–1901.

Calendar of Patent Rolls Preserved in the Public Record Office: Henry III. 6 vols. London, 1901–13.

Calendar of the Charter Rolls Preserved in the Public Record Office. 6 vols. London, 1903–27.

Calendar of the Close Rolls Preserved in the Public Record Office: Edward I. 5 vols. London, 1900–1908.

Calendar of the Close Rolls Preserved in the Public Record Office: Henry III. 14 vols. London, 1902–38.

Calendar of the Entries in the Papal Register relating to Great Britain and Ireland. Vol. 1, *1198–1304.* Ed. W. H. Bliss. London, 1893.

Calendar of the Fine Rolls Preserved in the Public Record Office. Vol. 1, *1272–1307.* London, 1911.

Calendarium rotulorum patentium in turri Londinensi. Ed. T. Astle and J. Caley. London, 1802.

Cartae Antiquae Rolls 11–20, The. Ed. J. Conway Davies. PR, NS, no. 33. London, 1960.

Chronica pontificum ecclesiae Eboracensis (The Historians of the Church of York and its Archbishops). Ed. James Raine. RS, no. 71. London, 1886. Reprint, 1965.

Chronica regia Coloniensis. Ed. G. Waitz. MGH SS rer. Germ., no. 18. Hanover, 1880; Reprint, 1978.

Chronicle of Bury St. Edmunds. Ed. Antonia Gransden. Nelson Medieval Texts. London, 1964.

Chronicles and Memorials of the Reign of Richard I. Ed. William Stubbs. 2 vols. RS, no. 38. London, 1864–65.

Chronicon Henrici de Hervordia. Ed. August Potthast. Göttingen, 1859.

Chronicon vulgo dictum Thomae Wykes. Ed. Henry Richards Luard. RS, no. 36, 4:6–354. London, 1869. Reprint, 1965.

Close Rolls (Supplementary) of the Reign of Henry III Preserved in the Public Record Office, 1244–1266. Ed. Ann Morton. London, 1975.

Constitutiones et acta publica imperatorum et regum inde ab anno 911 usque ad annum 1197. Ed. Ludwig Weiland. MGH Leges, no. 4, 1. Hanover, 1893. Reprint, 1963.

Constitutiones et acta publica imperatorum et regum inde ab anno 1198 usque ad annum 1272. Ed. Ludwig Weiland. MGH Leges, no. 4, 2. Hanover, 1896. Reprint, 1963.

Constitutiones et acta publica imperatorum et regum inde ab anno 1273 usque ad annum 1298. Ed. Jakob Schwalm. MGH Leges, no. 4, 3. Hanover, 1904–6. Reprint, 1980.

Constitutiones et acta publica imperatorum et regum inde ab anno 1298 usque ad annum 1313. Ed. Jakob Schwalm. 2 vols. MGH Leges, no. 4, 4. Hanover, 1906–11. Reprint, 1981.

Constitutiones regum Germaniae. Ed. G. Pertz. MGH Leges, no. 1, 2. Hanover, 1837. Reprint, 1965.

De expugnatione Lyxbonensi. Ed. Charles Wendell David. Records of Civilization, no. 24. New York, 1936.

De expugnatione Lyxbonensi. Ed. William Stubbs. RS, no. 38, 1:cxlii–clxxxii. London, 1864. Reprint, 1964.

Devon, Frederick, ed. *Issues of the Exchequer; being a collection of payments made out of His Majesty's revenue, from Henry III to Henry VI inclusive.* London, 1837.

Die Admonter Briefsammlung. Ed. Günter Hödl and Peter Classen. MGH Epistolae: Die Briefe der deutschen Kaiserzeit, no. 6. Munich, 1983.

Die Ältere Wormser Briefsammlung. Ed. Walther Blust. MGH Epistolae: Die Briefe der deutschen Kaiserzeit, no. 3. Weimar, 1949.

Die Kaiserurkunden des 10., 11. und 12. Jahrhunderts. Ed. Karl Friedrich Stumpf-Brentano. Innsbruck, 1865–83. Reprint, Aalen, 1964.

Die Regesten der Erzbischöfe von Köln im Mittelalter. PGRG 21. Vol. 1 (A.D.

313–1099). Ed. Friedrich Wilhelm Oediger. Bonn, 1954–61. Vol. 2 (A.D. 1100–1205). Ed. Richard Knipping. Bonn, 1901. Vol. 3, Part 1 (A.D. 1205–61). Ed. Richard Knipping. Bonn, 1909. Vol. 3, Part 2 (A.D. 1261–1303). Ed. Richard Knipping. Bonn, 1913. Vol. 4 (A.D. 1304–32). Ed. Wilhelm Kisky. Bonn, 1915.

Die Urkunden der deutschen Könige und Kaiser: Die Urkunden Friedrichs I. Einleitung. Ed. Heinrich Appelt. MGH DD, no. 10, 5. Hanover, 1990.

Die Urkunden der deutschen Könige und Kaiser: Die Urkunden Friedrichs I. 1152–1158. Ed. Heinrich Appelt. MGH DD, no. 10, 1. Hanover, 1975.

Die Urkunden der deutschen Könige und Kaiser: Die Urkunden Friedrichs I. 1158–1167. Ed. Heinrich Appelt. MGH DD, no. 10, 2. Hanover, 1979.

Die Urkunden der deutschen Könige und Kaiser: Die Urkunden Friedrichs I. 1168–1180. Ed. Heinrich Appelt. MGH DD, no. 10, 3. Hanover, 1985.

Die Urkunden der deutschen Könige und Kaiser: Die Urkunden Heinrich Raspes und Wilhelms von Holland, 1246–1252. Ed. Dieter Hägermann and Jaap G. Kruisheer. MGH DD, no. 18, 1. Hanover, 1989.

Die Urkunden der deutschen Könige und Kaiser: Die Urkunden Konrads III. und Seines Sohnes Heinrich. Ed. Friedrich Hausmann. MGH DD no. 9. Vienna, Cologne, and Graz, 1969.

Die Urkunden Heinrichs des Löwen Herzogs von Sachsen und Bayern. Ed. Karl Jordan. MGH DD. Weimar, 1949.

Die Urkunden Philipps von Schwaben und Ottos IV. (1198–1212). Ed. Paul Zinsmaier. Veröffentlichungen der Kommission für Geschichtliche Landeskunde in Baden-Württemberg, Reihe B: Forschungen, no. 53. Stuttgart, 1969.

Die Vita Brunonis des Ruotger. Ed. F. Lotter. Bonn, 1958.

Die Welfen Urkunden des Tower zu London und des Exchequer zu Westminster. Ed. Hans Friedrich Georg Julius Sudendorf. Hanover, 1844.

Diplomatic Documents Preserved in the Public Record Office. Vol. 1, 1107–1272. Ed. Pierre Chaplais. London, 1964.

Documents Illustrative of English History in the 13th and 14th Centuries. Ed. Henry Cole. London, 1844.

Eckertz, Gottfried, ed. "Cronica presulum et Archiepiscoporum ecclesie Coloniensium." *Annalen* 4 (1857): 181–250.

Ekkehard of Aura. *Chronica.* Ed. F. J. Schmale and Irene Schmale-Ott. Ausgewählte Quellen zur Deutschen Geschichte des Mittelalters, Freiherr von Stein-Gedächtnisausgabe, no. 15. Darmstadt, 1972.

Ellenhardi Chronicon. Ed. Ph. Jaffé. MGH SS, no. 17, 118–41. Hanover, 1861. Reprint, 1987.

Florence and John of Worcester. *Chronicon ex chronicis.* Ed. Benjamin Thorpe. 2 vols. English Historical Society Publications. London, 1848–49.

Foedera, conventiones, litterae et cuiuscumque generis acta publica inter reges Angliae et alios quosvis imperatores, reges, pontifices vel communitates ab ineunte saeculo duodecimo, viz. ab anno 1101 ad nostra usque tempora. Ed. Thomas Rymer. 2d rev. ed. by George Holmes. 20 vols. London, 1727–35.

Gerald of Wales. *Giraldi Cambrensis opera.* Ed. J. S. Brewer, J. F. Dimock, and G. F. Warner, 8 vols. RS, no. 21. London, 1861–91.

Gervase of Canterbury. *Chronicle of the Reigns of Stephen, Henry II, and Richard I.* Ed. William Stubbs. RS, no. 73, 1. London 1879. Reprint, 1965.

———. *Gesta regum continuata.* Ed. William Stubbs. RS, no. 73, 2:106–324. London, 1880. Reprint, 1965.

Gesta Treverorum continuatio tertia. Ed. G. Waitz. MGH SS, no. 24, 380–89. Hanover, 1879. Reprint, 1974.

Great Roll of the Pipe for the Fifth Year of the Reign of King Henry III, Michaelmas 1221, The. Ed. David Crook. PR, no. 65. London, 1990.

Great Rolls of the Pipe for the 5th–34th Years of the Reign of King Henry II. PR, nos. 1–2, 4–9, 11–13, 15–16, 18–19, 21–22, 25–34, 36–38, *The.* London, 1884–1925.

Great Roll of the Pipe for the First Year of the Reign of King Richard the First, A.D. 1189–1190, The. Ed. Joseph Hunter. London, 1844.

Great Rolls of the Pipe for the 1st–14th, 16th, and 17th Years of the Reign of King John. PR, NS, nos. 10, 12, 14–16, 18–20, 22–24, 26, 28, 30, 35, 37, *The.* London, 1933–64.

Great Roll of the Pipe for the Second, Third, and Fourth Years of the Reign of King Henry the Second, A.D. 1155–1158, The. Ed. Joseph Hunter. London, 1844. Reprint, 1931.

Great Rolls of the Pipe for the 2nd–4th and 14th Years of the Reign of King Henry III. PR, NS, nos. 4, 39, 42, 47, *The.* London, 1927–87.

Great Rolls of the Pipe for the 2nd–10th Years of the Reign of King Henry I. PR, NS, nos. 1–3, 5–9, *The.* London, 1925–32.

Great Roll of the Pipe for the Twenty-Sixth Year of the Reign of King Henry the Third, A.D. 1241–1242, The. Ed. Henry Lewin Cannon. Yale Historical Publications: Manuscripts and Edited Texts, no. 5. New Haven, 1918.

Giselbert of Mons. *Chronicon Hanoniense.* Ed. G. Pertz. MGH SS rer. Germ., no. 29. Hanover, 1869.

Hanseakten aus England 1271 bis 1472. Ed. Karl Kunze. Hansische Geschichtsquellen, no. 6. Halle, 1891.

Hanserecesse: Die Recesse und andere Akten der Hansetage von 1256–1430. Vol. 1, *1256–1370.* Ed. Karl Koppmann. Leipzig, 1870.

Hansisches Urkundenbuch. Vols. 1–3. Ed. Konstantin Höhlbaum. Halle, 1876–86. Vols. 4–6. Ed. Karl Kunze. Halle and Leipzig, 1896–1905. Vol. 7. Ed. H. G. Runstedt. Weimar, 1939. Vols. 8–11. Ed. W. Stein. Leipzig and Munich, 1899–1916.

Hearne, T., ed. *Hemingi Chartularium Ecclesiae Wigornensis.* Oxford, 1723.

Helmold of Bosau. *Slawenchronik.* Ed. Heinz Stoob. Ausgewählte Quellen zur deutschen Geschichte des Mittelalters, Freiherr von Stein-Gedächtnisausgabe, no. 19. Darmstadt, 1973.

Henry of Huntingdon. *Historia Anglorum.* Ed. Thomas Arnold. RS, no. 74. London, 1879.

Historia Diplomatica Friderici Secundi. Ed. J. L. A. Huillard-Bréholles. 6 vols. Paris, 1852–61.

Hugh the Chanter. *The History of the Church of York, 1066–1127.* Ed. Charles Johnson, M. Brett, Christopher Brooke, and M. Winterbottom. Oxford Medieval Texts. Oxford, 1990.

Lampert of Hersfeld. *Lamperti monachi Hersfeldensis opera.* Ed. Oswald Holder-Egger. MGH SS rer. Germ., no. 38. Hanover and Leipzig, 1894. Reprint, 1984.

Letters of John of Salisbury, The. Vol. 1, *1153–1161.* Ed. W. J. Millor, H. E. Butler, and Christopher Brooke. 2 vols. Oxford Medieval Texts. Oxford, 1979–86.

Letters of John of Salisbury, The. Vol. 2, *The Later Letters (1163–1180).* Ed. W. J. Millor and Christopher Brooke. Oxford, 1967.

Materials for the History of Thomas Becket, Archbishop of Canterbury. Ed. James C. Robertson and J. B. Shepard, 7 vols. RS, no. 67. London, 1875–85. Reprint, 1965.

Matthew Paris. *Chronica majora.* Ed. Henry Richards Luard. 7 vols. RS, no. 57. London, 1872–73. Reprint, 1964.

———. *Historia Anglorum sive historia minor.* Ed. Frederick Madden. 3 vols. RS, no. 44. London, 1866–69. Reprint, 1970.

Memoranda Roll for the Michaelmas Term of the First Year of the Reign of King John, 1199–1200, together with Fragments of the Originalia Roll of the Seventh Year of King Richard I, 1195–1196, the Liberate Roll of the Second Year of King John, 1200–1201, and the Norman Roll of the Fifth Year of King John, 1203. Ed. H. G. Richardson. PR, NS, no. 21. London, 1943.

Memoranda Roll for the Tenth Year of the Reign of King John, 1207–1208, together with the Curia Regis Rolls of Hilary 7 Richard I, 1196, and Easter 9 Richard I, 1198, a Roll of Plate Held by Hugh de Neville, 9 John, 1207–1208, and Fragments of the Close Rolls of 16 and 17 John, 1215–1216. Ed. R. Allen Brown. PR, NS, no. 31. London, 1956.

Ordericus Vitalis. *The Ecclesiastical History.* Ed. Marjorie Chibnall. 6 vols. Oxford Medieval Texts. Oxford, 1969–80.

Otto of Freising. *The Two Cities.* Ed. and trans. C. C. Mierow. New York, 1928.

Otto of Freising and Rahewin. *Gesta Frederici seu rectius Cronica.* Ed. Franz-Josef Schmale. Ausgewählte Quellen zur deutschen Geschichte des Mittelalters, Freiherr von Stein-Gedächtnisausgabe, no. 17. Berlin, 1965.

———. *Gesta Friderici I. imperatoris.* Ed. G. Waitz. MGH SS rer. Germ., no. 46. Hanover, 1912. Reprint, 1978.

Patrologiae cursus completus, series latina. Ed. J. P. Migne. 234 vols. Paris, 1844–1955.

Pipe Roll of 31 Henry I, Michaelmas 1130, The. Ed. Joseph Hunter. London, 1929.

Quellen zur Geschichte der Stadt Köln. Ed. Leonard Ennen and Gottfried Eckertz. 6 vols. Cologne, 1860–79.

Quellen zur Geschichte des Kölner Handels und Verkehrs im Mittelalter. Ed. Bruno Kuske. PGRG 33:1–4. Bonn, 1917–34.

Ralph de Diceto. *Ymagines historiarum (The Historical Works of Ralph de Diceto).* Ed. William Stubbs. 2 vols. RS, no. 68. London, 1876. Reprint, 1965.

Ralph of Coggeshall. *Abbreviationes Chronicorum*. Ed. William Stubbs. RS, no. 68, 1. London, 1876. Reprint, 1964.

———. *Chronicon Anglicanum*. Ed. Joseph Stevenson. RS, no. 66. London, 1875. Reprint, 1965.

Receuil des actes de Henri II roi d'Angleterre et duc de Normandie concernant les provinces et les affairs de France. Ed. Léopold Delisle and Élie Berger. Introd. and 3 vols. Chartes et Diplômes Relatifs à L'Histoire de France, no. 7. Paris, 1909–27.

Red Book of the Exchequer, The. Ed. Hubert Hall. RS, no. 99. London, 1896. Reprint, 1965.

Regesta Imperii. Vol. 3, pt. 1, *Die Regesten des Kaiserreichs unter Konrad II. (1024–1039)*. Ed. J. F. Böhmer. Reedited with additions by N. von Bischoff and Heinrich Appelt. Vienna, Cologne, and Graz, 1951.

Regesta Imperii. Vol. 3, pt. 2. *Die Regesten des Kaiserreichs unter Heinrich IV. (1056 [1050]–1065)*. Ed. J. F. Böhmer. Reedited with additions by Tilman Struve. Vienna, Cologne, and Graz, 1984.

Regesta Imperii. Vol. 4, pt. 2. *Die Regesten des Kaiserreichs unter Friedrich I. (1152 [1122]–1190)*. Ed. J. F. Böhmer. Reedited with additions by Ferdinand Opll. Vienna, Cologne, and Graz, 1980.

Regesta Imperii. Vol. 4, pt. 3. *Die Regesten des Kaiserreichs unter Heinrich VI. (1165 [1190]–1197)*. Ed. J. F. Böhmer. Reedited with additions by Gerhard Baaken. 2 vols. Vienna, Cologne, and Graz, 1972–79.

Regesta Imperii. Vol. 5, pts. 1–5. *Die Regesten des Kaiserreichs unter Philipp, Otto IV., Friedrich II., Heinrich (VII), Conrad IV. Heinrich Raspe, Wilhelm und Richard (1198–1272)*. Ed. J. F. Böhmer. Reedited with additions by Julius Ficker and Eduard Winkelmann. 3 vols. Innsbruck, 1881–1901.

Regesta Imperii. Vol. 5, pt. 4. *Die Regesten des Kaiserreichs unter Philipp, Otto IV., Friedrich II., Heinrich (VII.), Conrad IV., Heinrich Raspe, Wilhelm und Richard*. Ed. J. F. Böhmer. Reedited with further additions by Paul Zinsmaier. Vienna, Cologne, and Graz, 1983.

Regesta Imperii. Vol. 6, pt. 1. *Die Regesten des Kaiserreichs unter Rudolf I. von Hapsburg (1273–1291)*. Ed. J. F. Böhmer. Reedited with additions by O. Redlich. Innsbruck, 1898. Reprint, with appendix, 1969.

Regesta Imperii. Vol. 6, pt. 2. *Die Regesten des Kaiserreichs unter Adolf von Nassau (1291–1298)*. Ed. J. F. Böhmer. Reedited with additions by Vincenz Samanek. Innsbruck, 1933–48.

Regesta Regum Anglo-Normannorum, 1066–1154. Vol. 1, *Regesta Willelmi Conquestoris et Willelmi Rufi, 1066–1100*. Ed. H. W. C. Davis. Oxford, 1913.

Regesta Regum Anglo-Normannorum, 1066–1154. Vol. 2, *Regesta Henrici Primi*. Ed. Charles Johnson and H. A. Cronne. Oxford, 1956.

Regesten der Reichstadt Aachen I, 1250–1300. Ed. Wilhelm Mummenhoff. PGRG, no. 47. Bonn, 1961.

Regestum Innocentii III papae super negotio Romani imperii. Ed. Friedrich Kempf. Miscellanea Historiae Pontificiae, no. 12. Rome, 1947.

Robert of Torigni. *Chronica*. Ed. Richard Howlett. RS, no. 82. London, 1882. Reprint, 1964.

Roger of Howden. *Chronica magistri Rogeri de Hovedene.* Ed. William Stubbs. 4 vols. RS, no. 51. London, 1868–71. Reprint, 1964.

———. *Gesta regis Henrici secundi Benedicti abbatis.* Ed. William Stubbs. 2 vols. RS, no. 49. London, 1867. Reprint, 1965.

Roger of Wendover. *Flores historiarum.* Ed. Henry G. Hewlett. 3 vols. RS, no. 84. London, 1886–89. Reprint, 1965.

Rotuli chartarum in turri Londinensi asservati. Vol. 1, pt. 1. *Ab anno MCXCIX ad annum MCCXVI.* Ed. Thomas Duffus Hardy. London, 1837.

Rotuli de liberate ac de misis et praestitis regnante Johanne. Ed. Thomas Duffus Hardy. London, 1844.

Rotuli de oblatis et finibus in turri Londinensi asservati tempore Regis Johanni. Ed. Thomas Duffus Hardy. London, 1835.

Rotuli litterarum clausarum in turri Londinensi asservati. Ed. Thomas Duffus Hardy. 2 vols. London, 1833–34.

Rotuli litterarum patentium in turri Londinensi asservati. Vol. 1, pt. 1 *Ab anno MCCI ad annum MCCXVI.* Ed. Thomas Duffus Hardy. London, 1835.

Rotulus cancellarii vel antigraphum magni rotuli pipae de tertio anno regni Regis Johannis. Ed. Joseph Hunter. London, 1833.

Royal and other Historical Letters Illustrative of the Reign of Henry III. Ed. Walter W. Shirley. 2 vols. RS, no. 27. London, 1862–68.

Sancti Anselmi Cantuariensis Archiepiscopi Opera Omnia. Ed. F. S. Schmitt. Edinburgh, 1951.

Simeon of Durham. *Historia regum (Symeonis monachi opera omnia).* Ed. Thomas Arnold. 2 vols. RS, no. 75. London, 1882–85. Reprint, 1965.

Syllabus of the Documents relating to England and other Kingdoms Contained in the Collection known as Rymer's Foedera. Ed. Thomas Duffus Hardy. 3 vols. London, 1869–85.

Thomas de Papia. *Gesta imperatorum et pontificum.* Ed. E. Ehrenfeuchter. MGH SS, no. 22, 483–528. Hanover, 1872. Reprint, 1976.

Treaty Rolls Preserved in the Public Record Office. Vol. 1, *1234–1325.* Ed. Pierre Chaplais. London, 1955.

Urkundenbuch für die Geschichte des Niederrheins. Ed. Theodor Josef Lacomblet. 4 vols. Düsseldorf, 1840–58.

Vita Annonis archiepiscopi Coloniensis. Ed. R. Koepke. MGH SS, no. 11, 462–514. Hanover, 1854.

Vita Annonis minor. Ed. Mauritius Miller. Siegburger Studien, no. 10. Siegburg, 1975.

William of Malmesbury. *De gestis pontificum Anglorum.* Ed. N. E. S. A. Hamilton. RS, no. 52. London, 1870. Reprint, 1964.

William of Malmesbury. *De gestis regum Anglorum.* Ed. William Stubbs. 2 vols. RS, no. 90. London, 1887. Reprint, 1964.

William of Newburgh. *Historia rerum Anglicarum.* Ed. Richard Howlett. RS, no. 82, 1. London, 1844. Reprint, 1964.

William of Poitiers. *Histoire de Guillaume le Conquérant.* Ed. Raymonde Foreville. Paris, 1952.

Secondary Literature

Abulafia, David. *Frederick II*. London, 1988.

Ahlers, Jens. *Die Welfen und die englischen Könige 1165–1235*. Quellen und Darstellungen zur Geschichte Niedersachsens, no. 102. Hildesheim, 1987.

Althoff, Gerd. *Amicitiae und pacta: Bündnis, Einung, Politik und Gebetsgedenken im beginnenden 10. Jahrhundert*. MGH Shriften, no. 37. Hanover, 1992.

———. *Spielregeln der Politik im Mittelalter. Kommunikation in Frieden und Fehden*. Darmstadt, 1997.

Appelt, Heinrich. *Die Kaiseridee Friedrich Barbarossas*. Österreichische Akademie der Wissenschaften, Philosophisch-Historische Klasse. Sitzungsberichte Band 252, Abhandlung 4. Vienna, 1967.

Appleby, John T. *England without Richard (1190–1199)*. London, 1965.

———. *The Troubled Reign of King Stephen*. London, 1969.

Arnold, Benjamin. *Count and Bishop in Medieval Germany: A Study of Regional Power, 1100–1350*. Middle Ages Series. Philadelphia, 1991.

———. "England and Germany, 1050–1350." In *England and Her Neighbours, 1066–1453: Essays in Honour of Pierre Chaplais*, ed. Michael Jones and Malcolm Vale, 43–51. London, 1989.

———. "German Bishops and Their Military Retinues in the Medieval Empire." *German History: The Journal of the German History Society* 7, no. 2 (1989): 161–83.

———. *German Knighthood, 1050–1300*. Oxford, 1985.

———. "Germany and England, 1066–1453." In *England in Europe, 1066–1453*, ed. Nigel Saul, 76–87. New York, 1994.

———. *Medieval Germany, 500–1500: A Political Interpretation*. Toronto, 1997.

———. *Princes and Territories in Medieval Germany*. Cambridge, 1991.

Assmann, E. "Friedrich Barbarossas Kinder." *DA* 33 (1977): 435–72.

Bappert, J. F. *Richard von Cornwall seit seiner Wahl zum deutschen König 1257–1272*. Bonn, 1905.

Barlow, Frank. "The English, French, and Norman Councils Called to Deal with the Papal Schism of 1159." *EHR* 51 (1936): 264–68.

———. *The Feudal Kingdom of England, 1042–1216*. New York, 1988.

———. *Thomas Becket*. London, 1987.

———. *William Rufus*. London, 1983.

Barraclough, Geoffrey. "Edward I and Adolf of Nassau, a Chapter of Medieval Diplomatic History." *Cambridge Historical Journal* 6 (1940): 225–62.

———. "Frederick Barbarossa and the Twelfth Century." In *History in a Changing World*, 73–96. Oxford, 1955; reprint, 1957.

———. *The Origins of Modern Germany*. 2d ed. Oxford, 1947.

———, ed. *Mediaeval Germany, 911–1250: Essays by German Historians*. 2 vols. Studies in Mediaeval Germany, nos. 1 and 2. Oxford, 1948.

Barrow, Julia. "Cathedrals, Provosts, and Prebends: A Comparison of Twelfth-

Century German and English Practice." *Journal of Ecclesiastical History* 37, no. 4 (October 1986): 536–64.

———. "Education and the Recruitment of Cathedral Canons in England and Germany, 1100–1225." *Viator* 20 (1989): 118–37.

Bates, David. *William the Conqueror.* London, 1989.

Bayley, Charles C. "The Diplomatic Preliminaries of the Double Election of 1257 in Germany." *EHR* 62 (1947): 457–83.

———. *The Formation of the German College of Electors in the Mid-Thirteenth Century.* Toronto, 1949.

Benson, Robert L. *The Bishop-Elect: A Study in Medieval Ecclesiastical Office.* Princeton, 1968.

———. "Political *Renovatio:* Two Models." In *Renaissance and Renewal in the Twelfth Century,* ed. Robert L. Benson and Giles Constable with Carol D. Lanham, 339–86. Cambridge, MA, 1982.

Berg, Dieter. *England und der Kontinent: Studien zur auswärtigen Politik der anglonormannischen Könige im 11. und 12. Jahrhundert.* Bochum, 1987.

———. "Imperium und Regna. Beiträge zur Entwicklung der deutsch-englischen Beziehungen im Rahmen der auswärtigen Politik der römischen Kaiser und deutschen Könige im 12. und 13. Jahrhundert." In *Zeitschrift für Historische Forschung Beiheft 5: "Bündnissyteme" und "Außenpolitik" im späteren Mittelalter,* ed. Peter Moraw, 13–37. Berlin, 1987.

Bloch, Marc. "A Contribution towards a Comparative History of European Societies." In *Land and Work in Medieval Europe: Selected Papers by Marc Bloch,* trans. J. E. Anderson, 44–81. Berkeley, 1967.

Bock, F. "Englands Beziehungen zum Reich unter Adolf von Nassau." *MIÖG Ergänzungsband* 12 (1933): 198–257.

Böhm, Franz. *Das Bild Friedrich Barbarossas und seines Kaisertums in den ausländischen Quellen seiner Zeit.* Historische Studien, no. 289. Berlin, 1936. Reprint, 1965.

Brackmann, A. "The Birth of the National State in Medieval Germany and the Norman Monarchies." In *Mediaeval Germany, 911–1250: Essays by German Historians,* ed. Geoffrey Barraclough, 281–300. Studies in Mediaeval Germany, no. 2. Oxford, 1948.

Brandi, K. "Die Urkunde Friedrichs II. vom August 1235 für Otto von Lüneberg." In *Festschrift für Paul Zimmerman,* 33–46. Wolfenbüttel, 1914.

Brooke, Christopher. *From Alfred to Henry III (871–1272).* New York, 1969.

Buszello, Horst. "Köln und England (1468–1509): *Köln, das Reich und Europe MSAK* 60 (1971) 431–67.

Butterfield, Herbert. *The Whig Interpretation of History.* London, 1931. Reprint, 1959.

Cantor, Norman F. "Medieval Historiography as Modern Political and Social Thought." *Journal of Contemporary History* 3 (1968): 55–73.

Cardauns, Hermann. *Konrad von Hochstaden, Erzbischof von Köln (1238–1261).* Cologne, 1880.

Carpenter, D. A. *The Minority of Henry III*. Berkeley, 1990.
———. *The Reign of Henry III*. London and Rio Grande, OH, 1996.
Cartellieri, Alexander. "Die Machtstellung Heinrichs II. von England." *Neue Heidelberger Jahrbücher* 8 (1898): 269–83.
———. *Die Schlacht bei Bouvines*. Leipzig, 1914.
———. *Philip II. August, König von Frankreich*. 4 vols. Leipzig, 1899–1922.
Chaplais, Pierre. *English Medieval Diplomatic Practice*. 2 vols. London, 1975–82.
———. *Essays in Medieval Diplomacy and Administration*. London, 1981.
Chibnall, Marjorie. *The Empress Matilda: Queen, Consort, Queen Mother, and Lady of the English*. Oxford, 1992.
Colvin, Ian. *The Germans in England, 1066–1598*. London, 1915.
Constable, Giles. "A Note on the Route of the Anglo-Flemish Crusaders of 1147." *Speculum* 28 (1953): 525–26.
Cuttino, G. P. *English Diplomatic Administration, 1259–1339*. 2d ed. Oxford, 1971.
———. *English Medieval Diplomacy*. Bloomington, 1985.
Davis, R. H. C. *King Stephen (1135–1154)*. Berkeley, 1967.
Decker-Hauff, H. "Das staufische Haus." In *Die Zeit der Staufer: Katalog der Ausstellung im württembergischen Landesmuseum*, ed. Reiner Hausherr, 3: 358–59, 366. Stuttgart, 1977.
Denholm-Young, N. *Richard of Cornwall*. Oxford, 1947.
Deutsche Könige und Kaiser des Mittelalters. Ed. Eva Maria Engel and Eberhard Holtz. Cologne and Vienna, 1989.
Dibben, L. B. "Secretaries in the Thirteenth and Fourteenth Centuries." *EHR* 25 (1910): 430–44.
Diederich, Toni. *Die alten Siegel der Stadt Köln*. Cologne, 1980.
di Miranda, Armin: "Richard von Cornwallis und sein Verhältnis zur Krönungstadt Aachen." *Annalen* 35 (1880): 65–92.
Dollinger, Philippe. *La Hanse*. Paris, 1964. Reprinted as *Die Hanse* (Stuttgart, 1966). Translated as *The German Hansa* (London, 1970).
Douglas, David C. *William the Conqueror*. Berkeley, 1964.
Duby, Georges. *Le dimanche de Bouvines 27 Juillet 1214*. Trente journées qui ont fait la France, no. 5. La Flèche, 1973. Reprint, 1986.
———. *The Legend of Bouvines*. Berkeley, 1990.
Dunbabin, Jean. *France in the Making (843–1180)*. Oxford, 1985.
Eberhard, Otto. "Friedrich Barbarossa in seinen Briefen." *DA* 5 (1942): 72–111.
Ehlers, Joachim. "Die Deutsche Nation des Mittelalters als Gegenstand der Forschung." In *Ansäzte und Diskontinuität Deutscher Nationsbildung im Mittelalter*, ed. Joachim Ehlers, 11–58. Nationes: Historische und philologische Untersuchungen zur Entstehung der europäischen Nationen des Mittelalter, no. 8. Sigmaringen, 1989.
Engels, Odilo. *Der Niederrhein und das Reich im 12. Jahrhundert*. Gesellschaft für Rheinische Geschichtskunde Vorträge, no. 23. Sonderausdruck from *Königtum und Reichsgewalt am Niederrhein*, Klever Archiv, 4 (1983): 93–96.
———. "Des Reiches heilger Gründer: Die Kanonisation Karls des Großen und

ihre Beweggründe." In *Karl der Große und sein Schrein in Aachen: Eine Festschrift,* ed. Hans Müllejans, 37–46. Aachen and Mönchengladbach, 1988.

———. *Die Staufer.* 3d rev. ed. Stuttgart, 1984.

———. "Zur Entmachtung Heinrichs des Löwen." In *Festschrift für Andreas Kraus zum 60. Geburtstag,* ed. Pankraz Fried and Walter Ziegler, 45–59. Münchener historische Studien, Abteilung Bayerische Geschichte, no. 10. Kallmünz, 1982.

Ennen, Edith. "Erzbischof und Stadtgemeinde in Köln bis zur Schlacht von Worringen (1288)." In *Gesammelte Abhandlungen,* ed. Georg Droege, 1:388–404. Veroffentlichung des Instituts fur Geschichtliche Landeskunde der Rheinlande an der Universitat Bonn. Bonn, 1977. Reprinted from *Bischofs- und Kathedralstädte des Mittelalters und der frühen Neuzeit,* ed. F. Petri, Stadteforschung, Reihe A, Darstellungen, no. 1 (Cologne and Vienna, 1976).

———. "Europäische Züge der mittelalterlichen Kölner Stadtgeschichte." *Köln, das Reich und Europa, MSAK* 60 (1971): 1–48.

———. "Kölner Wirtschaft im Früh- und Hochmittelalter." in *Zwei Jahrtausende Kölner Wirtschaft,* ed. Hermann Kellenbenz, 89–94, 119–23, 151–60. Rheinisch-Westfälisches Wirtschaftsarchiv zu Köln. Cologne, 1975.

Ennen, Leonard. *Geschichte der Stadt Köln.* 6 vols. Cologne, 1860–79.

Erdmann, C. "Der Kreuzzugsgedanke in Portugal." *Historische Zeitschrift* 141 (1930): 23–53.

Erkens, Franz-Reiner. *Der Erzbischof von Köln und die deutsche Königswahl: Studien zur Kölner Kirchengeschichte, zum Krönungsrecht und zur Verfassung des Reiches.* Studien zur Kölner Kirchengeschichte, no. 21. Siegburg, 1987.

———. *Siegfried von Westerburg (1274–1297): Die Reichs- und Territorialpolitik eines Kölner Erzbischofs im ausgehenden 13. Jahrhundert.* Rheinisches Archiv, no. 114. Bonn, 1982.

Esser, Gertrud Maria. *England, Frankreich und die römische Kurie in der Vorbereitung des Dritten Kreuzuges.* Ph.D. diss., Cologne, 1953.

Eyton, Robert William. *Court, Household, and Itinerary of King Henry II.* London, 1878. Reprint, 1974.

Fahne, A. *Geschichte der Kölnischen, Jülichschen und Bergischen Geschlechter.* 2 vols. Bonn, 1843–53.

Fawtier, Robert. *The Capetian Kings of France: Monarchy and Nation (987–1328).* London, 1960.

Ficker, Julius. *Engelbert der Heilige, Erzbischof von Köln und Reichsverweser.* Cologne, 1853.

———. *Reinald von Dassel.* Cologne, 1850.

Flink, Klaus. "Köln, das Reich und die Stadtentwicklung im nordlichen Rheinland (1100–1250)." *Blätter für deutsche Landesgeschichte* 120 (1984): 155–93.

Föhl, Walther. "Studien zu Rainald von Dassel." *JKGV* 17 (1935): 234–63; 20 (1938): 238–60.

Franzl, Johann. *Rudolf I.* Graz, Vienna, and Cologne, 1986.

Freed, John B. "The Counts of Falkenstein: Noble Self-Consciousness in Twelfth-Century Germany." *Transactions of the American Philosophical Society* 74, no. 6 (1984): 1–70.

———. *The Friars and German Society in the Thirteenth Century.* Publications of the Medieval Academy of America, no. 86. Cambridge, MA, 1977.

———. "Medieval German Social History: Generalizations and Particularism." *Central European History* 25, no. 1 (1992): 1–26.

———. *Noble Bondsmen: Ministerial Marriages in the Archdiocese of Salzburg, 1100–1343.* Ithaca, 1995.

———. "The Origins of the Medieval Nobility: The Problem of the Ministerials." *Viator* 7 (1976): 211–41.

———. "Reflections on the Medieval German Nobility." *American Historical Review* 91, no. 3 (1986): 553–75.

Fried, Johannes. "Die Wirtschaftspolitik Friedrich Barbarossas in Deutschland." *Blätter für deutsche Landesgeschichte* 120 (1984): 195–239.

Fuhrmann, Horst. *Deutsche Geschichte im hohen Mittelalter.* Deutsche Geschichte, no. 2. Göttingen, 1978; 2d ed., 1983. Translated into English as *Germany in the High Middle Ages (c. 1050–1200),* trans. Timothy Reuter (Cambridge, 1986).

———. " 'Quis Teutonicos constituit iudices nationum?' The Trouble with Henry." *Speculum* 60, no. 2 (April 1994): 344–58.

Ganshof, François. *Le Moyen âge: Histoire des relations internationales I.* Paris, 1953. Translated into English as *The Middle Ages: A History of International Relations,* trans. Rémy Inglis Hall (New York, 1970).

Georgi, Wolfgang. *Friedrich Barbarossa und die auswärtigen Mächte: Studien zur Außenpolitik, 1159–1180.* Europäische Hochschulschriften, no. 3/442. Frankfurt am Main, 1990.

Gescher, Franz. "Die erzbischöfliche Kurie in Köln von ihren ersten Anfängen bis zur Gegenwart: Eine rechtsgeschichtliche Skizze." *Annalen* 118 (1931): 1–31.

Gillingham, John. "Elective Kingship and the Unity of Medieval Germany." *German History: The Journal of the German History Society* 9 (1991): 124–35.

———. "The Fall of the Angevin Empire." In *England in Europe, 1066–1453,* ed. Nigel Saul, 88–96. New York, 1994.

———. *The Kingdom of Germany in the High Middle Ages, 900–1200.* Historical Association Pamphlet no. G77. London, 1971.

———. *Richard Coeur de Lion: Kingship, Chivalry, and War in the Twelfth Century.* London and Rio Grande, OH, 1994.

———. *Richard the Lionheart.* London, 1978.

———. "The Unromantic Death of Richard I." *Speculum* 54 (1979): 18–41.

Given, James. *State and Society: Gwynedd and Languedoc under Outside Rule.* Ithaca, 1990.

Gransden, Antonia. *Historical Writing in England, c. 550 to c. 1307.* Ithaca, 1974.

Grebe, Werner. "Erzbischof Arnold I von Köln in der Rechts- und Territorialpolitik." *JKGV* 42 (1968): 1–80; 43 (1971): 1–76.

———. "Rainald von Dassel als Reichskanzler Friedrich Barbarossas (1156–1159)." *JKGV* 49 (1978): 49–74.

———. "Studien zur geistigen Welt Rainalds von Dassel." *Annalen* 171 (1969): 5–44.

Gronen, Editha. *Die Machtpolitik Heinrichs des Löwen.* Historische Studien, no. 139. Berlin, 1919.

Groten, Manfred. "Die Anfänge des Kölner Schreinswesens." *JKGV* 56 (1985): 1–21.

———. *Köln im 13. Jahrhundert: Gesellschaftlicher Wandel und Verfassungsentwicklung.* Städteforschung Veröffentlichungen des Instituts für vergleichende Städtegeschichte in Münster Reihe A: Darstellungen, no. 36. Cologne, 1995; 2d ed. Cologne, 1998.

———. "Konrad von Hochstaden und die Wahl Richards von Cornwall." In *Köln, Stadt und Bistum in Kirche und Reich des Mittelalters: Festschrift für Odilo Engels zum 65. Geburtstag,* ed. Hanna Vollrath and Stefan Weinfurter, 483–510. Kölner historische Abhandlungen, no. 39. Cologne, 1993.

———. "Studien zum Aachener Karlssiegel und zum gefälschten Dekret Karls des Großen." *Zeitschrift des Aachener Geschichtsvereins* 93 (1986): 15–29.

———. "Untersuchungen zum Urkundenwesen unter den Erzbischöfen Arnold I und Arnold II von Köln (1138–1156)." *JKGV* 50 (1979): 11–38.

Haller, Johannes. *Das Papsttum: Idee und Wirklichkeit.* 5 vols. Basel, 1951–53. Reprint, Esslingen am Neckar, 1962.

Hamilton, Bernard. "Prester John and the Three Kings of Cologne." In *Studies in Medieval History Presented to R. H. C. Davis,* ed. H. Mayr-Harting, 177–92. London, 1985.

Hampe, Karl. *Germany under the Salian and Hohenstaufen Emperors.* Trans. Ralph Bennett. Oxford, 1973.

Hardegen, Friedrich. *Imperialpolitik König Heinrichs II. von England.* Heidelberger Abhandlungen, no. 12. Heidelberg, 1905.

Harding, Alan. *England in the Thirteenth Century.* Cambridge Medieval Textbooks. Cambridge, 1993.

Haverkamp, Alfred, ed. *Friedrich Barbarossa: Handlungsspielräume und Wirkungsweisen des staufischen Kaisers.* Vorträge und Forschungen, no. 40. Sigmaringen, 1992.

———. *Medieval Germany (1056–1273).* Trans. Helga Braun and Richard Mortimer. 2d ed. Oxford, 1992.

Haverkamp, Alfred, and Hanna Vollrath, eds. *England and Germany in the High Middle Ages.* Oxford, 1996.

———. "Germany and England in the High Middle Ages: A Comparative Approach." *Bulletin of the German Historical Institute of London* 10, no. 2 (May 1988): 23–26.

Hechberger, Werner. *Staufer und Welfen 1125–1190: Zur Verwendung von Theorien in der Geschichtswissenschaft.* Passauer historische Forschungen, no. 10. Cologne, Weimar, and Vienna, 1996.

Hecker, Hermann. *Die Territorialpolitik des Erzbischofs Philip I. von Köln (1167–1191).* Historische Studien, no. 10. Berlin, 1883.

Heinemeyer, Walter. "Die Verhandlungen an der Sâone im Sommer 1162." *DA* 20 (1964): 155–89.

Hentze, Carl. *England, Frankreich und König Adolf von Nassau 1294–1298.* Kiel, 1914.

Herborn, Wolfgang. *Die politische Führungsschicht der Stadt Köln im Spätmittelalter.* Rheinisches Archiv, no. 100. Bonn, 1977.

Herkenrath, Rainer Maria. *Rainald von Dassel: Reichskanzler und Erzbischof von Köln.* Graz, 1963.

Heydal, W. J. "Das Itinerar Heinrichs des Löwen." *Niedersächsisches Jahrbuch* 6 (1929): 1–166.

Hiller, H. *Heinrich der Löwe: Herzog und Rebell.* Munich, 1978.

Hilpert, Hans-Eberhard. "Richard of Cornwall's Candidature for the German Throne and the Christmas 1256 Parliament at Westminster." *Journal of Medieval History* 6 (1980): 185–98.

———. "Zwei Briefe Kaiser Ottos IV. an Johann Ohneland." *DA* 38 (1982): 123–40.

Höhlbaum, Konstantin. "Kölns älteste Handelsprivilegien für England." *HGB* 3 (1882): 41–48.

Holtzmann, Walter. "Zur Geschichte des Investiturstreites: (Englische Analekten II, 3) England, Unteritalien und der Vertrag von Ponte Mammolo." *Neues Archiv* 50 (1935): 246–319.

Huckenbeck, Ernst. *Der deutsche Thronstreit 1198–1208 und die Westmächte.* Cologne, 1952.

Hucker, Bernd U. *Kaiser Otto IV.* MGH Schriften, no. 34. Hanover, 1990.

Huffman, Joseph P. "*Anglicus in Colonia:* Die juristische, soziale und ökonomische Stellung der Engländer in Köln während des 12. und 13. Jahrhunderts." *JKGV* 62 (1991): 1–62.

———. "Documentary Evidence of Anglo-German Currency Movement in the Central Middle Ages: Cologne and English Sterling." *British Numismatic Journal* 65 (1995): 32–45.

———. *Family, Commerce, and Religion in London and Cologne: Anglo-German Emigrants, c. 1000–c. 1300.* Cambridge Studies in Medieval Life and Thought, 4th ser., no. 39. Cambridge, 1998.

———. "Prosopography and the Anglo-Imperial Connection: A Cologne *Ministerialis* Family and Its English Relations." *Medieval Prosopography* 11, no. 2 (autumn 1990): 53–134.

Huyskens, Albert. "Der Plan des Königs Richard von Cornwallis zur Niederlegung eines deutschen Krönungsschatzes in Aachen." *Annalen* 115 (1929): 180–204.

———. "Noch Einmal der Krönungsschatz des Königs Richard von Cornwallis." *Annalen* 118 (1931): 136–43.

Jenal, Georg. *Erzbischof Anno II. von Köln (1056–1075) und sein politisches Wirken: Ein Beitrag zur Geschichte der Reichs- und Territorialpolitik im 11. Jahrhundert.* Monographien zur Geschichte des Mittelalters, no. 8, parts 1 and 2. Stuttgart, 1974–75.

Jordan, Karl. "Aspekte der Mittelalterforschung in Deutschland in den letzten fünfzig Jahren." In *Ausgewählte Aufsätze zur Geschichte des Mittelalters*, 329–44. Kieler historische Studien, no. 29. Stuttgart, 1980.

———. "Die Gestalt Heinrichs des Löwen im Wandel des Geschichtsbildes." *Geschichte im Wissenschaft und Unterricht* 26, no. 4 (1975): 226–41.

———. *Henry the Lion: A Biography*. Trans. P. S. Falla. Oxford, 1986.

Kallen, Gerhard. "Das Kölner Erzstift und der 'ducatus Westfalie et Angarie' (1180)." *JKGV* 31/32 (1956–57): 78–107.

———. "Philipp von Heinsberg, Erzbischof von Köln (1169–1191)." In *Im Schatten von St. Gereon*, 183–205. Veröffentlichungen des Kölnischen Geschichtsvereins, no. 25. Cologne, 1960.

Kantorowicz, Ernst. *Kaiser Friedrich II.* Berlin, 1927.

———. "Petrus von Vinea in England." *MIÖG* 51 (1937): 43–88.

Kellenbenz, Hermann. "Der Aufstieg Kölns zur mittelalterlichen Handelsmetropole." *JKGV* 41 (1967): 1–30.

———, ed. *Zwei Jahrtausende Kölner Wirtschaft*. 2 vols. Rheinisch-Westfälisches Wirtschaftsarchiv zu Köln. Cologne, 1975.

Keller, Hagen. *Zwischen regionaler Begrenzung und universalem Horizont: Deutschland im Imperium der Salier und Staufer, 1024 bis 1250*. Propylaen Geschichte Deutschlands, no. 2. Berlin, 1986.

Keussen, Hermann. *Köln im Mittelalter: Topographie und Verfassung*. 2 vols. Bonn, 1918. Reprint, Düsseldorf, 1986.

Kienast, Walter. *Deutschland und Frankreich in der Kaiserzeit (900–1270): Weltkaiser und Einzelkönige*. Monographien zur Geschichte des Mittelalters, no. 9, parts 1–3. Stuttgart, 1974–75.

———. "Die Anfänge des europäischen Staatensystem im späteren Mittelalter." *Historische Zeitschrift* 153 (1936): 229–71.

———. "Die Deutschen Fürsten im Dienste der Westmächte bis zum Tode Philipps des Schönen von Frankreich." *Bijdragen van het Instituut voor Middeleeuwsche Geschiedenis der Rijks-Universiteit te Utrecht*, nos. 10, 16. Utrecht and Munich, 1924–31.

Kirfel, Hans. *Weltherrschaftsidee und Bündnispolitik: Untersuchungen zur Auswärtigen Politik der Staufer*. Bonner historische Forschungen, no. 12. Bonn, 1959.

Kirn, Paul. "Mit welcher Krone wurde König Sigmund in Aachen gekrönt?" *Annalen* 118 (1931): 132–36.

Kluger, Helmuth, and Edgar Pack, eds. *Series episcoporum ecclesiae catholicae occidentalis ab initio usque ad anno MCXCVIII*. Series 5, Germania, vol. 1, *Archiepiscopatus Coloniensis*. Stuttgart, 1982.

Knipping, Richard. *Die Kölner Stadtrechnungen des Mittelalters mit einer Darstellung der Finanzverwaltung*. 2 vols. PGRG, no. 15. Bonn, 1897–98.

Köhler, Ruth. *Die Heiratsverhandlungen zwischen Eduard I. von England und Rudolf von Habsburg: Ein Beitrag zur english-deutschen Bündnispolitik am Ausgang des 13. Jahrhunderts*. Meisenheim am Glan, 1969.

Kurth, Friedrich. "Der Anteil Niederdeutscher Kreuzfahrer an den Kämpfen der Portugiesen gegen die Mauren." *MIÖG Ergänzungsband* 8 (1911): 131–252.

Ladner, Gerhart B. "Formularbehelfe in der Kanzlei Kaiser Friedrichs II. und die 'Briefe des Petrus de Vinea.' " *MIÖG Ergänzungsband* 12 (1933): 92–198, 415.

Landon, Lionel. *The Itinerary of King Richard I, with Studies on Certain Matters of Interest Connected with His Reign.* PR, NS, no. 13. London, 1935.

Lappenberg, Johann Martin. *Urkundliche Geschichte des Hansischen Stahlhofes zu London.* Hamburg, 1851; reprint Osnabrück, 1967.

Laudage, Johannes. *Alexander III. und Friedrich Barbarossa.* Forschungen zur Kaiser- und Papstgeschichte des Mittelalters, Beihefte zu J. F. Böhmer, Regesta Imperii, no. 16. Cologne, Weimar, and Vienna, 1997.

Levison, Wilhelm. *England and the Continent in the Eighth Century.* Ford Lectures 1943. Oxford, 1946.

Lewald, Ursula. "Köln im Investiturstreit." In *Investiturstreit und Reichsverfassung,* ed. Josef Fleckenstein, 373–93. Vorträge und Forschungen, no. 17. Sigmarigen, 1973.

Lewis, F. R. "Beatrix von Falkenburg, the Third Wife of Richard of Cornwall." *EHR* 52 (1937): 279–82.

Leyser, Karl. "The Anglo-Norman Succession, 1120–1125." *Anglo-Norman Studies* 13 (1991 for 1990): 233–39. Reprinted in *Communications and Power: The Gregorian Revolution and Beyond,* 97–114.

———. *Communications and Power in Medieval Europe: The Carolingian and Ottonian Centuries.* Ed. Timothy Reuter. London and Rio Grande, OH, 1994.

———. *Communications and Power in Medieval Europe: The Gregorian Revolution and Beyond.* Ed. Timothy Reuter. London and Rio Grande, OH, 1994.

———. "Concepts of Europe in the Early and High Middle Ages." *Past and Present* 137 (November 1992): 25–47. Reprinted in *Communications and Power in Medieval Europe: The Carolingian and Ottonian Centuries,* 1–18.

———. *The Crisis of Medieval Germany.* Raleigh Lectures on History. London, 1984. Reprinted in *Communications and Power: The Gregorian Revolution and Beyond,* 21–50.

———. "The Emperor Frederick II." *The Listener,* August 16, 1973. Reprinted in *Medieval Germany and Its Neighbours, 900–1250,* 269–76.

———. "England and the Empire in the Early Twelfth Century." *TRHS,* 5th ser., 10 (1960): 61–83. Reprinted in *Medieval Germany and Its Neighbours, 900–1250,* 191–214.

———. "Frederick Barbarossa and the Hohenstaufen Polity." *Viator* 19 (1988): 154–76. Reprinted in *Communications and Power: The Gregorian Revolution and Beyond,* 115–42.

———. "Frederick Barbarossa, Henry II, and the Hand of St. James." *EHR* 40 (1975): 481–506. Reprinted in *Medieval Germany and Its Neighbours, 900–1250,* 215–40.

———. "Friedrich Barbarossa—Hof und Land." In *Friedrich Barbarossa: Handlungsspielräume und Wirkungsweisen des Staufischen Kaisers,* ed. Alfred Haverkamp, 519–30. Sigmaringen, 1992. Translated into English as "Frederick Barbarossa: Court and Country," in *Communications and Power: The Gregorian Revolution and Beyond,* 143–56.

———. "Gregory VII and the Saxons." In *La Riforma Gregoriana e l'Europa,* ed.

Alphonso M. Stickler, 231–38. Studi Gregoriani, no. 14, 2. Rome, 1991. Reprinted in *Communications and Power: The Gregorian Revolution and Beyond*, 69–76.

———. *Medieval Germany and Its Neighbours, 900–1250.* London, 1982.

———. "A Recent View of the German College of Electors." *Medium Aevum* 23 (1954): 76–87. Reprinted in *Communications and Power in Medieval Europe: The Gregorian Revolution and Beyond*, 177–88.

———. "Some Reflections on Twelfth-Century Kings and Kingship." In *Medieval Germany and Its Neighbours, 900–1250*, 241–69.

Liebeschütz, Hans. *Die Beziehungen Kaisers Friedrichs II. zu England seit der Jahre 1235.* Ph.D. diss., Heidelberg, 1920.

Lloyd, Simon. *English Society and the Crusades, 1216–1307.* New York, 1988.

Lomax, D. W. "The First English Pilgrims to Santiago de Compostela." In *Studies in Medieval History Presented to R. H. C. Davis*, ed. H. Mayr-Harting and R. I. Moore, 165–79. London and Ronceverte, 1985.

Lucas, Henry S. "John of Avesnes and Richard of Cornwall." *Speculum* 23 (1948): 81–101.

———. "The Machinery of Diplomatic Intercourse." In *The English Government at Work*, ed. James F. Willard and William A. Morris, 1:300–303. Cambridge, 1940

Lunt, William. *Financial Relations of the Papacy with England to 1327.* Cambridge, MA, 1939.

Lyon, Bruce. "The Money Fief under the English Kings, 1066–1485." *EHR* 66 (1951): 161–93.

Matthew, D. J. A. "Reflections on the Medieval Roman Empire." *History* 77, no. 251 (October 1992): 363–90.

Mayer, Hans Eberhard. *The Crusades.* Trans. John Gillingham. 2d ed. Oxford, 1988.

———. "Staufische Weltherrschaft? Zum Brief Heinrichs II. von England an Friedrich Barbarossa von 1157." In *Festschrift Karl Pivec*, ed. Anton Haidacher and Hans Eberhard Mayer, 265–78. Innsbrucker Beiträge zur Kulturwissenschaft, no. 12. Innsbruck, 1966. Reprinted in *Friedrich Barbarossa*, ed. G. Wolf, Wege der Forschung, no. 390 (Darmstadt, 1975).

Mayr-Harting, H. "Henry II and the Papacy, 1170–1189." *Journal of Ecclesiastical History* 16 (1965): 39–53.

Mitteis, Heinrich. *Der Staat des hohen Mittelalters.* 8th ed. Weimar, 1968.

———. *Die deutsche Königswahl: Ihre Rechtsgrundlagen bis zur Goldenen Bulle.* Darmstadt, 1977.

Mortimer, Richard. *Angevin England, 1154–1258.* Oxford, 1994.

Müller, Heribert. *Heribert, Kanzler Ottos III. und Erzbischof von Köln.* Cologne, 1977.

Munz, Peter. *Frederick Barbarossa.* Ithaca, 1969.

Nelson, Janet L. "England and the Continent in the Anglo-Saxon Period." In *England in Europe, 1066–1453*, ed. Nigel Saul, 21–35. New York, 1994.

Nitschke, A. "German Politics and Medieval History." *Journal of Contemporary History* 3 (1968): 75–92.

Norgate, Kate. *The Minority of Henry III*. London, 1912.

Oediger, Friedrich Wilhelm. *Das Bistum Köln von den Anfängen bis zum Ende des 12. Jahrhunderts*. 2d ed. Geschichte des Erzbistums Köln, no. 1. Cologne, 1972.

Offler, H. S. "England and Germany at the Beginning of the Hundred Years' War." *EHR* 54 (1939): 608–31.

Opll, Ferdinand. *Friedrich Barbarossa*. Gestalten des Mittelalters und der Renaissance. Darmstadt, 1990.

Ortenberg, Veronica. *The English Church and the Continent in the Tenth and Eleventh Centuries: Cultural, Spiritual, and Artistic Exchanges*. Oxford, 1992.

Painter, Sidney. *The Reign of King John*. Baltimore, 1949.

Patze, Hans. "Die Welfen in der mittelalterlichen Geschichte Europas." *Blätter für deutsche Landesgeschichte* 117 (1981): 139–66.

Peters, Arnold. *Die Reichspolitik des Erzbischofs Philip von Köln (1167–1191)*. Ph.D. diss., Marburg, 1899.

Peters, Edward. "More Trouble with Henry: The Historiography of Medieval Germany in the Angloliterate World, 1888–1995." *Central European History* 28, no. 1 (1995): 47–72.

Peters, Inge-Maren. *Hansekaufleute als Gläubiger der Englischen Krone (1294–1350)*. Quellen und Darstellungen zur Hansischen Geschichte, NF, no. 24. Cologne and Vienna, 1978.

Petersohn, Jürgen. "Die päpstliche Kanonisationsdelegation des 11. und 12. Jahrhunderts und die Heiligsprechung Karls des Großen." In *Proceedings of the Fourth International Congress of Medieval Canon Law*, ed. Stefan Kuttner, 163–206. Monumenta Iuris Canonici, ser. C, Subsidia, no. 5. Vatican City, 1976.

———. "Saint Denis–Westminster–Aachen: Die Karls-Translatio von 1165 und ihre Vorbilder." *DA* 31 (1975): 420–54.

Poole, Austin Lane. "Die Welfen in der Verbannung." *Deutsches Archiv für Geschichte des Mittelalters* 2 (1938): 129–48.

———. *Henry the Lion*. Oxford, 1912.

———. "Richard the First's Alliances with the German Princes in 1194." In *Studies in Medieval History Presented to F. M. Powicke*, ed. R. W. Hunt, W. A. Pantin, and R. W. Southern, 90–99. Oxford, 1948.

Poole, R. L. "Burgundian Notes: The Alpine Son-in-Law of Edward the Elder." *EHR* 26 (1911): 313–17.

Pötter, Wilhelm. *Die Ministerialität der Erzbischöfe von Köln vom Endes des 11. bis zum Ausgang des 13. Jahrhunderts*. Studien zur Kölner Kirchengeschichte, no. 9. Düsseldorf, 1967.

Powicke, F. M. *King Henry III and the Lord Edward*. 2 vols. Oxford, 1947.

———. *The Loss of Normandy*. 2d ed. Manchester, 1961.

Prestwich, Michael. *Edward I*. Berkeley, 1988.

———. *English Politics in the Thirteenth Century*. New York, 1993.

Queller, Donald E. *The Office of the Ambassador in the Middle Ages*. Princeton, 1967.

Ramsay, J. H. *The Angevin Empire or the Three Reigns of Henry II, Richard I, and John*. London, 1903.

Rassow, P. *Honor Imperii: Die neue Politik Friedrich Barbarossas 1152–1159.* Munich, 1940.

Rauschen, Gerhard. *Die Legende Karls des Großen im 11. und 12. Jahrhundert.* PGRG, no. 7. Leipzig, 1890.

Reese, Werner. *Die Niederlande und das deutsche Reich.* Berlin, 1941.

Reisinger, Roswitha. *Die römisch-deutschen Könige und ihr Wahler 1189–1273.* Untersuchungen zur deutschen Staats- und Rechtsgeschichte, NF, no. 21. Aalen, 1977.

Reuter, Timothy. " *'Episcopi cum sua militia':* The Prelate as Warrior in the Early Staufer Era." In *Warriors and Churchmen in the High Middle Ages: Essays Presented to Karl Leyser,* ed. Timothy Reuter, 79–94. London, 1992.

———. *Germany in the Early Middle Ages, c. 800–1056.* London and New York, 1991.

———. "John of Salisbury and the Germans." In *The World of John of Salisbury,* ed. Michael Wilks, 415–25. Studies in Church History, Subsidia, no. 3. Oxford, 1984.

———. "The Medieval German *Sonderweg*? The Empire and Its Rulers in the High Middle Ages." In *Kings and Kingship in Medieval Europe,* ed. Anne J. Duggan, 179–211. King's College, London, Medieval Studies, no. 10. London, 1993.

———. "The Papal Schism of 1159–1169, the Empire, and the West." D. Phil. diss., Oxford University, 1975.

———. "Past, Present, and No Future in the Twelfth-Century *Regnum Teutonicum.*" In *The Perception of the Past in Twelfth-Century Europe,* ed. Paul Magdalino, 15–36. London, 1992.

———. "Pre-Gregorian Mentalities." *Journal of Ecclesiastical History* 45, no. 3 (July 1994): 465–74.

———, ed. *Warriors and Churchmen in the High Middle Ages: Essays Presented to Karl Leyser.* London, 1992.

———, ed. and trans. *The Medieval Nobility: Studies on the Ruling Classes of France and Germany from the Sixth to the Twelfth Century.* Europe in the Middle Ages, no. 14. Amsterdam and New York, 1979.

Reynolds, Susan. *Kingdoms and Communities in Western Europe, 900–1300.* 2d ed. Oxford, 1997.

Rill, G. "Zur Geschichte der Würzburger Eide von 1165." *Würzburger Diözesan-Geschichtsblätter* 20 (1960): 7–19.

Roche, T. W. E. *The King of Almayne.* London, 1966.

Röhrich, Victor. *Adolf I. Erzbischof von Köln. I Teil: Adolf als Reichsfürst.* Ph.D. diss., Königsberg, 1886.

Rössler, O. *Kaiserin Mathilde, Mutter Heinrichs von Anjou, und das Zeitalter der Anarchie in England.* Historische Studien, no. 7. Berlin, 1897.

Runciman, Steven. *A History of the Crusades.* 3 vols. Cambridge, 1954.

Samanek, Vincenz. "Der angebliche Verrat Adolfs von Nassau." *Historische Vierteljahrschrift* 29 (1935): 302–41.

Sawyer, P. H. "The Wealth of England in the Eleventh Century." *TRHS,* 5th ser., 15 (1965): 145–64.

Schaible, Karl Heinrich. *Geschichte der Deutschen in England von den ersten germanischen Ansiedlungen in Britannien bis zum Ende des 18. Jahrhunderts.* Strasbourg, 1885.

Schambach, C. "Das Verhalten Rainalds von Dassel zum Empfang der höchsten Weihen." *Zeitschrift des Historischen Vereins für Niedersachsen* 80 (1915): 173–95.

Scheibelreiter, Georg. "Der deutsche Thronstreit 1198–1208 im Spiegel der Datierung von Privaturkunden." *MIÖG* 84 (1976): 337–77; 85 (1977): 36–76.

Schmale, Franz Josef. "Friedrich I. und Ludwig VII. im Sommer des Jahres 1162." *Zeitschrift für Bayerische Landesgeschichte* 31 (1968): 315–68.

Schmandt, Raymond H. "The Election and Assassination of Albert of Louvain, Bishop of Liège, 1191–1192." *Speculum* 42 (1967): 639–60.

Schmidt, U. *Königswahl und Thronfolge im 12. Jahrhundert.* Forschungen zur Kaiser- und Papstgeschichte des Mittelalters, Beihefte zu J. F. Böhmer, Regesta Imperii, no. 7. Cologne and Vienna, 1987.

Schmugge, Ludwig. "Über 'nationale' Vorurteile im Mittelalter." *DA* 38, no. 2 (1982): 439–59.

Schnath, Georg. "Das Welfenhaus als europäische Dynastie." In *Streifzüge durch Niedersachsens Vergangenheit: Gesammelte Aufsätze und Vorträge von G. Schnath,* 126–45. Hildesheim, 1968.

Schneider, Friedrich. *Arnold II. Erzbischof von Cöln 1151–1156.* Ph.D. diss., Halle, 1884.

Schreiber, Albert. "Drei Beiträge zur Geschichte der deutschen Gefangenschaft des Könige Richard Löwenherz." *Historische Vierteljahrschrift* 26 (1931): 268–94.

Schrohe, H. "Die politischen Bestrebungen Erzbischof Siegfrieds von Köln." *Annalen* 67 (1899): 1–108.

Schultze, Aloys. *Der hohe Adel im Leben des mittelalterlichen Köln.* Sitzungsberichte der Bayerischen Akademie der Wissenschaft, Philosophisch-philologische und Historische Klasse, no. 8. Munich, 1919.

Schwineköper, B. "Eine unbekannte heraldische Quelle zur Geschichte Ottos IV. und seiner Anhänger." In *Festschrift für Hermann Heimpel zum 70. Geburtstag,* 2:959–1022. Veroffentlichungen des Max-Planck-Instituts fur Geschichte, no. 36. Göttingen, 1972.

Spatz, Wilhelm. *Die Schlacht von Hastings.* Historische Studien, no. 3. Berlin, 1896. Reprint, 1965.

Spörl, Johannes. "Rainald von Dassel auf dem Konzil von Reims 1148 und sein Verhältnis zu Johannes von Salisbury." *Historisches Jahrbuch* 60 (1940): 250–57.

Stacey, Robert C. *Politics, Policy, and Finance under Henry III (1216–1245).* Oxford, 1987.

Stehkämper, Hugo. "Der Kölner Erzbischof Adolf von Altena und die deutsche Königswahl (1195–1205)." In *Historische Zeitschrift, Beiheft NF 2,* ed. Theodor Schneider, 5–83. Beiträge zur Geschichte des mittelalterlichen deutschen Königtums. Munich, 1973.

————. "Der Reichsbischof und Territorialfürst (12. und 13. Jahrhundert)." In *Der Bischof in seiner Zeit, Bischofstypus und Bischofsideal im Spiegel der Kölner Kirche: Festgabe für Joseph Kardinal Höffner, Erzbischof von Köln,* ed. P. Berglar and Odilo Engels, 95–184. Cologne, 1986.

————. "Die Stadt Köln in der Salierzeit." In *Die Salier und das Reich,* ed. Stefan Weinfurter, 3:75–152. Sigmaringen, 1991.

————. "England und die Stadt Köln als Wahlmacher König Ottos IV." *Köln, das Reich und Europa,* MSAK 60 (1971): 213–44.

————. "England und Köln." *Vierteljahrschrift für die Freunde der Stadt* 3 (1965): 1–5.

————. *England und Köln: Beziehungen durch die Jahrhunderte in archivalischen Zeugnissen. Ausstellung im Historischen Archiv der Stadt Köln Mai-Juni 1965.* Cologne, 1965.

————. "Friedrich Barbarossa und die Stadt Köln: Ein Wirtschaftskrieg am Niederrhein." In *Köln, Stadt und Bistum in Kirche und Reich des Mittelalters: Festschrift für Odilo Engels zum 65. Geburtstag,* ed. Hanna Vollrath and Stefan Weinfurter, 367–414. Kölner historische Abhandlungen, no. 39. Cologne, 1993.

————. "Geld bei deutschen Königswahlen des 13. Jahrhunderts." In *Wirtschaftskräfte und Wirtschaftswege,* vol. 1, *Mittelmeer und Kontinent: Festschrift für Hermann Kellenbenz,* ed. Jürgen Schneider, 83–135. Beiträge zur Wirtschaftsgeschichte, no. 4. Bamberg, 1978.

————. "Konrad von Hochstaden, Erzbischof von Köln (1238–1261)." *JKGV* 36/37 (1961/62): 95–116.

Stelzmann, Arnold. "Rainald von Dassel und seine Reichspolitik." *JKGV* 25 (1960): 60–82.

Strait, Paul. *Cologne in the Twelfth Century.* Gainesville, 1974.

Strayer, Joseph. *On the Medieval Origins of the Modern State.* Princeton, 1970.

Stringer, Keith J. *The Reign of Stephen: Kingship, Warfare, and Government in Twelfth-Century England.* Lancaster Pamphlets. London and New York, 1993.

Thierfelder, Hildegard. *Köln und die Hanse.* Kölner Vorträge zur Sozial- und Wirtschaftsgeschichte, no. 7. Cologne, 1970.

Toeche, Theodor. *Kaiser Heinrich VI.* Leipzig, 1867.

Töpfer, Bernard. *Deutsche Könige und Kaiser des Mittelalters.* Cologne and Vienna, 1989.

Tout, T. F. *Chapters in the Administrative History of Medieval England.* 6 vols. Publications of the University of Manchester Historical Series, nos. 34–35, 48–49, 57, 64. Manchester, 1920–33.

Trautz, Fritz. *Die Könige von England und das Reich 1271–1377: Mit einem Rückblick auf ihr Verhältnis zu den Staufern.* Heidelberg, 1961.

Turner, Ralph V. *King John.* London, 1994.

————. *Men Raised from the Dust: Administrative Service and Upward Mobility in Angevin England.* Middle Ages Series. Philadelphia, 1988.

Tyerman, Christopher. *England and the Crusades, 1095–1588.* Chicago, 1988.

Ullmann, Walter. "Cardinal Roland and Besançon." In *Sacerdozio e Regno da*

Gregorio VII a Bonifacio VIII, ed. Friedrich Kempf, 107–26. Miscellanea Historiae Pontificae, no. 18. Rome, 1954.

Van Cleve, Thomas Curtis. *The Emperor Frederick II of Hohenstaufen.* Oxford, 1972.

Van Engen, John H. *Rupert of Deutz.* Publications of the Center for Medieval and Renaissance Studies, no. 18. Berkeley, 1983.

van Houtte, J. A. *An Economic History of the Low Countries (800–1800).* London, 1977.

von Knonau, Meyer. *Jahrbücher des deutschen Reiches unter Heinrichs IV und Heinrich V.* Leipzig, 1894.

Wand, Karl. "Die Englandpolitik der Stadt Köln und ihrer Erzbischöfe im 12. und 13. Jahrhundert." In *Aus Mittelalter und Neuzeit: Festschrift zum 70. Geburtstag von Gerhard Kallen,* ed. Josef Engel and Hans Martin Klinkenbert, 77–95. Bonn, 1975.

Warren, W. L. *The Governance of Norman and Angevin England, 1086–1272.* Stanford, 1987.

———. *Henry II.* Berkeley, 1973. Reprint, 1977.

———. *King John.* Berkeley, 1961. Reprint, 1978.

Weiner, A. "Early Commercial Intercourse between England and Germany." *Economica* 11 (1922): 127–48.

Weinfurter, Stefan. "Erzbischof Phillip von Köln und der Sturtz Heinrichs des Löwen." In *Köln, Stadt und Bistum in Kirche und Reich des Mittelalters: Festschrift für Odilo Engels zum 65. Geburtstag,* ed. Hanna Vollrath and Stefan Weinfurter, 455–82. Kölner historische Abhandlungen, no. 39. Cologne, 1993.

Werle, H. "Staufische Hausmachtpolitik am Rheim im 12. Jahrhundert." *Zeitschrift für die Geschichte des Oberrheins* 110 (1962): 299–321.

Winkelmann, Eduard. *Kaiser Friedrich II.* 2 vols. Leipzig, 1889–97.

———. *Philip von Schwaben und Otto IV. von Braunschweig.* 2 vols. Jahrbücher der deutschen Geschichte. Leipzig, 1873–78.

Wissowa, Felix. *Politische Beziehungen zwischen England und Deutschland bis zum Untergang der Staufer.* Breslau, 1889.

Wolfschläger, Casper. *Erzbischof Adolf I. von Köln als Fürst und Politiker.* Münsterische Beiträge zur Geschichtsforschung, NF, no. 6. Münster, 1905.

Wolter, Heinz. *Arnold von Weid, Kanzler Konrads III. und Erzbischof von Köln.* Veröffentlichungen des Kölnischen Geschichtsvereins, no. 32. Cologne, 1973.

———. "Erzbischof Friedrich I. von Köln (1156–1158)." *JKGV* 46 (1975): 1–50.

Wood, Charles. "The Return of Medieval Politics." *American Historical Review* 94 (1989): 391–404.

Wurster, W. "Das Bild Heinrichs des Löwen in der mittelalterlichen Chronistik Deutschlands und Englands." In *Heinrich der Löwe,* ed. W. D. Mohrmann, 407–39. Göttingen, 1980.

Zatschek, Heinz. *England und das Reich.* Vienna, 1942.

Zöllner, Erich. "Das Projekt einer babenbergischen Heirat König Heinrichs III. von England." *Archiv für Österreichische Geschichte* 125 (1966): 54–75.

Index